FREE Study Skills D\/~ ~~~~

Dear Customer,

Thank you for your purchase from Mometrix! We consider it an honor and a privilege that you have purchased our product and we want to ensure your satisfaction.

As a way of showing our appreciation and to help us better serve you, we have developed a Study Skills DVD that we would like to give you for <u>FREE</u>. This DVD covers our best practices for getting ready for your exam, from how to use our study materials to how to best prepare for the day of the test.

All that we ask is that you email us with feedback that would describe your experience so far with our product. Good, bad, or indifferent, we want to know what you think!

To get your FREE Study Skills DVD, email <u>freedvd@mometrix.com</u> with FREE STUDY SKILLS DVD in the subject line and the following information in the body of the email:

- The name of the product you purchased.
- Your product rating on a scale of 1-5, with 5 being the highest rating.
- Your feedback. It can be long, short, or anything in between. We just want to know your impressions and experience so far with our product. (Good feedback might include how our study material met your needs and ways we might be able to make it even better. You could highlight features that you found helpful or features that you think we should add.)
- Your full name and shipping address where you would like us to send your free DVD.

If you have any questions or concerns, please don't hesitate to contact me directly.

Thanks again!

Sincerely,

Jay Willis
Vice President
<u>jay.willis@mometrix.com</u>
1-800-673-8175

TExES

Special Education EC-12 (161)

SECRETS

Study Guide
Your Key to Exam Success

TExES Test Review for the
Texas Examinations of Educator Standards

Published by

Mometrix Test Preparation

Mometrix Texas Teacher Certification Test Team

Written and edited by the Mometrix Texas Teacher Certification Test Team

Printed in the United States of America

This paper meets the requirements of ANSI/NISO Z39.48-1992 (Permanence of Paper).

Mometrix offers volume discount pricing to institutions. For more information or a price quote, please contact our sales department at sales@mometrix.com or 888-248-1219.

Paperback
ISBN 13: 978-1-61072-981-9
ISBN 10: 1-61072-981-1

Ebook
ISBN 13: 978-1-62120-460-2
ISBN 10: 1-62120-460-X

Hardback
ISBN 13: 978-1-5167-0560-3
ISBN 10: 1-5167-0560-2

Dear Future Exam Success Story:

First of all, **THANK YOU** for purchasing Mometrix study materials!

Second, congratulations! You are one of the few determined test-takers who are committed to doing whatever it takes to excel on your exam. **You have come to the right place.** We developed these study materials with one goal in mind: to deliver you the information you need in a format that's concise and easy to use.

In addition to optimizing your guide for the content of the test, we've outlined our recommended steps for breaking down the preparation process into small, attainable goals so you can make sure you stay on track.

We've also analyzed the entire test-taking process, identifying the most common pitfalls and showing how you can overcome them and be ready for any curveball the test throws you.

Standardized testing is one of the biggest obstacles on your road to success, which only increases the importance of doing well in the high-pressure, high-stakes environment of test day. Your results on this test could have a significant impact on your future, and this guide provides the information and practical advice to help you achieve your full potential on test day.

Your success is our success

We would love to hear from you! If you would like to share the story of your exam success or if you have any questions or comments in regard to our products, please contact us at **800-673-8175** or **support@mometrix.com**.

Thanks again for your business and we wish you continued success!

Sincerely,
The Mometrix Test Preparation Team

Need more help? Check out our flashcards at: http://MometrixFlashcards.com/TExES

TABLE OF CONTENTS

Introduction

Thank you for purchasing this resource! You have made the choice to prepare yourself for a test that could have a huge impact on your future, and this guide is designed to help you be fully ready for test day. Obviously, it's important to have a solid understanding of the test material, but you also need to be prepared for the unique environment and stressors of the test, so that you can perform to the best of your abilities.

For this purpose, the first section that appears in this guide is the **Secret Keys**. We've devoted countless hours to meticulously researching what works and what doesn't, and we've boiled down our findings to the five most impactful steps you can take to improve your performance on the test. We start at the beginning with study planning and move through the preparation process, all the way to the testing strategies that will help you get the most out of what you know when you're finally sitting in front of the test.

We recommend that you start preparing for your test as far in advance as possible. However, if you've bought this guide as a last-minute study resource and only have a few days before your test, we recommend that you skip over the first two Secret Keys since they address a long-term study plan.

If you struggle with **test anxiety**, we strongly encourage you to check out our recommendations for how you can overcome it. Test anxiety is a formidable foe, but it can be beaten, and we want to make sure you have the tools you need to defeat it.

Secret Key #1 – Plan Big, Study Small

There's a lot riding on your performance. If you want to ace this test, you're going to need to keep your skills sharp and the material fresh in your mind. You need a plan that lets you review everything you need to know while still fitting in your schedule. We'll break this strategy down into three categories.

Information Organization

Start with the information you already have: the official test outline. From this, you can make a complete list of all the concepts you need to cover before the test. Organize these concepts into groups that can be studied together, and create a list of any related vocabulary you need to learn so you can brush up on any difficult terms. You'll want to keep this vocabulary list handy once you actually start studying since you may need to add to it along the way.

Time Management

Once you have your set of study concepts, decide how to spread them out over the time you have left before the test. Break your study plan into small, clear goals so you have a manageable task for each day and know exactly what you're doing. Then just focus on one small step at a time. When you manage your time this way, you don't need to spend hours at a time studying. Studying a small block of content for a short period each day helps you retain information better and avoid stressing over how much you have left to do. You can relax knowing that you have a plan to cover everything in time. In order for this strategy to be effective though, you have to start studying early and stick to your schedule. Avoid the exhaustion and futility that comes from last-minute cramming!

Study Environment

The environment you study in has a big impact on your learning. Studying in a coffee shop, while probably more enjoyable, is not likely to be as fruitful as studying in a quiet room. It's important to keep distractions to a minimum. You're only planning to study for a short block of time, so make the most of it. Don't pause to check your phone or get up to find a snack. It's also important to **avoid multitasking**. Research has consistently shown that multitasking will make your studying dramatically less effective. Your study area should also be comfortable and well-lit so you don't have the distraction of straining your eyes or sitting on an uncomfortable chair.

The time of day you study is also important. You want to be rested and alert. Don't wait until just before bedtime. Study when you'll be most likely to comprehend and remember. Even better, if you know what time of day your test will be, set that time aside for study. That way your brain will be used to working on that subject at that specific time and you'll have a better chance of recalling information.

Finally, it can be helpful to team up with others who are studying for the same test. Your actual studying should be done in as isolated an environment as possible, but the work of organizing the information and setting up the study plan can be divided up. In between study sessions, you can discuss with your teammates the concepts that you're all studying and quiz each other on the details. Just be sure that your teammates are as serious about the test as you are. If you find that your study time is being replaced with social time, you might need to find a new team.

Secret Key #2 – Make Your Studying Count

You're devoting a lot of time and effort to preparing for this test, so you want to be absolutely certain it will pay off. This means doing more than just reading the content and hoping you can remember it on test day. It's important to make every minute of study count. There are two main areas you can focus on to make your studying count:

Retention

It doesn't matter how much time you study if you can't remember the material. You need to make sure you are retaining the concepts. To check your retention of the information you're learning, try recalling it at later times with minimal prompting. Try carrying around flashcards and glance at one or two from time to time or ask a friend who's also studying for the test to quiz you.

To enhance your retention, look for ways to put the information into practice so that you can apply it rather than simply recalling it. If you're using the information in practical ways, it will be much easier to remember. Similarly, it helps to solidify a concept in your mind if you're not only reading it to yourself but also explaining it to someone else. Ask a friend to let you teach them about a concept you're a little shaky on (or speak aloud to an imaginary audience if necessary). As you try to summarize, define, give examples, and answer your friend's questions, you'll understand the concepts better and they will stay with you longer. Finally, step back for a big picture view and ask yourself how each piece of information fits with the whole subject. When you link the different concepts together and see them working together as a whole, it's easier to remember the individual components.

Finally, practice showing your work on any multi-step problems, even if you're just studying. Writing out each step you take to solve a problem will help solidify the process in your mind, and you'll be more likely to remember it during the test.

Modality

Modality simply refers to the means or method by which you study. Choosing a study modality that fits your own individual learning style is crucial. No two people learn best in exactly the same way, so it's important to know your strengths and use them to your advantage.

For example, if you learn best by visualization, focus on visualizing a concept in your mind and draw an image or a diagram. Try color-coding your notes, illustrating them, or creating symbols that will trigger your mind to recall a learned concept. If you learn best by hearing or discussing information, find a study partner who learns the same way or read aloud to yourself. Think about how to put the information in your own words. Imagine that you are giving a lecture on the topic and record yourself so you can listen to it later.

For any learning style, flashcards can be helpful. Organize the information so you can take advantage of spare moments to review. Underline key words or phrases. Use different colors for different categories. Mnemonic devices (such as creating a short list in which every item starts with the same letter) can also help with retention. Find what works best for you and use it to store the information in your mind most effectively and easily.

Secret Key #3 – Practice the Right Way

Your success on test day depends not only on how many hours you put into preparing, but also on whether you prepared the right way. It's good to check along the way to see if your studying is paying off. One of the most effective ways to do this is by taking practice tests to evaluate your progress. Practice tests are useful because they show exactly where you need to improve. Every time you take a practice test, pay special attention to these three groups of questions:

- The questions you got wrong
- The questions you had to guess on, even if you guessed right
- The questions you found difficult or slow to work through

This will show you exactly what your weak areas are, and where you need to devote more study time. Ask yourself why each of these questions gave you trouble. Was it because you didn't understand the material? Was it because you didn't remember the vocabulary? Do you need more repetitions on this type of question to build speed and confidence? Dig into those questions and figure out how you can strengthen your weak areas as you go back to review the material.

Additionally, many practice tests have a section explaining the answer choices. It can be tempting to read the explanation and think that you now have a good understanding of the concept. However, an explanation likely only covers part of the question's broader context. Even if the explanation makes sense, **go back and investigate** every concept related to the question until you're positive you have a thorough understanding.

As you go along, keep in mind that the practice test is just that: practice. Memorizing these questions and answers will not be very helpful on the actual test because it is unlikely to have any of the same exact questions. If you only know the right answers to the sample questions, you won't be prepared for the real thing. **Study the concepts** until you understand them fully, and then you'll be able to answer any question that shows up on the test.

It's important to wait on the practice tests until you're ready. If you take a test on your first day of study, you may be overwhelmed by the amount of material covered and how much you need to learn. Work up to it gradually.

On test day, you'll need to be prepared for answering questions, managing your time, and using the test-taking strategies you've learned. It's a lot to balance, like a mental marathon that will have a big impact on your future. Like training for a marathon, you'll need to start slowly and work your way up. When test day arrives, you'll be ready.

Start with the strategies you've read in the first two Secret Keys—plan your course and study in the way that works best for you. If you have time, consider using multiple study resources to get different approaches to the same concepts. It can be helpful to see difficult concepts from more than one angle. Then find a good source for practice tests. Many times, the test website will suggest potential study resources or provide sample tests.

Practice Test Strategy

When you're ready to start taking practice tests, follow this strategy:

Untimed and Open-Book Practice

Take the first test with no time constraints and with your notes and study guide handy. Take your time and focus on applying the strategies you've learned.

Timed and Open-Book Practice

Take the second practice test open-book as well, but set a timer and practice pacing yourself to finish in time.

Timed and Closed-Book Practice

Take any other practice tests as if it were test day. Set a timer and put away your study materials. Sit at a table or desk in a quiet room, imagine yourself at the testing center, and answer questions as quickly and accurately as possible.

Keep repeating timed and closed-book tests on a regular basis until you run out of practice tests or it's time for the actual test. Your mind will be ready for the schedule and stress of test day, and you'll be able to focus on recalling the material you've learned.

Secret Key #4 – Pace Yourself

Once you're fully prepared for the material on the test, your biggest challenge on test day will be managing your time. Just knowing that the clock is ticking can make you panic even if you have plenty of time left. Work on pacing yourself so you can build confidence against the time constraints of the exam. Pacing is a difficult skill to master, especially in a high-pressure environment, so **practice is vital**.

Set time expectations for your pace based on how much time is available. For example, if a section has 60 questions and the time limit is 30 minutes, you know you have to average 30 seconds or less per question in order to answer them all. Although 30 seconds is the hard limit, set 25 seconds per question as your goal, so you reserve extra time to spend on harder questions. When you budget extra time for the harder questions, you no longer have any reason to stress when those questions take longer to answer.

Don't let this time expectation distract you from working through the test at a calm, steady pace, but keep it in mind so you don't spend too much time on any one question. Recognize that taking extra time on one question you don't understand may keep you from answering two that you do understand later in the test. If your time limit for a question is up and you're still not sure of the answer, mark it and move on, and come back to it later if the time and the test format allow. If the testing format doesn't allow you to return to earlier questions, just make an educated guess; then put it out of your mind and move on.

On the easier questions, be careful not to rush. It may seem wise to hurry through them so you have more time for the challenging ones, but it's not worth missing one if you know the concept and just didn't take the time to read the question fully. Work efficiently but make sure you understand the question and have looked at all of the answer choices, since more than one may seem right at first.

Even if you're paying attention to the time, you may find yourself a little behind at some point. You should speed up to get back on track, but do so wisely. Don't panic; just take a few seconds less on each question until you're caught up. Don't guess without thinking, but do look through the answer choices and eliminate any you know are wrong. If you can get down to two choices, it is often worthwhile to guess from those. Once you've chosen an answer, move on and don't dwell on any that you skipped or had to hurry through. If a question was taking too long, chances are it was one of the harder ones, so you weren't as likely to get it right anyway.

On the other hand, if you find yourself getting ahead of schedule, it may be beneficial to slow down a little. The more quickly you work, the more likely you are to make a careless mistake that will affect your score. You've budgeted time for each question, so don't be afraid to spend that time. Practice an efficient but careful pace to get the most out of the time you have.

Secret Key #5 – Have a Plan for Guessing

When you're taking the test, you may find yourself stuck on a question. Some of the answer choices seem better than others, but you don't see the one answer choice that is obviously correct. What do you do?

The scenario described above is very common, yet most test takers have not effectively prepared for it. Developing and practicing a plan for guessing may be one of the single most effective uses of your time as you get ready for the exam.

In developing your plan for guessing, there are three questions to address:

- When should you start the guessing process?
- How should you narrow down the choices?
- Which answer should you choose?

When to Start the Guessing Process

Unless your plan for guessing is to select C every time (which, despite its merits, is not what we recommend), you need to leave yourself enough time to apply your answer elimination strategies. Since you have a limited amount of time for each question, that means that if you're going to give yourself the best shot at guessing correctly, you have to decide quickly whether or not you will guess.

Of course, the best-case scenario is that you don't have to guess at all, so first, see if you can answer the question based on your knowledge of the subject and basic reasoning skills. Focus on the key words in the question and try to jog your memory of related topics. Give yourself a chance to bring the knowledge to mind, but once you realize that you don't have (or you can't access) the knowledge you need to answer the question, it's time to start the guessing process.

It's almost always better to start the guessing process too early than too late. It only takes a few seconds to remember something and answer the question from knowledge. Carefully eliminating wrong answer choices takes longer. Plus, going through the process of eliminating answer choices can actually help jog your memory.

Summary: Start the guessing process as soon as you decide that you can't answer the question based on your knowledge.

How to Narrow Down the Choices

The next chapter in this book (**Test-Taking Strategies**) includes a wide range of strategies for how to approach questions and how to look for answer choices to eliminate. You will definitely want to read those carefully, practice them, and figure out which ones work best for you. Here though, we're going to address a mindset rather than a particular strategy.

Your chances of guessing an answer correctly depend on how many options you are choosing from.

How many choices you have	How likely you are to guess correctly
5	20%
4	25%
3	33%
2	50%
1	100%

You can see from this chart just how valuable it is to be able to eliminate incorrect answers and make an educated guess, but there are two things that many test takers do that cause them to miss out on the benefits of guessing:

- Accidentally eliminating the correct answer
- Selecting an answer based on an impression

We'll look at the first one here, and the second one in the next section.

To avoid accidentally eliminating the correct answer, we recommend a thought exercise called **the $5 challenge**. In this challenge, you only eliminate an answer choice from contention if you are willing to bet $5 on it being wrong. Why $5? Five dollars is a small but not insignificant amount of money. It's an amount you could afford to lose but wouldn't want to throw away. And while losing $5 once might not hurt too much, doing it twenty times will set you back $100. In the same way, each small decision you make—eliminating a choice here, guessing on a question there—won't by itself impact your score very much, but when you put them all together, they can make a big difference. By holding each answer choice elimination decision to a higher standard, you can reduce the risk of accidentally eliminating the correct answer.

The $5 challenge can also be applied in a positive sense: If you are willing to bet $5 that an answer choice *is* correct, go ahead and mark it as correct.

Summary: Only eliminate an answer choice if you are willing to bet $5 that it is wrong.

Which Answer to Choose

You're taking the test. You've run into a hard question and decided you'll have to guess. You've eliminated all the answer choices you're willing to bet $5 on. Now you have to pick an answer. Why do we even need to talk about this? Why can't you just pick whichever one you feel like when the time comes?

The answer to these questions is that if you don't come into the test with a plan, you'll rely on your impression to select an answer choice, and if you do that, you risk falling into a trap. The test writers know that everyone who takes their test will be guessing on some of the questions, so they intentionally write wrong answer choices to seem plausible. You still have to pick an answer though, and if the wrong answer choices are designed to look right, how can you ever be sure that you're not falling for their trap? The best solution we've found to this dilemma is to take the decision out of your hands entirely. Here is the process we recommend:

Once you've eliminated any choices that you are confident (willing to bet $5) are wrong, select the first remaining choice as your answer.

Whether you choose to select the first remaining choice, the second, or the last, the important thing is that you use some preselected standard. Using this approach guarantees that you will not be enticed into selecting an answer choice that looks right, because you are not basing your decision on how the answer choices look.

This is not meant to make you question your knowledge. Instead, it is to help you recognize the difference between your knowledge and your impressions. There's a huge difference between thinking an answer is right because of what you know, and thinking an answer is right because it looks or sounds like it should be right.

Summary: To ensure that your selection is appropriately random, make a predetermined selection from among all answer choices you have not eliminated.

Test-Taking Strategies

This section contains a list of test-taking strategies that you may find helpful as you work through the test. By taking what you know and applying logical thought, you can maximize your chances of answering any question correctly!

It is very important to realize that every question is different and every person is different: no single strategy will work on every question, and no single strategy will work for every person. That's why we've included all of them here, so you can try them out and determine which ones work best for different types of questions and which ones work best for you.

Question Strategies

Read Carefully

Read the question and answer choices carefully. Don't miss the question because you misread the terms. You have plenty of time to read each question thoroughly and make sure you understand what is being asked. Yet a happy medium must be attained, so don't waste too much time. You must read carefully, but efficiently.

Contextual Clues

Look for contextual clues. If the question includes a word you are not familiar with, look at the immediate context for some indication of what the word might mean. Contextual clues can often give you all the information you need to decipher the meaning of an unfamiliar word. Even if you can't determine the meaning, you may be able to narrow down the possibilities enough to make a solid guess at the answer to the question.

Prefixes

If you're having trouble with a word in the question or answer choices, try dissecting it. Take advantage of every clue that the word might include. Prefixes and suffixes can be a huge help. Usually they allow you to determine a basic meaning. Pre- means before, post- means after, pro - is positive, de- is negative. From prefixes and suffixes, you can get an idea of the general meaning of the word and try to put it into context.

Hedge Words

Watch out for critical hedge words, such as *likely, may, can, sometimes, often, almost, mostly, usually, generally, rarely*, and *sometimes*. Question writers insert these hedge phrases to cover every possibility. Often an answer choice will be wrong simply because it leaves no room for exception. Be on guard for answer choices that have definitive words such as *exactly* and *always*.

Switchback Words

Stay alert for *switchbacks*. These are the words and phrases frequently used to alert you to shifts in thought. The most common switchback words are *but, although*, and *however*. Others include *nevertheless, on the other hand, even though, while, in spite of, despite, regardless of*. Switchback words are important to catch because they can change the direction of the question or an answer choice.

Face Value

When in doubt, use common sense. Accept the situation in the problem at face value. Don't read too much into it. These problems will not require you to make wild assumptions. If you have to go beyond creativity and warp time or space in order to have an answer choice fit the question, then you should move on and consider the other answer choices. These are normal problems rooted in reality. The applicable relationship or explanation may not be readily apparent, but it is there for you to figure out. Use your common sense to interpret anything that isn't clear.

Answer Choice Strategies

Answer Selection

The most thorough way to pick an answer choice is to identify and eliminate wrong answers until only one is left, then confirm it is the correct answer. Sometimes an answer choice may immediately seem right, but be careful. The test writers will usually put more than one reasonable answer choice on each question, so take a second to read all of them and make sure that the other choices are not equally obvious. As long as you have time left, it is better to read every answer choice than to pick the first one that looks right without checking the others.

Answer Choice Families

An answer choice family consists of two (in rare cases, three) answer choices that are very similar in construction and cannot all be true at the same time. If you see two answer choices that are direct opposites or parallels, one of them is usually the correct answer. For instance, if one answer choice says that quantity x increases and another either says that quantity x decreases (opposite) or says that quantity y increases (parallel), then those answer choices would fall into the same family. An answer choice that doesn't match the construction of the answer choice family is more likely to be incorrect. Most questions will not have answer choice families, but when they do appear, you should be prepared to recognize them.

Eliminate Answers

Eliminate answer choices as soon as you realize they are wrong, but make sure you consider all possibilities. If you are eliminating answer choices and realize that the last one you are left with is also wrong, don't panic. Start over and consider each choice again. There may be something you missed the first time that you will realize on the second pass.

Avoid Fact Traps

Don't be distracted by an answer choice that is factually true but doesn't answer the question. You are looking for the choice that answers the question. Stay focused on what the question is asking for so you don't accidentally pick an answer that is true but incorrect. Always go back to the question and make sure the answer choice you've selected actually answers the question and is not merely a true statement.

Extreme Statements

In general, you should avoid answers that put forth extreme actions as standard practice or proclaim controversial ideas as established fact. An answer choice that states the "process should be used in certain situations, if..." is much more likely to be correct than one that states the "process should be discontinued completely." The first is a calm rational statement and doesn't even make a definitive, uncompromising stance, using a hedge word *if* to provide wiggle room, whereas the second choice is a radical idea and far more extreme.

Benchmark

As you read through the answer choices and you come across one that seems to answer the question well, mentally select that answer choice. This is not your final answer, but it's the one that will help you evaluate the other answer choices. The one that you selected is your benchmark or standard for judging each of the other answer choices. Every other answer choice must be compared to your benchmark. That choice is correct until proven otherwise by another answer choice beating it. If you find a better answer, then that one becomes your new benchmark. Once you've decided that no other choice answers the question as well as your benchmark, you have your final answer.

Predict the Answer

Before you even start looking at the answer choices, it is often best to try to predict the answer. When you come up with the answer on your own, it is easier to avoid distractions and traps because you will know exactly what to look for. The right answer choice is unlikely to be word-for-word what you came up with, but it should be a close match. Even if you are confident that you have the right answer, you should still take the time to read each option before moving on.

General Strategies

Tough Questions

If you are stumped on a problem or it appears too hard or too difficult, don't waste time. Move on! Remember though, if you can quickly check for obviously incorrect answer choices, your chances of guessing correctly are greatly improved. Before you completely give up, at least try to knock out a couple of possible answers. Eliminate what you can and then guess at the remaining answer choices before moving on.

Check Your Work

Since you will probably not know every term listed and the answer to every question, it is important that you get credit for the ones that you do know. Don't miss any questions through careless mistakes. If at all possible, try to take a second to look back over your answer selection and make sure you've selected the correct answer choice and haven't made a costly careless mistake (such as marking an answer choice that you didn't mean to mark). This quick double check should more than pay for itself in caught mistakes for the time it costs.

Pace Yourself

It's easy to be overwhelmed when you're looking at a page full of questions; your mind is confused and full of random thoughts, and the clock is ticking down faster than you would like. Calm down and maintain the pace that you have set for yourself. Especially as you get down to the last few minutes of the test, don't let the small numbers on the clock make you panic. As long as you are on track by monitoring your pace, you are guaranteed to have time for each question.

Don't Rush

It is very easy to make errors when you are in a hurry. Maintaining a fast pace in answering questions is pointless if it makes you miss questions that you would have gotten right otherwise. Test writers like to include distracting information and wrong answers that seem right. Taking a little extra time to avoid careless mistakes can make all the difference in your test score. Find a pace that allows you to be confident in the answers that you select.

Keep Moving

Panicking will not help you pass the test, so do your best to stay calm and keep moving. Taking deep breaths and going through the answer elimination steps you practiced can help to break through a stress barrier and keep your pace.

Final Notes

The combination of a solid foundation of content knowledge and the confidence that comes from practicing your plan for applying that knowledge is the key to maximizing your performance on test day. As your foundation of content knowledge is built up and strengthened, you'll find that the strategies included in this chapter become more and more effective in helping you quickly sift through the distractions and traps of the test to isolate the correct answer.

Now it's time to move on to the test content chapters of this book, but be sure to keep your goal in mind. As you read, think about how you will be able to apply this information on the test. If you've already seen sample questions for the test and you have an idea of the question format and style, try to come up with questions of your own that you can answer based on what you're reading. This will give you valuable practice applying your knowledge in the same ways you can expect to on test day.

Good luck and good studying!

Understanding Individuals with Disabilities and Evaluating Their Needs

Types of Disability Categories

Specific Learning Disabilities (SLD) is the umbrella term for children who struggle with issues in their abilities to read, write, speak, listen, reason, or do math. *Other Health Impairment (OHI)* is another umbrella term for a disability that limits a child's strength, energy, or alertness. *Autism Spectrum Disorder (ASD)* is a disability that mostly affects a child's social and communication skills, and sometimes behavior. *Emotional Disturbance (ED)* is a disability category for a number of mental disorders. *Speech or Language Impairment* covers children with language impairments. *Visual Impairment or Blindness* is a disability category for children with visual impairments that significantly impair their abilities to learn. *Deafness*, *Hearing Impairment*, and *Deaf-Blindness* cover children diagnosed with these disabilities. Children with *Orthopedic Impairments* have impairments to their bodies. An *Intellectual Disability* is the diagnosis for students with below-average intellectual abilities. *Traumatic Brain Injury (TBI)* covers children who have suffered from TBIs. A diagnosis of *Multiple Disabilities* means a child has more than one disability defined by IDEA.

Interventions for Students with Physical Disabilities

A physical disability refers to any disability that limits gross mobility and prevents normal body movement. For example, muscular dystrophy is a physical disability that weakens the muscles of the human body over time. Students with physical disabilities require early interventions before grade school, if applicable. When students with physical disabilities enter grade school, they may receive interventions and related services if they qualify for special education and receive Individualized Education Programs or 504 Plans. When physical disabilities do not affect the students' academic success, they may be put on 504 Plans to receive appropriate related services, accommodations, or modifications. When physical disabilities are present with other disabilities, or the physical disabilities affect academic performance, students may be put on Individualized Education Programs. They may also receive appropriate related services, accommodations, and modifications. Teachers, intervention specialists, physiotherapists, occupational therapists, and speech language pathologists are all team members that work with students with physical disabilities by assisting and implementing appropriate accommodations, modifications, and related services.

Dyslexia and Dysgraphia Disorders

Students with dyslexia are eligible for special education with a specific learning disability under the Individuals with Disabilities Education Act if their educational performances are significantly impacted by their disabilities. Dyslexia is a permanent condition that makes it difficult for people to read. This affects reading accuracy, fluency, and comprehension. Dyslexia also generalizes to difficulties in the content areas of writing, mathematics, spelling, and reading comprehension. Children who have dyslexia often have difficulties with phonemic awareness skills and decoding. It is not a disability that affects vision or the way people see letters. Dyslexia may coexist with other conditions such as dysgraphia, which is a disorder that causes issues with written expression. With dysgraphia, children often struggle with holding pencils and writing letters accurately. It is difficult for students with dysgraphia to distinguish shapes, use correct letter spacing, read maps, copy text, understand spelling rules, and more.

Behavioral Issues for Students with Autism

Autism is a spectrum disorder, which means the characteristics associated with the disability vary depending on the student. However, there are common repetitive and patterned behaviors associated with communication and social interactions for this population of students. Students with autism may demonstrate delayed or different speech patterns, the inability to understand body language or facial expressions, and the inability to exhibit appropriate speech patterns, body language, or facial expressions. In a classroom environment, students with autism may demonstrate repetitive behaviors that are distracting, such as hand flapping or making vocalizations. Some students with autism demonstrate preoccupation with doing activities, tasks, or routines in certain ways. This preoccupation can lead to difficulties when the students are asked to make changes to the activities, tasks, or routines. Furthermore, some students with autism prefer to participate in a limited range of activities and may get upset when asked to participate in activities outside of their self-perceived ranges. Repetitive behaviors may translate into obsessions or excessive knowledge relating to one particular topic. Extreme interests in one topic can turn into disruptions when students with autism are asked to speak or write about different topics.

Effect of Hearing Loss on Language Development

Hearing language is part of learning language. Children with hearing loss miss out on sounds associated with language, and this can affect their listening, speaking, reading, social skills, and overall school success. Hearing loss can sometimes lead to delayed speech and language, learning disabilities in school, insecurities, and issues with socialization and making friends. Children with hearing loss may:

- have trouble learning abstract vocabulary (i.e. since, before).
- omit article words in sentences (i.e. a, an).
- fall behind on core components of learning and development without early interventions.
- have difficulty speaking in and/or understanding sentences.
- speak in shorter sentences.
- have difficulty including word endings (i.e. -ing, -s).
- have issues speaking clearly because they cannot accurately hear sounds.
- omit quiet sounds, like *p, sh,* or *f.*
- be unable to hear what their own voices sound like.

Children with hearing loss are more likely to fall behind in school due to their hearing deficits. They can easily fall behind without support from interventions, teachers, and their families. Early hearing testing is essential to ensure that interventions, such as sign language, can be introduced to promote school and life success for children with hearing loss.

Receptive Language Disorders

Children with receptive language disorders often demonstrate appropriate expressive language skills and hear and read at age-appropriate levels. They may seem like they are not paying attention or engaging in activities, or appear to have difficulties following or understanding directions. They may refrain from asking questions or interrupt frequently during activities, especially during read aloud activities. It may appear as if they are not listening, but children with receptive language disorders cannot perceive meaning from what they hear. Children with this disorder may consistently leave tasks incomplete unless the tasks are broken down into smaller steps. This is due to issues with directions, especially verbal directions. Children with receptive language disorders may not respond appropriately or at all to questions from peers or adults. Answers to comprehension questions, especially when texts are read aloud, may be off topic or incorrect. Children with receptive language disorders have trouble gathering and connecting meaning to what they hear. A receptive language disorder is not exclusively a learning disability. However, children who have receptive disorders may have learning disabilities.

Types of Disabilities

Medical disabilities include problems related to diseases, illnesses, and trauma. Medical disabilities can also include problems related to genetics. Physical disabilities include problems related to fine and gross motor skills and can include sensory input or sensory perception disorders. Medical and physical disabilities often manifest with other disabilities, such as learning disabilities. Medical disabilities, such as a student whose health issue affects educational performance, are usually categorized under the Other Health Impaired or Traumatic Brain Injury eligibility categories under the Individuals with Disabilities Education Act (IDEA). People with physical disabilities, such as cerebral palsy, can be eligible for special education under IDEA under the Orthopedic Impairment category. However, for both medical and physical disabilities to qualify, a student's medical or physical disability must adversely affect educational performance. For example, a student with cerebral palsy may not be eligible for special education or an Individualized Education Program if the disability does not affect educational performance. The student would receive accommodations and modifications under a 504 Plan.

Educational Implications of a Diagnosis of SLD, OHI, ASD, and ED

Students with Specific Learning Disability (SLD) may struggle with instruction in general education classrooms and require specific instruction fine-tuned to their individual needs. Their annual IEP goals may target specific skills that are not age appropriate but are appropriate to their unique learning needs. An OHI (Other Health Impairment) diagnosis can include children with ADHD, diabetes, HIV/AIDS, heart conditions, and more. Students with OHI receive accommodations for their unique health or educational needs on a case by case basis. Students with Autism Spectrum Disorder (ASD) may rely on the use of visuals or access to other ways to express feelings or communicate. Students with ASD may not respond to everyday conversations or classroom situations the same ways their peers do. They require supports to learn how to express their needs within the general education classroom. Students with emotional disturbances (ED) exhibit an inability to learn that is not due to intellectual, sensory, or health problems. Students with ED also exhibit inability to form and maintain appropriate relationships with peers and adults, demonstrate inappropriate behaviors, and may exhibit depression or general unhappiness.

Early Characteristics Indicating a Child Has a Specific Learning Disability

Early characteristics that indicate a specific learning disability (SLD) include factors like medical history, speech acquisition, problems with socialization, academic delays, and behavioral delays. Delays in certain milestones may indicate learning disabilities, but these delays may also be due to other causes. Premature birth, serious childhood illnesses, frequent ear infections, and sleep disorders are medical factors that can influence the development of learning disabilities. Children that develop SLDs may demonstrate early delays in oral speech. For example, late speech development, pronunciation problems, and stuttering may indicate SLDs, but these issues may also sometimes be addressed by individualized speech instruction. Students with SLDs may also have problems adjusting socially. They may demonstrate social skills that are not age appropriate. Depending on when the children enter academic settings, they may demonstrate academic delays compared to similar-aged peers. These delays are usually determined using formal and informal assessments in educational settings. Behaviors such as hyperactivity or difficulty following

- 17 -

directions may also indicate a child has a SLD. However, these indicators do not definitely mean a child has a learning disability, and some of the indicators overlap with characteristics of other disabilities.

Instructional Strategies for Teaching Students with Specific Learning Disabilities

While there is no one strategy that works effectively with all students with specific learning disabilities, there are some strategies that tend to produce positive outcomes for these students. Direct instruction, learning strategy instruction, and a multi-sensory approach are three large-scale interventions that can be used to promote student learning. Direct instruction is teacher-driven instruction that targets specific skills. Direct instruction is sometimes delivered in resource rooms. Learning strategy instruction is a method for teaching students with disabilities different tools and techniques useful for learning new content or skills. Learning strategy instruction includes techniques like chunking the content, sequencing tasks, and small group instruction. A multi-sensory approach ensures that students are receiving and interacting with new information and skills using more than one sense at a time. This approach is helpful for students with learning disabilities because it targets many different ways of learning.

Children with Emotional Disturbances

A diagnosis of an emotional disturbance can also be referred to as a behavioral disorder or mental illness. Causes of emotional disturbances are generally unclear. However, heredity, brain disorders, and diet are some factors that influence the development of emotional disturbances. Emotional disturbance is the general term for children with anxiety disorders, bipolar disorder, eating disorders, obsessive-compulsive disorder, or any other psychotic disorders. The Individuals with Disabilities Education Act states that emotional disturbances can affect children beyond emotion and make them eligible for special education with this diagnosis. Children's cognitive, physical, or social behaviors may also be affected. Indicators of emotional disturbances include hyperactivity, aggression, withdrawal, immaturity, and academic difficulties. While many children demonstrate these indicators throughout their development, a strong indicator of an emotional disturbance is a prolonged demonstration of these behaviors. Children who have emotional disorders demonstrate behaviors associated with particular disorders. For example, a child with obsessive-compulsive disorder will demonstrate uncontrolled, reoccurring thoughts and behaviors.

Issues Students with ED Experience in the Instructional Setting

Students with the diagnosis of emotional disturbance (ED) as defined by the Individuals with Disabilities Education Act require emotional and behavioral support in the classroom. Students with ED may also require specialized academic instruction in addition to behavioral and emotional support. The amount of support given varies according to the needs of individual students. These students also need scaffolded instruction in social skills, self-awareness, self-esteem, and self-control. Students with ED often exhibit behaviors that impede their learning or the learning of others. Positive Behavioral Support (PBS) is a preventative instructional strategy that focuses on promoting positive behaviors in students. With PBS, teachers or other professionals make changes to students' environments in order to decrease problem behaviors. PBS involves the process of collecting information on the behavior, identifying positive ways to support the behavior, and implementing a support to decrease the behavior. Supports can be implemented schoolwide or in the classroom. However, for students with ED, classroom supports are more effective because they can be individualized.

Signs Indicating a Child Has a Speech or Language Impairment

Speech and language impairments, sometimes referred to as communication disorders, are disabilities recognized by the Individuals with Disabilities Education Act. Students diagnosed with communication disorders are eligible for special education if they qualify for services. Early indicators of communication disorders include but are not limited to:

- not smiling or interacting with others.
- lack of babbling or cooing in infants.
- lack of age-appropriate comprehension skills.
- speech that is not easily understood.
- issues with age-appropriate syntax development.
- issues with age-appropriate social skills.
- deficits in reading and writing skills.

Stuttering, beginning or ending words with incorrect sounds, and hearing loss are also indicators of possible communication disorders. These are symptoms of communication disorders, but they can also be linked to other disabilities, such as hearing impairments or autism. A prolonged demonstration of these indicators may suggest communication disorders. However, children can demonstrate delays and self-correct as they grow.

Qualifications to Be Eligible for Special Education Under the Category of OHI

The category of Other Health Impaired (OHI) under the Individuals with Disabilities Education Act (IDEA) indicates that a child has limited strength, vitality, or alertness. This includes hyper-alertness or hypo-alertness to environmental stimuli. In order to be eligible for special education under this category according to IDEA, the disability must adversely affect educational performance. It must also be due to chronic or acute health problems, such as attention deficit disorder (ADD), attention deficit hyperactivity disorder (ADHD), diabetes, epilepsy, heart conditions, hemophilia, lead poisoning, leukemia, nephritis, rheumatic fever, sickle cell anemia, or Tourette's Syndrome. It is important to note that in order to be eligible under this category, the disability must be affecting a child's academic performance. Since the OHI category encompasses a number of different disabilities, teachers and parents must rely on a student's Individualized Education Program to ensure that individual academic needs are met, and appropriate accommodations and modifications are provided.

Educational Implications and Limitations of Students Eligible for Special Education

According to the Individuals with Disabilities Education Act (IDEA), students who are eligible for special education under the category of Intellectual Disability have significantly lower intellectual abilities, along with adaptive behavior deficits. Previously, intellectual disability was referred to as mental retardation. In 2010, President Obama signed Rosa's Law, which changed the term to intellectual disability. The definition of the disability category remained unchanged. Educational implications of a diagnosis of an intellectual disability differ depending on students' needs as determined by their Individualized Education Programs (IEPs). Students with intellectual disabilities often display limitations to mental functioning in skills like communication, self-care, and social skills (adaptive behavior). In many cases, these skills must be addressed in the educational environments in addition to any academic skill deficits. Learning adaptive behaviors and academic skills takes longer for students with intellectual disabilities, so their special education placements depend upon what environments are least restrictive. This depends on the individual student and is determined in the IEP.

Components of the Multiple Disability Eligibility Category According to IDEA

A diagnosis of multiple disabilities according to the Individuals with Disabilities Education Act (IDEA) indicates two or more disabilities occurring simultaneously. The difference between a diagnosis of intellectual disability and multiple disabilities is that students with multiple disabilities present with such severe educational needs that they cannot be accommodated in special education settings that address only one disability. Students with multiple disabilities require assistance for more than one disability. Their educational performances are adversely affected by their disabilities. Placement in special education programs is determined by students' least restrictive environments and defined in their Individualized Education Programs. The multiple disability category does not encompass deaf-blindness, which has its own category under IDEA. Students with multiple disabilities often present with communication deficits and difficulties, mobility challenges, deficits in adaptive behavior, and the need for one-on-one instruction or assistance when performing daily activities.

Qualifications to Receive Special Education for Orthopedic Impairment

A student who qualifies to receive special education under the Individuals with Disabilities Education Act category for Orthopedic Impairment has a disability that adversely affects educational performance. This includes children with congenital anomalies, impairments caused by disease, or impairments from other causes, such as cerebral palsy or amputations. An orthopedic impairment alone does not qualify a student for special education and an Individualized Education Program. Once a student's educational performance is proven to be affected by the orthopedic impairment, the student can be eligible for special education and placed on an IEP. The IEP determines the student's least restrictive environment, individualized goals for academic skills or adaptive behavior, and any appropriate accommodations or modifications. Students with orthopedic impairments whose educational performances are not affected may receive accommodations and modifications on 504 Plans if appropriate for their disabilities. Strategies for instruction should be determined and implemented on a case by case basis, as the orthopedic impairment category covers a broad range of disabilities.

Strategies Facilitating Learning in Students with Speech or Language Impairments

In order to teach students with speech or language impairments, also referred to as communication disorders, special educators and professionals can use certain strategies to ensure learning takes place. Teachers and other professionals can use the strategies listed below.

- Use visuals and concrete examples to help students with communication disorders take in new information visually. Link the visuals with spoken words or phrases.
- Use visuals or photographs to introduce or reinforce vocabulary.
- Use repetition of spoken words to introduce or reinforce vocabulary.
- Model conversational and social skills, which helps students with communication disorders become familiar with word pronunciation.
- Speak at a slower rate when necessary, especially when presenting new information.
- Consistently check for understanding.
- Be aware that communication issues may sometimes result in other issues, such as behavioral or social skill issues.
- Pair actions and motions with words to emphasize meaning, especially for students with receptive language disorders.

Determining If a Child May Have an Intellectual Disability

Students diagnosed with intellectual disabilities (ID) demonstrate deficits in academic skills, abstract thinking, problem solving, language development, new skill acquisition, and retaining information. Students with intellectual disabilities do not adequately meet developmental or social milestones. They demonstrate deficits in functioning with one or more basic living skills. Students with intellectual disabilities struggle conceptually and sometimes demonstrate delays in language development. They may also have difficulties with time and money concepts, short-term memory, time management skills, pre-academic and academic skills, planning, and strategizing. Socially, this population of students may also grasp concrete concepts over abstract concepts, but in a process that is significantly behind their similar-aged, regular education peers. Students with ID demonstrate poor social judgement and decision-making skills because they have trouble understanding social cues and rules. These students also tend to struggle with self-care skills, household tasks, and completing tasks that may be easy for similar-aged peers.

Promoting a Positive Educational Performance for Students with Intellectual Disabilities

Students with intellectual disabilities often present skills that are far below the skill levels of similar-aged peers. Due to skill deficits in academic, behavioral, and social skills, these students require specialized instruction to address specific skills. The skills addressed vary depending on the needs of each individual student. An effective strategy for promoting a positive educational performance is to collect observations and data on the academic, behavioral, and social skill levels of the individual student. Teachers usually work with related services members, like speech language pathologists, to address needs and implement educational interventions that work for this population of students. These students can benefit from communication interventions focused on interactions the students may have with adults and peers. Students may benefit from augmentative communication devices, visual activity schedules, visual supports, and computer-based instruction to teach communication and social skills. Students with ID may also require behavioral interventions to teach appropriate behaviors or decrease negative behaviors. They may also benefit from increased peer interactions through structured social groups in order to promote appropriate communication skills.

Early Indications of Visual Impairment or Blindness

A visual impairment ranges from low vision to blindness. The Individuals with Disabilities Education Act defines a visual impairment as an impairment in vision that is great enough to affect a child's educational performance. Blindness is defined as a visual acuity of 20/200 or less in the dominant eye. Some people diagnosed with blindness still have minimal sight. Early indicators of a visual impairment or blindness for children include:

- holding things closely to their eyes or faces.
- experiencing fatigue after looking at things closely.
- misaligned eyes or squinting.
- tilting heads or covering eyes to see things up close or far away.
- demonstrating clumsiness.
- appearing to see better during the day.

Students who are diagnosed with visual impairments or blindness who are also eligible for special education benefit the most from early interventions, especially when the impairments are present with other disabilities. Appropriate interventions vary based on each student and whether or not the impairments are paired with other disabilities. Modifications, such as magnified text, Braille, auditory support, and text-tracking software, also help level the learning plane for these students.

Early Communication and Social Skill Delays in Students with ASD

Students with delays in communication development often need and receive some type of assistance or instruction with communication and social skills. For students with Autism Spectrum Disorder (ASD), the need for communication and social skill instruction varies depending on the individual student. Early intervention for these students is key, as communication difficulties are an early symptom of Autism Spectrum Disorder. Key characteristics of early communication difficulties for a student with ASD may include not responding to his/her name, not pointing at objects of interest, avoiding eye contact, not engaging in pretend play, delayed speech or language skills, or repeating words or phrases. Children with ASD may also exhibit overreaction or underreaction to environmental stimuli. Key characteristics of early social skill difficulties for a student with ASD may include preferring to play alone, trouble understanding personal feelings or the feelings of others, not sharing interests with others, and difficulty with personal space boundaries. Infants with ASD may not respond to their names and demonstrate reduced babbling and reduced interest in people. Toddlers with ASD may demonstrate decreased interest in social interactions, difficulty with pretend play, and a preference for playing alone.

Characteristics of Social Skill Delays in Students with ASD

Autism Spectrum Disorder (ASD) is a disability that can affect a student's social, communication, and behavioral abilities. Social skill delays and deficits are common for students with ASD. Characteristics of social skill delays go hand-in-hand with communication limitations for students with ASD. This includes conversational focus on one or two narrow topics or ideas. This limits their conversations to one or two subject areas, and it is difficult for them to hold two-way conversations about things that do not interest them. Some students with ASD engage in repetitive language or echolalia or rely on standard phrases to communicate with others. Their speech and language skills may be delayed compared to their similar-aged peers. This may also affect their abilities to engage in effective, two-way conversations. The nonverbal skills of students with ASD may also be misinterpreted, such as avoiding eye contact while speaking or being spoken to.

Early Signs of a Child Having ASD

Early signs of Autism Spectrum Disorder (ASD) include impairments or delays in social interactions and communication, repetitive behaviors, limited interests, and abnormal eating habits. Students with ASD typically do not interact in conversations in the same ways as similar-aged peers without ASD. They may demonstrate inability to engage in pretend play and may pretend they don't hear when being spoken to. Hand flapping, vocal sounds, or compulsive interactions with objects are repetitive behaviors sometimes demonstrated by students with ASD. They may only demonstrate interest in talking about one topic or be interested in interacting with one object. They may also demonstrate self-injurious behavior or sleep problems, in addition to having a limited diet of preferred foods. Early intervention is key for these students in order to address and improve functioning. These students may also benefit from applied behavior analysis to target specific behaviors and require speech and language therapy, occupational therapy, social skills instruction, or other services geared toward improving intellectual functioning.

Low-Incidence Disabilities and High-Incidence Disabilities

Low-incidence disabilities account for up to 20% of all students' disabilities. Students with low-incidence disabilities have sometimes received assistance for their disabilities starting from an early age. This group includes students with intellectual disabilities and significant developmental delays. Low-incidence disabilities can include intellectual disabilities, multiple disabilities, hearing impairments, orthopedic impairments, other health impairments, visual impairments, autism, deaf-blindness, traumatic brain injury, and developmental delays. High-incidence disabilities account for up to 80% of all students' disabilities. Students with high-incidence disabilities present with academic, social, and/or behavioral problems and can often be held to the same standards as their regular education peers. Children with high-incidence disabilities may perform at the same capacities as their similar-aged peers but have deficits in reading, math, writing, handwriting, or maintaining attention. They may also present with limitations in communication, adaptive behavior, and social skills. Examples of high-incidence disabilities include speech and language impairments, learning disabilities, attention deficit hyperactivity disorder, emotional disorders, mild intellectual disabilities, certain spectrums of autism, and cognitive delays.

Sensory Processing Disorders

When a person experiences a deficit with handling sensory information interpreted by the brain, this is called a sensory processing disorder (SPD). In brains without SPD, people can experience sensory input, and their brain receptors can interpret them to demonstrate appropriate reactions. In brains of people with SPD, the brains experience sensory input, but the brains' receptors are blocked, resulting in abnormal reactions. Previously known as a sensory integration disorder, SPD is not a disability specifically defined or eligible under the Individuals with Disabilities Education Act (IDEA). However, many students with disabilities defined by IDEA, like autism, also experience some sort of sensory processing disorder. Students with SPD may display oversensitive or under-sensitive responses to their environments, stimuli, and senses. Students with SPD may not understand physical boundaries, such as where their bodies are in space. They may bump into things and demonstrate clumsiness. These students may get upset easily, throw tantrums, demonstrate high anxiety, and not handle changes well.

Characteristics and Causes of ADHD and ADD

Children with Attention Deficit Hyperactivity Disorder (ADHD) may demonstrate hyperactivity, inattention, and impulsivity. However, they may demonstrate hyperactivity and inattention only or hyperactivity and impulsivity. Children with Attention Deficit Disorder (ADD) demonstrate inattention and impulsivity, but not hyperactivity. Students with either ADHD or ADD may have difficulties with attention span, following instructions, and concentrating to the point that educational performance is affected. Since ADD and ADHD symptoms are common among children, their presence does not necessarily indicate that a child needs a diagnosis of ADD or ADHD. ADD and ADHD are not caused by certain environmental factors, such as diet or watching too much television. Symptoms may be exacerbated by these factors, but the real causes can be heredity, chemical imbalances, issues with brain functions, environmental toxins, or prenatal trauma, such as the mother smoking or drinking during pregnancy.

Importance of Adaptive Behavior Skills Instruction for Students with Disabilities

Adaptive behavior skills refer to age-appropriate behaviors that people need to live independently and function in daily life. Adaptive behavior skills include self-care skills, following rules, managing money, making friends, and more. For students with disabilities, especially severely limiting disabilities, adaptive behavior skills may need to be included in daily instruction. Adaptive behavior skills can be separated into conceptual skills, social skills, and practical life skills. Conceptual skills include academic concepts, such as reading, math, money, time, and communication skills. Social skills instruction focuses on teaching students to get along with others, communicate appropriately, and maintain appropriate behavior inside and outside the school environment. Practical life skills are skills needed to perform the tasks of daily living. Adaptive behavior assessments are useful in assessing what adaptive behavior skills need to be addressed for each student. These assessments are usually conducted using observations and questionnaires completed by parents, teachers, or students.

Effect of Environmental Factors on Social-Emotional Development

A person's environment has a large impact on social-emotional environment. Factors that impact a child's social-emotional development include:

- family relationships and environment.
- play-based learning.
- a nurturing environment.
- verbal skills.

Children who grow up with strong, solid family relationships in stable environments tend to develop appropriate social-emotional skills. Children who experience family or environmental stress and trauma, such as divorce or constant fighting, may demonstrate deficits in their social-emotional growth. Play-based learning fosters important skills and brain development when children observe adults demonstrating acceptable social behavior. In positive, nurturing environments, children learn by watching adults interacting appropriately with one another. They learn skills that foster social and emotional well-being. The first sounds infants hear are voices. Children first grasp a sense of spoken language in their home environments. Caregivers that speak to their children consistently help them develop strong verbal skills.

Physical Stages of Gross Motor Development in Children

Gross motor skills refer to larger motor skills that require movement of the body as a whole. Gross motor skills begin developing in infancy as children learn to crawl and walk. At ages two to three, children transition from toddling to walking, then learn to jump, run, hop, throw, catch, and push themselves in riding toys with their feet. Children ages three to four become skilled at stair climbing. They also jump higher and develop better upper body mobility. Additionally, they develop the ability to ride a small bike or tricycle and kick large balls accurately. At ages four to five, children can go up and down stairs with ease. They also develop running mobility skills and speed and have more control when riding bikes or tricycles. Children ages five to six fine tune previously learned gross motor skills. They are more adept at physical play skills, such as those needed to play on jungle gyms or swings independently. Children in this age range demonstrate interest in organized sports and other extracurricular activities. Children develop and refine their gross motor skills as they grow. Sometimes a child will demonstrate a delay in a gross motor skill, but this does not always indicate a disability. Some disabilities are characterized by specific delays in gross motor skills. Parents and educators should be familiar with gross motor skill milestones in order to pinpoint any significant delays in students.

Fine Motor Abilities of Children

Fine motor skills are skills focused on smaller movements, usually involving the hands and fingers. Children ages two to three begin to make things using their hands, such as block towers. They can scribble with writing utensils and manipulate playdough. They demonstrate conceptual knowledge of basic puzzles, fitting appropriate pieces into their correct locations. At this age, children begin to demonstrate a right or left-hand dominance. Adjusting fasteners, such as buttons and snaps, independently dressing and undressing, and cutting paper with scissors are fine motor milestones for children ages three to four. These children also fine tune their eating skills and use larger writing tools, maintaining a specific grip instead of a grasp. Children ages four to five refine their fine motor skills. Their artistic skills become more refined as they become more confident in hand dominance and drawing. Children ages five to seven begin to demonstrate fine motor abilities, such as writing letters and numbers and creating shapes. They use utensils and writing tools with greater ease. Children in this age range can complete self-care tasks independently, such as teeth brushing. A child with a fine motor delay would demonstrate a significant deficit in one or more fine motor skills at one or more stages of development.

Classroom Strategies Promoting Social-Emotional Development and Growth

Classroom environments should emanate positivity and growth. Classrooms that promote social-emotional development and growth provide security for students and create environments where learning takes place. Teachers can promote social-emotional development and growth by creating predictable classroom routines with visual reminders, keeping classrooms free of dangerous objects and materials, and arranging for learning to take place in large and small groups. They can also rotate activities and materials to keep students engaged, provide appropriate materials for learning centers, and create opportunities for children to engage socially. Teachers can act as nurturing adults by encouraging social interactions and problem solving, modeling appropriate language and social skills, encouraging and validating children's thoughts and feelings, and using clear signals to indicate transitions between activities. Teachers should build community environments in their classrooms, build appropriate relationships with students by getting to know their strengths and weaknesses, and demonstrate good conflict resolution and problem-solving abilities.

Educational Implications of Instructing Children with ADHD or ADD

The Individuals with Disabilities Education Act (IDEA) does not recognize Attention Deficit Hyperactivity Disorder (ADHD) or Attention Deficit Disorder (ADD) in any of its 13 major disability categories. Students may be diagnosed with ADHD or ADD only by a physician, but this diagnosis is not enough to qualify the student for special education services. When ADHD or ADD are present with another disability, such as a learning disability, the student qualifies for special education services under the learning disability. A student whose ability to learn is affected by ADHD or ADD can receive services with a 504 Plan in place. Section 504 provides services for any child whose disability affects a major life activity and makes the child eligible for accommodations and modifications in the classroom. This ensures that the child receives appropriate accommodations and/or modifications in the learning environment in order to be successful. Parents who think a child's disability adversely affects educational functioning may request a formal evaluation to be performed by the school. If a child is found to qualify for special education services, the child receives services under the Other Health Impaired category of IDEA.

Effect of Emotional and Psychological Needs on Students with a Disabilities

When a child is diagnosed with a disability, educators often primarily focus on the educational implications. However, students with disabilities also have emotional needs associated with their disabilities. These needs vary by student and disability. Generally, students with disabilities struggle emotionally. Symptoms may include low self-esteem, anxiety, acting out, reduced intrinsic motivation, and physical symptoms like headaches. Educators, parents, and other professionals can manage the emotional needs of students with disabilities by talking about the disability diagnoses and educational implications of the diagnoses with the students. Educators can increase their awareness of how students might be feeling about the diagnoses and identify situations that may cause anxiety or acting out. Educators can also help by praising students consistently, even for small actions, which can help with confidence. Parents, educators, and other professionals can also work together to ensure that the students receive instruction in the most appropriate educational environments for their disabilities.

Determining Severe, Profound, and Mild Intellectual Disabilities

69b. There are three levels of intellectual disabilities: severe, profound, and mild. Specific factors are used to determine whether a disability is severe, profound, or mild. Intellectual levels are measured using cognitive-based and research-based assessments. An intellectual disability is defined as having significant cognitive deficits to intellectual functioning, such as reasoning, problem solving, abstract thinking, and comprehension. A mild to moderate intellectual disability (ID) is the most common type of intellectual disability. People with mild to moderate ID can generally participate in independent living skills and learn practical life skills and adaptive behavior. People diagnosed with severe intellectual disabilities demonstrate major developmental delays. They struggle with simple routines and self-care skills. Additionally, they often understand speech but have trouble with expressive communication. People with profound ID cannot live independently and depend heavily on care from other people and resources. They are likely to have congenital disorders that affect their intellectual functioning.

Social Cognitive Learning Theory

Albert Bandura's social cognitive learning theory features four stages or processes of observational learning: attention, retention, production, and motivation. Observational learning is based on the idea that a person modifies behavior after being provided with a model for the behavior. Not to be confused with exact imitation of behavior, observational learning occurs when a behavior is witnessed then demonstrated at a later time as a result of witnessing the behavior. For example, a child learns how to hold eating utensils by watching an adult hold the utensils. Attention refers to a person paying attention to what is happening in the environment. In the retention stage, a person not only observes the behavior, but stores it in memory to perform later. Production requires the person to be physically and mentally able to reproduce the behavior. The motivation stage means the person must be motivated or have an incentive to reproduce the behavior. Students with disabilities may struggle with one or more of the observational stages as a characteristic of their disabilities. Limitations, such as attention difficulties, present barriers to appropriately moving through the observational learning processes.

Educational Implications of a Diagnosis of an Impairment

Speech or Language Impairment and Visual Impairment or Blindness adversely affect a student's educational performance. Students with Speech or Language Impairments and Visual Impairments or Blindness are provided with accommodations, modifications, and related services specific to their disabilities. Students with these impairments may be educated alongside peers and provided with related services outside of the general education classroom. Similar to these disabilities, the educational performances of students with Deafness or Hearing Impairments are also affected by their disabilities. Accommodations, modifications, and related services are provided based on the severity of the disability.

An OI severely impairs mobility or motor activity. Accommodations, modifications, and related services in the classroom environments may be appropriate for students with Orthopedic Impairments. Students with ID, such as students with Down Syndrome, often need supports in place for communication, self-care, and social skills. The educational implications of a student with TBI are unique to the individual and are therefore treated on a case by case basis. Students with MD have needs that cannot be met in any one program. Sometimes their needs are so great that they must be educated in partial inclusion or self-contained settings.

Autism Spectrum Disorder vs. Specific Learning Disabilities

Autism Spectrum Disorder (ASD) and learning disabilities can exist concurrently. Students with ASD may also have a lot in common with students with learning disabilities. However, ASD is a spectrum disorder that affects children in different ways. ASD is often confused with learning and attention issues, but students with ASD can have IQs ranging from significantly delayed to above average or gifted. Students with learning disabilities often have consistently lower IQs. Students with attention issues like Attention Deficit Hyperactivity Disorder also have varying needs, depending on if the ADHD exists with a learning disability or ASD. Students with learning disabilities and students with ASD may both have difficulties recognizing and reading nonverbal cues, staying organized, problem solving, and expressing themselves. They may also have issues with desiring or rejecting sensory input. These disabilities are different because ASD involves struggles with social understanding and communication, along with repetitive routines or behaviors. These struggles are not associated with students with learning disabilities.

Role of Cultural Competence in Schools and Special Education

Schools have a duty to abide by cultural competence in order to ensure avoidance of cultural and linguistic bias. Schools that demonstrate cultural competence have an appreciation of families and their unique backgrounds. Cultural competence is important because it assists with incorporating knowledge and appreciation of other cultures into daily practices and teaching. This helps increase the quality and effectiveness of how students with unique cultural and linguistic backgrounds are provided with services. It also helps produce better outcomes for these students. In special education, being culturally competent means being aware of cultural and linguistic differences, especially when considering children for the identification process. Adapting to the diversity and cultural contexts of the surrounding communities allows teachers to better understand flags for referrals. Teachers that continually assess their awareness of the cultures and diversity of the communities where they teach demonstrate cultural competence. In order for schools and teachers to be described as culturally competent, they should have a process for recognizing diversity. They should also learn about and incorporate knowledge of cultural diversity into their classrooms.

Cultural and Linguistic Differences vs. Learning Difficulties

Many schools are enriched with cultural diversity. It is important for special educators to identify if a suspected learning disability may instead be a cultural or linguistic difference in a student. Teachers and schools must increase awareness of cultural and linguistic differences in order to avoid overidentification of this population as having learning difficulties. Some ways a child's behavior may represent cultural or linguistic differences are demonstrated in the interactions between teachers and students. In some cultures, children are asked to make eye contact to ensure they are listening, whereas in other cultures, children are taught to look down or away when being spoken to by an adult. Certain facial expressions and behaviors may be interpreted differently by students due to their cultural backgrounds. Additionally, teaching methods that are comfortable and effective for some students may be ineffective for others due to differing cultural backgrounds. Cultural values and characteristics may vary between teachers and students and contribute to the students' school performances. It is important for teachers to be self-aware and constantly assess whether ineffective teaching methods are due to learning difficulties or differences in cultural and linguistic diversity.

Instructional Strategies for Teaching ESL Students and Students with Disabilities

English as a Second Language (ESL) students are often at risk for being referred for special education services. This is frequently a result of inadequate planning for the needs of English language learners rather than skill deficits. To ensure that the needs of ESL students are met and discrimination is avoided, educators can implement strategies for targeting their learning processes. Strategies similar to those utilized in inclusive special education settings are helpful, such as using visuals to supplement instruction. This type of nonlinguistic representation helps convey meaning to ESL students. Working in groups with peers helps students with disabilities and ESL students demonstrate communication and social skills while working toward common goals. Allowing students to write and speak in their first languages until they feel comfortable speaking in English is a scaffolding strategy that can also be implemented. Sentence frames that demonstrate familiar sentence formats are helpful for all students to practice speaking and writing in structured, formal ways.

Teaching Appropriate Communication Skills

Students with disabilities who are also English Language Learners (ELLs) have the additional challenge of language barriers affecting their access to learning. These barriers, combined with the disabilities, can also make instruction for these students challenging. For ELL students with disabilities, it is important for teachers to rely on appropriate instructional strategies in order to determine what is affecting the students' access to information. Instructional strategies for teaching ELL students are similar to teaching strategies used for nonverbal students. Pairing visuals with words helps students make concrete connections between the written words and the pictures. The consistency of seeing the words paired with the visuals increases the likelihood of the students beginning to interpret word meanings. Using sign language is another way teachers can facilitate word meaning. When used consistently, students make connections between the visual word meanings and the written words. Teachers can also provide opportunities for ELL students to access language by having all classroom students communicate in a consistent manner. The goal of this instructional strategy is for peers to model appropriate verbal communication as it applies to different classroom situations.

Benefits the Socratic Method

With the Socratic method of teaching, students are guided by their teachers in their own educational discovery learning processes. This involves students intrinsically seeking knowledge or answers to problems. This method can be helpful for facilitating and enhancing the social and emotional abilities of students with disabilities, particularly Autism Spectrum Disorder (ASD). The Socratic method requires dialogue in order to successfully facilitate the teacher/student guided learning process. This is beneficial for students with autism who generally struggle with appropriate communication and social skills. This method emphasizes information seeking and communication skills by engaging students in class discussions, assignment sharing, and group work. Communication for information-seeking purposes is often a deficit of students with ASD. Sharing of ideas is a concept that develops naturally in guided learning and often requires flexibility in the thought process, another skill that students with ASD struggle with. These skills can be taught and reinforced to students with and without disabilities in order to develop skills essential to life-long learning processes.

Erikson's Four Earliest Social Stages of Human Development

The stages of human development and behavior are separated into seven human age groups, with the four earliest being infancy (birth to 2 years old), early childhood (3 to 8 years old), middle childhood (9 to 11 years old), and adolescence (12 to 18 years old). As children age, they build upon each stage. Growth is unique to each individual. According to Erikson's theory of psychosocial development, each developmental stage is characterized by crises. During infancy, babies learn trust versus mistrust (hope). This is when a nurtured and loved infant would develop trust, and a mistreated infant would not. The infancy stage is also formed by autonomy versus shame (will). This stage is characterized by the exertion of will and the seeking of independence by small children. Early childhood is characterized by learning initiative versus guilt (purpose). During this stage, children begin to develop their interpersonal skills. Industry versus inferiority (competence) also develops during early childhood. During this stage, teachers begin to play an important role, as school-aged children learn competence in new skills. Throughout middle childhood and adolescence, children learn identity versus role confusion (fidelity). The identity stage is when adolescents seek to form their individual identities.

Values of the Social Cognitive Theory

The three values or valuables of the social cognitive theory are behavioral factors, personal factors (intrinsic), and environmental factors (extrinsic). The social cognitive behavior theory suggests that these three variables are connected to each other and therefore promote learning. The basic concepts of the social cognitive theory can become evident in infancy, childhood, and adulthood. These concepts include observational learning, reproduction, self-efficacy, emotional coping, and self-regulatory capability. Observational learning is the process by which people learn behavior by observing other behaviors. This is especially influenced by a person's environment. Reproduction occurs when a person repeats modeled behavior. Reproduction can be impeded by a person's limited abilities. Self-efficacy is when a person puts new knowledge or behavior into action. Emotional coping is a learning process where people develop coping skills for dealing with stressful environments and negative influences. The development of good emotional coping skills influences learning processes. Self-regulatory capability describes a person's ability to manage choices and behavior even when influenced by negative environments.

Gardner's Theory of Multiple Intelligences

Howard Gardner developed the theory of multiple intelligences, which outlines seven different ways he believes people can learn. Gardner's theory was based on the idea that everyone understands the world through different intelligences, and our individual intelligence strengths are what make people different. The multiple intelligences are described below.

- Visual-spatial thinkers think about things visually. They are very aware of their environments. They are good at activities like completing puzzles, drawing, and reading maps. They learn best through the use of visuals, such as graphs and diagrams.
- Bodily-kinesthetic thinkers learn best with a hands-on approach. They process information by doing. They learn best through physical activities.
- Musical thinkers are sensitive to music, sound, and rhythm in their environments. They learn best when lesson concepts are turned into musical features like lyrics and songs.
- Interpersonal thinkers like to learn by interacting with others. They find learning easy in group environments like seminars and lecture halls.
- Intrapersonal thinkers are independent learners. They learn best using introspection.

- Linguistic thinkers are efficient and use words to express themselves. They are auditory learners who enjoy reading, word games, and making up stories.
- Logical-mathematical thinkers learn best through familiar patterns and relationships. They think conceptually and reasonably.

Cognitive Behavioral Theory

The cognitive behavioral theory states that people form their own negative or positive concepts that affect their behaviors. The cognitive behavioral theory involves a cognitive triad of human thoughts and behaviors. This triad refers to human thoughts about the self, the world and environment, and the future. In times of stress, people's thoughts can become distressed or dysfunctional. Sometimes cognitive behavioral therapy, based on the cognitive behavioral theory model, is used to help people address and manage their thoughts. This process involves people examining their thoughts more closely in order to bring them back to more realistic, grounded ways of thinking. People's thoughts and perceptions can often affect their lives negatively and lead to unhealthy emotions and behaviors. Cognitive behavioral therapy helps people to adjust their thinking, learn ways to access healthy thoughts, and learn behaviors incompatible with unhealthy or unsafe behaviors.

Social and Emotional Skill Expectations and Milestones of Toddlers and Preschoolers

Toddlers 18 months to 2 years old typically begin to demonstrate their independence and show an increasing interest in communication. Toddlers exhibit temper tantrums and an increase in defiant behavior. Children in this age group begin to imitate the actions of familiar adults and engage in pretend play. They also demonstrate an interest in playing with other children but engage in side-by-side play (parallel play) instead of cooperative play. Preschoolers ages 3 and 4 continue to demonstrate independence and build on their communication skills. They may also demonstrate temper tantrums and defiant behavior. Preschoolers are able to verbalize a wider range of emotions, especially when they do not get what they want or have trouble communicating what they want. They begin to engage with their peers in cooperative play and start to play independently. Preschoolers are still interested in and engage in pretend play. At this age, they begin to recognize adults' moods or feelings. They begin to exhibit moments of helpfulness and kindness.

Social and Emotional Skill Expectations and Milestones of Grade Schoolers

Children typically enter kindergarten at ages 5 to 6. They begin to exert their independence and test boundaries at home and school. They show a preference to playing with kids their own ages and sometimes their own genders. Their conversational language grows as they interact with other students. At ages 7 to 8, children start to become aware of what others might think of them. They may be more sensitive to interpersonal relationships with their peers. They can aptly express their feelings but get frustrated when they do not have the right words. At ages 9-10, children begin getting selective with their peer friendships. They may prefer a few close friends over getting along with everyone. They begin to demonstrate more independence and start attempting to develop their own identities. Children in this age group are able to communicate their feelings but can still get frustrated. They demonstrate a wide range of emotions in adult and peer interactions.

Piaget's Four Stages of Cognitive Development

Piaget's four stages of cognitive development are sensorimotor (birth to 18 months), preoperational (18-24 months to age 7), concrete operational (ages 7 to 12), and formal operational (adolescence to adulthood). During the sensorimotor stage, newborn infants only have a minute awareness. As they grow, they begin to interact with their environments before developing object permanence at 7-9 months. Another important milestone that develops during this stage is early language development. During the preoperational stage, infants grow into young children and their language becomes more meaningful. They develop memory and imagination but cannot yet grasp complex concepts such as cause and effect. The concrete operational stage is characterized by concrete reasoning. Children in this stage become more aware of the world around them and are less egocentric. They cannot yet think abstractly or hypothetically. During the formal operational stage, adolescents are able to engage in abstract thinking. They are now able to formulate hypotheses and demonstrate logical thought and deductive reasoning.

Rights and the Roles Families in the Educations of Children with Disabilities

Under IDEA, parents and legal guardians of children with disabilities have procedural safeguards that protect their rights. The safeguards also provide parents and legal guardians of children with disabilities with the means to resolve any disputes with school systems. Families serve as advocates for their children with disabilities. Parents and legal guardians may underestimate their importance to Individualized Education Program teams. However, they are important members of the Individualized Education Program teams and integral parts of the decision-making processes for their children's educational journeys. Parents and legal guardians often work more closely with their children than other adults. Therefore, as part of the IEP teams, parents and legal guardians often provide insight regarding the children's backgrounds, educational histories, developmental histories, strengths, and weaknesses. Parents and legal guardians are also important decision makers in transition meetings, when students with disabilities move from one level of school to another. Parent and legal guardian input in transition meetings ensures that appropriate services and supports are in place within the next levels of school in order to ensure student success.

Targeting and Implementing Social Skills Instruction

Developing good social skills is essential for lifelong student success, and people with disabilities often struggle with these skills. Addressing social skill behavior is most effective when:

- social skill needs are specifically identified.
- social skills instruction is implemented as a collaborative effort between parents and teachers.

Evaluating developmental milestones is helpful in targeting social skills that need to be addressed and taught. If a child with a disability is not demonstrating a milestone, such as back and forth communication, this skill can be evaluated to determine if it should be taught. However, meeting milestones is not a surefire way to measure a student's social skill ability, as some children naturally progress more slowly. Social skill deficits may be acquisition deficits, performance deficits, or fluency deficits. Acquisition deficits occur when a student demonstrates an absence of a skill or behavior. Performance deficits occur when a student does not implement a social skill consistently. A fluency deficit means a student needs assistance with demonstrating a social skill effectively or fluently. Once the student's social skill need is identified, teachers, parents, and other professionals can collaborate to incorporate an established routine or behavior contract or to implement applied behavior analysis.

Purposes and Benefits of Social Skills Groups

Social skills groups are useful for helping students with social skill deficits learn and practice appropriate skills with their peers. Social skills groups are primarily composed of similar-aged peers with and without disabilities. An adult typically leads the group and teaches students skills needed for making friends, succeeding in school and life, and sometimes obtaining and maintaining a job. Other professionals, such as school psychologists or speech language pathologists, may also lead social skills groups. Social skills groups work by facilitating conversation and focusing on skill deficits, such as reading facial cues. Social skills groups have many benefits. They can help students learn to appropriately greet others, begin conversations, respond appropriately, maintain conversations, engage in turn-taking, and request help when needed.

Receiving Special Education Services in the Least Restrictive Environment

The Individuals with Disabilities Education Act (IDEA) requires a free and appropriate public education (FAPE) to be provided in a student with a disability's least restrictive environment (LRE). This means that a student who qualifies for special education should be educated in a free, appropriate, and public setting and be placed in an instructional setting that meets the LRE principle. IDEA states that LRE means students with disabilities should participate in the general education classroom "to the maximum extent that is appropriate." Mainstreaming and inclusion are two words that are associated with LRE because these are the two settings where students with disabilities can participate in the general education classroom while receiving appropriate accommodations, modifications, interventions, and/or related services. The amount of time a student spends in an LRE suitable for his or her individual needs is stated in the Individualized Education Program (IEP). The accommodations, modifications, interventions, and/or related services the student should receive are also outlined in the IEP. Students who need special education services for more than 50% of the day may be placed in instructional settings that meet their LRE needs, such as resource rooms or self-contained classrooms.

Continuum of Special Education Services

IDEA mandates that school systems must educate students with disabilities with students who do not have disabilities to the maximum extent that is appropriate. IDEA also mandates that schools may not take students out of regular education classes unless the classes are not benefitting the students. Supplementary aids and support services must be in place before students can be considered for removal. Schools must offer a continuum of special education services that offer a restrictive to least restrictive range. In a typical continuum of services, regular education classrooms offer the least restrictive access to students with disabilities. After regular education classrooms, students can be educated in resource rooms, then special classes that target specific deficits. Special schools, homebound services, and hospitals and institutions are the last three least restrictive educational options for children with disabilities. The number of students in these continuum settings decreases as restriction increases. Fewer students benefit from being educated in hospitals or institutions than in resource rooms.

Evidence-Based Methods for Promoting Self-Determination

Students with disabilities often need to be taught skills for promoting self-determination and self-advocacy. These skills may not come easily to students with specific disorders like autism. Self-determination involves a comprehensive understanding of one's own strengths and limitations. Self-determined people are goal-oriented and intrinsically motivated to improve themselves. Teachers can facilitate the teaching of these skills in a number of ways, starting in early elementary school. In early elementary school, teachers can promote self-determination by teaching choice-making skills and providing clear consequences for these choices. Teacher can also promote problem-solving and self-management skills, like having students evaluate their own work. At the middle school and junior high level, students can be taught to evaluate and analyze their choices.

They can also learn academic and personal goal-setting skills and decision-making skills. At the high school level, teachers can promote decision-making skills, involvement in educational planning (i.e. attending their Individualized Education Program meetings), and strategies like self-instruction, self-monitoring, and self-evaluation. Throughout the educational process, teachers should establish and maintain high standards for learning, focus on students' strengths, and create positive learning environments that promote choice and problem-solving skills.

Teaching Self-Awareness Skills

Students engage in private self-awareness and public self-awareness. Some students with disabilities have the additional challenge of needing instruction in self-awareness skills. Special educators and other professionals can facilitate the instruction of self-awareness skills by teaching students to be aware of their thoughts, feelings, and actions. Self-awareness also means teaching students how their thoughts, feelings, and actions affect other people. Students can be taught self-awareness by identifying their own strengths and weaknesses and learning to self-monitor errors in assignments. They can also be taught to identify what materials or steps are needed to complete tasks. Additionally, students can learn to recognize that other people have needs and feelings and recognize how their behaviors affect others. Students can also learn self-awareness by recognizing the limitations of their disabilities and learning to advocate for accommodations or strategies that work for them. Special educators or other professionals should frequently talk with students about their performances and encourage students to discuss their mistakes without criticism.

Importance of Learning Self-Advocacy Skills

Self-advocacy is an important skill to learn for people entering adulthood. For students with disabilities, self-advocacy skills are especially important for success in post-secondary environments. Teaching and learning self-advocacy skills should begin when students enter grade school and be reinforced in the upper grade levels. Students with disabilities who have the potential to enter post-secondary education or employment fields need to learn self-advocacy skills in order to communicate how their disabilities may affect their educational or job performances. They must also communicate the need for supports and possible accommodations in the educational, training, or employment fields. Students with disabilities who graduate or age out of their Individualized Education Programs do not receive the educational supports they received at the grade school level. It is essential for students to advocate for themselves in the absence of teachers or caregivers advocating for them, especially when students independently enter post-secondary employment, training, or educational environments. Many colleges, universities, communities, and work environments offer services to students with disabilities who need them, but it is up to the students to advocate for themselves and seek them out.

Providing Instruction in the Area of Functional Living Skills

Also known as life skills, functional skills are skills students need to know to live independently. Ideally, students leave high school having gained functional skills. For students with special needs, functional skills instruction is needed to gain independent living skills. Students with developmental disabilities or cognitive disabilities sometimes need to acquire basic living skills, such as self-feeding or toileting. Applied behavior analysis is a process where these skills can be broken down, modeled, and taught. These students must also learn functional math and language arts skills, such as managing money and reading bus schedules. Students may also participate in community-based instruction to learn skills while completing independent living tasks in the community. These skills include grocery shopping, reading restaurant menus, and riding public transportation. Social skills instruction is also important for these students, as learning appropriate social interactions is necessary to function with community members.

Types of Developmental Assessments

Developmental assessments measure the development of infants, toddlers, and preschoolers. These norm-referenced tests measure fine and gross motor skills, communication and language, and social, cognitive, and self-help milestones that young children should achieve at certain ages. When a child is suspected of having a developmental delay, a developmental assessment is useful in identifying the child's strengths and weaknesses. Developmental assessments map out the progress of a child compared to the progress of similar-aged children. Developmental assessments are also useful in identifying if the delay is significant or can be overcome with time. These assessments can be used to determine what educational placement is most appropriate for a child with a developmental delay. Developmental assessments are administered via observations and questionnaires. Parents, legal guardians, caregivers, and instructors who are most familiar with the child provide the most insight on developmental strengths and weaknesses.

Screening Tests for Identifying Students

When determining if a child needs special education, screening tests are the first step. The Individuals with Disabilities Education Act (IDEA) offers guidance for schools to implement screening tests. Districts and schools often have school-wide processes in place for screening students for special education. Screening tests can also be used to identify students who are falling behind in class. The advantage of screening tests is that they are easily administered. They require few materials and little time and planning in order to administer. Additionally, they can be used to quickly assess students' strengths and weaknesses. They do not have to be administered one-on-one and can be used class wide. Screening tests can be as simple as paper and pencil quizzes assessing what students know. Screening tests are used for measuring visual acuity, auditory skills, physical health, development, basic academic skills, behavioral problems, children at risk for behavioral problems, language skills, and verbal and nonverbal intelligence.

Individual Intelligence Tests vs. Individual Academic Achievement Tests

Intelligence tests measure a student's capacity for abstract thinking, mental reasoning, judgement, and decision making. These norm-referenced tests help determine a student's overall intelligence, which correlates with potential academic performance. Intelligence tests can be used to determine if a student's deficits are due to intellectual disabilities or related to specific learning disabilities or emotional disorders. Intelligence tests are also known as intelligence quotient tests (IQ tests). IQ tests should be administered by trained professionals in order to ensure the tests are administered accurately. Intelligence tests can also measure verbal skills, motor performance, and visual reasoning. Unlike intelligence tests, individual academic tests measure a student's strengths and weaknesses in individual skills. They are also norm referenced and used to determine if a student needs special education services. Results from individual academic tests help determine areas of concern or possible deficits for an individual student. Unlike intelligence tests, individual academic tests can be administered by teachers.

Adaptive Behavior Scale Assessments

Adaptive behavior scales are useful for diagnosing a student with an intellectual disability that affects the development or progression of adaptive behavior. They are used in preschools and for determining eligibility for special education in grade schools. They are also used in planning curriculum for students with intellectual disabilities. Adaptive behavior scales are standardized but not always norm referenced because of difficulties comparing expectations for some adaptive and maladaptive skills exhibited by similar-aged peers. In terms of curriculum planning, these assessments can determine what type and how much assistance a student may need. Adaptive behavior scale assessments identify a student's level of independence. Adaptive behavior scales can be used to determine skill abilities associated with daily living, community functioning, social skills, communication, motor functions, and basic academic skills. Teachers and other professionals can administer adaptive behavior scales to students with intellectual disabilities to determine starting points for improving their adaptive behavior deficits.

Curriculum Based Measurement for Measuring Student Academic Progress

Curriculum Based Measurement (CBM) is a way for teachers to track how students are progressing in mathematics, language arts, social studies, science, and other skills. CBM is useful for addressing how students with special needs are progressing on their Individualized Education Program (IEP) goals. It is also useful for communicating progress to parents or legal guardians. CBM results can determine whether or not current instructional strategies are effective for particular students. In the same respect, CBM can determine if students are meeting the standards laid out in their IEP goals. If instructional strategies are not effective or their goals are not being met, CBM progress (or lack of progress) signals that the teachers should change instructional strategies. CBM can be revisited to determine whether or not the newly implemented strategies are effective. Progress can sometimes be charted to present a visual for how a student is progressing in a particular content area or with a specific skill.

Woodcock Johnson Achievement Tests and Identifying Children with High-Incidence Disabilities

Woodcock Johnson achievement tests can be used as diagnostic tools for identifying children with high-incidence disabilities. The Woodcock Johnson Tests of Achievement and the Woodcock Johnson Tests of Cognitive Abilities are comprehensively useful for assessing children's:

- intellectual abilities.
- cognitive abilities.
- aptitude.
- oral language.
- academic achievements.

These norm-referenced tests are valuable in understanding children's strengths and weaknesses and how they compare to cohorts of normally progressing, similar-aged peers. For example, Woodcock Johnson Tests (WJ tests) are useful in identifying children with language disorders because children with language disorders typically score lower on the Listening Comprehension and Fluid Reasoning test sections. The WJ tests are useful diagnostic tools for identifying children with Attention Deficit Hyperactivity Disorder (ADHD) as well. While children with ADHD may perform similarly to children with learning disabilities, their key deficits are in the Cognitive Efficiency, Processing Speed, Academic Fluency, Short-Term Memory, and Long-Term Retrieval test sections.

Woodcock Johnson Achievement Tests and Identifying Students with Learning Disabilities in Reading and Mathematics

The Woodcock Johnson achievement tests (WJ tests) include a test of achievement and a test of cognitive abilities. Together, these assessments are useful in the diagnostic process of identifying a student with a disability. Additionally, they are helpful for identifying specific deficits in a student's reading or math skills. WJ tests are norm referenced and compare the results of a child's performance to that of a cohort of children of similar chronological age and average intellectual abilities. These assessments provide information about a child's reading disorder, such as dyslexia, because they measure phonological awareness, rapid automatized naming, processing speed, and working memory. WJ tests report on a child's cognitive functioning in these test areas. These assessments also provide useful information for students with learning deficits in mathematics. Performances on the Math Calculation Skills and Math Reasoning test sections provide information on specific deficits in general comprehension, fluid reasoning, and processing speed. Children that have deficits in these areas demonstrate relationships to learning disabilities in mathematics.

Evaluating Students with Special Needs Using the Weschler Intelligence Scale

The Weschler Intelligence Scale is an assessment that measures the cognitive abilities of children and adults. The Weschler Intelligence Scale for Children (WISC) measures a child's verbal intelligence (including comprehension and vocabulary) and performance intelligence (including reasoning and picture completion). The WISC is an intelligence quotient test that is useful for helping diagnose a student with a cognitive disability. A score below 100 indicates below-average intelligence. WISC results are useful tools for evaluating a student with a disability. Tests results can be used to measure and report on a student's general intelligence and provide insight into the student's cognitive abilities in order to determine an appropriate educational pathway. Results can be reported in a student's Evaluation Team Report and Individualized Education Program in order to justify special education services or have a starting point for Individualized Education Program goals. WISC results are especially important in an Evaluation Team Report, generally completed every 3 years or less, because they contribute to describing the overall performance profile of a student with a disability.

Kaufman Assessment Battery for Children

The Kaufman Assessment Battery for Children (K-ABC) is a unique standardized test because it is used to evaluate preschoolers, minority groups, and children with learning disabilities. The K-ABC can be used to assess children ages 2-18 and is meant to be used with children who are nonverbal, bilingual, or English speaking. However, it is especially useful in assessing the abilities of students who are nonverbal. The K-ABC can be used to help determine students' educational placements and assist with their educational planning. This assessment has four components that measure students' abilities, which are described below.

- The sequential processing scale assesses short-term memory and problem-solving skills when putting things in sequential order.
- The simultaneous processing scale assesses problem-solving skills for completing multiple processes simultaneously, such as identifying objects and reproducing design shapes using manipulatives.
- The achievement component measures expressive vocabulary, mathematics skills, and reading and decoding skills.
- The mental processing component assesses the abilities a student demonstrates on the sequential and simultaneous processing scales.

The K-ABC is also unique because it includes a nonverbal scale that can be administered to children with hearing or speech impairments and children who do not speak English.

Vineland Adaptive Behavior Scale

The Vineland Adaptive Behavior Scale (VABS) assesses the personal and social skills of children and adults. Adaptive behavior refers to the skills needed for day-to-day activities and independent living. Children with disabilities sometimes have deficits in adaptive behavior, and the VABS is useful for planning their educational pathways. It is an especially useful tool for developing transition plans and goals for students of appropriate ages on Individualized Education Programs. The VABS is a process that involves people who know the students best, like parents and/or teachers. The teacher version and parent version of this assessment can be delivered via interview or survey. The parent version focuses on a student's adaptive behavior at home, while the teacher version focuses on adaptive behavior in the school setting. Version II of the VABS assesses four domains: communication, daily living skills, socialization, and social skills. A student's comprehensive score from both the teacher and parent version are used to report abilities in the four domains.

Types of Cognitive Assessments

Cognitive tests assess the cognitive functioning abilities of children and adults. They are useful tools for diagnosing and/or identifying children with disabilities who are eligible for special education services under the Individuals with Disabilities Education Act. Examples of cognitive tests used in diagnosing or identifying children with disabilities include aptitude tests and intelligence quotient (IQ) tests. There are also cognitive assessments that measure verbal reasoning, numerical reasoning, abstract reasoning, spatial ability, verbal ability, and more. Children's cognitive abilities are related to how quickly they process information. Assessment results can be good measurements of how quickly children may learn new information or tasks. Cognitive assessments provide specific information about children's cognitive functioning by providing measurements of their intelligence, attention, concentration, processing speed, language and communication, visual-spatial abilities, and short and long-term memory capabilities. Individual assessment results can be used to evaluate a child's need for special education services. Results can also be used on a child's Evaluation Team Report or for developing goals on the Individualized Education Program.

Prenatal, Perinatal, and Neonatal Disabilities

Prenatal, perinatal, and neonatal risk factors can be genetic or environmental. These risk factors put infants at risk for developing intellectual disabilities that affect their day-to-day lives. An intellectual disability (ID) is a disability that significantly limits a child's overall cognitive abilities. Prenatal risk factors include genetic syndromes (i.e. Down Syndrome), brain malformation, maternal diseases, and environmental influences. Drugs, alcohol, or poison exposure can all affect an unborn child. Perinatal (during delivery) risk factors include labor and delivery trauma or anoxia at birth. Neonatal (post-birth) risk factors include hypoxic ischemic injury (brain injury), traumatic brain injury, infections, seizure disorders, and toxic metabolic syndromes. Early screening and applicable assessments are tools used to identify young children with intellectual disabilities. Early screening and assessments can assist with providing a child with ID with special education services under the Individuals with Disabilities Education Act. These tools can also help assess the severity of need, deficit areas, and need for special services, such as occupational therapy.

Advantages and Disadvantages of Curriculum-Based Assessments

Curriculum-based assessments (CBAs) are assessments that determine if students are making adequate progress through the curriculum. They can be administered by a teacher, special educator, or school psychologist. CBAs have advantages over norm-referenced assessments, like developmental assessments, because they are not used to compare performances between students. Other types of assessments measure a student's cumulative abilities across multiple skills instead of assessing individual skills. CBAs measure student progress in more individualized ways. They are especially useful for measuring Individualized Education Program (IEP) goal progress. Since CBAs are teacher-created assessments, they provide opportunities to assess students informally and formally on IEP goals. For example, a teacher may verbally quiz a student on ten addition problems to determine if the student is making progress on math IEP goals. CBAs are also used in the Response to Intervention process to identify students with special needs by measuring the effectiveness of interventions provided to them.

Advantages and Disadvantages of Using Formal Assessments

Formal assessments are assessments that measure whether or not students are learning what they are supposed to be learning. Formal assessments help teachers determine what their students know. They typically measure how students are performing compared to their similar-aged peers. Examples of formal assessments include quizzes, tests, standardized tests, achievement tests, aptitude tests, and norm-referenced tests.

Formal assessments have the same set of expectations for all students and are graded using the same criteria. However, students with disabilities do not always learn or retain previously taught content in the same ways as their similar-aged peers. Using universal criteria to assess what students have learned is one disadvantage to formal assessments for students with disabilities. An advantage of formal assessments is that they allow teachers to collect baseline data on students' educational performances by comparing their performances to age or grade-based performance criteria. Additionally, students with disabilities can receive accommodations and modifications on these types of assessments. Accommodations and modifications are implemented based on needs specific to each student. The goal is to level the playing field for these students on formal assessments, like standardized state tests.

Uses, Advantages, and Disadvantages of Using Informal Assessments

Informal assessments can provide teachers with a lot of information about students' educational strengths and weaknesses. Informal assessments are also used to guide teachers' daily instruction by providing constant and immediate feedback about students' learning processes. Examples of informal assessments include observations and rating scales, checks of daily work, homework, group projects, checklists, and rubrics.

Informal assessments offer some advantages. They are often easy to implement and allow teachers to gather useful data. Informal assessments may naturally be less stressful for students because they do not realize they are being tested. When test stress factors are removed, results from informal assessments may provide the best reflections of students' abilities.

Disadvantages of informal assessments include hidden bias or stereotypes within the person administering the assessment. Teachers implementing informal assessments must be conscious of and avoid bias in order to receive accurate information about students' educational performances. Another disadvantage is that students may also feel more pressure to perform well on formal assessments versus informal assessments, affecting their performances on the informal assessments.

How Formative Assessments Work

The goals of formative assessments are to provide ongoing feedback and monitor students' learning. These assessments are a process of informal assessment strategies that help educators gather information about student learning. Formative assessments help differentiate instruction and are considered part of the student learning process. Formative assessments communicate what the students are learning and also check for understanding. They provide information needed to adjust teaching and learning while it is happening.

Formative assessments also provide opportunities for students to receive feedback on their individual performances and engage in their paths to success. Teachers can use formative assessments to allow students to participate in the learning process, outside of sitting and listening to lectures. Discussions are examples of formative assessments, where teachers can initiate discussions about topics and gauge students' understanding. Exit slips are written questions posed by teachers at the ends of their classes, intended to determine what the students have learned. The think, pair, share method requires students to work together to solve problems. Students are asked to brainstorm answers to questions posed by the teachers, then they are paired with other students before sharing their thinking with their partners.

How Summative Assessments Work

Summative assessments are less flexible than formative assessments due to how performance data is collected. The goal of summative assessment is to evaluate what a student has learned at the end of an instructional section or unit. Summative assessments often measure the mastery of learning standards.

Summative assessments use standards or benchmarks to measure student success at certain checkpoints during the learning process. They are almost always high stakes, heavily weighted (unlike formative assessments), and formally graded. Information from summative assessments can be used to report on student progress. Teachers can use a variety of summative assessments to determine where students are in the learning process. These types of assessments also play a role in identifying benchmarked progress and the educational needs of students with disabilities.

These types of assessments feature a narrower range of question types, such as multiple choice, short answer, and essay questions. Examples of summative assessments include state tests, end of unit or chapter tests, end of semester exams, and assessments that formally measure the mastery of a particular benchmark.

Alternate Assessments

Students with and without disabilities are typically expected to take the same standardized tests, sometimes with accommodations and/or modifications. Some students with disabilities take alternate assessments, which are forms of the standardized tests that other students take. Students that participate in alternate assessments are unable to participate in state standardized tests even with accommodations. Less than 1% of students in public school districts participate in alternate assessments. They are mostly intended for students with intellectual disabilities or severe cognitive delays. Alternate assessments are based on Alternate Achievement Standards (AAS), which are modified versions of state achievement standards. Alternate assessments are a way for students' progress to be assessed with standards that are more appropriate for their skills. Teachers, parents, and students work collaboratively to demonstrate that the achievement standards are met. For example, a state standard for math may not be appropriate for a student with an intellectual disability. Instead, the student may have the alternative standard of demonstrating the ability to count money to make a purchase.

Role Formal Assessments Play in the Education of a Student with Disabilities

Formal assessments measure how well a student has mastered learning material and are useful in detecting if a student is falling behind in general or at the end of a taught unit. Formal test results can be used to compare the performance of a student with disabilities against other students of similar demographics. Developmental assessments are norm-referenced tests that are designed to assess the development of small children. Developmental assessments are used to identify the strengths and weaknesses of a child suspected of having a disability. Intelligence tests are another type of norm-referenced test that can determine a student's potential to learn academic skills. Intelligence tests, sometimes called IQ tests, also indicate a student's specific level of intelligence. This is helpful in knowing if a student's learning problems are associated with sub-average intellectual abilities or other factors, such as an emotional disturbance. A student with an emotional disturbance or specific learning disability would have an average or above-average intelligence score, whereas a student with intellectual disabilities would have a sub-average score. Curriculum-based assessments are also helpful in determining where, specifically, a student needs the most help within a content area.

Interest Inventories

Interest inventories are tools for measuring people's interests or preferences in activities. They are useful for gathering information about a student's likes and dislikes. In special education, interest inventories are sometimes used to help develop the transition portion of an Individualized Education Plan (IEP). A student's interests as determined by an interest inventory can be used to drive the entire IEP. For an older student with a driving interest in mind, interest inventories can also be reflected in the annual IEP goals. Interest inventories can come in the form of observations, ability tests, or self-reporting inventories. They can also work as age-appropriate transition assessments used in the transition statement section of the IEP. An advantage of interest inventories is they help students get to know their strengths and interests. They are also useful in guiding students with disabilities into thinking about post-secondary careers, education, or independent living.

Role Informal Assessments Play in the Education of a Student with Disabilities

Informal assessments are a little more flexible for teachers, particularly in the ways they can be administered in the classroom. In special education, informal assessments play an important role in adjusting instruction to meet the specific needs of the student. Using informal assessment outcomes to drive instruction ensures that academic or behavioral student needs are met. Informal assessments are also helpful in adjusting instruction to meet specific goals or objectives on a student's Individualized Education Program. Checklists, running records, observations, and work samples are all informal assessments from which data for IEP goals can be collected. Checklists can include a list of behaviors or academic skills the student is meant to achieve. Checklists enable the teacher to check off skills that a student can do. Running records help provide insight into student behavior over time by focusing on a sequence of events. Work samples are helpful in providing a concrete snapshot of a student's academic capabilities.

Developing and Writing Measurable IEP Goals

According to the Individuals with Disabilities Education Act (IDEA), Individualized Education Program goals must contain specific components for students eligible for special education and placed on IEPs. Components of a measurable IEP goal include condition, performance, criteria, assessment, and standard. Condition refers to when, where, and how the disability will be addressed. For example, an IEP goal may state, "By the end of this IEP, Jacob will use appropriate skills to communicate his needs in 4/5 trials." "By the end of this IEP" is the condition of the goal. Performance is what the student is expected to accomplish during the condition of the goal. "Jacob will use appropriate skills to communicate his needs" is a performance example in the goal above. The last part of the goal stating "in 4/5 trials" is the criteria that outlines how well the goal will be performed. Measurable goals also include how skill mastery will be assessed, such as through observations or work samples. Goals should also be standards based, and goals must be connected to state standards.

Determining the Placement of a Student with a Disability

With every student, the goal is placement in the general education classroom as much as possible, while still meeting the student's educational needs and ensuring a successful educational experience. IDEA does not require that students be placed in the regular education classroom. However, this is the first option that should be considered by a student's IEP team. Ultimately, the IEP determines what environment best suits the student based on the student's specific needs. The IEP is responsible for determining what educational environment would provide the student with the maximum appropriate educational benefit. While justification for removing a student from the regular education classroom is common and appropriate, as occurs when a student is placed in a resource room, the IEP team must explain the reasoning on the student's IEP. Justification must specifically list why the student cannot be educated with accommodations and services in the regular education classroom during any part of the school day. Justification for removal cannot be due to perceived instructional limitations of the regular education teacher or concerns over extra instructional time needed to educate a student with a disability.

Roles/Responsibilities of the Special Education Instructor in Full/Partial Inclusion Setting vs. a Self-Contained Classroom

Students with mild to moderate disabilities are often placed in inclusion or partial inclusion classrooms. The responsibilities of the special educator include assisting and collaborating with the general education teacher to create a curriculum with modifications that meets the learning styles and needs of the students with disabilities. The special educator may circulate during lessons or classwork to help students when needed and provide modifications to the general education curriculum to best meet the individual needs of each student.

The role of a special educator in a self-contained classroom is much different. Students in a self-contained classroom typically have disabilities that severely limit their abilities to receive quality education in inclusion or partial inclusion settings. Students with moderate disabilities in self-contained classrooms receive modified instruction with accommodations. The special educator is usually assisted by teaching assistants or paraprofessionals who help the educator meet the needs of individual students.

Special educators in inclusion, partial inclusion, and self-contained classrooms share some similar responsibilities. These responsibilities include monitoring IEP data on annual goals for each student, giving standardized pretests and posttests, facilitating parent-teacher conferences, completing annual IEP reviews, and developing curriculum.

Specially Designed Instruction

Specially Designed Instruction (SDI) in special education refers to the teaching methods and strategies used by special educators to teach students with learning disabilities and other learning disorders. SDI is used to meet the specific needs of learners who may not be successful learning in the same ways as their similar-aged peers. SDI should be adapted to the unique learning needs of students, address the learning issues specific to a child's disability, and ensure student access to the general education classroom. In SDI, the teaching methodology should be changed without sacrificing content aligned with the state standards.

Universal Design for Learning

The universal design for learning is a flexible approach to learning that keeps students' individual needs in mind. Teachers that utilize UDL offer different ways for students to access material and engage in content. This approach is helpful for many students, but particularly those with learning and attention issues. The three main principles of UDL are representation, action and expression, and engagement. Through these principles, UDL ensures multiple means of representation, multiple ways for students to interact with the material, and multiple ways to motivate students.

Role of Local Education Agency Members in the IEP Meetings

Local education agency (LEA) representatives represent local educational agencies and are knowledgeable about special education curriculum, general education curriculum, and community resources. An LEA member is also referred to as a district representative. An LEA member is a member of the school district where any special education meetings take place. In an Individualized Education Program (IEP) meeting, LEAs are members of the school district that referred the student for special education services. LEAs contribute their knowledge during the IEP meeting. An LEA member must be a licensed professional who knows the student and is familiar with the IEP process. The role of LEA members in IEP meetings is to make sure the information presented is compliant with the Individuals with Disabilities Education Act (IDEA) standards. LEAs are also responsible for ensuring that the school district is compliant with procedural components of IDEA and that eligible students are receiving free and appropriate public educations (FAPEs).

Involvement of Students on IEPs in the Transition Process in High School

Most states require transition statements to be made when students reach age 14 during the Individualized Education Program (IEP) year. Federal law requires students 16 years of age or older to have transition statements, post-secondary goals for independent living, employment, and education, and summaries of performance that include the results of the most recent transition assessments. Per federal law, students of transition age must be invited to their IEP meetings. It is important for students on IEPs to participate in the transition process because it helps them figure out what they want to do after they graduate from high school. Participation in the process gets them thinking about living independently, post-secondary education options, and employment options. Students usually have opportunities to participate in formal and informal assessments like interest inventories that help them narrow their interests. Transition goals for independent living, employment, and education should be based on the results of these assessments and any other interests the students have expressed. The students participate in the implementation of the transition goals by completing activities associated with their indicated interests.

Role of the Support Team in the Education of a Child with a Disability

A student support team (SST) assists with identifying and supporting a student needing special education services. In this support team model, a group of educators works to identify and provide early intervention services for any student exhibiting academic or behavioral problems. Most schools have a system by which the interventions for the student are implemented. The purpose of this SST is to offer different supports, such as monitoring student progress, developing intervention plans, and referring students for intervention services. While the primary goal of this SST is to provide support for students struggling with school, it can also shift focus to supporting students at risk of dropping out of school.

A support team can also be a team of professionals in charge of the implementation of an IEP for a student with a disability. A student-based support team is created for any student with an IEP. The purpose of this SST is to enhance a student's learning process and development. Members of this type of SST include the child, parent or legal guardian, special educator, a general educator, and a representative of the school system. The SST may also include relevant service professionals, student or parent advocates, school psychologists, or any others with knowledge or expertise about the student.

Amendments to an Individualized Education Program

A student's Individualized Education Program (IEP) is in effect for one year. Academic goals, objectives, benchmarks, transition goals, and any accommodations and modifications are to be in place for the student for the duration of the IEP. An amendment can be made when a change needs to be made to the IEP before the year is over. An amendment is an agreement between the student, parents or legal guardians, and the IEP team. IEP meetings for amendments can be requested at any time. IEP amendments can be requested if a student is not making adequate progress toward the goals, if the goals become inappropriate in some way for the student, or when the student has met all IEP goals and requires new ones. If new information about the student becomes available, the IEP can be amended. Students who need accommodations and modifications added or removed can also request amendment meetings.

How Needs of Students with IEPs Are Met in the School Environment

IEPs communicate what services are to be provided for children with disabilities in the school setting, the children's present levels of performance (PLOPs), and how their disabilities affect academic performance. IEPs also specify annual goals appropriate to the students' specific needs and any accommodations or modifications that need to be provided. Schools and teachers working with students with disabilities have the responsibility to implement these IEP components when working with the students. Additionally, schools and teachers working with students with disabilities must ensure that the students' individualized annual goals are met within a year of the students' IEP effective dates. It is up to the IEP teams to determine what classroom settings would most benefit the students, while also appropriately meeting their IEP goals with the fewest barriers. Special educators must determine how data is collected, then record and obtain data on how the students are meeting their IEP goals. Special educators are responsible for providing intervention services based on the data results. They must also ensure that any accommodations or modifications listed on the IEPs are implemented in both general education and self-contained classrooms.

Accommodation Vs. Modification in IEPs

Formal accommodations and modifications for a student with a disability are listed on the Individualized Education Program. Accommodations change *how* a student learns the material, while a modification changes *what* a student is taught or expected to learn. In classroom instruction, accommodations level the playing field for students with disabilities by helping them learn the same material and have the same expectations as their classmates. For example, a student with a reading difficulty might receive the accommodation of being able to listen to the text being read. Modifications are for students who are academically far behind their peers. An example of a classroom instructional modification would be a student receiving a shorter reading assignment or an assignment catered to the student's reading level.

Accommodations for tests look a little different because the tests are assessing what the students learned. An appropriate example of a test accommodation is giving the student extra time to complete the test. Classroom test modifications may involve giving the students less to learn and including less material on the tests. For state standardized tests, accommodations like extra time and frequent breaks can be provided. Students that need modifications to state tests may complete alternate assessments that may not cover the same material as the standard exams.

Ensuring a SMART Annual Goal in an IEP

A good IEP goal describes how far the student is expected to progress toward the IEP goal by the next IEP. Since IEPs should be revised once a year, a good annual IEP goal should describe what the student is capable of doing in a one-year time frame. Creating SMART IEP goals can help the student determine realistic expectations for what can be achieved in a year. SMART IEP goals are specific, measurable, attainable, results oriented, and timebound. Goals are specific when they list the targeted result of the skill or subject area. Goals should also be specific to the student's needs. Goals that are measurable state the way a student's progress will be measured. Measurable goals list how accurately a student should meet the goal. Attainable goals mean the goal is realistic for the student to achieve in one year. Results-oriented goals outline what a student needs to do to accomplish the goal. For example, a SMART goal may state, "During the school week, Robert will use his device to communicate greetings 80% of the time in 4/5 trials." Time-bound goals include a timeframe for the student to achieve the goal. They also list when and how often progress will be measured.

Role an Initial Evaluation Assessment Plays in Qualifying a Student for Special Education

When a student is determined to need special education, it means the student has a disability or disabilities adversely affecting educational performance. It may also mean the student's needs cannot be addressed in the general education classroom with or without accommodations, and specially designed instruction (SDI) is required. An initial evaluation of the student is required for special education eligibility. The evaluation is comprehensive and includes existing data collected on the student and additional assessments needed to determine eligibility. Individual school districts decide what assessments should be completed for the student's initial evaluation. Each district is responsible for and should provide assessments that measure functional, developmental, and academic information. The student's parents or legal guardians are responsible for providing outside information relevant to the student's education, such as medical needs assessed outside of the school district by qualified providers.

Purpose of an IEP for an Individual Student

The purpose of an Individualized Education Program is to guide the learning of a student with a disability in the educational environment. An Individualized Education Program is a written statement for a student eligible for special education. An initial IEP is implemented once the child has been evaluated and determined as needing special education. After the initial IEP, IEP meetings are conducted annually (or more) in order to update the plan to meet the needs of the student. IEPs are created, reviewed, and revised according to individual state and federal laws. These plans include the amount of time the student will spend in the special education classroom based on the level of need. It also includes any related services the student might need, such as speech-language therapy, and academic and behavioral goals for the year. As the student learns and changes, performance levels and goals change as well. A student's present levels of performance are included and updated yearly, as are the academic and behavioral goals.

Members of an Individualized Education Program Team

Individualized Education Programs are conducted annually, following the initial IEP. IEP team members meet at least once a year to discuss a student's progress and make changes to the IEP. The required members of a student's IEP team include the student's parents or legal guardians, one of the student's general education teachers, the special education teacher, a school representative, an individual who can interpret the instructional implications of evaluation results, anyone else who has knowledge or expertise about the student, and, if appropriate, the student. Parents and legal guardians contribute unique expertise about the student, typically having the benefit of knowing the child well. General education teachers can speak on behalf of how the student is performing in the general education classroom. The special education teacher can report on progress made toward academic and behavioral goals and present levels of performance. A school representative must be qualified to provide or supervise specially designed instruction, be knowledgeable of the general education curriculum, and be knowledgeable about school resources. The individual who can interpret evaluation results can be an existing team member or someone else who is qualified to report on evaluation results. Advocates, such as counselors or therapists who see the student outside the school day, can also attend the meeting to speak on the student's behalf.

Legal Rights for Parents or Legal Guardians

Individualized Education Program (IEP) meetings occur annually for each student. However, it is a parent or legal guardian's right to request a meeting at any point during the school year. The student's school is responsible for identifying and evaluating the child, developing, reviewing, and/or revising the IEP, and determining what placement setting best suits the needs of the student. It is within the parent or legal guardian's rights to have input in all processes related to the student. Under the Individuals with Disabilities Education Act (IDEA), parents have the right to participate in IEP meetings, have an independent evaluation outside the one the school provides, give or deny consent for the IEP, contest a school's decision, and obtain private education paid for by the public school. In specific circumstances, if the student is determined to need services that the public school cannot provide, the public school district may need to pay for the student's tuition at a private school where the student's needs can be met.

Collaborative Consultation Between Educational Professionals

Collaborative consultation refers to the special educator or other professional providing advice to the general education teacher about the student on the Individualized Education Program. Special educators and other IEP team members, such as school psychologists and related service professionals, serve as the experts and have knowledge about how individual students learn and behave. This is especially important when students with IEPs are included in the general education classroom. Special educators and general education teachers must work collaboratively to ensure that students are reaching their potential in the general education setting. Examples of collaborative consultation include the special educator serving as a consultant to the general education teacher by providing advice on a student's IEP, accommodations, modifications, skill techniques, and IEP goal tracking. Another way the special educator or other professional can assist the general educator is by providing skill and strategy instruction to students on IEPs outside the general education classroom. The idea behind this method is for students to generalize these skills and strategies to the general education classroom.

Public School Responsibilities to Parents and Legal Guardians of Students on IEPs

The school must invite the parents or legal guardians to any IEP meetings and provide advance notice of the meetings. Each meeting notice is required to include the purpose of the meeting, its time and location, and who will attend. The location of the meeting is likely the student's school, but legally it must be held at a mutually agreed upon place and time. If the parent or legal guardian cannot attend the IEP meeting, the school must ensure participation in another way, such as video or telephone conference. The meeting can be conducted without the parent or legal guardian if the school district cannot get the parent or legal guardian to attend. A parent or legal guardian can request a meeting, and the school can refuse or deny the request. If denied, the school must provide a Prior Written Notice explaining their refusal. A Prior Written Notice is a document outlining important school district decisions about a student on an IEP.

Environmental Modifications for Students with Disabilities in the Classroom

Students with disabilities may need environmental modifications in order to be successful in their classrooms, homes, and communities. Environmental modifications are adaptations that allow people with disabilities to maneuver through their environments with as little resistance as possible. They allow for more independent living experiences, especially for those with limited mobility. Environmental modifications ensure the health, safety, and welfare of the people who need them. Examples of environmental modifications in the home, community, or school include ramps, hydraulic lifts, widened doorways and hallways, automatic doors, hand rails, and grab bars. Roll-in showers, water faucet controls, worktable or work surface adaptations, and cabinet and shelving adaptations are also environmental modifications that can be provided if necessary. Other adaptations include heating and cooling adaptations and electrical adaptations to accommodate devices or equipment. Environmental modifications in the home are typically provided by qualified agencies or providers. The Americans with Disabilities Act ensures that environmental modifications are provided in the community to avoid the discrimination of a person with a disability.

Promoting Student Learning and Development

Teaching Strategies and Accommodations for Students with Working Memory Deficits

Working memory is critical for remembering letters and numbers, listening to short instructions, reading and understanding content, completing homework independently, and understanding social cues. When working memory skills are absent or slow to develop, learning may be difficult. This may get worse for children over time. As they fail to develop or retain working memory capabilities, their overall cognitive abilities begin to suffer. Working memory deficits differ from person to person with disabilities, but accommodations can be made to make up for missing or developing skills. Educators can implement strategies like reducing the children's workload, providing visual cues, being aware of when children might be reaching memory overload, providing positive feedback, providing testing alternatives, and providing extra time. Accommodations on an Individualized Education Program for a student with working memory deficits might include frequent breaks, small group instruction, and extended time for tests and assignments.

Classroom Accommodations That Allow Students with Disabilities to Be Successful

Accommodations are flexible classroom tools because they can be used to provide interventions without time or location boundaries. They remove barriers to learning for students with disabilities, and they change how students learn. Accommodations do not change what the students are learning or expected to know. Classroom accommodations may be outlined in students' Individualized Education Programs or 504 Plans, or simply provided on the spot by the special educators or general educators. Accommodations are put into place to ensure that the students with disabilities are accessing the learning process with the fewest barriers, putting them on the same levels as their peers without disabilities. Presentation accommodations include allowing students to listen to instructions orally, providing written lists of instructions, and allowing students to use readers to assist with comprehension. Response accommodations include allowing students to provide oral responses, capture responses via audio recording, and/or use spelling dictionaries or spell checkers when writing. Accommodations to setting include special seating (wherever the students learn best), use of sensory tools, and/or use of special lighting.

Effect of Home Life Factors on Learning and Development

Students' home lives are interconnected with their school lives. Home and life factors, especially negative ones, are difficult for students to avoid generalizing to the school environment. Home stressors can often develop into dysfunction at school for children with disabilities. Factors that affect the learning and development of students with disabilities include academic factors, environmental factors, intellectual factors, medical factors, perceptual factors, social factors, and psychological factors. Academic factors include developmental delays in core content areas, lack of basic skills, and apparent inconsistency of learning in certain stages of development. Environmental factors occur when children are exposed to home life trauma, such as divorce, drug abuse, alcoholism, parental fighting, or family illness. Intellectual factors include limited intellectual abilities or unnoticed gifted abilities. Language factors include issues with language barriers or language acquisition, such as aphasia, bilingualism, expressive language disorder, or pragmatic language disorder. Medical factors include Attention Deficit Hyperactivity Disorder, muscular problems, or hearing problems. Perceptual factors include any factors that affect or slow down students' processing of information. Psychological factors include depression, anxiety, or conduct disorders.

Social Skill Deficits That Occur in Students with Disabilities

Social skills are a concept that needs to be taught to some students with disabilities, such as students with autism. Social skills instruction involves the teaching of basic communication skills, empathy and rapport skills, interpersonal skills, problem-solving skills, and accountability. Basic communication skills include listening skills, following directions, and avoiding speaking out of turn. Empathy and rapport skills involve teaching students how to demonstrate empathy and build rapport. Interpersonal skills must be learned by teaching students to demonstrate skills like sharing, joining activities, and participating in turn taking. Problem-solving skills sometimes need to be taught as well. These include teaching students to ask for help, apologize to others, make decisions, and accept consequences. Accountability must be taught to students so they can learn to follow through on promises and accept criticisms appropriately. These are skills that do not come naturally to students with social skill deficits.

Obtaining Accommodations in the Classroom Setting

When parents or legal guardians of children with disabilities believe that accommodations may help their children, they can arrange to speak with the teachers about informal supports. Informal supports are strategies the teachers can put into place to assist the students with their learning processes. These changes do not require paperwork and can be provided during classroom instruction. Teachers can experiment with informal supports to determine what will be most helpful for removing the barriers to learning the students might be experiencing. If it is determined that students need bigger changes to how they learn, formal evaluations can take place. If the students are not already on Individualized Education Programs or 504 Plans, these needs may lead to initial evaluations to collect data on the students' needs. For students with IEPs or 504 Plans, accommodations that help the students can be included on their next IEPs or 504 Plans. The IEPs or 504 Plans can also be amended if the need for the accommodations is immediate, such as if they need to be put in place before standardized testing time. In both situations, data supporting the need for the accommodations must be provided and listed in the comprehensive initial evaluations, initial IEPs or 504 Plans, or the students' amended IEPs or 504 Plans.

Informal Supports vs. Formal Accommodations

Informal supports are generally easier to implement in the classroom setting. They do not necessarily have to be implemented only for students on Individualized Education Programs or students with disabilities. Students who have not been evaluated for special education services can receive informal supports to ensure classroom success. When teachers see students struggling with the ways they are learning, the teachers may use informal supports to help the students. They may demonstrate that the students are able to learn with the accommodations in place. Informal supports are often the first step to indicating that students are in need of special education services. Formal accommodations come into place when students become eligible for IEPs or 504 Plans. Formal supports are written into the IEPs or 504 Plans and then required by law to be provided. Examples of informal supports include frequent breaks, special seating, quiet areas for test taking or studying, teacher cues, and help with basic organizational skills. These informal supports may eventually turn into formal supports if and when students become eligible for special education services.

Inclusion Classroom Setting

The Individuals with Disabilities Education Act does not expressly define a least restrictive environment for each specific disability. Typically, it is up to the Individualized Education Program

- 48 -

team of professionals, including the student's parent or legal guardian, to determine the best case LRE setting possible for an individual student. Mainstreaming is a term that is often used interchangeably with inclusion. A mainstreaming or inclusion setting means the student with a disability is included in the general education setting the entire school day. The student may receive supports and services like an aide, related services, assistive technology, accommodations, or modifications that are appropriate for the individual student. These supports and services seek to help the student with a disability gain access to the general education curriculum with the fewest barriers. This model essentially seeks to level the playing field for the student with a disability so that he or she may learn alongside general education peers. For these students, the LRE setting must be justified in the Individualized Education Program.

Self-Contained Classroom Setting

The Individuals with Disabilities Education Act states that according to least restrictive environment standards, students in an LRE are ideally spending as much time as possible with their non-disabled peers in the general education setting. IDEA states that LRE means a student should receive general education "to the maximum extent that is appropriate," and that special classes, special schools, or removal from the general education classroom should only happen when a child's needs are greater than what can be provided by supplementary aids and services. A self-contained classroom setting can be a separate class of students within a school or a separate school that specifically addresses the needs of children with disabilities. In both settings, the needs of the students are greater than what can be offered in the general education classroom, even with educational supports. Settings like these may be specialized in instruction and support for students with similar needs. For these children, their placements in self-contained classrooms must be justified on their Individualized Education Programs.

Partial Mainstream/Inclusion Classroom Setting

It is generally up to the Individualized Education Program team of professionals and the student's parent or legal guardian to determine a least restrictive environment that best suits the needs of the student. In a partial mainstream/inclusion classroom setting, a student spends part of the day in the general education classroom. The student receives part of his or her education in a separate, special education classroom. This type of LRE is determined when a student's needs are greater than what services can be provided in the general education classroom, even with educational supports or services in place. For example, a student with severe deficits in mathematical skills may be placed in a classroom outside the general education classroom that targets specific needs and skills. The student may also get pulled out of the general education classroom to receive one-on-one instruction or small group instruction. For these children, their placements in partial mainstream/inclusion classrooms must be justified on their Individualized Education Programs.

Specialized Educational Settings

School districts sometimes offer specialized educational settings for students with disabilities, such as special preschools. Preschools for children with disabilities typically focus on children ages 3-5. They are important resources for teaching early learning, communication, and social skills that are essential for children with disabilities. Life skills settings are where students with disabilities can receive specialized instruction in academic, social, behavioral, or daily living skills. Social behavior skills settings are sometimes called applied behavior skills or behavior skills. In this type of setting, the primary focus is on social and decision-making skills. Transition settings are available for students making the transition from high school to life after high school. Students with Individualized Education Programs can stay in high school until the age of 21 or 22, depending on the calendar month they turn 22. Transition settings assist students with work experiences, post-secondary education experiences, and independent living skills.

Parents/Legal Guardians Ensuring Accommodations Are Being Provided

Accommodations are changes to the ways children with disabilities learn, not changes to what the children are learning. Parents can ensure that accommodations are being provided in a number of ways. Unless specifically stated on the students' Individualized Education Programs or 504 Plans, parents and legal guardians may only receive formal updates on how accommodations are being provided or helping the students during specified reporting times. However, parents and legal guardians can ask for reports on goal progress or accommodations for their students at any time. Parents and legal guardians can ensure that accommodations are successfully implemented by using the schools' progress reports and by asking the right questions. Parents and legal guardians can advocate for their students' accommodations by making sure the accommodations are being implemented on a regular basis. Parents and legal guardians also have the right to ask if students are using the accommodations on a regular basis. If they are being used on a regular basis, parents and legal guardians can explore options that might also help the students. Parents and legal guardians can work with the special education teachers and/or the IEP teams to ensure that their students' accommodations are being received and are effective.

Evaluating, Modifying, and Adapting the Classroom Setting Using the UDL

The Universal Design for Learning (UDL) model is most successful when the classroom teacher prepares a classroom setting that encourages the success of students with and without disabilities. Knowledge of the characteristics of students with different disabilities, as well as the unique learning needs of these students, ensures that the classroom teacher is aware of and addresses these needs in the classroom setting. Setting clear short and/or long-term goals for students to achieve is one way to meet the UDL standards. A traditional classroom may offer one assignment for all students to complete, but a UDL compliant classroom may offer different assignments or different ways for students to complete the assignment. UDL compliant classrooms also offer flexible work spaces for the students to complete their classwork. Students may have access to quiet spaces for individual work or group tables for group work. Students in a UDL compliant classroom also receive regular feedback throughout their classwork rather than receiving one grade upon assignment completion. UDL compliant teachers recognize that students access information differently and provide different ways for students to gain access, such as audio text.

Evaluating, Modifying, and Adapting the Classroom Curriculum Using the UDL

In order for a Universal Design for Learning (UDL) model classroom to be successful, the classroom teacher must evaluate, modify, and adapt the classroom curriculum to best suit the needs of the individual students. UDL contrasts with a one-size-fits-all concept of curriculum planning, where lesson plans are developed and implemented strictly based on how teachers expect students to learn. Instead, a successful UDL model addresses the many specific needs of a classroom of students. These needs may vary depending on the unique abilities each classroom of students presents. UDL compliant teachers can evaluate the success of lessons by checking the achievement of students using formal and informal assessments. UDL compliant teachers utilize these assessments throughout the lessons, instead of upon lesson completion. These teachers use the results of the evaluations to modify and/or adapt classroom instruction to best meet the needs of the students. Evaluation methods given informally can provide a lot of information about whether or not students are grasping the concepts. UDL compliant teachers use evaluation results to reflect upon lessons and determine how to move forward with future lessons.

Evaluating, Modifying, and Adapting the Classroom Materials and Equipment Using the UDL

In order for a Universal Design for Learning (UDL) classroom to be successful, the classroom teacher must evaluate, modify, and adapt the classroom materials and equipment to best suit the needs of the individual students. When teachers are UDL compliant, they are observing the needs of the students and making necessary changes to materials and/or equipment to ensure student success. A way for teachers to determine the success of classroom materials or equipment is through formal and informal assessments. Informal assessments in particular are helpful for receiving immediate feedback as to whether materials are appropriate for student learning. A UDL compliant teacher may offer multiple ways for students to present what they learned, instead of completing pencil and paper assignments. Multiple assignment completion options ensure that the unique abilities of students are being targeted, instead of just targeting one or two specific skills. Equipment such as audio or digital text, when paired with words, can assist students who have issues with listening or comprehension. A UDL compliant teacher may choose to pair audio output and text during a reading assignment for all students in order to target students with listening or comprehension difficulties.

Principles of the Universal Design for Learning Model

The UDL model contains three principles that aim to level the playing field for all learners. Principle I of the Universal Design for Learning model primarily focuses on what representation or version of information is being taught. This principle aims to target an audience of diverse learners. By providing multiple ways for students to approach content, teachers can ensure that the unique needs of all learners in their classrooms are met. Principle II examines the how of learning. This principle focuses on the concept that students learn best when provided with multiple ways to demonstrate what they have learned. In Principle II compliant classrooms, students are given more than one option for expressing themselves. Principle III maintains a focus on providing multiple ways for students to engage in the learning process. Principle III compliant teachers provide options for keeping content interesting and relevant to all types of learners. In effective UDL model classrooms, these principles are generally met by providing multiple ways to learn the content, express what was learned, and engage in lesson content.

Implementing Modifications and Accommodations in an Inclusive Classroom Setting

General educators can work with special educators to create an effective co-teaching model. In an effective co-teaching model, both the general educator and special educator demonstrate the Universal Design for Learning Framework. This ensures that the needs of the diverse group of learners are being met. For students using Individualized Education Programs, modifications such as reduced work would be expressly written in their IEPs. In a co-teaching model, student modifications would be communicated to the general educator. The special educator can work with the general educator to provide the modifications in the inclusive classroom setting. Students using IEPs may have accommodations expressly written in their IEPs. These accommodations may or may not be used in an inclusive setting, depending on the relevancy of the accommodation. For example, the accommodation of using a calculator would be utilized in a math class but not a social studies class. In addition to expressly written accommodations, special educators and general educators can work together in the setting to provide appropriate accommodations during the learning process. These types of accommodations may be part of informal assessments used to adjust instruction.

Role of Paraeducators

Paraeducators, sometimes referred to as aides or paraprofessionals, are part of students' educational teams. Paraeducators work under the supervision of special educators or principals and are key contributors to the learning process for certain students. Their primary role, especially if their positions are funded by the Individuals with Disabilities Education Act, is to provide educational support for students. For students using Individualized Education Programs, the use of paraeducators is typically included in the IEPs. Paraeducators can facilitate the learning process for students by removing learning barriers, keeping track of goal progress, or organizing goal-tracking activities. Paraeducators cannot introduce new concepts or take over the role of highly qualified teachers. Paraeducators cannot make changes to what students are learning, unless specific modifications are listed in the students' IEPs. They cannot provide accommodations unless the accommodations are appropriate for what is written in the students' IEPs. The paraeducators may also be instructed by supervising teachers or principals to facilitate and monitor accommodations or modifications for students and reinforce learned concepts.

Benefits of Collaborative Teaching and the Co-Teaching Model

If determined by an Individualized Education Program (IEP), a student with a disability may participate in an inclusive setting. In some classrooms, students participate in co-taught settings. In this collaborative teaching environment, the general educator and special educator work together to meet the goals of the students with disabilities in the regular education classroom. Students in this setting are all taught to the same educational standards. However, accommodations and modifications may be implemented for students with disabilities. In a successful collaborative teaching model, the special educator and general educator may cooperatively implement the accommodations and modifications for these students. A two-teacher setting also gives students more opportunities to receive individualized instruction, work in small groups, or receive one-on-one attention. Collaborative teaching in the co-taught setting can facilitate differentiated instruction, help the teachers meet the Universal Design for Learning framework, and provide individualized learning opportunities.

Fostering the Communication Development of Students with ASD

Students with Autism Spectrum Disorder (ASD) vary in their need for communication and social skill assistance and instruction. Some students with ASD may demonstrate slight to extreme delays in language, difficulty sustaining conversations, and the inability to understand body language, tone of voice, and facial expressions. Since ASD is a spectrum disorder, there typically is no single instructional strategy or technique that works for all students with the disorder. Some evidence-based strategies are effective for teaching appropriate communication skills to students with ASD. Applied behavioral analysis (ABA) is an evidence-based strategy that involves providing an intervention and analyzing its effectiveness for a student with ASD. Discrete trial training (DTT) is a teaching strategy that is more structured than ABA. It focuses on teaching and reinforcing skills in smaller increments. Pivotal response treatment (PRT) is an ABA-derived approach that focuses more on meaningful reinforcement when general behaviors occur. PRT targets progress in areas of development rather than focusing on decreasing specific behaviors.

Managing Distractions That May Affect Learning and Development

Managing distractions is a part of good teaching practices. Special educators demonstrate good classroom management strategies when they:

- create positive learning environments by getting to know students' individual emotional, intellectual, social, and physical needs.
- remove or accommodate environmental triggers specific to students.
- remove or accommodate behavioral triggers.
- encourage students to help with classroom jobs and small tasks.
- create preemptive lesson plans for anticipated behaviors.
- attempt verbal de-escalation first when behavioral issues arise.
- set clear, consistent rules.
- set and follow through with consequences for breaking the rules.
- take time to get to know students and their triggers.
- create seating arrangements that minimize distractions.
- teach social skills, thinking skills, test-taking skills, problem-solving skills, and self-regulation skills alongside academic content.
- use visual aids in lessons.
- utilize peer-instructional opportunities.
- provide opportunities for breaks.
- incorporate computer-based programs, which can hold the attention of students with disabilities like autism.

Strategies for Planning, Implementing, and Facilitating Intrinsic Motivation

Intrinsic motivation is a person's inner drive to engage in an activity or behavior. Students with special needs often struggle with intrinsic motivation as a skill. This requires special educators and other professionals to promote and/or teach students to be intrinsically motivated. Teachers can promote intrinsic motivation by giving students opportunities to demonstrate achievement. This can be done by challenging students with intellectual risks and helping them focus on challenging classwork or tasks. Teachers should also build upon students' strengths by providing daily opportunities in the classroom for students to demonstrate their strengths instead of focusing on their weaknesses. Offering choices throughout the day provides students with ownership of their decision making and communicates that they have choices in the classroom environment. Teachers should also allow students to fail without criticism and instead promote self-reflection in order to build students' confidence. Teachers should also instruct students on how to break down tasks and promote other self-management skills and organizational skills.

Instructional Methods for Teaching Students with Social Skills Deficits

Students with social skills deficits often need instruction in social skill areas. These deficits can be addressed in inclusive settings and may not necessarily require explicit social skills instruction. Social skills instruction can be delivered to entire classes or individual students, depending on the needs of the students. Students will sometimes also receive one-on-one or small group social skills instruction from professionals like speech-language pathologists, especially when this is written in students' Individualized Education Programs (IEPs). In these situations, the idea is for the students to generalize learned concepts to their school and home environments. In both settings, it is important to model appropriate manners, hold students responsible for their actions, and have clear and concise rules and consequences. This solidifies educational environments that are both predictable and safe. Social situations that produce undesired outcomes can be remediated by role-playing the situations and teaching students positive responses. Social stories are another way to foster social skills growth. Often, these social stories demonstrate how people should respond to specific social situations appropriately.

Promoting Learning and Development

Educators that practice effective strategies for promoting learning and development create successful learning environments and help struggling learners. Teachers should take the time to know the strengths and weaknesses of individual students in order to plan and implement instructional matches, including curriculum that challenges students without frustrating them. Scaffolding is a strategy that breaks larger concepts into smaller chunks. This process helps students learn new concepts and apply prior knowledge. Instruction should be broken up into step-by-step strategies in order to allow students to follow steps or remediate certain concepts. Modeling and demonstrating tasks or lessons is useful for demonstrating problem-solving abilities. Students mastering new content should also receive consistent, positive feedback for their achievements. Additionally, students should be given opportunities to talk through their processes with peers or in teacher-led groups when learning new concepts.

Selecting Developmentally Appropriate Curriculum

Choosing a developmentally appropriate curriculum is challenging for educators. Special educators have the additional challenge of finding a curriculum that meets the needs of the individual students with disabilities. The end result is not usually a one-size-fits-all curriculum because that goes against the intentions of individualized education programs that meet the needs of students with special needs. Instead, special educators often pick and choose curriculum components that best meet the needs of differing abilities in the classroom. When selecting appropriate curriculum, special educators should consider:

- standards and goals that are appropriate to the needs of the classroom students.
- best practices that have been found effective for classroom students.
- curriculum that is engaging and challenging.
- instruction and activities that are multi-modal.
- Individualized Education Program (IEP) goals.
- real-world experiences.
- different ways of learning that help teachers understand students' learning processes.
- collaboration with co-teachers to deliver appropriate instruction.

In some special education settings, the curriculum is already chosen. In these settings, teachers can collaborate with co-teachers to find ways to provide instruction that meets standards and the individual needs of the classroom students.

Accessibility Components of a Picture Exchange Communication System

A Picture Exchange Communication System (PECS) is a communication system for people with little or no communicative abilities. This system is a way for the students to access their environments using a unique communication system. PECS is a way for people with limited communicative abilities to use picture symbols to communicate meaning, wants, and needs. Children can learn a PECS system by using pictures to request and receive items. For example, a child may point to a picture symbol to request a book. PECS is a way for students with communication disorders to develop their verbal communication without actually speaking. It eliminates frustration and problem behaviors by providing students with an avenue to express what they want to say. It is commonly used for students with Autism Spectrum disorder in the form of augmentative communication devices. It can also be used for students with other impairments whose communicative abilities are affected. PECS focuses on functional communication skills and can be practiced in the home, school, and community environments.

Using Visual Supports to Facilitate Instruction and Self-Monitoring Strategies

Many students learn best when provided with instruction and activities that appeal to multiple senses. A multi-modal approach is especially important for students with developmental disabilities who may need supports that meet their individual ways of learning. Visual supports are concrete representations of information used to convey meaning. Visual supports can be used by teachers of students with developmental disabilities to help them understand what is being taught and communicated to them. Visual supports can help students with understanding classroom rules, making decisions, communicating with others, staying organized, and reducing frustrations. Visual schedules show students visual representations of their daily schedules. This assists with transitions between activities, which can sometimes be difficult for students with disabilities. Visuals can be used to help students share information about themselves or their school days with their peers and parents. Visual supports can also be used with checklists to help facilitate independence, and behavior checklists can be used to help students self-monitor their behaviors.

Using Instructional Methods to Address Independent Living Skills

When applicable, goals for independent living skills are included in the transition section of students' Individualized Education Plans. However, independent living skills education should begin well before students reach high school, regardless of whether or not these skills are addressed in their IEP goals. Functional skills instruction is necessary to teach students skills needed to gain independence. Instructional methods used to address independent living skills for students with disabilities include making life skills instruction part of the daily curriculum. An appropriate task analysis can be used to determine what skills need to be taught. Functional academic skills, especially in the areas of math and language arts, should also be included in the curriculum. Basic skills like telling time, balancing a bank account, and recognizing signs and symbols are just some examples of skills that students can generalize outside of the classroom environment. The goal of community-based instruction is to help students develop skills needed to succeed in the community, such as skills needed when riding a bus or shopping. This type of instruction may be harder to implement than basic social skills training, which should take place in the daily curriculum.

Teaching Strategies for Students Learning at Different Educational Levels

Learning styles of students differ, regardless of whether or not the students have disabilities. When addressing groups of students in inclusion settings, it is important for teachers to organize and implement teaching strategies that address learning at different educational levels. Students generally fall into one or more learning modes. Some are visual learners, some are auditory learners, some are kinesthetic or tactile learners, and some learn best using a combination of these approaches. Teachers can address students' educational levels by creating lessons that allow learning to take place visually, auditorily, and kinesthetically. Visual learners have preferences for seeing information that has been visually organized, such as seeing information presented in graphic organizers or diagrams. Auditory learners prefer information presented in spoken words. Lessons that target auditory learners provide opportunities for students to engage in conversations and/or question material. Kinesthetic learners prefer a hands-on approach to learning. These learners prefer to try out new tasks and learn as they go. Lessons that include opportunities for these three types of learning to occur can successfully target different educational levels.

Components of a Differentiated Curriculum

Differentiated instruction is different from individualized instruction. It targets the strengths of classroom students and can work well in both special education and general education settings. Differentiated instruction is also useful for targeting the needs of students with learning and attention deficits. With differentiated instruction, teachers adjust their instructional processes to meet the needs of the individual students. Teaching strategies and classroom management skills are based largely on each particular class of students instead of using methods that may have been successful in the past. Teachers can differentiate content, classroom activities, student projects, and the learning environments. For example, students may be encouraged to choose topics of personal interest to focus on for projects. Students are held to the same standards but have many choices in terms of project topics. Differentiated content means teachers provide access to a variety of resources to encourage student choice over what and how they learn. Differentiated learning environments are flexible to meet the ever-changing needs of the students.

Differentiated Instruction

Differentiated instruction is effective in general education settings, team-teaching settings, and special education settings because it targets the strengths of classroom students. Differentiated instruction is used to target the different ways that students learn instead of taking a one-size-fits-all approach. Differentiated instruction is used in lieu of individualized instruction because it uses a variety of instructional approaches and allows students access to a variety of materials to help them access the curriculum. Effective differentiated instruction includes small group work, reciprocal learning, and continual assessment.

Small group work allows for the individual learning styles and/or needs of students to be addressed. In small groups, students receive instruction by rotating through different sized groups. In reciprocal learning, students play the role of the teacher, instructing the class by sharing what they know and asking content questions of their peers. Teachers that practice continual assessment can determine if their differentiated instructional methods are effective or if they need to be changed. Assessments can determine what needs to be changed in order for students to participate in effective classroom environments.

Teaching Communication to Students Who Are Nonverbal

Nonverbal students have extra challenges in addition to learning content. These students may need extra instruction in academic areas as well as specialized instruction in the area of communication skills. Students with nonverbal disabilities may also need social skills instruction, struggle with abstract concepts, and dislike changes to their routines. Teachers can facilitate learning for nonverbal students by making changes to their classroom environments, teaching strategies for comprehending concepts, and providing materials to accommodate their needs. Teachers can also provide accommodations and/or modifications to classwork and tests to make the content accessible to nonverbal students. Additionally, teachers can assist nonverbal students by taking measures to prevent undesirable behaviors from occurring. Using visuals to represent actions, words, or concepts is a helpful instructional strategy for teaching nonverbal students, especially when teaching new material.

Co-Teaching Models

Co-teaching models are utilized in collaborative, inclusive teaching settings that include students with and without disabilities. General educators teach alongside special educators and hold all students to the same educational standards. In successful co-teaching settings, these models are used interchangeably. In the One Teach-One Support model, one instructor teaches a lesson while the other instructor supports students who have questions or need assistance. A Parallel Teaching model involves a class being split into two groups, with one instructor teaching each group. The Alternative Teaching model may be appropriate in situations where it is necessary to instruct small groups of students. In this model, one instructor teaches a large group of students while the other provides instruction to a smaller group of students. In Station Teaching, students are split into small groups and work in several teaching centers while both instructors provide support. Teachers participating in Team-Teaching collaboratively plan, implement lesson content, facilitate classroom discussions, and manage discipline. These models all take place in the inclusive classroom setting and are intended to meet the needs of diverse groups of learners.

Intervention Strategies for the Instruction of Students with Multiple Disabilities

Working with students with multiple disabilities can be challenging to manage. However, strategies used in other special education settings can be implemented to promote the success of students with multiple disabilities. Effective strategies include:

- setting long-term goals, which may last for a few years depending on how long students are in the same classrooms.
- working collaboratively with team members, like paraprofessionals and related services professionals, to ensure that the students' educational objectives are carried out consistently between all adults.
- developing and maintaining group goals that the adults and students in the classrooms can strive to achieve together.
- working with students and paraprofessionals and consulting paraprofessionals frequently for feedback.
- demonstrating patience when waiting for children to respond or complete tasks.
- learning about how students communicate, which may involve gestures, a Picture Exchange Communication System, or other methods.
- driving instructional and educational goals based on how students learn best.
- considering how students will respond when designing lessons, including accounting for response time during instruction.

Remedial Instruction vs. Special Education

Though the terms are sometimes used interchangeably, receiving remedial instruction does not always equal special education. The difference between remedial instruction and special education has a lot to do with the intellectual levels of the students. In remedial instruction, a student has average or better than average intellectual abilities but may struggle with skills in one or more content areas. When schools or teachers offer remedial instructional programs or opportunities in the classroom, they offer one-on-one instruction to students who are falling behind. Remedial programs are often mainstreamed into general education classrooms to address the varying learning abilities of classroom students. Remedial instruction can be delivered by general education teachers. Special education programs address the needs of students who may have lower intellectual abilities that require individualized instruction. Students in special education have disabilities that are eligible according to the Individuals with Disabilities Education Act and use

Individualized Education Programs. Unlike remedial instruction, special education requires qualified and credentialed special educators to decide how to best provide interventions in classroom settings for students with disabilities.

Teaching Social Interactions to Students Who Are Nonverbal

Students who are nonverbal may have access to communication systems implemented by trained professionals. Teachers, caretakers, and other professionals work with the students to use the communication systems effectively. The goal of a communication system is to teach a nonverbal student how to "talk" and engage in age-appropriate social skills. In order for nonverbal students to learn appropriate social interactions, they must spend time learning communication skills, just as they learn academic content. Communication skills can be taught in isolation or occur within students' daily activities. Giving nonverbal students opportunities to foster communication skills in familiar environments ensures that they learn how to socially interact appropriately. Teachers, caregivers, and other professionals must demonstrate how to use communication systems to engage in conversations, make requests, and answer questions. Most importantly, nonverbal students must be instructed to access their "words" (communication systems) at all times throughout the school and home environments.

Remedial Instruction vs. Compensatory Approaches to Intervention

Compensatory interventions can be offered in the form of programs or services that help children with special needs or children who are at risk. The compensatory approach is different from remedial instruction because remedial instruction involves the breaking of concepts or tasks into smaller chunks and reteaching information. The remedial approach focuses on repetition and developing or reinforcing certain skills. The compensatory approach is implemented when a remedial approach is not working. It focuses on building upon children's strengths and working with or around their weaknesses. Tools such as audiobooks, text-to-speech software, speech recognition software, and other types of assistive technology are compensatory accommodations that provide free and appropriate educations for children with disabilities who might otherwise continue to demonstrate skill deficits without these tools. Compensatory approaches and remedial instruction can and should be delivered at the same time to ensure that children with disabilities are meeting their potential.

Levels of Bloom's Taxonomy of Learning Domains

Bloom's Taxonomy of Learning Domains is a tool that can be used for instructional planning, curriculum planning, and assessment. It is used to promote and elicit higher levels of thinking instead of relying on rote memorization. Bloom's Taxonomy can enhance instructional experiences for students by helping them to extend their thinking skills. This taxonomy is a useful tool for teachers wanting to improve students' thinking abilities. The taxonomy includes a list of cognitive skills ranking from lower-order thinking to higher-order thinking. Remembering is the lowest level on the taxonomy. This involves simply remembering or recalling information. Comprehending is the next level, which involves thinking about and understanding information. When students demonstrate application, the next level, they show that they can use information and apply it to real-life interactions. In the analyzing level, students are able to categorize, compare, and contrast information. Students demonstrate the second to last level, evaluating, by making decisions and demonstrating judgement. Creating is the last level, which involves using prior knowledge and generalizing it to new concepts.

Mapping

Concept maps are visual organizers that help students with understanding and comprehension. They are generally easy to create and implement. Concept maps should be used before approaching new learning concepts. The purpose of a concept map is to help students organize new information and make connections between other content, thoughts, and ideas. Concept maps can be constructed as part of teacher-led instruction, which is a strategy that may be beneficial for younger grades. They can also be constructed independently or in small groups and then discussed as a class, which is a strategy more beneficial for children in higher grades. Concept mapping starts with identifying major concepts from reading selections or texts. Then the major ideas are sorted into categories, which can be adjusted as the process continues. Arrows or other visuals can be used to demonstrate how the ideas are connected. The last integral part of the concept mapping process is the sharing piece, when students reflect and talk about the processes and concept maps.

Culturally Responsive Teaching and Instruction

Culturally responsive teaching (CRT) involves teachers implementing instruction in a variety of culturally diverse ways in order to target all students. CRT teachers respect their own cultures and the cultures of others by taking the applicable cultures into consideration during planning and instruction. CRT instruction is student centered, considers students' unique abilities and strengths, and helps build and maintain student confidence in their specific cultures. CRT instruction is about reflecting cultural pride, learning styles, and tools. Successful CRT instruction allows all students to engage more and comprehend content that applies to them. Games created to address learning objectives require attention and processing and can teach skills that emphasize use of cultural tools to solve problems. Social learning helps students become responsible for their own learning processes and develop cultural skills. Benefits of CRT include establishing inclusive classroom environments, encouraging individual development and decision making, assisting with overall comprehension, and putting a greater emphasis on the value of learning.

Voice Recognition Software

Voice recognition software and communication software can assist students who struggle with speaking or communicating. Voice recognition software works through computers and allows people to speak commands into microphones instead of using keyboards. This feature creates a least restrictive environment for a student with a disability because it removes the sometimes challenging aspect of using a keyboard while working on a computer. Voice recognition software allows users to carry out commands such as opening documents, saving documents, and moving the mouse cursor. It also allows users to "write" sentences and paragraphs by speaking into the microphones in word processing programs. In order for voice recognition software to be effective, the user must learn to dictate words separately into a microphone. This ensures that the correct word is heard and dictated by the voice-to-text software. Some programs collect information and familiarize themselves with people's particular voice qualities. Over time, the systems learn to adapt to people's voices, and the systems become more efficient.

Effectively Instructing Students Using Assistive Technology

Assistive technology (AT) refers to tools effective for teaching students with learning disabilities, as they address a number of potential special needs. The purpose of AT is to level the playing field for students with learning disabilities, particularly when they are participating in general education classrooms. AT can address learning difficulties in math, listening, organization, memory, reading, and writing. AT for listening can assist students who have difficulties processing language. For example, a personal listening device can help a student hear a teacher' voice more clearly. AT for organization and memory can help students with self-management tasks, such as keeping assignment calendars or retrieving information using hand-held devices. AT for reading often include text-to-speech devices that assist with students' reading fluency, decoding, comprehension, and other skill deficits. AT for writing assists students who struggle with handwriting or writing development. Some AT writing devices help with actual handwriting, while others assist with spelling, punctuation, grammar, word usage, or text organization.

Types of Assistive Technology Tools

Assistive technology (AT) tools can be separate objects and devices or tools readily available on the Internet to assist in the learning of students with disabilities. The purpose of AT tools is to provide students with disabilities equal access to the curriculum by accommodating their individual needs to promote positive outcomes. Personal listening devices (PLDs), sometimes called FM systems, are devices that clarify teachers' words. With a PLD, a teacher speaks into a small microphone, and the words transmit clearly into a student's headphone or earpiece. Sound field systems amplify teachers' voices to eliminate sound issues in the classroom environments. Noise-cancelling headphones are useful for students who need to work independently and limit distractions or behavioral triggers. Audio recorders allow students to record lectures or lessons and refer back to the recordings at their own pace. Some note-taking applications will transcribe audio into written words. Captioning is available to pair visual words with spoken words. Text-to-speech (TTS) software lets students see and hear words at the same time. TTS and audiobook technology can help students with fluency, decoding, and comprehension skills.

Instructing Nonverbal Students on the Use of Augmentative and Alternative Communication Systems

Students with communication disorders may often require the use of augmentative or alternative communication systems. Communication systems are used to help the students effectively demonstrate expressive and receptive language and engage in social skills. Teaching appropriate communication skills is a collaborative effort between the students' caretakers, teachers, and other professionals. Typically, speech services are written into students' Individualized Education Programs (IEPs), and the services are delivered by speech language pathologists (SLPs). Depending on how it is written in the IEPs, the SLPs may work one-on-one with students or work with the teachers to incorporate speech and language skills throughout students' school days. In order for communication systems to work for nonverbal students, measures must be taken to ensure that the particular systems are appropriate for what the students need. It is important for the caretakers, teachers, other professionals, and even classmates to model using the devices so the students can learn how to "talk" appropriately. Students must also have constant access to the systems and receive consistent opportunities to communicate with the systems at home and at school.

Use of Visual Representation Systems with Students with Autism

Assistive technology (AT) helps increase learning opportunities for students with autism by eliminating educational barriers to learning. AT can help improve students' expressive communication skills, attention skills, motivational skills, academic skills, and more. Visual representation systems in the form of objects, photographs, drawings, or written words provide concrete representations of words for students with autism. Visual representations, such as simple pictures paired with words, can be used to create visual schedules for students with autism. Photographs can be used to help students learn the names of people, places, or vocabulary words. Written words should be paired with the visual representations in order to create links between the concrete objects and the actual words. The goal is for the students to eventually recognize the words without the pictures. Visual representation systems can also help facilitate easier transitions between activities or places, which can be difficult for students with autism.

Benefits of Vocational/Career Education

Students with disabilities often participate in vocational or career and technical education in order to gain independent living skills. Often, schools and communities offer services for vocational or career and technical education that provide vocational or career training for people with disabilities. These programs offer students job-specific skills training and opportunities to earn certifications, diplomas, or certificates. They often involve hands-on learning experiences focused on building skills specific to certain occupations. These programs are beneficial to students with disabilities, as they tend to struggle with grasping abstract concepts learned in typical classroom environments. Hands-on training in vocational or career education programs can be a meaningful way for students with disabilities to both learn academic concepts and gain living skills needed to function in post-graduate life. Vocational and technical education opportunities also offer alternatives for students with disabilities who might otherwise drop out of high school. These programs also serve as a viable option for younger students to work towards, as most vocational or career education programs are offered to students in upper grade levels.

Supporting Classroom Transitions

Transitioning to life after high school can be a difficult process, particularly for students with disabilities. It is important for teachers to facilitate and support these transitions before students exit their special education programs. Structured learning environments that include independent work stations and learning centers provide opportunities for independent learning to occur. Independent work stations give students chances to practice previously introduced concepts or perform previously introduced tasks. Learning centers provide small group settings where new skills can be taught. Students can also rotate through different learning centers that offer art lessons, focus on academic skills, or provide breaks or leisure activities. Classroom layout also plays an important role. Teachers should plan their classroom layouts based on individual student needs in order to create comfortable, predictable environments for students with disabilities. Visual schedules help students transition between centers by providing them with concrete schedule references.

Vocational Skills Needed to Be Successful in Work Environments

Informal vocational training often begins before students even get to high school. Teachers include informal vocational training skills in their classrooms by teaching academic and communication skills. Academic skills can both spark and strengthen students' career interests and provide learning platforms to build upon. Communication skills generalize to work environments when students learn appropriate communication skills, like how to give and follow instructions and process information. Social and interpersonal skills, like problem-solving abilities and learning how to participate in phone conversations, are important for teaching students how to perform in workplaces. Students also need to learn important vocational and occupational skills required by most jobs, such as how to interact appropriately with coworkers and keep track of worked hours. Students also need formal or informal training in completing resumes, cover letters, and tax forms. Training may also include interviewing practice and job search guidance.

Resources to Promote Successful Transitions to Life after High School

In some states, statements of transition should be included on Individualized Education Programs (IEPs) at age 14 for students with disabilities. In most states, the Individuals with Disabilities Education Act mandates that transition plans be put in place for students on IEPs at age 16 and every year thereafter. Some schools and communities have programs and/or resources available to facilitate students' successful transitions to life after high school. Throughout the transition process, it is important that students and their caregivers participate in any decision-making processes. Vocational education courses, sometimes called career and technical education (CTE) courses, offer academic course alternatives. The courses usually specialize in specific trades or occupations. They can serve to spark or maintain students' interests in vocational fields. Some schools offer post-secondary enrollment options (PSEO), where students can participate in college courses, earning both high school and college credits. Career assessments, including interest inventories and formal and informal vocational assessments, serve to gauge students' career interests. These can be worked into students' transitional goals on their IEPs and should be conducted frequently as students' interests change.

Components of a Transition Plan

Per federal law, transition plans are required to be part of a student's Individualized Education Program during the year the student turns 16 years old. The transition plan components include postsecondary goals and transition services. The purpose of the goals is to state what a student wants to achieve after high school. The four goal areas are vocational training, post-secondary education, employment, and independent living. Transition goals must be results oriented and measurable. Goals can be general, but the transition activities need to be quantified to reflect what the student can complete in the IEP year. It is common for interests to change from year to year. Therefore, goals and plans may change as well. Transition services are determined once the goals are established. Transition services include types of instruction the student will receive in school, related services, community experiences, career or college counseling, and help with adaptive behavior skills. Goals and transition services must be reviewed and updated each year. Academic goals in the IEP can also support transition goals. For example, academic math goals can focus on money management skills as part of a transition plan.

Purpose and Implications of a Transition Plan on the IEP

In most states, a transition plan should be included on the Individualized Education Program (IEP) for a student with a disability the year the student turns 16 years old. As mandated by the Individuals with Disabilities Education Act, a transition plan should include goals and services specific to the student's individual needs. The purpose of a transition plan on a student's IEP is to help guide and prepare the student for post-secondary employment, education, and independent living. A transition plan is driven by the student's interests, which can be gathered via formal and informal career assessments, such as interest inventories. A transition plan includes goals specific to a student's expressed interests, which can or will be achieved within the IEP year. Successful goals are objective, measurable, and specifically related to a student's expressed interests. These goals can include goals for post-secondary employment, education, and/or independent living, depending on the needs and interests of the specific student. Transition goals can also include student goals for vocational training.

Factors That Influence Successful Transitions to Post-Secondary Life

Students, parents or legal guardians, teachers, school professionals, and sometimes community members are key factors in successful transitions to post-secondary life for students with disabilities. Factors that influence students' successful transitions include participation in standards-based education, work preparation and career-based learning experiences, and experience with leadership skills. Other factors that influence successful transitions include access to and experience with community services, such as mental health and transportation services. Lastly, family involvement and support are key factors in facilitating successful transitions for students with disabilities. Standards-based education ensures that students receive consistent and clear expectations with curriculum that is aligned to the Universal Design for Learning standards. Exposure to work preparation and career-based learning experiences ensures that students receive opportunities to discover potential career interests and/or hobbies. Connections and experiences with community activities provide students with essential post-secondary independent living skills. Family involvement and support ensure that students have advocates for their needs and interests. Families can also help students connect with school and community-based supports that facilitate their career interests.

Including Measurable and Challenging Objectives in Lesson Plans

Lesson objectives should be SMART, meaning they should be specific, measurable, attainable, relevant, and time based. When teachers plan lessons, SMART objectives provide the framework to effectively execute the lesson plans. Specific objectives describe exactly what will be taught within the time frame of the lesson. Specific objectives answer "W" questions, such as the questions listed below.

- What do I want to accomplish?
- Why is this goal important?
- Who is involved?
- Where is it located?
- Which resources are available?

Measurable objectives are important for staying on task and tracking progress. Attainable objectives are created with students' strengths and needs in mind. Attainable objectives should keep in mind what students can realistically accomplish within the lesson time frame. Achievable objectives spell out how the goals will be accomplished. A good attainable objective is challenging but realistically achievable based on students' abilities. Relevant objectives should build upon prior knowledge and matter to the teacher and the students. Relevant objectives promote student interest and engagement. Time-bound objectives set deadlines and help prioritize objectives.

Characteristics of Effective Structured Learning Environments

A structured learning environment is an important component of good classroom management. Teachers that create environments that are conducive for teaching and learning create environments where students feel safe. In effective structured learning environments, teachers create solid relationships with students by getting to know them and their interests. Often, this information can be used to implement learning activities based on students' interests. Another way to promote effective structured learning environments is to consistently follow implemented rules and maintain consistency in procedures in order to communicate what to expect to students. Transitioning students appropriately between activities increases time spent learning. Additionally, teachers that spend time designing effective lesson plans that anticipate student behaviors create solid environments for their students. Teachers can also establish good learning environments by promoting target behaviors. This means promoting standards of behavior and clear consequences for breaking rules. Students that have clear expectations learn in effective structured learning environments.

Curriculum and Assignment Modifications in the Classroom for Students with Disabilities

Modifications are changes to what students are taught or expected to learn. Students with disabilities can receive curriculum modifications as determined by their specific needs and as written out in their Individualized Education Programs. Curriculum modifications allow students to learn material that is different from what their general education peers learn. For example, students with classroom modifications may receive assignments with fewer math problems or with reading samples appropriate for their reading levels. Students with curriculum modifications may receive different grading tiers than their peers. The ways teachers grade their assignments may be different from how the teachers grade their peers' assignments. Students may also be excused from particular projects or given project guidelines that are different and better suited to their individual needs. Assignment modifications include completing fewer or different homework problems than peers, writing shorter papers, answering fewer questions on classwork and tests, and creating alternate projects or assignments.

Purpose of Non-Traditional Classroom Seating Arrangements

Seating arrangements are part of good classroom management strategies, especially for students with disabilities. Special education settings and inclusion settings often require flexibility with instruction and versatility with seating arrangements. The traditional setting includes rows of desks facing the area where the teacher conducts instruction. More student-centered arrangements include a horseshoe seating arrangement, a group pod arrangement, or a paired arrangement. A horseshoe seating arrangement is conducive to student-centered instruction because it allows the students to face each other and the instructor to move around the classroom easily. This setup facilitates classroom discussions and encourages interactions between instructors and students and among peers. The group pod or paired-pod arrangement is useful for student-centered instruction like small group work. This arrangement is also helpful when students need to rotate through lesson stages or work in small groups on projects. Effective teachers do not use one seating arrangement for the entire year. Best practices indicate that seating arrangements should change and be tied to the intent of lesson objectives.

Determining the Special Education Setting Placement

Special education setting placement is determined in a student's Individualized Education Program (IEP), as specified by the Individuals with Disabilities Education Act (IDEA). IDEA requires that students be placed in general education classrooms to the maximum extent possible. Students should be placed in environments that are most appropriate for them, known as the least restrictive environment. If students can be educated in general education classrooms (inclusion) when provided with appropriate accommodations, they can be placed in general education classrooms. When students with disabilities need modifications to curriculum that are significantly below grade level or different than their peers, the students may be placed in resource rooms for remedial instruction. However, the students may also participate in the general education curriculum with modified work that meets their current abilities. For example, a student who struggles in math can use a calculator accommodation in the inclusion setting. A student whose math skills are two grade levels below the skills of same-aged peers may be placed in an inclusion setting with modifications or receive instruction in a resource room.

Function of a Multidisciplinary Team-Teaching Model

The three disciplinary team models include a multidisciplinary team, an interdisciplinary team, and a transdisciplinary team. The multidisciplinary team is usually composed of the special educator, general education teacher, parents, paraprofessionals, principal, and school psychologist. As a whole, this team presents a comprehensive group of expertise, qualifications, and skills. In the multidisciplinary team model, these professionals do not collaborate, but instead work alongside each other to pursue a common goal for the individual student with special needs. The multidisciplinary team model is effective for evaluating a student for referral for special education, completing pre-referral testing, and completing an Individualized Education Program or Evaluation Team Report. Sometimes this team is referred to as the child study team or student support team. In this model, professionals usually pull out students to work with them individually. Parents and legal guardians are a part of this process. Professionals working with the student should openly communicate their processes and the results of any evaluations or informal observations.

Interdisciplinary Team-Teaching Model

An interdisciplinary team model features the general education teacher providing all curriculum and accommodations for a student with an Individualized Education Program. In this model, the special educator and other professionals relevant to the education of the student collaborate to ensure that the curriculum meets the needs of the student and the accommodations are appropriate. This model is not a team-teaching model. Advantages of this model include the collaboration of all IEP team members towards a common goal and the student's needs being addressed by one teacher instead of several different teachers or professionals. The disadvantages of this model include difficulties with collaboration between professionals and issues with delivering related services to students who need them. Related service provision sometimes includes one-on-one instruction, which requires the student to be pulled out for a certain amount of time during general education instruction. This model may also not be appropriate for students with intense needs, as they often require individualized education in order to meet IEP goals. They may also require specific accommodations and modifications not suitable for the general education classroom.

Transdisciplinary Team-Teaching Model

131b. In this model, professionals working with the student work together collaboratively to ensure the individual needs of the student are met. The special educator may teach in the general education classroom delivering instruction to both students with and without disabilities. This model features a team-teaching experience for classroom students, where the special educator and general educator may take turns teaching. The presence of the special educator in the general education setting means the special educator can offer advice for accommodating the students with special needs in the classroom. Additionally, this model provides opportunities for teachers and other professionals to communicate consistently about students' progress, share ideas, and work collaboratively to solve any issues that arise. The effectiveness of this model relies heavily on the collaboration of the special educator and the general educator addressing the major features of this team-teaching model.

Advantages and Disadvantages of Team-Teaching Models

Students with and without disabilities present a variety of learning abilities in the general education classroom. One advantage of team-teaching models in this setting is being able to target the unique abilities, learning methods, and skills that each student brings to the classroom. Another advantage is effective classroom management. In an effective team-teaching model, one teacher provides the instruction, while the other practices classroom management skills to minimize disruptions and promote a safe learning environment. This model encourages class participation, facilitates group activities, and provides multiple means of engagement for learning content. One disadvantage is there may be an offset between the teachers sharing a class. When one teacher is not open to multiple methods of delivering instruction, the team-teaching approach is ineffective. Planning and making group decisions regarding curriculum can be time consuming and stressful in a team-teaching environment.

Lifting Guidelines for Students Who Require Physical Lifting

Teachers and paraprofessionals may encounter students with physical disabilities who require assisted transfers. In some circumstances, students must be lift-assisted from their wheelchairs in order to participate in physical therapy or floor activities. While this practice is more common in low-incidence classrooms and not always a job requirement, it is important to know school guidelines for lifting techniques to keep staff and students safe. Knowing school guidelines for lifting can also help prevent back injuries from occurring. Physical therapists working with the students should be consulted before attempting student lifts. They are trained professionals who know specific procedures for lifting students in order to keep the students and staff members safe. Every school district has policies for lift-assisted student transfers. Each student should be evaluated to determine if a one-person lift or two-person lift is needed. Two-person lifts are for heavier students, and some school districts do not allow two-person lifts for safety reasons.

How Cooperative Learning Works

Cooperative learning is an interpersonal group learning process where students learn concepts by working together in small groups. Cooperative learning involves collaboration among small groups to achieve common goals. With formal cooperative learning, an instructor oversees the learning of lesson material or completion of assignments for students in these small groups. With informal cooperative learning, the instructor supervises group activities by keeping students cognitively active but does not guide instruction or assignments. For example, a teacher might use a class period to show a movie but provide a list of questions for students to complete during the movie. In the special education classroom, cooperative learning is helpful when students need specific skills targeted or remediated. It is also helpful for separating students who are learning different content at different levels. For example, a cooperative learning activity may involve multiple groups of students with differing levels of mathematic abilities. Group work also promotes development of interpersonal skills as students interact with one another.

Benefit of Multiple Modality Instruction and Activities

The purpose of multiple modality instruction is to engage students by offering different ways to learn the same material. Multiple modality teaching also addresses students' unique learning styles. Learning modalities are generally separated into four categories: visual (seeing), auditory (hearing), kinesthetic (moving), and tactile (touch) modalities. This way of teaching targets students who may have deficits in one or more modalities. It is also helpful for students who struggle in one or more of the learning categories. If a student struggles with understanding content that is presented visually, a lesson that includes auditory, kinesthetic, and tactile components may engage learning. Additionally, presenting lesson material and activities in a multi-modal approach helps improve student memory and retention by solidifying concepts through multiple means of engagement. This approach is also useful for students with attention disorders who may struggle in environments where one mode of teaching is used. The multiple modality approach ensures that activities, such as kinesthetic or tactile activities, keep more than one sense involved with the learning process.

Components of a Successful Team-Teaching Model

A successful team-teaching model is one where the teachers involved set clear, effective, specific goals for performance. These goals must demonstrate clarity. All team-teaching members must be clear on the components of the goals and their potential outcomes. Clear goals allow team members and students to know what they are working towards as a classroom. Goals should be specific and measurable. Goal criteria should be qualified in percentages or quantities. This provides hard evidence for how effectively the team-teaching classroom is meeting the goals. Challenging goals set high expectations for what the team needs to work towards. Challenging goals ensure that team members and classroom students are working to achieve goals right outside their ability levels. Goals that are too challenging can be frustrating for all team members and students. A successful team-teaching model also reflects commitment from team members and any other professionals involved in the classroom.

Classroom Timing, Schedule, and Organization Accommodations

Timing, schedule, and organizational accommodations change the ways students with disabilities have access to classrooms with the fewest barriers to learning. Students who need these accommodations receive them as written statements in their Individualized Education Programs, 504 Plans, or as teachers see fit during classroom time. Timing accommodations allow students more time to complete tasks or tests and/or process instructions. They also allow students to access frequent breaks during assignments or tests. Schedule accommodations include taking tests in chunks over periods of time or several days, taking test sections in different orders, and/or taking tests during specific times of day. Organizational skill accommodations include assistance with time management, marking texts with highlighters, maintaining daily assignment or work schedules, and/or receiving study skills instruction. When accommodations are written in a student's IEP, the student has access to them for state standardized tests. When and how accommodations are put into place is left to the discretion of the teacher unless specifically written in the student's IEP or 504 Plan.

Creating Inclusive Learning Environments That Address Unique Needs

Effective inclusive environments abide by the Universal Design for Learning framework. Special educators and general educators can work together to create learning environments that are accessible to the unique needs of students with language or physical needs. This can be done by providing multiple ways for students to access lesson concepts, express learned concepts, and engage in the learning process. For students with language barriers, signs, symbols, pictures, and learning concepts may have different meanings than they do for students without language barriers. Keeping this in mind, teachers can address UDL guidelines for students with language barriers by providing diverse ways to activate prior knowledge, emphasizing key learning elements, and using visuals to guide the learning process. For students with physical barriers, teachers can level the learning process by making their physical classroom environments accessible and providing different ways for students to express what they have learned. In general, teachers abiding by UDL framework would have these supports in place in order to ensure that the needs of diverse learners are met.

Fostering Positive and Inclusive Learning Environments Addressing Students with Learning or Cognitive Needs

Whether in the general education classroom or special education classroom, the Universal Design for Learning model should foster positive and inclusive learning environments. General education and special education teachers can take measures to ensure the UDL concept is implemented to address the unique needs of students with cognitive or behavioral needs. Since each student presents different needs, a one-size-fits-all approach to learning is not suitable or UDL compliant for these students. Special educators and general educators should openly communicate about the unique learning needs of the students with learning or cognitive needs. General strategies include receiving regular input from special educators on how to best meet the needs of the students in the classroom. This includes sharing information with any paraprofessionals and aides regarding how to assist the students in the general education classroom. UDL base strategies include the general educators providing multiple means by which students can complete the assignments. Students with cognitive disabilities may also benefit from the use of concrete examples and instruction, especially when addressing abstract concepts.

Fostering Positive and Inclusive Learning Environments Addressing Students with Behavioral Needs

The Universal Design for Learning (UDL) concepts can be implemented to reduce challenging behavior in the classroom. They can also be used to help students with behavioral needs find success in the general education classroom. Lack of student engagement is compatible with the presentation of challenging behaviors. When UDL concepts are demonstrated appropriately, engagement can improve. Providing multiple means of representation is one UDL strategy for improving engagement and challenging behavior. This means the classroom teacher provides multiple ways of presenting the teaching material in order to engage as many students as possible. Teachers that provide multiple means of representation look to activate prior knowledge and help students make sense of the current content. UDL compliant strategies also include providing multiple means of expression. Teachers applying UDL principles recognize that differentiating activities and assignments addresses a variety of abilities and learning styles. UDL compliant teachers should also provide multiple means of engagement. Successful engagement in learning can often offset challenging behaviors by helping students focus on lesson material. Offering both challenging and simplistic work options and making engaging, solid connections to past and/or future lesson content can minimize the possibility of problems arising in the classroom.

Promoting Student Achievement in English Language Arts, Reading, and Mathematics

Pedagogical Concepts

Promoting Critical Thinking Skills

Critical thinking is a self-directed thinking process that helps people make logical, reasonable judgements. This is an especially challenging skill for students with developmental disabilities, who often demonstrate deficits in logical thinking and reasoning abilities. In order to teach these students critical thinking skills, the focus should be on encouraging critical thinking across home and school environments and providing opportunities for students to practice this type of thinking. Teachers and parents can encourage critical thinking by implementing teaching strategies focused on fostering creativity in students. Instead of providing outlines or templates for lesson concepts, students can use their prior knowledge to figure out the boundaries of the lessons independently and explore new concepts. Parents and teachers should not always be quick to jump in and help students who are struggling. Sometimes the best way to help is by facilitating ways for students to solve problems without doing things for them. Opportunities for brainstorming, classifying and categorizing information, comparing and contrasting information, and making connections between topics are teaching strategies that also facilitate critical thinking skills.

Metacognitive Approach to Teaching

Metacognition refers to people's awareness and understanding of their own thinking processes. The metacognitive approach to teaching helps students think about their thinking processes and make sense of the world around them. Increasing their levels of self-awareness allows students to gain an understanding of how they feel, think, and act. This helps them optimize their educational performances because by learning more about how they feel, think, and act, they begin to understand more about how they learn. Teachers can engage students in metacognitive thinking by teaching them how to think reflectively. Teachers should also encourage students to recognize what they do not understand. This allows them to be comfortable with a lack of understanding and learn how to work through it. Instructors can also provide time for students to keep learning journals that note their learning progress throughout the year. Reflecting on projects and assignments, monitoring their own skills, and providing tests that target higher level thinking objectives, like essay tests, also promote metacognitive thinking in students.

Teaching Participation in Career-Based Education

During their schooling years, students with disabilities have the additional challenge of determining possible career options for life after high school. Fortunately, instruction can be provided during the school day or within after-school programs that address career-based skills. Effective career-based programs for students with disabilities should work collaboratively with community and school resources. Students should receive information on career options, be exposed to a range of experiences, and learn how to self-advocate. Information regarding career options can be gathered via career assessments that explore students' possible career interests. Students should receive exposure to post-secondary education to determine if it is an option that aligns with their career interests. They should also learn about basic job requirements, such as what it means to earn a living wage and entry requirements for different types of jobs. Students should be given opportunities for job training, job shadowing, and community service. It is helpful to provide students with opportunities to learn and practice work and occupational skills that pertain to specific job interests. Students need to learn self-advocacy skills, such as communicating the implications of their disabilities to employers, in order to maintain success in post-secondary work environments.

Prior Knowledge

By the time children enter school, their life experiences have shaped their understandings about how the world around them works. Activating prior knowledge is a way to build upon and develop children's prior knowledge and apply it to new concepts. Prior knowledge can be a useful instructional tool for addressing concepts that might otherwise be especially challenging. Prior knowledge is a combination of children's beliefs and academic experiences that affect how students learn. Therefore, it is important for educators to gauge this knowledge in order to plan lessons accordingly. Know, Want to Know, and Learned charts (KWL) are useful tools to use before lessons begin. Students explore what they know and want to know about concepts. At the conclusion of the lessons, students examine what they have learned about the concepts. The Known and Unknown chart strategy works similarly. Teachers can ask what students know about concepts and write responses down in the known column. What students want to learn more about or do not know goes into the unknown column. Both strategies can be implemented as individual or group activities to introduce lessons.

Guided Learning

Guided learning is practice or instruction completed by the teacher and students together. The goal of guided learning is to help students engage in the learning process in order to learn more about how they think and acquire new information. Guided practice occurs when the teacher and students complete practice activities together. The advantage of guided practice is that students can learn ways to approach concepts they have just learned. It allows students to understand and ask questions about lesson-related activities before working independently. Guided practice is useful in classrooms for students with and without disabilities because it helps teachers gauge how students learn and what instructional methods work best for them. Additionally, guided practice allows teachers to understand how students are learning the material. It also allows teachers to revisit concepts that are unclear or fine tune any missed lesson objectives.

Diagnostic Prescriptive Method

The diagnostic prescriptive approach to teaching is based on the fact that all students are unique learners. The diagnostic prescriptive approach examines factors that impede student learning and how to remedy specific issues. A successful approach begins with a diagnosis of what students are bringing to the classroom. This can be completed through careful observations and assessments. Once the skill deficits are clear, prescriptive teaching can be put into effect. In this process, teachers examine what will help students the most. It may be switching materials, changing to group settings, or recognizing the need for specialized interventions due to disabilities. In order to address multiple needs in the classroom, lesson plans should be multi-modal. Developing strategies in advance to address students' needs is also a highlight of this method. Another important part of this method is evaluating results to determine what was effective or ineffective for entire classes and individual students.

Developmentally Appropriate Math Skills for Young Children

Starting in pre-kindergarten and first grade, children should be able to count to 100, learn how to write numbers, and demonstrate basic addition and subtraction skills. Older students can demonstrate skills associated with counting money and telling time, and they can also understand decimal, place value, and word problem concepts. Students with disabilities may or may not develop what are considered to be developmentally appropriate mathematics skills by certain ages or grades. In inclusive special education settings, the needs of these students can be addressed with a number of strategies. Scaffolding is the process of breaking down concepts into chunks. Scaffolding addresses the issues that arise when some students are well behind others by allowing students to work at their own pace and helping them connect prior knowledge to new information. This ensures that students have solidified knowledge of concepts before moving on to new concepts.

Teaching Mathematics

Students whose disabilities affect their performances in mathematics require specialized instruction. Eligible students will have Individualized Education Program goals to address their specific needs but are also expected to learn content connected to state standards. Additionally, accommodations and modifications are available for qualifying students to assist with mathematics instruction. Strategies that can be effective for math instruction for students with disabilities include:

- using the same instructional strategies in all settings, including the home environment and all school environments.
- using concrete objects to teach math concepts, such as using manipulatives to count out number values.
- providing assistive materials, such as calculators and scrap paper.
- explaining and modeling objectives clearly.
- allowing time for students to check their work.
- activating prior knowledge to assist students with learning new concepts.
- providing opportunities for extra tutoring or one-on-one instruction.
- assisting students with self-monitoring their progress.
- encouraging math games to engage learning and interest in math concepts.

Components of Direct Reading Instruction

The purpose of direct learning instruction is to specifically target the needs of students with learning disabilities. Direct learning instruction can be provided in many educational settings. Direct instruction breaks concept learning into specific tasks and processes, with focus on mastering one skill before moving onto another skill. With direct reading instruction, the key components are teaching phonemic awareness, phonics, fluency, vocabulary development, and comprehension. Effective reading programs address all five areas of reading instruction. Phonemic awareness focuses on breaking words into sound units (phonemes). Phonics focuses on connecting these sound units with letters (graphemes). Phonics instruction allows students to approach decoding by sounding words out instead of attempting to read the whole words. Fluency instruction focuses on teaching students to read unfamiliar words and texts quickly and accurately. Vocabulary development helps increase familiarity with frequently occurring words in texts. Comprehension instruction focuses on helping students to understand what they have read. In comprehension instruction, learners connect prior knowledge to the texts.

Benefits of the Direct Reading Process

Direct reading instruction is an approach to teaching reading which focuses on specific skill development for early readers. Students frequently enter their schooling years with deficits in reading skills, especially when they are identified as having disabilities. Effective direct reading programs include the teaching of phonemic awareness, phonics, fluency, vocabulary development, and comprehension. Teachers are generally trained to implement direct reading programs instead of creating direct instruction curriculum. Specific programs ensure that teachers use the same curriculum and methods in order to effectively implement direct reading instruction. Direct reading instruction and programs are especially helpful for skill remediation for at-risk students. Efficient direct reading instruction communicates high standards for learning, is replicable or able to be implemented across a variety of settings, and offers support materials, professional development, and implementation guidance. Direct reading instruction is also proven to be effective for the improvement of reading abilities in at-risk students.

Teaching Social Studies

Depending on their special education classroom placements, students with disabilities receive varying degrees of instruction in other core content areas like social studies and science. Students with mild disabilities, such as learning disabilities, likely participate in inclusive classroom settings or general education classroom settings. Depending on a student's grade level, the student may attend a classroom setting with one or two teachers or switch classes and attend settings with many different teachers. Across all settings, students with mild disabilities receive any accommodations or modifications explicitly written in their Individualized Education Programs. Students with mild to moderate disabilities may receive instruction in special education classrooms for part or most of the day. In these instances, general education social studies or science classes may not be the most appropriate educational settings. Special educators then teach the content in the special education classrooms, sometimes connecting it with related tasks or skills. Students with moderate disabilities may receive indirect instruction in these content areas that is loosely based on content standards and more appropriate for the ways they acquire knowledge.

Teaching Special Education

Special education classrooms, whether inclusive, self-contained, or resource room settings, often need to deliver instruction in multiple subject areas. Students in these settings also represent many levels of learning. Therefore, one instructional strategy is not always the most effective way to teach students in these settings. In order to provide quality instruction, special educators can place students with similar skill levels into small groups during instruction in the content areas. This way, small groups of students can be working on skills that cater to their specific needs. Classroom centers are another way to group students. Classroom centers often feature self-guided instruction in skill or content areas where students can work at their own pace. Rotating centers allows teachers to instruct groups of students while the other groups work independently on previously learned skills. Thematic instruction is a teaching strategy where multiple subject areas are connected and taught within one lesson unit. Themes are effective in special education classrooms because they tie multiple content areas together. Special educators should also provide multiple levels of materials and books for student learning to target different learning levels.

Modifying the Stages of Writing to Assist Students with Learning Disabilities

The writing process can be especially challenging for new learners but especially for students with disabilities. The writing process can be facilitated by special educators and general educators in order to build adequate writing skills. Teachers must first address the needs of their classes before engaging in the pre-writing stage. Getting to know students provides insight into their prior knowledge and abilities. In the pre-writing (brainstorming) stage, teachers help students prepare for the writing process by establishing good content or thinking of things that interest them to write about. In the writing stage, students should be taught to write their content using graphic organizers or diagrams that assist with using appropriate formatting, grammar, and punctuation. The rewriting/revising stage can be facilitated by providing checklists of errors and having students self-check and revise their own work. In the editing/proofreading stage, students can self-check their work or exchange their final written projects with other students or their teachers. This can also be facilitated using formatting checklists and/or grammar and punctuation checklists to monitor the writing process.

Implications of a Mathematics Disability

Disabilities like dyscalculia are specific learning disabilities associated with mathematics. Students that have specific learning disabilities in mathematics have trouble with number-related concepts and using symbols or functions. Symptoms of math disorders include difficulties with counting numbers, solving math word problems, sequencing events or information, recognizing patterns when adding, subtracting, multiplying or dividing, and understanding concepts associated with time, like days, weeks, seasons, etc. Recalling math facts is also difficult for students with math disabilities. The severity of the disability is impacted when it coexists with dyslexia, Attention Deficit Hyperactivity Disorder, anxiety, or other disabilities. Special educators, math tutors, or other professionals can help students with math deficits by providing multi-modal instruction to engage multiple senses and enhance the chances of the students learning the concepts. They may also receive supports according to 504 Plans or Individualized Education Programs that level the educational playing field, such as use of a calculator. Use of concrete examples, visual aids, graph paper, or scratch paper can also assist students with math disabilities.

Teaching Comprehension with Research-Based Reading Intervention Strategies

Comprehension refers to a person's understanding of something. As it pertains to reading, comprehension is the understanding of content that has been read. Students with disabilities often struggle with comprehension, which makes teaching comprehension strategies essential to their learning. Special educators should teach students to monitor their comprehension by being aware of what they have read, identifying what they do not understand, and implementing problem-solving strategies to address what they do not understand. Special educators can also teach students to demonstrate metacognitive strategies, such as identifying specifically what they do not understand in texts (i.e. identifying the page numbers or chapters where they are struggling), looking back through the texts to find answers to comprehension questions, rereading sentences or sections they do not understand, and putting sentences they do not understand into their own words. Graphic organizers, like story maps and Venn diagrams, also allow students to map out the information they have read by laying out important concepts.

Effects of Deficits in Language Development on the Learning Processes

Without interventions, children with deficits in language development will likely have issues with overall academic success. Academic success is inextricably linked with good language development. Good language development skills include the ability to understand spoken and written words, as well as literacy skills. When a core knowledge of language is developed in young children, it can be built upon as the children grow and develop during their grade school years. Reading and writing are language-based skills. Phonological awareness is an essential skill and key building block for language development. Phonological awareness is a term that refers to students' awareness of sounds, syllables, and words. Students that develop strong phonological skills typically develop good literacy skills. Students with deficits in reading, writing, or math may have difficulties with phonological awareness and miss some building blocks essential for academic success. These deficits generalize to core subject areas as students are required to demonstrate grade-level appropriate skills.

Helping Students with Disabilities Become Solid Emergent Readers

Emergent reading refers to the reading and writing abilities of young readers. They precede conventional literacy, which refers to older children's reading and writing behaviors, such as decoding, reading comprehension, oral reading fluency, spelling, and writing. Children with learning disabilities may demonstrate discrepancies between emergent literacy behaviors and conventional literacy behaviors. They may flip-flop between the two stages, showing progress one moment or day and then seeming to forget the next. Educators can foster skills in emergent and conventional reading by teaching phonological awareness and written letter/sound recognition. These are both baseline skills that affect students' future phonological awareness development. Additionally, educators can provide engaging, age-appropriate activities that facilitate connections between emergent literacy and conventional literacy skills. Activities that promote students' print awareness and knowledge of book conventions also help build solid emergent reader skills.

Helping Students Develop Oral Language Abilities

Children pick up oral language skills in their home environments and build upon these skills as they grow. Early language development is a combination of genetic disposition, environment, and individual thinking processes. Children with oral language acquisition difficulties often experience difficulties in their literacy skills. Engaging students in activities that promote good oral language skills is beneficial to these skills as well as their literacy skills. Strategies that help students develop oral language abilities include developing appropriate speaking and listening skills, providing instruction that emphasizes vocabulary development, providing students with opportunities to communicate wants, needs, ideas, and information, creating language learning environments, and promoting auditory memory. Developing appropriate speaking and listening skills includes teaching turn-taking, awareness of social norms, and basic rules for speaking and listening. Emphasizing vocabulary development is a strategy that familiarizes early learners with word meanings. Providing students with opportunities to communicate is beneficial for developing early social skills. Teachers can create language learning environments by promoting literacy in their classrooms with word walls, reading circles, or other strategies that introduce language skills to students. Promoting auditory memory means teaching students to listen to, process, and recall information.

Components of Oral Language Development

Oral language learning begins well before students enter educational environments. It is learned first without formal instruction, with environmental factors being a heavy influence. Children tend to develop their own linguistic rules as a result of genetic disposition, their environments, and how their individual thinking processes develop. Component of oral language development include phonological components, semantic components, and syntactic components. Phonological components focus on the rules for combining sounds. Semantic components focus on the smallest units of sounds, morphemes, and how they combine to make up words. Syntactic components focus on how morphemes combine to form sentences. This complex system of phonological, semantic, and syntactic components grows and develops as children grow. Oral language development can be nurtured by caregivers and teachers well before children enter educational environments. Caregivers and teachers can promote oral language development by providing environments full of language development opportunities. Additionally, teaching children how conversation works, encouraging interaction among children, and demonstrating good listening and speaking skills are good strategies for nurturing oral language development.

Helping Students Monitor Errors in Oral Language

Oral language is the way people express knowledge, ideas, and feelings. As oral language develops, so do speaking and listening skills, which have strong connections to reading comprehension and writing skills. Oral language first develops in infancy and becomes fine-tuned with instruction as students enter grade school. Teachers can monitor oral language errors with progress monitoring strategies. Teachers can also help students monitor their own oral language development as they progress through the reading curriculum. Students can monitor their oral language by listening to spoken words in their school and home environments, learning and practicing self-correction skills, and participating in reading comprehension and writing activities. Students can also monitor oral language errors by learning oral language rules for phonics, semantics, syntax, and pragmatics. These are rules for learning sounds, words, and meanings in the English language. Learning these oral language rules typically generalizes to developing appropriate oral language skills.

Expressive Language

Expressive language involves the ability to use vocabulary, sentences, gestures, and writing. Expressive language skills mean that people can label objects in their environments, put words in sentences, use appropriate grammar, demonstrate comprehension verbally by retelling stories, and more. This type of language is important because it allows people to express feelings, wants and needs, thoughts and ideas, and individual points of view. Expressive language helps people develop spoken and written language and promotes positive interactions with others. Expressive language goes hand in hand with receptive language, which is the understanding of language. Children can learn solid expressive language skills by:

- completing tasks that require attention and focus.
- developing pre-language skills, such as understanding gestures like nodding.
- developing good pragmatics.
- developing intrinsic social motivation skills.
- developing fine motor skills, which are required for students who use sign language or gestures to communicate.

Receptive Language

Receptive language refers to a person's ability to understand language. Good receptive language means a person is gathering information from the environment and processing it into meaning. People with good receptive language skills perceive visual information, sounds and words, basic cognitive concepts like colors and shapes, and written information (i.e. street signs) well. Receptive language is important for developing appropriate communication skills. Strategies to build receptive language skills in children include activities that maintain focus and attention. This requires children to participate in activities that require sustained attention free of distractions in order to improve receptive communication skills. Pre-language skills are skills that people use before they learn to communicate with words. Building appropriate pre-language skills is another strategy for building receptive language. Lastly, focusing on social skills and play skills instruction encourages opportunities for children to interact with their peers or adults. This fosters receptive language skills or targets deficits in these skills.

Stages of Language Development in Infants and Children

The first stage of language development and acquisition, the pre-linguistic stage, occurs during an infant's first year of life. It is characterized by the development of gestures, making eye contact, and sounds like cooing and crying. The holophrase, or one-word sentence stage, develops in infants between 10 and 13 months of age. In this stage, young children use one-word sentences to communicate meaning in language. The two-word sentence stage typically develops by the time a child is 18 months old. Each two-word sentence usually contains a verb and a modifier, such as "big balloon" or "green grass." Children in this stage use their two-word sentences to communicate wants and needs. Multiple-word sentences form by the time a child is two to two and a half years old. In this stage, children begin forming sentences with subjects and predicates, such as "tree is tall" or "rope is long." Grammatical errors are present, but children in this stage begin demonstrating how to use words in appropriate context. Children ages two and a half to three years old typically begin using more complex grammatical structures. They begin to include grammatical structures such as conjunctions and prepositions. For example, they may say, "Throw it, the ball," or "Bring me outside." By the age of five or six, children reach a stage of adult-like language development. They begin to use words in appropriate context and can move words around in sentences while maintaining appropriate sentence structure.

Stages of Literacy Development

The development of literacy in young children is separated into five stages. Names of these stages sometimes vary, but the stage milestones are similar. Stage 1 is the Emergent Reader stage. In this stage, young children ages 6 months to 6 years demonstrate skills like pretend reading, recognizing letters of the alphabet, retelling stories, and printing their names. Stage 2 is the Novice/Early Reader stage (ages 6-7 years). Children begin to understand the relationships between letters and sounds and written and spoken words, and they read texts containing high-frequency words. Children in this stage should develop orthographic conventions and semantic knowledge. In Stage 3, the Decoding Reader stage, children ages 7-9 develop decoding skills in order to read simple stories. They also demonstrate increased fluency. Stage 4 (ages 8-15 years) is called the Fluent, Comprehending/Transitional Reader stage. In this stage, fourth to eighth graders read to learn new ideas and information. In Stage 5, the Expert/Fluent Reader stage, children ages 16 years and older read more complex information. They also read expository and narrative texts with multiple viewpoints.

Implications of Literacy Development for Children with Disabilities

Literacy development is broken into five stages. Names of these stages sometimes vary.

- Stage 1 (ages 6 months to 6 years) Emergent Reader Stage
- Stage 2 (ages 6-7 years) Novice/Early Reader Stage
- Stage 3 (ages 7-9 years) Decoding Reader Stage
- Stage 4 (ages 8-15 years) Fluent, Comprehending/Transitional Reader Stage
- Stage 5 (16+ years) Expert/Fluent Reader Stage

Children may not always meet the literacy stage milestones during the specified ages. However, this does not always indicate a disability. Children that fall significantly behind in their literacy development, continually struggle with skill acquisition, or do not consistently retain skill instruction may be at higher risk of being identified as having disabilities. Furthermore, children with speech and language disorders are more likely to experience problems learning to read and write. These issues are typically apparent before children enter grade school but can also become evident during their early grade school years. Early warning signs include disinterest in shared book reading, inability to recognize or remember names of letters, difficulty understanding directions, and persistent baby talk.

Promoting Literacy During the Early Stages of Literacy Development

Teachers and parents can implement strategies at different stages of literacy development in order to build good reading skills in children with and without disabilities. During the Emergent Reader stage, teachers and parents can introduce children to the conventions of reading with picture books. They can model turning the pages, reading from left to right, and other reading conventions. Book reading at this stage helps children begin to identify letters, letter sounds, and simple words. Repetitive reading of familiar texts also helps children begin to make predictions about what they are reading. During the Novice/Early Reader and Decoding Reader stages, parents and teachers can help children form the building blocks of decoding and fluency skills by reading for meaning and emphasizing letter-sound relationships, visual cues, and language patterns. In these stages, increasing familiarity with sight words is essential. In Stage 4, the Fluent, Comprehending Reader/Transitional stage, children should be encouraged to read book series, as the shared characters, settings, and plots help develop their comprehension skills. At this stage, a good reading rate (fluency) is an indicator of comprehension skills. Expert/Fluent readers can independently read multiple texts and comprehend their meanings. Teachers and parents can begin exposing children to a variety of fiction and non-fiction texts before this stage in order to promote good fluency skills.

Relationship Between Language Development and Early Literacy Skills

Language development and early literacy skills are interconnected. Language concepts begin and develop shortly after birth with infant/parent interactions, cooing, and then babbling. These are the earliest attempts at language acquisition for infants. Young children begin interacting with written and spoken words before they enter their grade school years. Before they enter formal classrooms, children begin to make connections between speaking and listening and reading and writing. Children with strong speaking and listening skills demonstrate strong literacy skills in early grade school. The development of phonological awareness is connected to early literacy skills. Children with good phonological awareness recognize that words are made up of different speech sounds. For example, children with appropriate phonological awareness can break words (i.e. "bat") into separate speech sounds (i.e. "b-a-t"). Examples of phonological awareness include rhyming (when the ending parts of words have the same or similar sounds) and alliteration (when words all have the same beginning sound). Success with phonological awareness (oral language) activities depends on adequate development of speech and language skills.

Importance of Enforcing Word Recognition

Many students with specific learning disabilities demonstrate deficits in reading abilities. This includes word recognition abilities. Teaching word identification is important for these students because developing age-appropriate word recognition skills is one of the essential building blocks for creating efficient readers. Children who do not develop adequate reading skills in elementary school are generally below average readers as they age in school. Most districts and teachers use basal reading programs that teach word recognition and phonics. Teachers often supplement basal reading programs with instructional programs that can be used at home and at school. These are especially useful for students with disabilities or students who are at risk and struggle with word recognition abilities. Elements of basal and supplementary reading programs include instruction for helping students make connections between letters and sounds, opportunities to become comfortable with reading, alphabetic knowledge, phonemic awareness, letter-sound correlations, word identification strategies, spelling, writing, and reading fluency.

Characteristics of Expressive Language Disabilities

Expressive language refers to a person's ability to express wants and needs. Children with expressive language disabilities may have trouble conversing with peers and adults and have trouble with self-expression. Answers to questions may be vague or repetitive. They may not demonstrate age-appropriate social skills with peers and adults. Children with expressive language disabilities have a limited vocabulary range and rely on familiar vocabulary words in their expressive language. They can be very quiet and seclude themselves from classroom activities due to difficulties expressing their thoughts and feelings. They may not be able to accurately express what they understand because children with expressive language difficulties have trouble speaking in sentences. Expressive language disabilities indicate issues with language processing centers in the brain. Children with this disability can sometimes understand language but have trouble expressing it. Children with traumatic brain injury, dyslexia, autism, or learning disabilities demonstrate issues with expressive language.

English Language Arts

Impact of Reading Skills on Student Success

The ability to read is not simply one academic area; it is a basic skill set underlying all academic activity and determines whether students fail or succeed in school. Research shows that of first-graders with poor **reading skills**, 88% still read poorly in fourth grade. By this time, most information that students require is provided in text form. For this reason, the focus shifts from *learning to read* in the earlier grades, to *reading to learn* by fourth grade. Consequently, students with poor reading skills can find it harder to access and interact with the content in their schools' curricula. Moreover, reading abilities that are delayed or disordered usually are identified in higher elementary grades. Yet research finds remediation attempts then could be too late, because children acquire language and have literacy experiences from birth. Phonemic awareness, the alphabetic principle, and print awareness normally develop in early childhood. Children missing such early experiences will fall behind peers without extra instruction. This means elementary school teachers must give these children **literacy-rich environments**.

Reading Comprehension

The whole point of reading is to **comprehend** what someone else is trying to say through writing. Without comprehension, a student is just reading the words without understanding them or increasing knowledge of a topic. Comprehension results when the student has the vocabulary and reading skills necessary to make sense of the **whole picture**, not just individual words. Students can self-monitor because they know when they are comprehending the material and when they are not. Teachers can help students solve problems with comprehension by teaching them strategies such as pre-reading titles, sidebars, and follow-up questions; looking at illustrations; predicting what's going to happen in the story; asking questions to check understanding while reading; connecting to background knowledge; and relating to the experiences or feelings of the characters.

> **Review Video: Predicting What Will Happen in a Story**
> Visit mometrix.com/academy and enter code: 288778
>
> **Review Video: Predictions**
> Visit mometrix.com/academy and enter code: 437248
>
> **Review Video: Reading Comprehension Tips**
> Visit mometrix.com/academy and enter code: 280215

Skills Needed to Develop Literacy

According to studies by the National Reading Panel, for children to develop **literacy**, they must have developed skills in phonemic awareness, phonics, vocabulary, comprehension, and fluency. A prerequisite to developing these five skill areas is having an understanding of how literacy works, what it does, and how it is used. While young children exposed to spoken and printed language interactions from birth often develop this understanding of the functions and applications of literacy in a natural way, children with language and learning disabilities may not. A **literacy-rich environment** is defined as one that provides students having disabilities with stimulation to take part in activities involving language and literacy during their everyday life routines. Stimulating such participation in and integration of language and literacy into daily living is an effective way to help disabled students begin to develop understanding of how spoken and printed language function and are used. Teaching strategies to establish literacy-rich environments can not only remediate language and literacy deficits, but also benefit all elementary-level students.

Literacy-Rich Environment in Elementary School Classrooms

An elementary classroom constituting a **literacy-rich setting** would engage all students in various literacy activities, some working individually and others in groups. Students would explore different *genres* of books, not only during reading periods or in the library, but during math, social studies, and science periods or lessons. The teacher might read aloud to students from a book about math during math period, and lead class discussions of the book's content, and have students explore eyewitness science books during science time to learn about scientific concepts. These activities help students experience literacy across all curriculum subject content areas. Students also use books on tapes and CD-ROMs. The classroom includes adapted materials to motivate disabled students to read and help them interact with text. Students write in notebooks and journals, write reports in all subjects, and compose books. A literacy-rich classroom environment features *information resources* for students including dictionaries, encyclopedias, books in varied genres, word walls, and computers, as well as teachers and peers.

Vocabulary Instruction

There are a number of factors to consider when developing **vocabulary**, academic language, and background knowledge. To begin with, not all words should be given equal emphasis. Some words occur much more frequently and should therefore be of greater importance in instruction. This is yet another reason why the context of vocabulary and academic language is so important. It is a bad idea to find a list of difficult words and proceed through it alphabetically, because the students will have very little context for the words they are learning. Instead, teachers should approach vocabulary *thematically*. For instance, a teacher might spend one week teaching vocabulary words related to government, and the next teaching words related to legislation. It is a good idea to link new vocabulary to the lesson being covered in other content areas. The most important thing is to ensure that students have a context for new words, so that they will be able to incorporate them in their speaking and writing as soon as possible.

Word Analysis

Semantic and Syntactic Approaches

Word analysis instruction should be balanced and comprehensive. It is a good idea to let students approach unfamiliar words from both the semantic and syntactic perspectives. A **semantic approach** emphasizes the meaning of words. A child is using the semantic approach when he thinks about context and about what type of word would make sense in a given sentence. A teacher can guide the student towards an appreciation of semantics by asking questions about the meaning of the sentence and the likely meaning of an unfamiliar word. The **syntactic approach**, on the other hand, emphasizes the order of the words in a sentence. English has fairly regular syntax, so the reader can often predict what type of word (e.g., noun, verb) will appear next in a sentence. A teacher can stimulate students to think about syntax by asking the student to read a sentence and determine whether it makes sense. A teacher can ask the student whether the words in a sentence appear to be in the right order.

Differentiation of Word Analysis Instruction

Word analysis can be a challenge for many students, and so there is likely to be a great range of performance in the same class. Teachers must be able to address the strong and weak students in the class. In particular, teachers need to provide differentiated instruction for students who are struggling or have reading difficulties or disabilities. For instance, a teacher needs to be able to go back and focus on key skills and knowledge, like syllable patterns and morphemes that occur frequently. Some students need to have the same material approached from different perspectives before they fully master it. The teacher should be able to outline a number of real-world examples for an abstract concept. The use of songs and poems to illustrate syllabification is one helpful way to bring struggling students up to speed. Finally, a teacher should be able to provide differentiated practice situations for the skills that have been taught.

> **Review Video: Defining a Word**
> Visit mometrix.com/academy and enter code: 648080
>
> **Review Video: Denotation and Connotation**
> Visit mometrix.com/academy and enter code: 310092

Literal and Critical Comprehension

Literal comprehension refers to the skills a reader uses to deal with the actual words in a text. It involves skills such as identifying the topic sentence, main idea, important facts, and supporting details; using context clues to determine the meaning of a word; and sequencing events.

Critical comprehension involves prior knowledge and an understanding that written material, especially in nonfiction, is the author's version of the subject and not necessarily anybody else's. Critical comprehension involves analysis of meaning, evaluation, validation, questioning, and the reasoning skills a reader uses to recognize:

- Inferences and conclusions
- Purpose, tone, point of view, and themes

- The organizational pattern of a work
- Explicit and implicit relationships among words, phrases, and sentences
- Biased language, persuasive tactics, valid arguments, and the difference between fact and opinion

> **Review Video: Author's Main Point or Purpose**
> Visit mometrix.com/academy and enter code: 734339
>
> **Review Video: Author's Position**
> Visit mometrix.com/academy and enter code: 827954
>
> **Review Video: Inference**
> Visit mometrix.com/academy and enter code: 379203

Metacognition

Metacognition is thinking about thinking. For the student, this involves taking control of their own learning process, self-monitoring progress, evaluating the effectiveness of strategies, and making adjustments to strategies and learning behaviors as needed. Students who develop good metacognitive skills become more independent and confident about learning. They develop a sense of ownership about their education and realize that information is readily available to them.

Metacognitive skills can be grouped into three categories:

- **Awareness** – This involves identifying prior knowledge; defining learning goals; inventorying resources such as textbooks, libraries, computers, and study time; identifying task requirements and evaluation standards; and recognizing motivation and anxiety levels.
- **Planning** – This involves doing time estimates for tasks, prioritizing, scheduling study time, making checklists of tasks, gathering needed materials, and choosing strategies for problem solving or task comprehension.
- **Self-monitoring and reflection** – This involves identifying which strategies or techniques work best, questioning throughout the process, considering feedback, and maintaining focus and motivation.

Role of Metacognitive Skills in Literacy Development

In terms of literacy development, **metacognitive skills** include taking an active role in reading, recognizing reading behaviors and changing them to employ the behaviors that are most effective, relating information to prior knowledge, and being aware of text structures. For example, if there is a problem with comprehension, the student can try to form a mental image of what is described, read the text again, adjust the rate of reading, or employ other reading strategies such as identifying unknown vocabulary and predicting meaning. Being aware of **text structures** is critical to being able to follow the author's ideas and relationships among ideas. Being aware of difficulties with text structure allows the student to employ strategies such as hierarchical summaries, thematic organizers, or concept maps to remedy the problem.

Critical Thinking Tools

It is important to teach students to use critical thinking skills when reading. Three of the **critical thinking tools** that engage the reader are:

- **Summarization** – The student reviews the main point(s) of the reading selection and identifies important details. For nonfiction, a good summary will briefly describe the main arguments and the examples that support those arguments. For fiction, a good summary will identify the main characters and events of the story.
- **Question generation** – A good reader will constantly ask questions while reading about comprehension, vocabulary, connections to personal knowledge or experience, predictions, etc.
- **Textual marking** – This skill engages the reader by having him or her interact with the text. The student should mark the text with questions or comments that are generated by the text using underlining, highlighting, or shorthand marks such as "?," "!," and "*" that indicate lack of understanding, importance, or key points, for example.

Context Clues

Context clues are words or phrases that help the reader figure out the meaning of an unknown word. They are built into a sentence or paragraph by the writer to help the reader develop a clear understanding of the writer's message. Context clues can be used to make **intelligent guesses** about the meaning of a word instead of relying on a dictionary. Context clues are the reason most vocabulary is learned through reading. There are four types of commonly used context clues:

- **Synonyms** – A word with the same meaning as the unknown word is placed close by for comparison.
- **Antonyms** – A word with the opposite meaning as the unknown word is placed close by for contrast.
- **Explanations** – An obvious explanation is given close to the unknown word.
- **Examples** – Examples of what the word means are given to help the reader define the term.

> **Review Video: Synonyms and Antonyms**
> Visit mometrix.com/academy and enter code: 105612
>
> **Review Video: Multiple Meaning Words**
> Visit mometrix.com/academy and enter code: 371666

Topic Sentence

The **topic sentence** of a paragraph states the paragraph's subject. It presents the **main idea**. The rest of the paragraph should be related to the topic sentence, which should be explained and supported with facts, details, proofs, and examples. The topic sentence is more general than the **body sentences**, and should cover all the ideas in the body of the paragraph. It may contain words such as "many," "most," or "several." The topic sentence is usually the first sentence in a paragraph, but it can appear after an introductory or background sentence, can be the last sentence in a paragraph, or may simply be implied, meaning a topic sentence is not present. **Supporting sentences** can often be identified by their use of transition terms such as "for example" or "that is."

Supporting sentences may also be presented in numbered sequence. The topic sentence provides **unity** to a paragraph because it ties together the supporting details into a coherent whole.

> **Review Video: Topics and Main Ideas**
> Visit mometrix.com/academy and enter code: 407801
>
> **Review Video: Supporting Details**
> Visit mometrix.com/academy and enter code: 396297

Theme

Theme is the central idea of a work. It is the thread that ties all the elements of a story together and gives them purpose. The theme is not the subject of a work, but what a work says about a subject. A theme must be **universal**, which means it must apply to everyone, not just the characters in a story. Therefore, a theme is a comment about the nature of humanity, society, the relationship of humankind to the world, or moral responsibility. There may be more than one theme in a work, and the determination of the theme is affected by the viewpoint of the reader. Therefore, there is not always necessarily a definite, irrefutable theme. The theme can be implied or stated directly.

> **Review Video: Theme**
> Visit mometrix.com/academy and enter code: 732074

Types of Definition Paragraphs or Essays

A **definition paragraph** or essay describes what a word or term means. There are three ways the explanation can be presented:

- **Definition by synonym** – The term is defined by comparing it to a more familiar term that the reader can more easily understand (A phantom is a ghost or spirit that appears and disappears mysteriously and creates dread).
- **Definition by class** – Most commonly used in exams, papers, and reports, the class definition first puts the term in a larger category or class (The Hereford is a breed of cattle), and then describes the distinguishing characteristics or details of the term that differentiate it from other members of the class (The Hereford is a breed of cattle distinguished by a white face, reddish-brown hide, and short horns).
- **Definition by negation** – The term is defined by stating what it is not and then saying what it is (Courage is not the absence of fear, but the willingness to act in spite of fear).

Types of Paragraphs and Essays

Illustrative — An illustrative paragraph or essay explains a general statement through the use of specific examples. The writer starts with a topic sentence that is followed by one or more examples that clearly relate to and support the topic.

Narrative — A narrative tells a story. Like a news report, it tells the who, what, when, where, why, and how of an event. A narrative is usually presented in chronological order.

Descriptive — This type of writing appeals to the five senses to describe a person, place, or thing so that the readers can see the subject in their imaginations. Space order is most often used in descriptive writing to indicate place or position.

Process — There are two kinds of process papers: the "how-to" that gives step-by-step directions on how to do something and the explanation paper that tells how an event occurred or how something works.

Cause and Effect

Causes are reasons for actions or events. **Effects** are the results of a cause or causes. There may be multiple causes for one effect (evolutionary extinction, climate changes, and a massive comet caused the demise of the dinosaurs, for example) or multiple effects from one cause (the break-up of the Soviet Union has had multiple effects on the world stage, for instance). Sometimes, one thing leads to another and the effect of one action becomes the cause for another (breaking an arm leads to not driving, which leads to reading more while staying home, for example). The ability to identify causes and effects is part of critical thinking, and enables the reader to follow the course of events, make connections among events, and identify the instigators and receivers of actions. This ability improves comprehension.

Distinguishing Between Facts and Opinions

Facts are statements that can be verified through research. Facts answer the questions of who, what, when, and where, and evidence can be provided to prove factual statements. For example, it is a fact that water turns into ice when the temperature drops below 32 degrees Fahrenheit. This fact has been proven repeatedly. Water never becomes ice at a higher temperature. **Opinions** are personal views, but facts may be used to support opinions. For example, it may be one person's opinion that Jack is a great athlete, but the fact that he has made many achievements related to sports supports that opinion. It is important for a reader to be able to distinguish between fact and opinion to determine the validity of an argument. Readers need to understand that some unethical writers will try to pass off an opinion as a fact. Readers with good critical thinking skills will not be deceived by this tactic.

Inductive and Deductive Reasoning

Inductive reasoning is using particulars to draw a general conclusion. The inductive reasoning process starts with **data**. For example, if every apple taken out of the top of a barrel is rotten, it can be inferred without investigating further that all the apples are probably rotten. Unless all data is examined, conclusions are based on probabilities. Inductive reasoning is also used to make inferences about the universe. The entire universe cannot be examined, but inferences can be made based on observations about what can be seen. These inferences may be proven false when more data is available, but they are valid at the time they are made if observable data is used. **Deductive reasoning** is the opposite of inductive reasoning. It involves using general facts or premises to come to a specific conclusion. For example, if Susan is a sophomore in high school, and all sophomores take geometry, it can be inferred that Susan takes geometry. The word "all" does not allow for exceptions. If all sophomores take geometry, assuming Susan does too is a logical conclusion. It is important for a reader to recognize inductive and deductive reasoning so he or she can follow the line of an argument and determine if the inference or conclusion is **valid**.

Style, Tone, and Point of View

Style is the manner in which a writer uses language in prose or poetry. Style is affected by:

- Diction or word choices
- Sentence structure and syntax
- Types and extent of use of figurative language
- Patterns of rhythm or sound
- Conventional or creative use of punctuation

Tone is the attitude of the writer or narrator towards the theme of, subject of, or characters in a work. Sometimes the attitude is stated, but it is most often implied through word choices. Examples of tone are serious, humorous, satiric, stoic, cynical, flippant, and surprised.

Point of view is the angle from which a story is told. It is the perspective of the narrator, established by the author. Common points of view are:

- *Third person* – Third person points of view include omniscient (knows everything) and limited (confined to what is known by a single character or a limited number of characters). When the third person is used, characters are referred to as he, she, or they.
- *First person* – When this point of view is used, the narrator refers to himself or herself as "I."

> **Review Video: Style, Tone, and Mood**
> Visit mometrix.com/academy and enter code: 416961
>
> **Review Video: Point of View**
> Visit mometrix.com/academy and enter code: 383336

Types of Figurative Language

A **simile** is a comparison between two unlike things using the words "like" or "as." Examples are Robert Burn's sentence "O my love's like a red, red, rose" or the common expression "as pretty as a picture."

A **metaphor** is a direct comparison between two unlike things without the use of "like" or "as." One thing is identified as the other instead of simply compared to it. An example is D. H. Lawrence's sentence "My soul is a dark forest."

Personification is the giving of human characteristics to a non-human thing or idea. An example is "The hurricane howled its frightful rage."

Synecdoche is the use of a part of something to signify the whole. For example, "boots on the ground" could be used to describe soldiers in a field.

Metonymy is the use of one term that is closely associated with another to mean the other. An example is referring to the "crown" to refer to the monarchy.

Alliteration, Assonance, and Onomatopoeia

Alliteration is the repetition of the first sounds or stressed syllables (usually consonants) in words in close proximity. An example is: "Chirp, chirp," said the chickadee.

Assonance is the repetition of identical or similar vowel sounds, particularly in stressed syllables, in words in close proximity. Assonance is considered to be a form of near rhyme. An example is: the quiet bride cried.

Onomatopoeia refers to words that imitate sounds. It is sometimes called echoism. Examples are hiss, buzz, burp, rattle, and pop. It may also refer to words that correspond symbolically to what they describe, with high tones suggesting light and low tones suggesting darkness. An example is the *gloom* of night versus the *gleam* of the stars.

Parallelism, Euphemism, Hyperbole, and Climax

Parallelism — Subjects, objects, verbs, modifiers, phrases, and clauses can be structured in sentences to balance one with another through a similar grammatical pattern. Parallelism helps to highlight ideas while showing their relationship and giving style to writing.

Examples are:

- **Parallel words** – The killer behaved coldly, cruelly, and inexplicably.
- **Parallel phrases** – Praised by comrades, honored by commanders, the soldier came home a hero.
- **Parallel clauses** – "We shall fight on the beaches, we shall fight on the landing grounds, we shall fight in the hills." (Winston Churchill)

Euphemism — This is a "cover-up" word that avoids the explicit meaning of an offensive or unpleasant term by substituting a vaguer image. An example is using "expired" instead of "dead."

Hyperbole — This is an example or phrase that exaggerates for effect. An example is the extravagant overstatement "I thought I would die!" Hyperbole is also used in tall tales, such as those describing Paul Bunyan's feats.

Climax — This refers to the process of building up to a dramatic highpoint through a series of phrases or sentences. It can also refer to the highpoint or most intense event in a story.

Bathos, Oxymoron, Irony, and Malapropism

Bathos — This is an attempt to evoke pity, sorrow, or nobility that goes overboard and becomes ridiculous. It is an insincere pathos and a letdown. It is also sometimes called an anticlimax, although an anticlimax might be intentionally included for comic or satiric effect.

Oxymoron — This refers to two terms that are used together for contradictory effect, usually in the form of an adjective that doesn't fit the noun. An example is: a "new classic."

Irony — This refers to a difference between what is and what ought to be, or between what is said and what is meant. Irony can be an unexpected result in literature, such as a twist of fate. For example, it is ironic that the tortoise beat the hare.

Malapropism — This is confusing one word with another, similar-sounding word. For example, saying a movie was a cliff dweller instead of a cliffhanger is a malapropism.

Invalid Arguments

There are a number of **invalid or false arguments** that are used unethically to gain an advantage, such as:

- The "**ad hominem**" or "against the person" argument – This type attacks the character or behavior of a person taking a stand on an issue rather than the issue itself. The statement "That fat slob wants higher taxes" is an example of this type of argument.
- **Hasty generalizations** – These are condemnations of a group based on the behavior of one person or part. An example of this type of argument is someone saying that all McDonald's restaurants are lousy because he or she had a bad experience at one location.
- **Faulty causation** – This is assigning the wrong cause to an event. An example is blaming a flat tire on losing a lucky penny rather than on driving over a bunch of nails.
- **Bandwagon effect** – This is the argument that if everybody else is doing something, it must be a good thing to do. The absurdity of this type of argument is highlighted by the question: "If everybody else is jumping off a cliff, should you jump, too?"

It is important for a reader to be able to identify various types of invalid arguments to prevent being deceived and making faulty conclusions.

Fiction and Nonfiction

Fiction is a literary work usually presented in prose form that is not true. It is the product of the writer's imagination. Examples of fiction are novels, short stories, television scripts, and screenplays. **Nonfiction** is a literary work that is based on facts. In other words, the material is true. The purposeful inclusion of false information is considered dishonest, but the expression of opinions or suppositions is acceptable. Libraries divide their collections into works of fiction and nonfiction. Examples of nonfiction include historical materials, scientific reports, memoirs, biographies, most essays, journals, textbooks, documentaries, user manuals, and news reports.

> **Review Video: Reading Fiction**
> Visit mometrix.com/academy and enter code: 391411
>
> **Review Video: Historical Context**
> Visit mometrix.com/academy and enter code: 169770
>
> **Review Video: Interpretation of Expository or Literary Text**
> Visit mometrix.com/academy and enter code: 860442

Prose and Poetry

Prose is language as it is ordinarily spoken as opposed to verse or language with metric patterns. Prose is used for everyday communication, and is found in textbooks, memos, reports, articles, short stories, and novels. Distinguishing characteristics of prose include:

- It may have some sort of rhythm, but there is **no formal arrangement**.
- The common unit of organization is the **sentence**.
- It may include literary devices of repetition and balance.
- It must have more coherent relationships among sentences than a list would.

Poetry, or verse, is the manipulation of language with respect to meaning, meter, sound, and rhythm. A line of poetry can be any length and may or may not rhyme. Related groups of lines are called **stanzas**, and may also be any length. Some poems are as short as a few lines, and some are as long as a book. Poetry is a more ancient form of literature than prose.

Role of Emotions in Poetry

Poetry is designed to appeal to the physical and emotional senses. Using appeals to the **physical senses** through words that evoke sight, sound, taste, smell, and touch also causes the imagination to respond **emotionally**. Poetry appeals to the soul and memories with language that can be intriguingly novel and profoundly emotional in connotation. Poetry can focus on any topic, but the feelings associated with the topic are magnified by the ordered presentation found in poetry. Verse, however, is merely a matter of structure. The thing that turns words into poetry is the feeling packed into those words. People write poetry to express their feelings and people read poetry to try to experience those same feelings. Poetry interprets the human condition with understanding and insight. Children respond well to poetry because it has an inviting, entertaining sound that they are eager to mimic.

Short Story

A **short story** is prose fiction that has the same elements as a novel, such as plot, characters, and point of view. Edgar Allan Poe defined the short story as a **narrative** that can be read in **one sitting** (one-half to two hours), and is limited to a **single effect**. In a short story, there is no time for extensive character development, large numbers of characters, in-depth analysis, complicated plot lines, or detailed backgrounds. Historically, the short story is related to the fable, the exemplum, and the folktale. Short stories have become mainly an American art form. Famous short story writers include William Faulkner, Katherine Anne Porter, Eudora Welty, Flannery O'Connor, O. Henry, and J. D. Salinger.

Character Types

Readers need to be able to differentiate between **major and minor characters**. The difference can usually be determined based on whether the characters are round, flat, dynamic, or static. **Round characters** have complex personalities, just like real people. They are more commonly found in longer works such as novels or full-length plays. **Flat characters** display only a few personality traits and are based on stereotypes. Examples include the bigoted redneck, the lazy bum, or the absent-minded professor. **Dynamic characters** are those that change or grow during the course of the narrative. They may learn important lessons, fall in love, or take new paths. **Static characters** remain the same throughout a story. Usually, round characters are dynamic and flat characters are static, but this is not always the case. Falstaff, the loyal and comical character in Shakespeare's plays about Henry IV, is a round character in terms of his complexity. However, he never changes, which makes him a reliable figure in the story.

Line Structure in Poems

A **line of poetry** can be any length and can have any metrical pattern. A line is determined by the physical position of words on a page. A line is simply a group of words on a single line. Consider the following example:

> When I consider how my light is spent,

> E're half my days, in this dark world and wide,

These are two lines of poetry written by John Milton. Lines may or may not have punctuation at the end, depending, of course, on the need for punctuation. If these two lines were written out in a paragraph, they would be written with a **slash line** and a **space** in between the lines: "When I consider how my light is spent, / E're half my days, in this dark world and wide."

Blank Verse and Free Verse

Blank verse is unrhymed verse that consists of lines of iambic pentameter, which is five feet (sets) of unstressed and stressed syllables. The rhythm that results is the closest to natural human speech. It is the most commonly used type of verse because of its versatility. Well-known examples of blank verse are Shakespearean plays, Milton's epic poems, and T. S. Eliot's *The Waste Land*. **Free verse** lacks regular patterns of poetic feet, but has more controlled rhythm than prose in terms of pace and pauses. Free verse has no rhyme and is usually written in short lines of irregular length. Well-known examples of free verse are the King James translation of the Psalms, Walt Whitman's *Leaves of Grass*, and the poetry of Ezra Pound and William Carlos Williams.

> **Review Video: Forms of Poetry**
> Visit mometrix.com/academy and enter code: 451705

Stanza Structure in Poems

A **stanza** is a group of lines. The grouping denotes a relationship among the lines. A stanza can be any length, but the separation of lines into different stanzas indicates an intentional *pattern* created by the poet. The breaks between stanzas indicate a change of subject or thought. As a group of lines, the stanza is a melodic unit that can be analyzed for *metrical and rhyme patterns*. Various common rhyme patterns have been named. The Spenserian stanza, which has a rhyme pattern of a b a b b c b c c, is an example. Stanzas of a certain length also have names. Examples include the **couplet**, which has two lines; the **tercet**, which has three lines; and the **quatrain**, which has four lines.

Meter

A recurring pattern of stressed and unstressed syllables in language creates a rhythm when spoken. When the pattern is regular, it is called **meter**. When meter is used in a composition, it is called **verse**. The most common types of meter are:

- **Iambic** – An unstressed syllable followed by a stressed syllable
- **Anapestic** – Two unstressed syllables followed by a stressed syllable
- **Trochaic** – One stressed syllable followed by an unstressed syllable
- **Dactylic** – A stressed syllable followed by two unstressed syllables
- **Spondaic** – Two consecutive syllables that are stressed almost equally
- **Pyrrhic** – Two consecutive syllables that are equally unstressed

Types of Children's Literature

A **fairy tale** is a fictional story involving humans, magical events, and usually animals. Characters such as fairies, elves, giants, and talking animals are taken from folklore. The plot often involves impossible events (as in "Jack and the Beanstalk") and/or an enchantment (as in "Sleeping Beauty"). Other examples of fairy tales include "Cinderella," "Little Red Riding Hood," and "Rumpelstiltskin." A **fable** is a tale in which animals, plants, and forces of nature act like humans. A fable also teaches a moral lesson. Examples are "The Tortoise and the Hare," *The Lion King*, and *Animal Farm*. A **tall tale** exaggerates human abilities or describes unbelievable events as if the story were true. Often, the narrator seems to have witnessed the event described. Examples are fish stories, Paul Bunyan and Pecos Bill stories, and hyperboles about real people such as Davy Crockett, Mike Fink, and Calamity Jane.

Preadolescent and Adolescent Literature

Preadolescent literature is mostly concerned with the "tween" issues of changing lives, relationships, and bodies. **Adolescents** seeking escape from their sometimes difficult lives enjoy fantasy and science fiction. For both groups, books about modern, real people are more interesting than those about historical figures or legends. Boys especially enjoy nonfiction. Reading interests as well as reading levels for this group vary. Reading levels will usually range from 6.0 to 8.9. Examples of popular literature for this age group and reading level include:

- Series – Sweet Valley High, Bluford High, Nancy Drew, Hardy Boys, and Little House on the Prairie
- Juvenile fiction authors – Judy Blume and S. E. Hinton
- Fantasy and horror authors – Ursula LeGuin and Stephen King
- Science fiction authors – Isaac Asimov, Ray Bradbury, and H. G. Wells
- Classic books: Lilies of the Field, Charlie and the Chocolate Factory, Pippi Longstocking, National Velvet, Call of the Wild, Anne of Green Gables, The Hobbit, The Member of the Wedding, and Tom Sawyer

Grammatical Terms

The definitions for grammatical terms are as follows:

Adjective – This is a word that modifies or describes a noun or pronoun. Examples are a *green* apple or *every* computer.

Adverb – This is a word that modifies a verb (*instantly* reviewed), an adjective (*relatively* odd), or another adverb (*rather* suspiciously).

Conjunctions: There are three types of conjunctions:

- **Coordinating conjunctions** are used to link words, phrases, and clauses. Examples are and, or, nor, for, but, yet, and so.
- **Correlative conjunctions** are paired terms used to link clauses. Examples are either/or, neither/nor, and if/then.
- **Subordinating conjunctions** relate subordinate or dependent clauses to independent ones. Examples are although, because, if, since, before, after, when, even though, in order that, and while.

Gerund – This is a verb form used as a noun. Most end in "ing." An example is: *Walking* is good exercise.

Infinitive – This is a verbal form comprised of the word "to" followed by the root form of a verb. An infinitive may be used as a noun, adjective, adverb, or absolute. Examples include:

- *To hold* a baby is a joy. (noun)
- Jenna had many files *to reorganize.* (adjective)

- Andrew tried *to remember* the dates. (adverb)
- *To be honest*, your hair looks awful. (absolute)

Noun – This is a word that names a person, place, thing, idea, or quality. A noun can be used as a subject, object, complement, appositive, or modifier.

Object – This is a word or phrase that receives the action of a verb.

- A direct object states *to* whom/what an action was committed. It answers the question "to what?" An example is: Joan served *the meal*.
- An indirect object states *for* whom/what an action was committed. An example is: Joan served *us* the meal.

Preposition – This is a word that links a noun or pronoun to other parts of a sentence. Examples include above, by, for, in, out, through, and to.

Prepositional phrase – This is a combination of a preposition and a noun or pronoun. Examples include across the bridge, against the grain, below the horizon, and toward the sunset.

Pronoun – This is a word that represents a specific noun in a generic way. A pronoun functions like a noun in a sentence. Examples include I, she, he, it, myself, they, these, what, all, and anybody.

Sentence – This is a group of words that expresses a thought or conveys information as an independent unit of speech. A **complete sentence** must contain a noun and a verb (I ran). However, all the other parts of speech can also be represented in a sentence.

Verb – This is a word or phrase in a sentence that expresses action (Mary played) or a state of being (Mary is).

> **Review Video: Parts of Speech**
> Visit mometrix.com/academy and enter code: 899611

Capitalization and Punctuation

Capitalization refers to the use of capital letters. Capital letters should be placed at the beginning of:

- **Proper names** (Ralph Waldo Emerson, Australia)
- **Places** (Mount Rushmore, Chicago)
- Historical periods and holidays (Renaissance, Christmas)
- **Religious terms** (Bible, Koran)
- **Titles** (Empress Victoria, General Smith)
- All main words in **literary, art, or music titles** (Grapes of Wrath, Sonata in C Major)

Punctuation consists of:

Periods – A period is placed at the end of a sentence.

Commas – A comma is used to separate:

- Two adjectives modifying the same word (long, hot summer)
- Three or more words or phrases in a list (Winken, Blinken, and Nod; life, liberty, and the pursuit of happiness)
- Phrases that are not needed to complete a sentence (The teacher, not the students, will distribute the supplies.)

Colons and Semicolons

Colons – A colon is used to:

- Set up a **list** (We will need these items: a pencil, paper, and an eraser.)
- Direct readers to **examples or explanations** (We have one chore left: clean out the garage.)
- Introduce **quotations or dialogue** (The Labor Department reported on unemployment: "There was a 3.67% increase in unemployment in 2010."; Scarlett exclaimed: "What shall I do?")

> **Review Video: Colons**
> Visit mometrix.com/academy and enter code: 868673

Semicolons – A semicolon is used to:

- Join **related independent clauses** (There were five major hurricanes this year; two of them hit Florida.)
- Join **independent clauses connected by conjunctive adverbs** (Popular books are often made into movies; however, it is a rare screenplay that is as good as the book.)
- Separate items in a **series** if commas would be confusing (The characters include: Robin Hood, who robs from the rich to give to the poor; Maid Marian, his true love; and Little John, Robin Hood's comrade-in-arms.)

> **Review Video: Semicolon Usage**
> Visit mometrix.com/academy and enter code: 370605

Subject-Verb Agreement

A verb must **agree** in number with its subject. Therefore, a verb changes form depending on whether the subject is singular or plural. Examples include "I do," "he does," "the ball is," and "the balls are." If two subjects are joined by "and," the **plural** form of a verb is usually used. For example: *Jack and Jill want* to get some water (Jack wants, Jill wants, but together they want). If the compound subjects are preceded by each or every, they take the **singular** form of a verb. For example: *Each man and each woman brings* a special talent to the world (each brings, not bring). If one noun in a compound subject is plural and the other is singular, the verb takes the form of the subject **nearest** to it. For example: Neither the *students* nor their *teacher was* ready for the fire drill. **Collective nouns** that name a group are considered singular if they refer to the group acting as a unit. For example: The *choir is going* on a concert tour.

> **Review Video: Subject Verb Agreement**
> Visit mometrix.com/academy and enter code: 479190

- 92 -

Syntax

Syntax refers to the rules related to how to properly **structure** sentences and phrases. Syntax is not the same as grammar. For example, "I does" is syntactically correct because the subject and verb are in proper order, but it is grammatically incorrect because the subject and verb don't agree.

There are three types of sentence structures:

- **Simple** – This type is composed of a single independent clause with one subject and one predicate (verb or verb form).
- **Compound** – This type is composed of two independent clauses joined by a conjunction (Amy flew, but Brenda took the train), a correlative conjunction (Either Tom goes with me or I stay here), or a semicolon (My grandfather stays in shape; he plays tennis nearly every day).
- **Complex** – This type is composed of one independent clause and one or more dependent clauses joined by a subordinating conjunction (Before we set the table, we should replace the tablecloth).

Types of Paragraphs or Essays

A **comparison and contrast essay** examines the similarities and differences between two things. In a paragraph, the writer presents all the points about subject A and then all the points about subject B. In an essay, the writer might present one point at a time, comparing subject A and subject B side by side.

A **classification paper** sorts information. It opens with a topic sentence that identifies the group to be classified, and then breaks that group into categories. For example, a group might be baseball players, while a category might be positions they play.

A **cause and effect paper** discusses the causes or reasons for an event or the effects of a cause or causes. Topics discussed in this type of essay might include the causes of a war or the effects of global warming.

A **persuasive essay** is one in which the writer tries to convince the audience to agree with a certain opinion or point of view. The argument must be supported with facts, examples, anecdotes, expert testimony, or statistics, and must anticipate and answer the questions of those who hold an opposing view. It may also predict consequences.

Role of Purpose and Audience in Writing a Paper

Early in the writing process, the writer needs to definitively determine the **purpose** of the paper and then keep that purpose in mind throughout the writing process. The writer needs to ask: "Is the purpose to explain something, to tell a story, to entertain, to inform, to argue a point, or some combination of these purposes?" Also at the beginning of the writing process, the writer needs to determine the **audience** of the paper by asking questions such as: "Who will read this paper?" "For whom is this paper intended?" "What does the audience already know about this topic?" "How much does the audience need to know?" and "Is the audience likely to agree or disagree with my point of view?" The answers to these questions will determine the content of the paper, the tone, and the style.

Writing Processes

Drafting is creating an early version of a paper. A draft is a prototype or sketch of the finished product. A draft is a rough version of the final paper, and it is expected that there will be multiple drafts.

Revising is the process of making major changes to a draft in regards to clarity of purpose, focus (thesis), audience, organization, and content.

Editing is the process of making changes in style, word choice, tone, examples, and arrangement. These are more minor than the changes made during revision. Editing can be thought of as fine tuning. The writer makes the language more precise, checks for varying paragraph lengths, and makes sure that the title, introduction, and conclusion fit well with the body of the paper.

Proofreading is performing a final check and correcting errors in punctuation, spelling, grammar, and usage. It also involves looking for parts of the paper that may be omitted.

> **Review Video: Recursive Writing Process**
> Visit mometrix.com/academy and enter code: 951611

Title and Conclusion of an Essay

The **title** is centered on the page and the main words are capitalized. The title is not surrounded by quotation marks, nor is it underlined or italicized. The title is rarely more than four or five words, and is very rarely a whole sentence. A good title suggests the subject of the paper and catches the reader's interest. The **conclusion** should flow logically from the body of the essay, should tie back to the introduction, and may provide a summary or a final thought on the subject. New material should never be introduced in the conclusion. The conclusion is a wrap-up that may contain a call to action, something the writer wants the audience to do in response to the paper. The conclusion might end with a question to give the reader something to think about.

> **Review Video: Drafting Conclusions**
> Visit mometrix.com/academy and enter code: 209408

Introduction of an Essay

The **introduction** contains the **thesis statement**, which is usually the first or last sentence of the opening paragraph. It needs to be interesting enough to make the reader want to continue reading.

- Possible openings for an introduction include:
- The thesis statement
- A general idea that gives background or sets the scene
- An illustration that will make the thesis more concrete and easy to picture
- A surprising fact or idea to arouse curiosity
- A contradiction to popular belief that attracts interest
- A quotation that leads into the thesis

> **Review Video: Introduction**
> Visit mometrix.com/academy and enter code: 961328

Sentence Types

A **declarative sentence** makes a statement and is punctuated by a period at the end. An example is: The new school will be built at the south end of Main Street.

An **interrogative sentence** asks a question and is punctuated by a question mark at the end. An example is: Why will the new school be built so far out?

An **exclamatory sentence** shows strong emotion and is punctuated by an exclamation mark at the end. An example is: The new school has the most amazing state-of-the-art technology!

An **imperative sentence** gives a direction or command and may be punctuated by an exclamation mark or a period. Sometimes, the subject of an imperative sentence is you, which is understood instead of directly stated. An example is: Come to the open house at the new school next Sunday.

Transitional Words and Phrases

Transitional words are used to signal a relationship. They are used to link thoughts and sentences. Some types of transitional words and phrases are:

- **Addition** – Also, in addition, furthermore, moreover, and then, another
- **Admitting a point** – Granted, although, while it is true that
- **Cause and effect** – Since, so, consequently, as a result, therefore, thus
- **Comparison** – Similarly, just as, in like manner, likewise
- **Contrast** – On the other hand, yet, nevertheless, despite, but, still
- **Emphasis** – Indeed, in fact, without a doubt, certainly, to be sure
- **Illustration** – For example, for instance, in particular, specifically
- **Purpose** – In order to, for this purpose, for this to occur
- **Spatial arrangement** – Beside, above, below, around, across, inside, near, far, to the left
- **Summary or clarification** – In summary, in conclusion, that is, in other words
- **Time sequence** – Before, after, later, soon, next, meanwhile, suddenly, finally

Pre-Writing Techniques

Pre-writing techniques that help a writer find, explore, and organize a topic include:

- **Brainstorming** – This involves letting thoughts make every connection to the topic possible, and then spinning off ideas and making notes of them as they are generated. This is a process of using imagination, uninhibited creativity, and instincts to discover a variety of possibilities.
- **Freewriting** – This involves choosing items from the brainstorming list and writing about them nonstop for a short period. This unedited, uncensored process allows one thing to lead to another and permits the writer to think of additional concepts and themes.
- **Clustering/mapping** – This involves writing a general word or phrase related to the topic in the middle of a paper and circling it, and then quickly jotting down related words or phrases. These are circled and lines are drawn to link words and phrases to others on the page. Clustering is a visual representation of brainstorming that reveals patterns and connections.

- **Listing** – Similar to brainstorming, listing is writing down as many descriptive words and phrases (not whole sentences) as possible that relate to the subject. Correct spelling and grouping of these descriptive terms can come later if needed. This list is merely intended to stimulate creativity and provide a vibrant vocabulary for the description of the subject once the actual writing process begins.
- **Charting** – This prewriting technique works well for comparison/contrast purposes or for the examination of advantages and disadvantages (pros and cons). Any kind of chart will work, even a simple two-column list. The purpose is to draw out points and examples that can be used in the paper.

Purpose of Writing

Writing always has a purpose. The five reasons to write are:

- **To tell a story** – The story does not necessarily need to be fictional. The purposes are to explain what happened, to narrate events, and to explain how things were accomplished. The story will need to make a point, and plenty of details will need to be provided to help the reader imagine the event or process.
- **To express oneself** – This type of writing is commonly found in journals, diaries, or blogs. This kind of writing is an exercise in reflection that allows writers to learn something about themselves and what they have observed, and to work out their thoughts and feelings on paper.
- **To convey information** – Reports are written for this purpose. Information needs to be as clearly organized and accurate as possible. Charts, graphs, tables, and other illustrations can help make the information more understandable.
- **To make an argument** – This type of writing also makes a point, but adds opinion to the facts presented. Argumentative, or persuasive, writing is one of the most common and important types of writing. It should follow rules of logic and ethics.
- **To explore ideas** – This is speculative writing that is quite similar to reflective writing. This type of writing explores possibilities and asks questions without necessarily expecting an answer. The purpose is to stimulate readers to further consider and reflect on the topic.

> **Review Video: Author's Main Point or Purpose**
> Visit mometrix.com/academy and enter code: 734339

Arranging Information Strategically

The order of the elements in a writing project can be organized in the following ways:

- **Logical order** – There is a coherent pattern in the presentation of information, such as inductive or deductive reasoning or a division of a topic into its parts.
- **Hierarchical order** – There is a ranking of material from most to least important or least to most important, depending on whether the writer needs a strong start or a sweeping finish. It can also involve breaking down a topic from a general form into specifics.
- **Chronological order** – This is an order that follows a sequence. In a narrative, the sequence will follow the time order of beginning to middle to end. In a "how to," the sequence will be step 1, step 2, step 3, and so on.
- **Order defined by genre** – This is a pre-determined order structured according to precedent or professional guidelines, such as the order required for a specific type of research or lab report, a resume, or an application form.

- **Order of importance** – This method of organization relies on a ranking determined by priorities. For example, in a persuasive paper, the writer usually puts the strongest argument in the last body paragraph so that readers will remember it. In a news report, the most important information comes first.
- **Order of interest** – This order is dependent on the level of interest the audience has in the subject. If the writer anticipates that reader knowledge and interest in the subject will be low, normal order choices need to be changed. The piece should begin with something very appealing. This will hook the reader and make for a strong opening.

Beginning Stages of Learning to Write

The following are the beginning stages of learning to write:

- **Drawing pictures** is the first written attempt to express thoughts and feelings. Even when the picture is unrecognizable to the adult, it means something to the child.
- The **scribble stage** begins when the child attempts to draw shapes. He or she may also try to imitate writing. The child may have a story or explanation to go with the shapes.
- Children have the most interest in learning to **write their own names**, so writing lessons usually start with that. Children will soon recognize that there are other letters too.
- Children are learning the **alphabet** and how to associate a **sound with each letter**. Reversing letters is still common, but instruction begins with teaching children to write from left to right.
- Written words may not be complete, but will likely have the correct **beginning and end sounds/letters**.
- Children will make some attempt to use **vowels** in writing.
- Children will write with more ease, although spelling will still be phonetic and only some punctuation will be used.

Journal Writing

Writing in a **journal** gives students practice in writing, which makes them more comfortable with the writing process. Journal writing also gives students the opportunity to sort out their thoughts, solve problems, examine relationships and values, and see their personal and academic growth when they revisit old entries. The advantages for the teacher are that the students become more experienced with and accustomed to writing. Through reading student journals, the teacher can also gain **insight** into the students' problems and attitudes, which can help the teacher tailor his or her lesson plans. A journal can be kept in a **notebook** or in a **computer file**. It shouldn't be just a record of daily events, but an expression of thoughts and feelings about everything and anything. Grammar and punctuation don't matter since journaling is a form of private communication. Teachers who review journals need to keep in mind that they should not grade journals and that comments should be encouraging and polite.

Revising a Paper

Revising a paper involves rethinking the choices that were made while constructing the paper and then rewriting it, making any necessary changes or additions to word choices or arrangement of points. Questions to keep in mind include:

- Is the thesis clear?
- Do the body paragraphs logically flow and provide details to support the thesis?
- Is anything unnecessarily repeated?

- Is there anything not related to the topic?
- Is the language understandable?
- Does anything need to be defined?
- Is the material interesting?

Another consideration when revising is **peer feedback**. It is helpful during the revision process to have someone who is knowledgeable enough to be helpful and will be willing to give an honest critique read the paper.

> **Review Video:** <u>General Revision and Proofreading</u>
> Visit mometrix.com/academy and enter code: 385882

Paragraph Coherence

Paragraph coherence can be achieved by linking sentences by using the following strategies:

- **Repetition of key words** – It helps the reader follow the progression of thought from one sentence to another if key words (which should be defined) are repeated to assure the reader that the writer is still on topic and the discussion still relates to the key word.
- **Substitution of pronouns** – This doesn't just refer to using single word pronouns such as I, they, us, etc., but also alternate descriptions of the subject. For example, if someone was writing about Benjamin Franklin, it gets boring to keep saying Franklin or he. Other terms that describe him, such as that notable American statesman, this printer, the inventor, and so forth can also be used.
- **Substitution of synonyms** – This is similar to substitution of pronouns, but refers to using similar terms for any repeated noun or adjective, not just the subject. For example, instead of constantly using the word great, adjectives such as terrific, really cool, awesome, and so on can also be used.

Verbs

In order to understand the role of a verb and be able to identify the verb that is necessary to make a sentence, it helps to know the different types of verbs. These are:

- **Action verbs** – These are verbs that express an action being performed by the subject. An example is: The outfielder caught the ball (outfielder = subject and caught = action).
- **Linking verbs** – These are verbs that link the subject to words that describe or identify the subject. An example is: Mary is an excellent teacher (Mary = subject and "is" links Mary to her description as an excellent teacher). Common linking verbs are all forms of the verb "to be," appear, feel, look, become, and seem.
- **Helping verbs** – When a single verb cannot do the job by itself because of tense issues, a second, helping verb is added. Examples include: should have gone ("gone" is the main verb, while "should" and "have" are helping verbs), and was playing ("playing" is the main verb, while "was" is the helping verb).

Coordinating Conjunctions and Subordinating Conjunctions

There are different ways to connect two clauses and show their relationship:

- A **coordinating conjunction** is one that can join two independent clauses by placing a comma and a coordinating conjunction between them. The most common coordinating conjunctions are and, but, or, nor, yet, for, and so. Examples include: "It was warm, so I left my jacket at home" and "It was warm, and I left my jacket at home."
- A **subordinating conjunction** is one that joins a subordinate clause and an independent clause and establishes the relationship between them. An example is: "We can play a game after Steve finishes his homework." The dependent clause is "after Steve finishes his homework" because the reader immediately asks, "After Steve finishes, then what?" The independent clause is "We can play a game." The concern is not the ability to play a game, but "when?" The answer to this question is dependent on when Steve finishes his homework.

> **Review Video: Conjunctions**
> Visit mometrix.com/academy and enter code: 904603

Run-On Sentences and Comma Splices

A **run-on sentence** is one that tries to connect two independent clauses without the needed conjunction or punctuation and makes it hard for the reader to figure out where one sentence ends and the other starts. An example is: "Meagan is three years old she goes to pre-school." Two possible ways to fix the run-on would be: "Meagan is three years old, and she goes to pre-school" or "Meagan is three years old; however, she goes to pre-school." A **comma splice** occurs when a comma is used to join two independent clauses without a proper conjunction. The comma should be replaced by a period or one of the methods for coordination or subordination should be used. An example of a comma splice is: "Meagan is three years old, she goes to pre-school."

Fragments

A **fragment** is an incomplete sentence, which is one that does not have a subject to go with the verb, or vice versa. The following are types of fragments:

- **Dependent clause fragments** – These usually start with a subordinating conjunction. An example is: "Before you can graduate." "You can graduate" is a sentence, but the subordinating conjunction "before" makes the clause dependent, which means it needs an independent clause to go with it. An example is: "Before you can graduate, you have to meet all the course requirements."
- **Relative clause fragments** – These often start with who, whose, which, or that. An example is: "Who is always available to the students." This is a fragment because the "who" is not identified. A complete sentence would be: "Mr. Jones is a principal who is always available to the students."
- **The "-ing" fragment** lacks a subject. The "-ing" form of a verb has to have a helping verb. An example is: "Walking only three blocks to his job." A corrected sentence would be: "Walking only three blocks to his job, Taylor has no need for a car."

- **Prepositional phrase fragments** are ones that begin with a preposition and are only a phrase, not a complete thought. An example is: "By the time we arrived." "We arrived" by itself would be a complete sentence, but the "by" makes the clause dependent and the reader asks, "By the time you arrived, what happened?" A corrected sentence would be: "By the time we arrived, all the food was gone."
- **Infinitive phrase fragments** have the same problem as prepositional phrase ones. An example is: "To plant the seed." A corrected sentence would be: "To plant the seed, Isaac used a trowel."

> **Review Video: Fragments and Run-on Sentences**
> Visit mometrix.com/academy and enter code: 541989

Primary and Secondary Research Information

Primary research material is material that comes from the "horse's mouth." It is a document or object that was created by the person under study or during the time period under study. Examples of primary sources are original documents such as manuscripts, diaries, interviews, autobiographies, government records, letters, news videos, and artifacts (such as Native American pottery or wall writings in Egyptian tombs). **Secondary research material** is anything that is not primary. Secondary sources are those things that are written or otherwise recorded about the main subject. Examples include a critical analysis of a literary work (a poem by William Blake is primary, but the analysis of the poem by T. S. Eliot is secondary), a magazine article about a person (a direct quote would be primary, but the report is secondary), histories, commentaries, and encyclopedias.

Primary sources are the raw material of research. This can include results of experiments, notes, and surveys or interviews done by the researcher. Other primary sources are books, letters, diaries, eyewitness accounts, and performances attended by the researcher. **Secondary sources** consist of oral and written accounts prepared by others. This includes reports, summaries, critical reviews, and other sources not developed by the researcher. Most research writing uses both primary and secondary sources: primary sources from first-hand accounts and secondary sources for background and supporting documentation. The research process calls for active reading and writing throughout. As research yields information, it often calls for more reading and research, and the cycle continues.

Drafting Research Essays

Introduction

The **introduction** to a research essay is particularly important, as it sets the *context* for the essay. It needs to draw the reader into the subject and provide necessary background to understand the subject. It is sometimes helpful to open with the research question and explain how the question will be answered. The major points of the essay may be forecast or previewed to prepare readers for the coming arguments. In a research essay, it is a good idea to establish the writer's credibility by reviewing credentials and experience with the subject. Another useful opening involves quoting several sources that support the points of the essay, again to establish credibility. The tone should be appropriate to the audience and subject, maintaining a sense of careful authority while building the arguments. *Jargon* should be kept to a minimum, and language should be carefully chosen to reflect the appropriate tone.

Conclusion

The **conclusion** to a research essay helps readers summarize what they have learned. Conclusions are not meant to convince, as this has been done in the body of the essay. It can be useful to leave the reader with a memorable phrase or example that supports the argument. Conclusions should be both memorable and logical restatements of the arguments in the body of the essay. A *specific-to-general pattern* can be helpful, opening with the thesis statement and expanding to more general observations. A good idea is to restate the main points in the body of the essay, leading to the conclusion. An ending that evokes a vivid image or asks a provocative question makes the essay memorable. The same effect can be achieved by a call for action, or a warning. Conclusions may be tailored to the audience's background, in terms of language, tone, and style.

Reviewing the Draft

Checklist for Reviewing a Draft of a Research Essay

1. **Introduction**: Is the reader's attention gained and held by the introduction?
2. **Thesis**: Does the essay fulfill the promise of the thesis? Is it strong enough?
3. **Main points**: Are the main points listed and ranked in order of importance?
4. **Organization**: What is the organizing principle of the essay? Does it work?
5. **Supporting information**: Is the thesis adequately supported? Is the thesis convincing?
6. **Source material**: Are there adequate sources and are they smoothly integrated into the essay?
7. **Conclusion**: Does the conclusion have sufficient power? Does it summarize the essay well?
8. **Paragraphs, sentences, words**: Are these elements effective in promoting the thesis?
9. **Overall review**: Evaluate the essay's strengths and weaknesses. What revisions are needed?

Modern Language Association Style

The **Modern Language Association style** is widely used in literature and languages as well as other fields. The MLA style calls for noting brief references to sources in parentheses in the text of an essay and adding an alphabetical list of sources, called "Works Cited," at the end. Specific recommendations of the MLA include the following:

1. **"Works Cited"**: Include in this section only works actually cited. List on a separate page the author's name, title, and publication information, which must include the location of the publisher, the publisher's name, and the date of publication.
2. **Parenthetical citations**: MLA style uses parenthetical citations following each quotation, reference, paraphrase, or summary to a source. Each citation is made up of the author's last name and page reference, keyed to a reference in Works Cited.
3. **Explanatory notes**: Explanatory notes are numbered consecutively and identified by superscript numbers in the text. The full notes may appear as endnotes or as footnotes at the bottom of the page.

Literacy

Literacy is commonly understood to refer to the *ability to read and write*. UNESCO has further defined literacy as the "ability to identify, understand, interpret, create, communicate, compute, and use printed and written materials associated with varying contexts." Under the UNESCO definition, understanding cultural, political, and historical contexts of communities falls under the definition of literacy. While **reading literacy** may be gauged simply by the ability to read a newspaper, **writing literacy** includes spelling, grammar, and sentence structure. To be literate in a foreign language, one would also need to have the ability to understand a language by listening and to speak the language. Some argue that visual representation and numeracy should be included in the requirements one must meet to be considered literate. Computer literacy refers to one's ability to utilize the basic functions of computers and other technologies. Subsets of reading literacy include phonological awareness, decoding, comprehension, and vocabulary.

Phonological Awareness

A subskill of literacy, **phonological awareness** is the ability to perceive sound structures in a spoken word, such as syllables and the individual phonemes within syllables. **Phonemes** are the sounds represented by the letters in the alphabet. The ability to separate, blend, and manipulate sounds is critical to developing reading and spelling skills. Phonological awareness is concerned with not only syllables, but also **onset sounds** (the sounds at the beginning of words) and **rime** (the same thing as rhyme, but spelled differently to distinguish syllable rime from poetic rhyme). Phonological awareness is an auditory skill that does not necessarily involve print. It should be developed before the student has learned letter to sound correspondences. A student's phonological awareness is an indicator of future reading success.

Activities That Teach Phonological Awareness

Classroom activities that teach **phonological awareness** include language play and exposure to a variety of sounds and contexts of sounds. Activities that teach phonological awareness include:

- Clapping to the sounds of individual words, names, or all words in a sentence
- Practicing saying blended phonemes
- Singing songs that involve phoneme replacement (e.g., The Name Game)
- Reading poems, songs, and nursery rhymes out loud
- Reading patterned and predictable texts out loud
- Listening to environmental sounds or following verbal directions
- Playing games with rhyming chants or fingerplays
- Reading alliterative texts out loud
- Grouping objects by beginning sounds
- Reordering words in a well-known sentence or making silly phrases by deleting words from a well-known sentence (perhaps from a favorite storybook)

Alphabetic Principle and Alphabet Writing Systems

The **alphabetic principle** refers to the use of letters and combinations of letters to represent speech sounds. The way letters are combined and pronounced is guided by a system of rules that establishes relationships between written and spoken words and their letter symbols. Alphabet writing systems are common around the world. Some are **phonological** in that each letter stands for an individual sound and words are spelled just as they sound. However, there are other writing systems as well, such as the Chinese **logographic** system and the Japanese **syllabic** system.

Development of Language Skills

Children learn language through interacting with others, by experiencing language in daily and relevant context, and through understanding that speaking and listening are necessary for effective communication. Teachers can promote **language development** by intensifying the opportunities a child has to experience and understand language.

Teachers can assist language development by:

- Modeling enriched vocabulary and teaching new words
- Using questions and examples to extend a child's descriptive language skills
- Providing ample response time to encourage children to practice speech
- Asking for clarification to provide students with the opportunity to develop communication skills
- Promoting conversations among children
- Providing feedback to let children know they have been heard and understood, and providing further explanation when needed

Relationship Between Oral and Written Language Development

Oral and written language develops simultaneously. The acquisition of skills in one area supports the acquisition of skills in the other. However, oral language is not a prerequisite to written language. An immature form of oral language development is babbling, and an immature form of written language development is scribbling. **Oral language development** does not occur naturally, but does occur in a social context. This means it is best to include children in conversations rather than simply talk at them. **Written language development** can occur without direct instruction. In fact, reading and writing do not necessarily need to be taught through formal lessons if the child is exposed to a print-rich environment. A teacher can assist a child's language development by building on what the child already knows, discussing relevant and meaningful events and experiences, teaching vocabulary and literacy skills, and providing opportunities to acquire more complex language.

Print-Rich Environment

A teacher can provide a **print-rich environment** in the classroom in a number of ways. These include:

- **Displaying** the following in the classroom:
  o Children's names in print or cursive
  o Children's written work
  o Newspapers and magazines
  o Instructional charts
  o Written schedules
  o Signs and labels
  o Printed songs, poems, and rhymes
- Using **graphic organizers** such as KWL charts or story road maps to:
  o Remind students about what was read and discussed
  o Expand on the lesson topic or theme
  o Show the relationships among books, ideas, and words
- Using **big books** to:
  o Point out features of print, such as specific letters and punctuation
  o Track print from right to left
  o Emphasize the concept of words and the fact that they are used to communicate

Benefits of Print and Book Awareness

Print and book awareness helps a child understand:

- That there is a **connection** between print and messages contained on signs, labels, and other print forms in the child's environment
- That reading and writing are ways to obtain information and communicate ideas
- That **print** runs from left to right and from top to bottom
- That a book has **parts**, such as a title, a cover, a title page, and a table of contents
- That a book has an **author** and contains a **story**
- That **illustrations** can carry meaning
- That **letters and words** are different
- That **words and sentences** are separated by spaces and punctuation
- That different **text forms** are used for different functions
- That print represents **spoken language**
- How to **hold** a book.

Facts Children Should Know About Letters

To be appropriately prepared to learn to read and write, a child should learn:

- That each letter is **distinct** in appearance
- What **direction and shape** must be used to make each letter
- That each letter has a **name**, which can be associated with the shape of a letter
- That there are **26** letters in the English alphabet, and letters are grouped in a certain order
- That letters represent **sounds of speech**
- That **words** are composed of letters and have meaning
- That one must be able to **correspond** letters and sounds to read

Decoding

Decoding is the method or strategy used to make sense of printed words and figure out how to correctly pronounce them. In order to decode, a student needs to know the relationships between letters and sounds, including letter patterns; that words are constructed from phonemes and phoneme blends; and that a printed word represents a word that can be spoken. This knowledge will help the student recognize familiar words and make informed guesses about the pronunciation of unfamiliar words. Decoding is not the same as **comprehension**. It does not require an understanding of the meaning of a word, only a knowledge of how to recognize and pronounce it. Decoding can also refer to the skills a student uses to determine the meaning of a **sentence**. These skills include applying knowledge of vocabulary, sentence structure, and context.

Teaching of Reading Through Phonics

Phonics is the process of learning to read by learning how spoken language is represented by letters. Students learn to read phonetically by sounding out the **phonemes** in words and then blending them together to produce the correct sounds in words. In other words, the student connects speech sounds with letters or groups of letters and blends the sounds together to determine the pronunciation of an unknown word. Phonics is a commonly used method to teach **decoding and reading**, but has been challenged by other methods, such as the whole language approach. Despite the complexity of pronunciation and combined sounds in the English language, research shows that phonics is a highly effective way to teach reading. Being able to read or

- 104 -

pronounce a word does not mean the student comprehends the meaning of the word, but context aids comprehension. When phonics is used as a foundation for decoding, children eventually learn to recognize words automatically and advance to decoding multisyllable words with practice.

Role of Fluency in Literacy Development

Fluency is the goal of literacy development. It is the ability to read accurately and quickly. Evidence of fluency includes the ability to recognize words automatically and group words for comprehension. At this point, the student no longer needs to decode words except for complex, unfamiliar ones. He or she is able to move to the next level and understand the **meaning** of a text. The student should be able to self-check for comprehension and should feel comfortable expressing ideas in writing. Teachers can help students build fluency by continuing to provide: reading experiences and discussions about text, gradually increasing the level of difficulty; reading practice, both silently and out loud; word analysis practice; instruction on reading comprehension strategies; and opportunities to express responses to readings through writing.

Role of Vocabulary in Literacy Development

When students do not know the meaning of words in a text, their comprehension is limited. As a result, the text becomes boring or confusing. The larger a student's **vocabulary** is, the better their reading comprehension will be. A larger vocabulary is also associated with an enhanced ability to **communicate** in speech and writing. It is the teacher's role to help students develop a good working vocabulary. Students learn most of the words they use and understand from listening to the world around them (adults, other students, media, etc.) They also learn from their reading experiences, which include being read to and reading independently. Carefully designed activities can also stimulate vocabulary growth, and should emphasize useful words that students see frequently, important words necessary for understanding text, and difficult words such as idioms or words with more than one meaning.

Teaching Techniques Promoting Vocabulary Development

A student's **vocabulary** can be developed by:

- Calling upon a student's **prior knowledge** and making comparisons to that knowledge
- **Defining** a word and providing multiple examples of the use of the word in context
- Showing a student how to use **context clues** to discover the meaning of a word
- Providing instruction on **prefixes, roots, and suffixes** to help students break a word into its parts and decipher its meaning
- Showing students how to use a **dictionary and a thesaurus**
- Asking students to **practice** new vocabulary by using the words in their own writing
- Providing a **print-rich environment** with a word wall
- Studying a group of words related to a **single subject**, such as farm words, transportation words, etc. so that concept development is enhanced.

Affixes, Prefixes, and Root Words

Affixes are syllables attached to the beginning or end of a word to make a derivative or inflectional form of a word. Both prefixes and suffixes are affixes. A **prefix** is a syllable that appears at the beginning of a word that, in combination with the root or base word, creates a specific meaning. For example, the prefix "mis" means "wrong." When combined with the root word "spelling," the word "misspelling" is created, which means the "wrong spelling." A **root word** is the base of a word to which affixes can be added. For example, the prefix "in" or "pre" can be added to the root word "vent" to create "invent" or "prevent," respectively. The suffix "er" can be added to the root word "work" to create "worker," which means "one who works." The suffix "able," meaning "capable of," can be added to "work" to create "workable," which means "capable of working."

Suffixes

A suffix is a syllable that appears at the end of a word that, in combination with the root or base word, creates a specific meaning. There are three types of suffixes:

- **Noun suffixes** – There are two types of noun suffixes. One denotes the act of, state of, or quality of. For example, "-ment" added to "argue" becomes "argument," which is defined as "the act of arguing." The other denotes the doer, or one who acts. For example, "-eer" added to "auction" becomes "auctioneer," meaning "one who auctions." Other examples include "-hood," "-ness," "-tion," "-ship," and "-ism."
- **Verb suffixes** – These denote "to make" or "to perform the act of." For example, "-en" added to "soft" makes "soften," which means "to make soft." Other verb suffixes are "-ate" (perpetuate), "-fy" (dignify), and "-ize" (sterilize).
- **Adjectival suffixes** – These include suffixes such as "-ful," which means "full of." When added to "care," the word "careful" is formed, which means "full of care." Other examples are "-ish," "-less," and "-able."

Strategies to Improve Reading Comprehension

Teachers can model in a read-aloud the strategies students can use on their own to better comprehend a text. First, the teacher should do a walk-through of the story **illustrations** and ask, "What's happening here?" Based on what they have seen, the teacher should then ask students to **predict** what the story will be about. As the book is read, the teacher should ask open-ended questions such as, "Why do you think the character did this?" and "How do you think the character feels?" The teacher should also ask students if they can **relate** to the story or have background knowledge of something similar. After the reading, the teacher should ask the students to **retell** the story in their own words to check for comprehension. This retelling can take the form of a puppet show or summarizing the story to a partner.

Role of Prior Knowledge in Determining Appropriate Literacy Education

Even preschool children have some literacy skills, and the extent and type of these skills have implications for instructional approaches. Comprehension results from relating two or more pieces of information. One piece comes from the text, and another piece might come from **prior knowledge** (something from a student's long-term memory). For a child, that prior knowledge comes from being read to at home; taking part in other literacy experiences, such as playing computer or word games; being exposed to a print-rich environment at home; and observing examples of parents' reading habits. Children who have had **extensive literacy experience** are better prepared to further develop their literacy skills in school than children who have not been read to, have few books or magazines in their homes, are seldom exposed to high-level oral or written language activities, and seldom witness adults engaged in reading and writing. Children with a scant literacy background are at a disadvantage. The teacher must not make any assumptions about their prior knowledge, and should use intense, targeted instruction. Otherwise, reading comprehension will be limited.

Using Puppetry in the Classroom

Using puppets in the classroom puts students at ease and allows them to enjoy a learning experience as if it were play. The purpose of using puppetry is to generate ideas, encourage imagination, and foster language development. Using a puppet helps a child "become" the character and therefore experience a different **outlook. Language development** is enhanced through the student interpreting a story that has been read in class and practicing new words from that story in the puppet show. Children will also have the opportunity to practice using descriptive adjectives for the characters and the scene, which will help them learn the function of adjectives. **Descriptive adjectives and verbs** can also be learned by practicing facial expressions and movements with puppets. The teacher can model happy, sad, eating, sleeping, and similar words with a puppet, and then ask students to do the same with their puppets. This is an especially effective vocabulary activity for ESL children.

Using Drama or Story Theater in the Classroom

Drama activities are fun learning experiences that capture a child's attention, engage the imagination, and motivate vocabulary expansion. For example, after reading a story, the teacher could ask children to act it out as the teacher repeats the story. This activity, which works best with very young learners, will help children work on listening skills and their ability to pretend. The best stories to use for this passive improvisation are ones that have lots of simple actions that children will be able to understand and perform easily. Older children can create their own improvisational skits and possibly write scripts. **Visualization** also calls upon the imagination and encourages concentration and bodily awareness. Children can be given a prompt for the visualization and then asked to draw what they see in their mind's eye. **Charades** is another way to act out words and improve vocabulary skills. This activity can be especially helpful to encourage ESL students to express thoughts and ideas in English. These students should be given easier words to act out to promote confidence.

Classroom Practices Benefiting Second Language Acquisition

Since some students may have limited understanding of English, a teacher should employ the following practices to promote second language acquisition:

- Make all instruction as **understandable** as possible and use simple and repeated terms.
- Relate instruction to the **cultures** of ESL children.
- Increase **interactive activities** and use gestures or non-verbal actions when modeling.
- Provide language and literacy development instruction in **all curriculum areas**.
- Establish **consistent routines** that help children connect words and events.
- Use a **schedule** so children know what will happen next and will not feel lost.
- Integrate ESL children into **group activities** with non-ESL children.
- Appoint bilingual students to act as **student translators**.
- Explain actions as activities happen so that a **word to action relationship** is established.
- Initiate opportunities for ESL children to **experiment** with and practice new language.
- Employ multisensory learning.

Theories of Language Development

Four theories of language development are:

- **Learning approach** – This theory assumes that language is first learned by imitating the speech of adults. It is then solidified in school through drills about the rules of language structures.
- **Linguistic approach** – Championed by Noam Chomsky in the 1950s, this theory proposes that the ability to use a language is innate. This is a biological approach rather than one based on cognition or social patterning.
- **Cognitive approach** – Developed in the 1970s and based on the work of Piaget, this theory states that children must develop appropriate cognitive skills before they can acquire language.
- **Sociocognitive approach** – In the 1970s, some researchers proposed that language development is a complex interaction of linguistic, social, and cognitive influences. This theory best explains the lack of language skills among children who are neglected, have uneducated parents, or lives in poverty.

Teaching Strategies to Promote Listening Skills of ESL Students

Listening is a critical skill when learning a new language. Students spend a great deal more time listening than they do speaking, and far less time reading and writing than speaking. Two ways to encourage ESL students to listen are to:

- Talk about topics that are of **interest** to the ESL learner. Otherwise, students may tune out the speaker because they don't want to put in that much effort to learn about a topic they find boring.
- Talk about content or give examples that are **easy** to understand or are **related** to a topic that is familiar to ESL students. Culturally relevant materials will be more interesting to ESL students, will make them feel more comfortable, and will contain vocabulary that they may already be familiar with.

Considerations Relevant to ESL Students Related to Learning by Listening

Listening is not a passive skill, but an **active** one. Therefore, a teacher needs to make the listening experience as rewarding as possible and provide as many auditory and visual clues as possible. Three ways that the teacher can make the listening experience rewarding for ESL students are:

- Avoid **colloquialisms** and **abbreviated or slang terms** that may be confusing to the ESL listener, unless there is enough time to define them and explain their use.
- Make the spoken English understandable by stopping to **clarify** points, **repeating** new or difficult words, and **defining** words that may not be known.
- Support the spoken word with as many **visuals** as possible. Pictures, diagrams, gestures, facial expressions, and body language can help the ESL learner correctly interpret the spoken language more easily and also leaves an image impression that helps them remember the words.

Top-Down and Bottom-Up Processing

ESL students need to be given opportunities to practice both top-down and bottom-up processing. If they are old enough to understand these concepts, they should be made aware that these are two processes that affect their listening comprehension. In **top-down processing**, the listener refers to

background and global knowledge to figure out the meaning of a message. For example, when asking an ESL student to perform a task, the steps of the task should be explained and accompanied by a review of the vocabulary terms the student already understands so that the student feels comfortable tackling new steps and new words. The teacher should also allow students to ask questions to verify comprehension. In **bottom-up processing**, the listener figures out the meaning of a message by using "**data**" obtained from what is said. This data includes sounds (stress, rhythm, and intonation), words, and grammatical relationships. All data can be used to make conclusions or interpretations. For example, the listener can develop bottom-up skills by learning how to detect differences in intonation between statements and questions.

Listening Lessons

All students, but especially ESL students, can be taught **listening** through specific training. During listening lessons, the teacher should guide students through three steps:

- **Pre-listening activity** – This establishes the purpose of the lesson and engages students' background knowledge. This activity should ask students to think about and discuss something they already know about the topic. Alternatively, the teacher can provide background information.
- **The listening activity** – This requires the listener to obtain information and then immediately do something with that information. For example, the teacher can review the schedule for the day or the week. The students are being given information about a routine they already know, but need to be able to identify names, tasks, and times.
- **Post-listening activity** – This is an evaluation process that allows students to judge how well they did with the listening task. Other language skills can be included in the activity. For example, this activity could involve asking questions about who will do what according to the classroom schedule (Who is the lunch monitor today?) and could also involve asking students to produce whole sentence replies.

Helping ESL Students Understand Subject Matter

Speaking

To help ESL students better understand subject matter, the following teaching strategies using spoken English can be used:

- **Read aloud** from a textbook, and then ask ESL students to **verbally summarize** what was read. The teacher should assist by providing new words as needed to give students the opportunity to practice vocabulary and speaking skills. The teacher should then read the passage again to students to verify accuracy and details.
- The teacher could ask ESL students to explain why the subject matter is important to them and where they see it fitting into their lives. This verbalization gives them speaking practice and helps them relate to the subject.
- Whenever small group activities are being conducted, ESL students can be placed with **English-speaking students**. It is best to keep the groups to two or three students so that the ESL student will be motivated by the need to be involved. English-speaking students should be encouraged to include ESL students in the group work.

<u>Reading</u>

There are supplemental printed materials that can be used to help ESL students understand subject matter. The following strategies can be used to help ESL students develop English reading skills.

- Make sure all ESL students have a **bilingual dictionary** to use. A thesaurus would also be helpful.
- Try to keep **content area books** written in the ESL students' native languages in the classroom. Students can use them side-by-side with English texts. Textbooks in other languages can be ordered from the school library or obtained from the classroom textbook publisher.
- If a student lacks confidence in his/her ability to read the textbook, the teacher can read a passage to the student and have him or her **verbally summarize** the passage. The teacher should take notes on what the student says and then read them back. These notes can be a substitute, short-form, in-their-own-words textbook that the student can understand.

General Teaching Strategies to Help ESL Students

Some strategies can help students develop more than one important skill. They may involve a combination of speaking, listening, and/or viewing. Others are mainly classroom management aids. General teaching strategies for ESL students include:

- **Partner** English-speaking students with ESL students as study buddies and ask the English-speaking students to share notes.
- Encourage ESL students to ask **questions** whenever they don't understand something. They should be aware that they don't have to be able to interpret every word of text to understand the concept.
- Dictate **key sentences** related to the content area being taught and ask ESL students to write them down. This gives them practice in listening and writing, and also helps them identify what is important.
- **Alternate** difficult and easy tasks so that ESL students can experience academic success.
- Ask ESL students to **label** objects associated with content areas, such as maps, diagrams, parts of a leaf, or parts of a sentence. This gives students writing and reading experience and helps them remember key vocabulary.

Media Literacy

Media literacy is the ability to access, read, and interpret information from various parts of the media. Parts of the media can include the Internet, artifacts, printed materials, primary source documents, and visual media. A student who has achieved media literacy can effectively navigate the Internet (and other facets of media) without losing focus or accessing information deemed inappropriate or unsafe. Students with media literacy also develop the ability to question the validity of the information they are accessing by questioning the source and accuracy of the information being presented. In addition, students with media literacy can identify the key components of what they are accessing without becoming overwhelmed by the amount of information available.

Key Points Related to Speaking

The following are key points to remember about volume, pace, pronunciation, body language, word choice, and visual aids as they relate to speaking:

- **Volume** – Voice volume should be appropriate to the room and adjusted according to whether or not a microphone is used. The speaker should not shout at the audience, mumble, or speak so softly that his or her voice is inaudible.
- **Pace and pronunciation** – The speaker shouldn't talk so fast that his or her speech is unintelligible, nor should the speaker speak so slowly as to be boring. The speaker should enunciate words clearly.
- **Body language and gestures** – Body language can add to or distract from the message, so annoying, repetitive gestures such as waving hands about, flipping hair, or staring at one spot should be avoided. Good posture is critical.
- **Word choice** – The speaker should use a vocabulary level that fits the age and interest level of the audience. Vocabulary may be casual or formal depending on the audience.
- **Visual aids** – The speaker should use whatever aids will enhance the presentation, such as props, models, media, etc., but should not use anything that will be distracting or unmanageable.

Communicating Emotions

The majority of communications taking place in academic and business settings involve **factual information**. Unfortunately, individuals who are adept at communicating facts may struggle when attempting to communicate **personal feelings** in a relationship. Personal relationships, which are basic to happiness, can develop only when feelings are openly and honestly shared. In order to do this, people should work on asking straight-forward questions and honestly answering questions about themselves. Being a good listener, asking the right questions, and respecting the other person's answers are necessary parts of establishing good emotional communication. Sometimes, though, this may mean putting aside your own opinions so that you can fully engage with another person and come to understand the other's point of view.

Nonverbal Communication

Even though we normally think of communication as something we do through spoken or written language, we are constantly sending messages to one another with our **bodies** and **tone of voice**. Often, physical messages are sent and interpreted without either party being aware. Some of the signals that are used are consistent across cultures, whereas others are unique to a particular culture. For instance, slumped shoulders generally mean passivity and submission in every society. Alternatively, some cultures interpret eye contact as a sign of respect, and others see it as a sign of hostility. One should try to be aware of the messages one is sending with one's posture and gestures to avoid sending messages that are insulting or self-defeating.

Self-Concept in Interpersonal Communication

During **interpersonal communication**, all the participating parties filter information through their own **self-concept**. Everyone naturally applies new information to his or her own self-concept. Often, however, self-interested concerns can make it difficult for a listener to get a true sense of what the other person is saying. As much as possible, listeners should strive to understand and take into account their own self-image, so they can be as objective as possible when evaluating an incoming message. Although a slight degree of egotism or self-centeredness is natural, these traits can hinder accurate and insightful listening. Therefore, the goal of speech communication education is to mitigate these distorting factors.

Images of Self and Others Existing During Two-Person Conversations

When two individuals have a conversation, their **self-images** and the **images they hold of each other** exert a great influence on the course of the conversation. For instance, imagine you are talking to your teacher. You have a self-image and an image of the teacher. You also have an image of how you hope your teacher sees you. Finally, you have an image of how you think your teacher actually sees you. Similarly, your teacher holds his or her own set of four images in mind. Obviously, then, even carrying on a simple conversation becomes a complicated event. Speech communication theorists assert that conversations tend to go better when there is less discrepancy between these various images. For instance, if your self-image is similar to the image you imagine your teacher has of you, you are less likely to have trouble coming up with appropriate things to say. Similarly, if your impression of what the teacher thinks of you is similar to what you *hope* the teacher would think of you, you are less likely to make outlandish claims or try to justify yourself.

Self-Disclosure

According to speech communication theorists, conversations work best when both parties are as honest and forthcoming about themselves as possible. In other words, when engaged in conversation, a person should strive to be as accurate as possible in revealing his or her self-image. This process is known as **self-disclosure**. To the degree that we hide information about ourselves, we prevent others from truly understanding us. There are a number of reasons why a person might not engage in total self-disclosure. Propriety, pride, and fear are probably the most common reasons for hiding information about oneself. Difficulty can also arise when one individual in a conversation has information about the other without the other party being aware of it. This kind of asymmetrical knowledge can create underlying but unexpressed tension in a conversation. Ideally, people should attempt to continually increase their level of self-disclosure while encouraging their interlocutor to do the same.

Encoding Meaning

When one person speaks to another, he or she is "**encoding**" the verbal message with supplemental nonverbal forms of communication. The precise "**code**" the speaker uses is the particular set of words, with their agreed-upon meaning, as well as syntax and grammar. To the degree that the speaker has a command of vocabulary and a strong sense of meaning, he or she will be able to construct a subtle and effective code. The process of encoding meaning is also influenced by individual bias, desire, and perception. People encode meaning differently based on the personal "agenda" they bring to any conversation. Two people speaking to one another should be able to increase the complexity and accuracy of their message encoding as the conversation progresses because they will be acquiring more and better information about one another's intentions, knowledge, and character.

Interpreting Meaning

When we listen to another person speak in conversation, we are attempting to **decode** their meaning through the **filter** of our own prejudices and perceptions. Speech communication theorists assert that listeners tend to emphasize the components of a message that are associated with their own pre-existing knowledge or interests. In particular, we all tend to emphasize the importance of those aspects of a message that directly pertain to us. Starting out, we are more likely to make mistakes in the interpretation of what a speaker is saying. As we acquire more information and

- 112 -

become more familiar with the other person's speaking style, however, we tend to make beneficial adjustments to our interpretation. The more time we spend with another person, the better we are able to correctly interpret the meanings of their communications.

Communication Appropriate to Cooperating on Tasks

For people to **cooperate** effectively on a task, they all need good **communication skills**. This is especially true in the adult professional world. Without effective communication among those involved, success will be more difficult to achieve, but many people do not learn to work effectively with others until late childhood. For the most part, any job-related task is most easily accomplished when all parties know enough about the task-related tools, ideas, and skills to communicate effectively among themselves. In some cases, two individuals working together on a task may have unequal power, such as in the case of an employer and employee collaborating on a work-related project. Such unequal distribution of power also has a strong effect on communication.

Classroom Materials That Support Literacy Across the Curriculum

In a classroom that supports literacy, the teacher should provide **labels** combining words and pictures on all objects. This continually stimulates students to associate written language with the objects and concepts it represents. Especially to support disabled students, teachers should use their particular interests and needs as a guide for labeling things. Printed directions, signs, calendars, and schedules are materials that students should use regularly in the classroom. These help students realize how language is used in everyday life. When the class is studying a certain topic, theme, or book, the teacher and students can work together to redesign the classroom using printed/written materials that reflect that topic, theme, or book. This enables students to experience fully and "live" the lesson rather than just observing it. All of the materials must be adapted for any students' special needs. For instance, in a class including blind/visually impaired students, labels, signs and other print materials can incorporate Braille words and textured surfaces.

Addressing Diverse Student Abilities and Needs

Teachers must consider the **diversity** among the skills and needs of their students as they design their classroom learning environments. The teachers should **individualize** the setting and their instruction so that these represent every student. Individualization and instructional differentiation should not only address disabled students' needs; they should also regularly provide suitable opportunities for these students to participate on an ongoing basis in activities that involve literacy and integrate it into all content areas. According to research, a salient need of students with diverse literacy backgrounds is that they often have trouble connecting new information to their existing knowledge. This ability is a critical component of learning. When teachers plan and organize their classrooms to offer literacy activities that are accessible to disabled students—and that immerse them in literacy experiences and give them opportunities to connect both new with old information, and spoken with printed language—these students can then access the general education curriculum.

Activities for Students with Disabilities to Develop Literacy Skills and Participate in General Curriculum

To participate in the general curriculum, students with disabilities need to understand the **alphabetic principle**, i.e. that printed language represents spoken language; connect print with speech; and be able to relate new information to their prior knowledge. Teachers can support these developments by designing classrooms as literacy-rich settings, immersing special-needs and other students in **accessible literacy activities** across all content areas. For example, students can interact with alphabet-letter magnets, cookie-cutters, and stamps: concrete manipulatives allow students not developmentally ready for exclusively abstract thought to understand concepts using real objects. Discussing daily schedules requires students to read and comprehend printed language, and then use spoken language to demonstrate and apply their understanding. Playing letter/word games like Bingo, Pictionary, Boggle, and Scrabble gives practice with creating and manipulating language, enhancing recognition and cognitive flexibility. Providing photos of peers, teachers, staff, and classroom activities and having students label them helps students connect written language with familiar, meaningful images. Daily communication notebooks help students further integrate literacy into their school days.

Implications of Cultural and Linguistic Differences Regarding Literacy Development

Educational research shows that the **cultural values** of families and/or communities influence children's literacy development, and also that culture is a significant factor to understanding children's home literacy environments. Researchers have also found that cultural purposes, perspectives, and contexts affect how students with disabilities in particular interact with the literacy environments they encounter. They say children's preparation levels entering formal education reflect their families'/communities' values and beliefs about literacy. Cultural attitudes about literacy then influence how schools deliver instruction and literacy experiences. Teachers must assess culturally diverse students' interactions with the environment, and design literacy-rich classrooms, with students' diverse backgrounds in mind. Students learning English (ELL/ESL) enter school either not knowing English or just learning it, lacking exposure to specific vocabulary and literature. Literacy-rich classrooms help them participate in regular curriculum. Teacher should read aloud often to these students; include print in their native language in classrooms; permit mistakes during student attempts to use English; encourage students to reread books repeatedly; and plan activities entailing language use.

Drawbacks of Whole-Class and Small-Group Reading, and Flexible Grouping Model

A major disadvantage of **whole-class reading** is that students who read above the average class level go unchallenged and can become bored, while students reading below average level are lost. Yet the **small-group method** intended to remedy this also has the drawback that, as traditionally implemented, most time is used for skill instruction, leaving far too little time for students actually to read the text. One solution is a **flexible grouping model**, e.g., Grouping Without Tracking (Paratore, 1990). This model uses a "sandwich" structure: teachers give students shared-reading processes at the beginning and end of the lesson, but provide differentiated instruction to two groups in the middle as they read the text. Teachers give indirect guidance to students who can read more independently, and more direct support to struggling readers. Teachers reunite the groups to lead them in a final discussion. Students with reading difficulties gain reading proficiency and comprehension from direct teacher support, enabling them to contribute better to the whole-class discussion, so all share this experience equally.

Jigsaw Approach to Shared Reading

Students reading below grade level may be able to access and comprehend some texts or portions of them, but have difficulty with harder parts/texts—for example, informational texts with more challenging subject matter and specialized vocabulary. When a text intended for the whole class contains such challenging material, one solution the teacher can use is a **jigsaw approach**. The teacher selects various portions of the text that are less difficult and assigns them to students reading below grade level. Whereas such texts overall might present struggles for these students, they find the easier portions more manageable when they tackle only these parts, as selected and assigned by the teacher, in small groups of students with comparable reading levels. The teacher makes each small student group responsible for comprehension of their assigned portion of text. Then the teacher brings the class back together, having each group report what they read, understood, and learned. The whole class then collaborates to help each other make connections among the learning each group reported.

Using Themes to Connect Texts

Any inclusive classroom will contain students who read at various age/grade levels. As a result, some books used as core texts are going to present difficulties for some of the students, who read below grade level and/or lack background knowledge and vocabulary of the subject. One way a teacher can facilitate all students' comprehension of such texts is to provide **supplementary texts** that allow readers at different levels easier access—texts on the same subject or theme as the more difficult core text. Teachers have students read these more accessible texts independently during small-group reading periods. This makes it easier for students with less reading proficiency to learn the core vocabulary and build their background knowledge. Thus, they are more prepared to tackle the more difficult core text during whole-class shared reading periods. With such preparation, less proficient readers are more likely to become engaged and active participants in the shared reading of a difficult text in the whole-group setting.

Assigning Students to Small Groups for Guided Reading Exercises

Expert educators and researchers recommend that when teachers divide classes into small student groups for **guided reading**, they should not be overly concerned with assigning students to exact reading levels. Rather, though they will want to group students whose literacy development is similar and who read around a similar level, they should give more attention to organizing groups according to the students' *areas of need*. For example, a teacher might identify students who share in common a need for help with noticing changes in setting; other students who share difficulties with recognizing and differentiating characters; some students who demonstrate problems with following and/or reproducing events they read in a text in the correct chronological sequence; some students who have trouble identifying and/or articulating the main idea in a text portion, etc. The teacher can create a group of students sharing one of these challenges; announce to the class what this group's focus is; and then invite other students to join this group by choice if they experience the same need.

Helping Teachers Provide More Equitable Learning Opportunities Using Word Counts

Books designed for lower reading levels typically contain fewer words, both per page and overall. Yet students who are reading below their grade levels require not fewer reading opportunities, but more, to practice and improve their reading skills. For example, within one class of second-grade students, the teacher might have one group using a text with over 80 words on just the first page, while another group uses a text with a total of 80 words in the entire book. This difference shows that the teacher will need to use several texts within certain groups to give them equal amounts of reading material and practice as readers of denser/longer texts during group reading times. Teachers can look at the backs of the books they assign during guided reading sessions, and maintain simple logs of their **word counts**. Comparing these word counts among groups can help teachers to equalize the numbers of words that each student group actually works with during small-group guided reading periods.

Connecting Text Sets for Small-Group Guided Reading Across Different Reading Difficulty Levels

When teachers select textbooks to teach a unit/lesson on a certain topic, they often compile **text sets**—groups of books all related to the same topic/theme. Because classes usually include students reading at different levels, teachers also often gather books at different reading levels for text sets. When collecting books representing multiple reading levels, the teacher can also intentionally organize the text set so all books are connected. For example, the books might share similar content; similar language, style, and vocabulary words; or similar layouts. Selecting books sharing such a commonality at different reading levels makes it easier for students to draw useful connections between easier and harder texts. It also facilitates students' flexibility in working across multiple reading levels, which builds their skills and confidence for faster progress. Additionally, to prepare some students to read books that teachers felt would prove too difficult otherwise, they can use easier texts with similar themes/language/formats to establish contexts for the harder ones.

Enhancing Students' Independent Reading Through the Reading Material Provided

In addition to whole-class and small-group reading exercises, students need some time reading **texts of their own choice**, which they can easily read with little/no support, to attain comfort, fluency, and confidence. To ensure more opportunities for practice, with equal time for all students, teachers should provide text sets at multiple reading levels for each content area. Experts suggest 70% of books should be easily accessible; and, in addition to classroom libraries, using rolling carts lets book collections travel among classrooms. Multiple reading levels let more advanced readers peruse a harder text, while less advanced readers read several easier texts; this equalizes the time and words they have for practicing. Because critics find some leveled readers lack variety in gender/race/class/other sociocultural aspects of characters, teachers should build diverse book collections representing all students. Teachers can inform their selections via student interest surveys; and familiarity with students' individual identities, personalities, and special interests. Knowing individual students can help match them to texts as effectively as leveled book lists.

Engaging Students in Reading

Experts find excessive attention to **leveling** as a way of matching texts to students can be restrictive, undermining high-quality instruction that balances the needs of the reader with the demands of the text. Teachers must consider that assigning certain texts will cause students to disengage from reading and avoid it rather than engage in it. In the real world, people read many different kinds of materials. Therefore, a teacher has better chances of finding texts that engage students, and that motivate them to read and allow them to perceive themselves as readers, by mindfully selecting **varied text genres** with **varied difficulty**. In classrooms incorporating various student reading levels, this can be the best method to procure classroom acceptability of accessible texts. Teachers can also use **individualized instructional formats**, such as Readers Workshop (Atwell, 1998), which balance issues of difficulty, choice, and engagement; develop reader communities affording more reading experiences with authenticity, meaning, and enjoyment; and stronger positive teacher-student relationships via individualized consultations. Teachers should also incorporate **accessible alternative texts** for independent activities.

Alternative Reading and Writing Forms to Help Students Attain Greater Progress in Reading

When students read and write outside of school, they choose many alternative forms of reading and writing. To engage these students while they are in school, teachers should think about adding such

alternative materials to their own instructional programs. For example, teachers might incorporate such media as graphic novels, magazines, newspapers, plays, anthologies of poetry, e-books and other digital/online content, and text that students have written themselves. Educational experts advise that just because it can be harder to determine the reading levels of such alternative text formats, teachers should not shy away from using them. Because they represent examples of text that people (including students) read in real life, they provide not only excellent practice for students' present and future reading of real-world materials, but also motivation to read and meaningful experiences in reading. Another boon of using these authentic, alternative texts is that they frequently incorporate multiple reading levels, so that nearly every student can read some portions of them.

Viewing Skills

Viewing skills can be sharpened by having students look at a single image, such as a work of art or a cartoon, and simply asking students what they **see**. The teacher can ask what is happening in the image, and then elicit the details that clue the students in to what is happening. Of course, there may be more than one thing happening. The teacher should also question the students about the message of the image, its purpose, its point of view, and its intended audience. The teacher should ask for first impressions, and then provide some background or additional information to see if it changes the way students look at or interpret the image. The conclusion of the lesson should include questions about what students learned from the exercise about the topic, themselves, and others.

Benefits

Students are exposed to multiple **images** every day. It is important for them to be able to effectively **interpret** these images. They should be able to make sense of the images and the spoken and print language that often accompany them. Learning can be enhanced with images because they allow for quicker connections to prior knowledge than verbal information. Visuals in the classroom can also be motivational, can support verbal information, and can express main points, sometimes resulting in instant recognition.

Some of the common types of images that students see every day include: bulletin boards, computer graphics, diagrams, drawings, illustrations, maps, photographs, posters, book covers, advertisements, Internet sites, multimedia presentations, puppet shows, television, videos, print cartoons, models, paintings, animation, drama or dance performances, films, and online newscasts and magazines.

Activities to Strengthen Skills

Activities at school that can be used to strengthen the **viewing skills** of students of varying ages include:

- **Picture book discussions** – Students can develop an appreciation of visual text and the language that goes with it through guided discussions of picture books that focus on the style and color of the images and other details that might capture a child's attention.
- **Gallery walks** – Students can walk around a room or hallway viewing the posted works of other students and hear presentations about the works. They can also view a display prepared by the teacher. Students are expected to take notes as they walk around, have discussions, and perhaps do a follow-up report.

- **Puppet theater and drama presentations** – Students can learn about plots, dialogue, situations, characters, and the craft of performance from viewing puppet or drama presentations, which also stimulate oral communication and strengthen listening skills. Discussions or written responses should follow performances to check for detail acquisition.

Classroom Viewing Center

A **classroom viewing center** should contain magazines, CD-ROMs, books, videos, and individual pictures (photographs or drawings). Students should have a **viewing guide** that explains expectations related to the viewing center (before, during, and after using the center). For younger students, the teacher can ask questions that guide them through the viewing rather than expecting them to read the guidelines and write responses.

- **Before** viewing, students should think about what they already know about the subject and what they want to learn from the viewing.
- **During** the viewing, students should make notes about whatever interests them or is new to them.
- **After** viewing, students could discuss or individually write down what they found to be the most interesting idea or striking image and explain why it caught their attention.

Types of Questions to Ask If Viewing Is a Narrative

A teacher should make students responsible for gaining information or insight from the **viewing**. Setting expectations increases student attention and critical thinking. As with any viewing, the students should consider what they already know about the topic and what they hope to gain by watching the narrative before viewing it. During the viewing, the students should take notes (perhaps to answer questions provided by the teacher).

After the viewing, students should be able to answer the following questions:

- What was the time period and setting of the story?
- Who were the main characters?
- How effective was the acting?
- What was the problem or goal in the story?
- How was the problem solved or the goal achieved?
- How would you summarize the story?
- What did you learn from the story?
- What did you like or dislike about the story or its presentation?
- Would you recommend this viewing to others?
- How would you rate it?

Difficulties Related to Learning by Listening

It is difficult to learn just by listening because the instruction is presented only in spoken form. Therefore, unless students take notes, there is nothing for them to review. However, an active listener will anticipate finding a **message** in an oral presentation and will listen for it, **interpreting** tone and gestures as the presentation progresses. In group discussions, students are often too busy figuring out what they will say when it is their turn to talk to concentrate on what others are saying. Therefore, they don't learn from others, but instead come away knowing only what they already knew. Students should be required to respond directly to the previous speaker before launching into their own comments. This practice will force students to listen to each other and learn that their own responses will be better because of what can be added by listening to others.

Graphic Organizers

The purpose of **graphic organizers** is to help students classify ideas and communicate more efficiently and effectively. Graphic organizers are visual outlines or templates that help students grasp key concepts and master subject matter by simplifying them down to basic points. They also help guide students through processes related to any subject area or task. Examples of processes include brainstorming, problem solving, decision making, research and project planning, and studying. Examples of graphic organizers include:

- **Reading** – These can include beginning, middle, and end graphs or event maps.
- **Science** – These can include charts that show what animals need or how to classify living things.
- **Math** – These can include horizontal bar graphs or time lines.
- **Language arts** – These can include alphabet organizers or charts showing the components of the five-paragraph essay.
- **General** – These can include KWL charts or weekly planners.

Speaking Skills Children in Elementary/Intermediate School Should Have

Children of elementary/intermediate school age should be able to:

- Speak at an appropriate volume, tone, and pace that is understandable and appropriate to the audience
- Pronounce most words accurately
- Use complete sentences
- Make eye contact
- Use appropriate gestures with speech
- Exhibit an awareness of audience and adjust content to fit the audience (adjust word choices and style to be appropriate for peers or adults)
- Ask relevant questions
- Respond appropriately when asked questions about information or an opinion, possibly also being able to provide reasons for opinions
- Speak in turn, not interrupt, and include others in conversations
- Provide a summary or report orally
- Participate in small and large group discussions and debates
- Read orally before an audience
- Conduct short interviews
- Provide directions and explanations orally, including explanations of class lessons

Viewing Skills Elementary/Intermediate School Children Should Have

Children of elementary school age should be developing or have attained the ability to understand the importance of **media** in people's lives. They should understand that television, radio, films, and the Internet have a role in everyday life. They should also be able to use media themselves (printing out material from the Internet or making an audio or video tape, for example). They should also be aware that the purpose of advertising is to sell. Children of intermediate school age should be developing or have attained the ability to **obtain and compare information** from newspapers, television, and the Internet. They should also be able to judge its **reliability and accuracy** to some extent. Children of this age should be able to tell the difference between fictional and non-fictional materials in media. They should also be able to use a variety of media, visuals, and sounds to make a presentation.

Listening Skills Children Should Develop Through Their Elementary/Intermediate School Years

Through the elementary/intermediate school years, children should develop the following listening skills:

- Follow oral instructions consistently
- Actively listen to peers and teachers
- Avoid creating distracting behavior or being distracted by the behavior of others most of the time
- Respond to listening activities and exhibit the ability to discuss, illustrate, or write about the activity and show knowledge of the content and quality of the listening activity
- Respond to listening activities and exhibit the ability to identify themes, similarities/differences, ideas, forms, and styles of activities
- Respond to a persuasive speaker and exhibit the ability to analyze and evaluate the credibility of the speaker and form an opinion describing whether they agree or disagree with the point made
- Demonstrate appropriate social behavior while part of an audience

Stages of Writing

The **three stages of writing** are drawing, dictating, and writing. During the **drawing stage**, young learners use scribbles or pictures to convey their message. When asked to "read" their drawing, children in the drawing stage will use their picture to tell a story, as if they were mimicking a book being read to them. In the **dictation stage**, learners will tell their thoughts to a literate person, who will in turn write the words for the child. During this stage, the student is aware that the written words on the page represent their thoughts and can sometimes recognize the beginning sounds of the words they are saying, including some sight words. In the third and final stage, the **writing stage**, students are able to write their own thoughts in a way that can be recognized by others. Both beginning and ending sounds are represented in the words, along with some vowels. Students in this stage also understand spacing between words and the idea of creating complete sentences.

Norm-Referenced and Criterion-Referenced Assessments

Norm-referenced assessments are used to gauge a student success by comparing his or her score to a theoretical "average" score achieved by students of the same age or grade level. With a norm-referenced assessment, a student's achievement is decided based on how much better or worse that student scored in comparison to his or her peers. In contrast, **criterion-referenced assessments** are scored based on each student's individual ability to show mastery of specific learning standards. Students are deemed successful if they are able to achieve mastery of concepts that are appropriate for their age or grade level, regardless of how their peers perform.

IRI

The **Informal Reading Inventory (IRI)**, also known as the **Qualitative Reading Inventory (QRI)** is a survey used to assess the instructional needs of individual readers. The IRI is used to determine a reader's grade-level reading, fluency, comprehension, vocabulary, oral reading accuracy, word recognition, word meaning, and reading strategies. The IRI is an ongoing assessment that should be administered several times a year starting from first grade through twelfth grade. Teachers should use the outcomes of these assessments to determine appropriate reading material for individual students and to identify and implement specific needs and strategies for individual learners or groups of learners.

Universal Screening Assessments, Diagnostic Assessments, and Progress Monitoring

Universal screening assessments are brief surveys given to all students at the beginning of each school year, which are used to determine the mastery of critical skills and concepts. These screenings should be repeated approximately three times a year to ensure that students are performing at age-appropriate levels. **Diagnostic assessments** are used to help educators make sense of universal screening assessment scores. Based on diagnostics, teachers can identify the specific educational gaps of individual students and use that information to modify and differentiate instruction. **Progress monitoring** is used to determine if the educational interventions and strategies put in place (based on the diagnostic testing) are actually working. Struggling students are often monitored more closely to ensure that educational gaps are being filled at an appropriate and sufficient rate.

Formal and Informal Assessments

Formal assessments, which include norm-based assessments, criterion-based assessments, intelligence tests, and diagnostic assessments are data driven. These types of assessments are used to determine a student's overall achievement and can be used to compare each student's abilities to his or her peers. Formal assessments are often shared with students and stakeholders to determine whether or not a student is performing at an appropriate level for his or her age or grade level. **Informal assessments**, which include running records, cloze tests, reading inventories, portfolios, and so on are not data driven. Instead, informal assessments use performance-driven tasks to guide instruction and provide informal ratings about each student's individual progress. During these assessments, each student's performance is used to monitor his or her progress and guide future instruction, often in preparation for a formal assessment.

Evaluating Appropriateness of Assessment Instrument or Practice

The two main factors that must be considered when evaluating the appropriateness of assessment instruction and practices are curriculum alignment and cultural bias. **Curriculum alignment** is the act of teaching students the concepts that they will eventually be tested on. To reach proficiency on the standards outlined by state or district mandates, teachers must continuously teach and assess the standards. Avoiding **cultural bias** ensures that all students are given access to all relevant lessons, instruction, and materials. Furthermore, avoiding cultural bias ensures that all students are given a fair opportunity to succeed on any given assessment. This includes accommodating students of certain subgroups with assessment modifications, such as additional testing time, taking the test in his or her native language, and creating types of assessments that are accessible and achievable for students of all backgrounds.

Example Evaluation of Scoring Method

A teacher is assessing a student's ability to identify the main idea of a text. The student correctly identifies the main idea but includes several spelling errors in her written response. The teacher lowers the student's grade, taking points off for misspellings. In this example, the teacher's scoring method is **inappropriate** for the concept being assessed. Although misspellings should be addressed and remedied, the question was designed to assess the student's ability to identify the main idea of the passage. It was not intended to assess the spelling abilities of the student. By lowering the student's score based on misspellings, the teacher is insinuating that the student is unable to correctly identify the main idea of a passage, which is not the case. When assessing a specific skill, it is important that teachers score students based on their ability to complete isolated skills for data to accurately drive future instruction.

Penmanship

Penmanship is a word used to describe a person's *handwriting*. The three main characteristics of penmanship are letter formation, size, and spacing. When teaching penmanship, teachers should start by helping students to correctly form each letter, using arrows to dictate the order and direction in which parts of each letter should be written. Once students have mastered each letter, teachers should focus on letter size or proportion. For example, smaller letters (like c, e, and n) should be half the size of larger letters (such as k, l, or t). Finally, proper spacing should be taught, both between letters and words. Once spacing between words has been mastered, students should begin to work on including punctuation and appropriate spacing between sentences.

Importance of Listening and Speaking Strategies

Both listening and speaking strategies are important skills for students in all areas of education. To achieve the highest success, students should be taught how to effectively **speak** and exchange dialogue in large- and small-group settings. In addition, students should be encouraged to question, retell, or reenact the words of others. Equally important, students must learn to actively **listen** and visualize the words of others so that they are able to understand the purpose of what someone else is saying. To check for listening, students should be encouraged to summarize what they have heard and complete graphic organizers outlining important concepts or facts. When given ample opportunity to both speak and listen, students are more likely to excel across all content areas.

Developing Listening and Speaking Skills with Dramatic Plays

Dramatic play is a type of play in which students are assigned specific roles and encouraged to act those roles out. In dramatic play, students are typically assigned a character but not a script. They are encouraged to take on the feelings and actions of the character they have been assigned and act as that character would act. Dramatic play is an excellent strategy for developing speaking skills as students must clearly identify and express the feelings of their characters. They must speak clearly and loud enough so that the other actors and audience can hear what they are saying. In addition, students must actively listen to what the other students in the play are saying to appropriately respond to the actions and words of the other characters in an effort to further develop the story line.

Numbers and Operations

Classifications of Numbers

- **Numbers** are the basic building blocks of mathematics. Specific features of numbers are identified by the following terms:
- **Integer** – any positive or negative whole number, including zero. Integers do not include fractions $\left(\frac{1}{3}\right)$, decimals (0.56), or mixed numbers $\left(7\frac{3}{4}\right)$.
- **Prime number** – any whole number greater than 1 that has only two factors, itself and 1; that is, a number that can be divided evenly only by 1 and itself.

- 122 -

- **Composite number** – any whole number greater than 1 that has more than two different factors; in other words, any whole number that is not a prime number. For example: The composite number 8 has the factors of 1, 2, 4, and 8.
- **Even number** – any integer that can be divided by 2 without leaving a remainder. For example: 2, 4, 6, 8, and so on.
- **Odd number** – any integer that cannot be divided evenly by 2. For example: 3, 5, 7, 9, and so on.
- **Decimal number** – any number that uses a decimal point to show the part of the number that is less than one. Example: 1.234.
- **Decimal point** – a symbol used to separate the ones place from the tenths place in decimals or dollars from cents in currency.
- **Decimal place** – the position of a number to the right of the decimal point. In the decimal 0.123, the 1 is in the first place to the right of the decimal point, indicating tenths; the 2 is in the second place, indicating hundredths; and the 3 is in the third place, indicating thousandths.
- The **decimal**, or base 10, system is a number system that uses ten different digits (0, 1, 2, 3, 4, 5, 6, 7, 8, 9). An example of a number system that uses something other than ten digits is the **binary**, or base 2, number system, used by computers, which uses only the numbers 0 and 1. It is thought that the decimal system originated because people had only their 10 fingers for counting.
- **Rational numbers** include all integers, decimals, and fractions. Any terminating or repeating decimal number is a rational number.
- **Irrational numbers** cannot be written as fractions or decimals because the number of decimal places is infinite and there is no recurring pattern of digits within the number. For example, pi (π) begins with 3.141592 and continues without terminating or repeating, so pi is an irrational number.
- **Real numbers** are the set of all rational and irrational numbers.

> **Review Video: Numbers and Their Classifications**
> Visit mometrix.com/academy and enter code: 461071

Place Value

Write the place value of each digit in the following number: 14,059.826

1: ten-thousands
4: thousands
0: hundreds
5: tens
9: ones
8: tenths
2: hundredths
6: thousandths

> **Review Video: Number Place Value**
> Visit mometrix.com/academy and enter code: 205433

Writing Numbers in Word Form

Example 1

Write each number in words.

29: twenty-nine

478: four hundred seventy-eight

9,435: nine thousand four hundred thirty-five

98,542: ninety-eight thousand five hundred forty-two

302, 876: three hundred two thousand eight hundred seventy-six

Example 2

Write each decimal in words.

0.06: six hundredths

0.6: six tenths

6.0: six

0.009: nine thousandths

0.113: one hundred thirteen thousandths

0.901: nine hundred one-thousandths

Rounding and Estimation

Rounding is reducing the digits in a number while still trying to keep the value similar. The result will be less accurate, but will be in a simpler form, and will be easier to use. Whole numbers can be rounded to the nearest ten, hundred or thousand.

Example 1

Round each number:

a. Round each number to the nearest ten: 11, 47, 118

b. Round each number to the nearest hundred: 78, 980, 248

c. Round each number to the nearest thousand: 302, 1274, 3756

Answer

a. Remember, when rounding to the nearest ten, anything ending in 5 or greater rounds up. So, 11 rounds to 10, 47 rounds to 50, and 118 rounds to 120

b. Remember, when rounding to the nearest hundred, anything ending in 50 or greater rounds up. So, 78 rounds to 100, 980 rounds to 1000, and 248 rounds to 200.

c. Remember, when rounding to the nearest thousand, anything ending in 500 or greater rounds up. So, 302 rounds to 0, 1274 rounds to 1000, and 3756 rounds to 4000.

When you are asked for the solution a problem, you may need to provide only an approximate figure or **estimation** for your answer. In this situation, you can round the numbers that will be calculated to a non-zero number. This means that the first digit in the number is not zero, and the following numbers are zeros.

Example 2

Estimate the solution to 345,932 + 96,369.

Start by rounding each number to have only one digit as a non-zero number: 345,932 becomes 300,000 and 96,369 becomes 100,000.

Then, add the rounded numbers: 300,000 + 100,000 = 400,000. So, the answer is approximately 400,000.

The exact answer would be 345,932 + 96,369 = 442,301. So, the estimate of 400,000 is a similar value to the exact answer.

Example 3

A runner's heart beats 422 times over the course of six minutes. About how many times did the runner's heart beat during each minute?

"About how many" indicates that you need to estimate the solution. In this case, look at the numbers you are given. 422 can be rounded down to 420, which is easily divisible by 6. A good estimate is 420 ÷ 6 = 70 beats per minute. More accurately, the patient's heart rate was just over 70 beats per minute since his heart actually beat a little more than 420 times in six minutes.

> **Review Video: Rounding and Estimation**
> Visit mometrix.com/academy and enter code: 126243

Measurement Conversion

When going from a larger unit to a smaller unit, multiply the number of the known amount by the **equivalent amount**. When going from a smaller unit to a larger unit, divide the number of the known amount by the equivalent amount.

Also, you can set up conversion fractions. In these fractions, one fraction is the **conversion factor**. The other fraction has the unknown amount in the numerator. So, the known value is placed in the denominator. Sometimes the second fraction has the known value from the problem in the numerator, and the unknown in the denominator. Multiply the two fractions to get the converted measurement.

Conversion Units

Metric Conversions

1000 mcg (microgram)	1 mg
1000 mg (milligram)	1 g
1000 g (gram)	1 kg
1000 kg (kilogram)	1 metric ton
1000 mL (milliliter)	1 L
1000 um (micrometer)	1 mm
1000 mm (millimeter)	1 m

100 cm (centimeter)	1 m
1000 m (meter)	1 km

U.S. and Metric Equivalents

Unit	U.S. equivalent	Metric equivalent
Inch	1 inch	2.54 centimeters
Foot	12 inches	0.305 meters
Yard	3 feet	0.914 meters
Mile	5280 feet	1.609 kilometers

Capacity Measurements

Unit	U.S. equivalent	Metric equivalent
Ounce	8 drams	29.573 milliliters
Cup	8 ounces	0.237 liter
Pint	16 ounces	0.473 liter
Quart	2 pints	0.946 liter
Gallon	4 quarts	3.785 liters

Weight Measurements

Unit	U.S. equivalent	Metric equivalent
Ounce	16 drams	28.35 grams
Pound	16 ounces	453.6 grams
Ton	2,000 pounds	907.2 kilograms

Fluid Measurements

Unit	English equivalent	Metric equivalent
1 tsp	1 fluid dram	5 milliliters
3 tsp	4 fluid drams	15 or 16 milliliters
2 tbsp	1 fluid ounce	30 milliliters
1 glass	8 fluid ounces	240 milliliters

Measurement Conversion Practice Problems

Example 1

a. Convert 1.4 meters to centimeters.

b. Convert 218 centimeters to meters.

Example 2

a. Convert 42 inches to feet.

b. Convert 15 feet to yards.

Example 3

a. How many pounds are in 15 kilograms?

b. How many pounds are in 80 ounces?

Example 4

a. How many kilometers are in 2 miles?

b. How many centimeters are in 5 feet?

Example 5

a. How many gallons are in 15.14 liters?

b. How many liters are in 8 quarts?

Example 6

a. How many grams are in 13.2 pounds?

b. How many pints are in 9 gallons?

Measurement Conversion Practice Solutions

Example 1

Write ratios with the conversion factor $\frac{100 \text{ cm}}{1 \text{ m}}$. Use proportions to convert the given units.

a. $\frac{100 \text{ cm}}{1 \text{ m}} = \frac{x \text{ cm}}{1.4 \text{ m}}$. Cross multiply to get $x = 140$. So, 1.4 m is the same as 140 cm.

b. $\frac{100 \text{ cm}}{1 \text{ m}} = \frac{218 \text{ cm}}{x \text{ m}}$. Cross multiply to get $100x = 218$, or $x = 2.18$. So, 218 cm is the same as 2.18 m.

Example 2

Write ratios with the conversion factors $\frac{12 \text{ in}}{1 \text{ ft}}$ and $\frac{3 \text{ ft}}{1 \text{ yd}}$. Use proportions to convert the given units.

a. $\frac{12 \text{ in}}{1 \text{ ft}} = \frac{42 \text{ in}}{x \text{ ft}}$. Cross multiply to get $12x = 42$, or $x = 3.5$. So, 42 inches is the same as 3.5 feet.

b. $\frac{3 \text{ ft}}{1 \text{ yd}} = \frac{15 \text{ ft}}{x \text{ yd}}$. Cross multiply to get $3x = 15$, or $x = 5$. So, 15 feet is the same as 5 yards.

Example 3

a. 15 kilograms $\times \frac{2.2 \text{ pounds}}{1 \text{ kilogram}} = 33$ pounds

b. 80 ounces $\times \frac{1 \text{ pound}}{16 \text{ ounces}} = 5$ pounds

Example 4

a. 2 miles $\times \frac{1.609 \text{ kilometers}}{1 \text{ mile}} = 3.218$ kilometers

b. 5 feet $\times \frac{12 \text{ inches}}{1 \text{ foot}} \times \frac{2.54 \text{ centimeters}}{1 \text{ inch}} = 152.4$ centimeters

Example 5

a. 15.14 liters $\times \frac{1 \text{ gallon}}{3.785 \text{ liters}} = 4$ gallons

b. 8 quarts $\times \frac{1 \text{ gallon}}{4 \text{ quarts}} \times \frac{3.785 \text{ liters}}{1 \text{ gallon}} = 7.57$ liters

Example 6

a. 13.2 pounds $\times \frac{1 \text{ kilogram}}{2.2 \text{ pounds}} \times \frac{1000 \text{ grams}}{1 \text{ kilogram}} = 6000 \text{ grams}$

b. 9 gallons $\times \frac{4 \text{ quarts}}{1 \text{ gallon}} \times \frac{2 \text{ pints}}{1 \text{ quarts}} = 72 \text{ pints}$

Operations

There are four basic mathematical operations:

Addition and Subtraction

Addition increases the value of one quantity by the value of another quantity. Example: $2 + 4 = 6$; $8 + 9 = 17$. The result is called the **sum**. With addition, the order does not matter. $4 + 2 = 2 + 4$.

Subtraction is the opposite operation to addition; it decreases the value of one quantity by the value of another quantity. Example: $6 - 4 = 2$; $17 - 8 = 9$. The result is called the **difference**. Note that with subtraction, the order does matter. $6 - 4 \neq 4 - 6$.

> **Review Video: Addition and Subtraction**
> Visit mometrix.com/academy and enter code: 521157

Multiplication and Division

Multiplication can be thought of as repeated addition. One number tells how many times to add the other number to itself. Example: 3×2 (three times two) $= 2 + 2 + 2 = 6$. With multiplication, the order does not matter. $2 \times 3 = 3 \times 2$ or $3 + 3 = 2 + 2 + 2$.

Division is the opposite operation to multiplication; one number tells us how many parts to divide the other number into. Example: $20 \div 4 = 5$; if 20 is split into 4 equal parts, each part is 5. With division, the order of the numbers does matter. $20 \div 4 \neq 4 \div 20$.

> **Review Video: Multiplication and Division**
> Visit mometrix.com/academy and enter code: 643326

Order of Operations

Order of operations is a set of rules that dictates the order in which we must perform each operation in an expression so that we will evaluate it accurately. If we have an expression that includes multiple different operations, order of operations tells us which operations to do first. The most common mnemonic for order of operations is **PEMDAS**, or "Please Excuse My Dear Aunt Sally." PEMDAS stands for parentheses, exponents, multiplication, division, addition, and subtraction. It is important to understand that multiplication and division have equal precedence, as do addition and subtraction, so those pairs of operations are simply worked from left to right in order.

Example

Evaluate the expression $5 + 20 \div 4 \times (2 + 3) - 6$ using the correct order of operations.

P: Perform the operations inside the parentheses: $(2 + 3) = 5$

E: Simplify the exponents.

The equation now looks like this: $5 + 20 \div 4 \times 5 - 6$

- 128 -

MD: Perform multiplication and division from left to right: $20 \div 4 = 5$; then $5 \times 5 = 25$

The equation now looks like this: $5 + 25 - 6$

AS: Perform addition and subtraction from left to right: $5 + 25 = 30$; then $30 - 6 = 24$

> **Review Video: Order of Operations**
> Visit mometrix.com/academy and enter code: 259675

Subtraction with Regrouping

<u>Example 1</u>

Demonstrate how to subtract 189 from 525 using regrouping.

First, set up the subtraction problem:

```
      525
  –   189
```

Notice that the numbers in the ones and tens columns of 525 are smaller than the numbers in the ones and tens columns of 189. This means you will need to use regrouping to perform subtraction.

```
      5    2    5
  –   1    8    9
```

To subtract 9 from 5 in the ones column you will need to borrow from the 2 in the tens columns:

```
      5    1    15
  –   1    8    9
                6
```

Next, to subtract 8 from 1 in the tens column you will need to borrow from the 5 in the hundreds column:

```
      4    11   15
  –   1    8    9
           3    6
```

Last, subtract the 1 from the 4 in the hundreds column:

```
      4    11   15
  –   1    8    9
      3    3    6
```

Example 2

Demonstrate how to subtract 477 from 620 using regrouping.

First, set up the subtraction problem:

```
      620
  –   477
```

Notice that the numbers in the ones and tens columns of 620 are smaller than the numbers in the ones and tens columns of 477. This means you will need to use regrouping to perform subtraction.

$$
\begin{array}{cccc}
 & 6 & 2 & 0 \\
- & 4 & 7 & 7 \\
\end{array}
$$

To subtract 7 from 0 in the ones column you will need to borrow from the 2 in the tens column.

$$
\begin{array}{cccc}
 & 6 & 1 & 10 \\
- & 4 & 7 & 7 \\
\hline
 & & & 3 \\
\end{array}
$$

Next, to subtract 7 from the 1 that's still in the tens column you will need to borrow from the 6 in the hundreds column.

$$
\begin{array}{cccc}
 & 5 & 11 & 10 \\
- & 4 & 7 & 7 \\
\hline
 & & 4 & 3 \\
\end{array}
$$

Lastly, subtract 4 from the 5 remaining in the hundreds column to get:

$$
\begin{array}{cccc}
 & 5 & 11 & 10 \\
- & 4 & 7 & 7 \\
\hline
 & 1 & 4 & 3 \\
\end{array}
$$

Real World One or Multi-Step Problems with Rational Numbers

Example 1

A woman's age is thirteen more than half of 60. How old is the woman?

"More than" indicates addition, and "of" indicates multiplication. The expression can be written as $\frac{1}{2}(60) + 13$. So, the woman's age is equal to $\frac{1}{2}(60) + 13 = 30 + 13 = 43$. The woman is 43 years old.

Example 2

A patient was given pain medicine at a dosage of 0.22 grams. The patient's dosage was then increased to 0.80 grams. By how much was the patient's dosage increased?

The first step is to determine what operation (addition, subtraction, multiplication, or division) the problem requires. Notice the keywords and phrases "by how much" and "increased." "Increased" means that you go from a smaller amount to a larger amount. This change can be found by subtracting the smaller amount from the larger amount: 0.80 grams– 0.22 grams = 0.58 grams.

Remember to line up the decimal when subtracting.

$$
\begin{array}{r}
0.80 \\
- \quad 0.22 \\
\hline
0.58 \\
\end{array}
$$

Example 3

At a hotel, $\frac{3}{4}$ of the 100 rooms are occupied today. Yesterday, $\frac{4}{5}$ of the 100 rooms were occupied. On which day were more of the rooms occupied and by how much more?

First, find the number of rooms occupied each day. To do so, multiply the fraction of rooms occupied by the number of rooms available:

$$\text{Number occupied} = \text{Fraction occupied} \times \text{Total number}$$

Today:

$$\text{Number of rooms occupied} = \frac{3}{4} \times 100 = 75$$

Today, 75 rooms are occupied.

Yesterday:

$$\text{Number of rooms occupied} = \frac{4}{5} \times 100 = 80$$

Yesterday, 80 rooms were occupied.

The difference in the number of rooms occupied is

$$80 - 75 = 5 \text{ rooms}$$

Therefore, five more rooms were occupied yesterday than today.

Review Video: Rational Numbers
Visit mometrix.com/academy and enter code: 280645

Example 4

At a school, 40% of the teachers teach English. If 20 teachers teach English, how many teachers work at the school?

To answer this problem, first think about the number of teachers that work at the school. Will it be more or less than the number of teachers who work in a specific department such as English? More teachers work at the school, so the number you find to answer this question will be greater than 20.

40% of the teachers are English teachers. "Of" indicates multiplication, and words like "is" and "are" indicate equivalence. Translating the problem into a mathematical sentence gives $40\% \times t = 20$, where t represents the total number of teachers. Solving for t gives $t = \frac{20}{40\%} = \frac{20}{0.40} = 50$. Fifty teachers work at the school.

Example 5

A patient was given blood pressure medicine at a dosage of 2 grams. The patient's dosage was then decreased to 0.45 grams. By how much was the patient's dosage decreased?

The decrease is represented by the difference between the two amounts:

$$2 \text{ grams} - 0.45 \text{ grams} = 1.55 \text{ grams}.$$

Remember to line up the decimal point before subtracting.

$$2.00$$
$$-\ \ \ \ 0.45$$
$$1.55$$

Example 6

Two weeks ago, $\frac{2}{3}$ of the 60 customers at a skate shop were male. Last week, $\frac{3}{6}$ of the 80 customers were male. During which week were there more male customers?

First, you need to find the number of male customers that were in the skate shop each week. You are given this amount in terms of fractions. To find the actual number of male customers, multiply the fraction of male customers by the number of customers in the store.

Actual number of male customers = fraction of male customers × total number of customers.

Two weeks ago: Actual number of male customers $= \frac{2}{3} \times 60$.

$$\frac{2}{3} \times \frac{60}{1} = \frac{2 \times 60}{3 \times 1} = \frac{120}{3} = 40$$

Two weeks ago, 40 of the customers were male.

Last week: Actual number of male customers $= \frac{3}{6} \times 80$.

$$\frac{3}{6} \times \frac{80}{1} = \frac{3 \times 80}{6 \times 1} = \frac{240}{6} = 40$$

Last week, 40 of the patients were customers.

The number of male customers was the same both weeks.

Example 7

Jane ate lunch at a local restaurant. She ordered a $4.99 appetizer, a $12.50 entrée, and a $1.25 soda. If she wants to tip her server 20%, how much money will she spend in all?

To find total amount, first find the sum of the items she ordered from the menu and then add 20% of this sum to the total.

In other words:

$$\$4.99 + \$12.50 + \$1.25 = \$18.74$$

Then 20% *of* $18.74 is $(20\%)(\$18.74) = (0.20)(\$18.74) = \$3.75$.

So, the total she spends is cost of the meal plus the tip or $18.74 + $3.75 = $22.49.

Another way to find this sum is to multiply 120% by the cost of the meal.

$$\$18.74(120\%) = \$18.74(1.20) = \$22.49.$$

- 132 -

Parentheses

Parentheses are used to designate which operations should be done first when there are multiple operations. Example: $4 - (2 + 1) = 1$; the parentheses tell us that we must add 2 and 1, and then subtract the sum from 4, rather than subtracting 2 from 4 and then adding 1 (this would give us an answer of 3).

> **Review Video: Mathematical Parentheses**
> Visit mometrix.com/academy and enter code: 978600

Exponents

An **exponent** is a superscript number placed next to another number at the top right. It indicates how many times the base number is to be multiplied by itself. Exponents provide a shorthand way to write what would be a longer mathematical expression. Example: $a^2 = a \times a$; $2^4 = 2 \times 2 \times 2 \times 2$. A number with an exponent of 2 is said to be "squared," while a number with an exponent of 3 is said to be "cubed." The value of a number raised to an exponent is called its power. So, 8^4 is read as "8 to the 4th power," or "8 raised to the power of 4." A negative exponent is the same as the **reciprocal** of a positive exponent. Example: $a^{-2} = \frac{1}{a^2}$.

> **Review Video: Exponents**
> Visit mometrix.com/academy and enter code: 600998

Roots

A **root**, such as a square root, is another way of writing a fractional exponent. Instead of using a superscript, roots use the radical symbol ($\sqrt{}$) to indicate the operation. A radical will have a number underneath the bar, and may sometimes have a number in the upper left: $\sqrt[n]{a}$, read as "the nth root of a." The relationship between radical notation and exponent notation can be described by this equation: $\sqrt[n]{a} = a^{\frac{1}{n}}$. The two special cases of $n = 2$ and $n = 3$ are called square roots and cube roots. If there is no number to the upper left, it is understood to be a square root ($n = 2$). Nearly all of the roots you encounter will be square roots. A square root is the same as a number raised to the one-half power. When we say that a is the square root of b ($a = \sqrt{b}$), we mean that a multiplied by itself equals b: ($a \times a = b$).

> **Review Video: Roots**
> Visit mometrix.com/academy and enter code: 795655
>
> **Review Video: Square Root and Perfect Square**
> Visit mometrix.com/academy and enter code: 648063

A **perfect square** is a number that has an integer for its square root. There are 10 perfect squares from 1 to 100: 1, 4, 9, 16, 25, 36, 49, 64, 81, 100 (the squares of integers 1 through 10).

Parentheses are used to designate which operations should be done first when there are multiple operations. Example: $4- (2 + 1) = 1$; the parentheses tell us that we must add 2 and 1, and then subtract the sum from 4, rather than subtracting 2 from 4 and then adding 1 (this would give us an answer of 3).

Absolute Value

A precursor to working with negative numbers is understanding what **absolute values** are. A number's absolute value is simply the distance away from zero a number is on the number line. The absolute value of a number is always positive and is written $|x|$.

Example
Show that $|3| = |-3|$.

The absolute value of 3, written as $|3|$, is 3 because the distance between 0 and 3 on a number line is three units. Likewise, the absolute value of –3, written as $|-3|$, is 3 because the distance between 0 and –3 on a number line is three units. So, $|3| = |-3|$.

> **Review Video: Absolute Value**
> Visit mometrix.com/academy and enter code: 314669

Operations with Positive and Negative Numbers

Addition

When adding signed numbers, if the signs are the same simply add the absolute values of the addends and apply the original sign to the sum. For example, $(+4) + (+8) = +12$ and $(-4) + (-8) = -12$. When the original signs are different, take the absolute values of the addends and subtract the smaller value from the larger value, then apply the original sign of the larger value to the difference. For instance, $(+4) + (-8) = -4$ and $(-4) + (+8) = +4$.

Subtraction

For subtracting signed numbers, change the sign of the number after the minus symbol and then follow the same rules used for addition. For example, $(+4) - (+8) = (+4) + (-8) = -4$.

Multiplication

If the signs are the same the product is positive when multiplying signed numbers. For example, $(+4) \times (+8) = +32$ and $(-4) \times (-8) = +32$. If the signs are opposite, the product is negative. For example, $(+4) \times (-8) = -32$ and $(-4) \times (+8) = -32$. When more than two factors are multiplied together, the sign of the product is determined by how many negative factors are present. If there are an odd number of negative factors then the product is negative, whereas an even number of negative factors indicates a positive product. For instance, $(+4) \times (-8) \times (-2) = +64$ and $(-4) \times (-8) \times (-2) = -64$.

Division

The rules for dividing signed numbers are similar to multiplying signed numbers. If the dividend and divisor have the same sign, the quotient is positive. If the dividend and divisor have opposite signs, the quotient is negative. For example, $(-4) \div (+8) = -0.5$.

The Number Line

A number line is a graph to see the distance between numbers. Basically, this graph shows the relationship between numbers. So, a number line may have a point for zero and may show negative numbers on the left side of the line. Also, any positive numbers are placed on the right side of the line.

<u>Example</u>

Name each point on the number line below:

Use the dashed lines on the number line to identify each point. Each dashed line between two whole numbers is $\frac{1}{4}$. The line halfway between two numbers is $\frac{1}{2}$.

> **Review Video: Negative and Positive Number Line**
> Visit mometrix.com/academy and enter code: 816439

Fractions, Decimals, and Percentages

Fractions

A **fraction** is a number that is expressed as one integer written above another integer, with a dividing line between them $\left(\frac{x}{y}\right)$. It represents the **quotient** of the two numbers "x divided by y." It can also be thought of as x out of y equal parts.

The top number of a fraction is called the **numerator**, and it represents the number of parts under consideration. The 1 in $\frac{1}{4}$ means that 1 part out of the whole is being considered in the calculation. The bottom number of a fraction is called the **denominator**, and it represents the total number of equal parts. The 4 in $\frac{1}{4}$ means that the whole consists of 4 equal parts. A fraction cannot have a denominator of zero; this is referred to as "*undefined.*"

Fractions can be manipulated, without changing the value of the fraction, by multiplying or dividing (but not adding or subtracting) both the numerator and denominator by the same number. If you divide both numbers by a common factor, you are **reducing** or simplifying the fraction. Two fractions that have the same value but are expressed differently are known as **equivalent fractions**. For example, $\frac{2}{10}, \frac{3}{15}, \frac{4}{20}$, and $\frac{5}{25}$ are all equivalent fractions. They can also all be reduced or simplified to $\frac{1}{5}$.

When two fractions are manipulated so that they have the same denominator, this is known as finding a **common denominator**. The number chosen to be that common denominator should be the least common multiple of the two original denominators. Example: $\frac{3}{4}$ and $\frac{5}{6}$; the least common multiple of 4 and 6 is 12. Manipulating to achieve the common denominator: $\frac{3}{4} = \frac{9}{12}$; $\frac{5}{6} = \frac{10}{12}$.

Proper Fractions and Mixed Numbers

A fraction whose denominator is greater than its numerator is known as a **proper fraction**, while a fraction whose numerator is greater than its denominator is known as an **improper fraction**. Proper fractions have values *less than one* and improper fractions have values *greater than one*.

A **mixed number** is a number that contains both an integer and a fraction. Any improper fraction can be rewritten as a mixed number. Example: $\frac{8}{3} = \frac{6}{3} + \frac{2}{3} = 2 + \frac{2}{3} = 2\frac{2}{3}$. Similarly, any mixed number can be rewritten as an improper fraction. Example: $1\frac{3}{5} = 1 + \frac{3}{5} = \frac{5}{5} + \frac{3}{5} = \frac{8}{5}$.

> **Review Video: Proper and Improper Fractions and Mixed Numbers**
> Visit mometrix.com/academy and enter code: 211077
>
> **Review Video: Fractions**
> Visit mometrix.com/academy and enter code: 262335

Decimals

Decimal Illustration

Use a model to represent the decimal: 0.24. Write 0.24 as a fraction.

The decimal 0.24 is twenty-four hundredths. One possible model to represent this fraction is to draw 100 pennies, since each penny is worth one-hundredth of a dollar. Draw one hundred circles to represent one hundred pennies. Shade 24 of the pennies to represent the decimal twenty-four hundredths.

To write the decimal as a fraction, write a fraction: $\frac{\text{\# shaded spaces}}{\text{\# total spaces}}$. The number of shaded spaces is 24, and the total number of spaces is 100, so as a fraction 0.24 equals $\frac{24}{100}$. This fraction can then be reduced to $\frac{6}{25}$.

> **Review Video: Decimals**
> Visit mometrix.com/academy and enter code: 837268

Percentages

Percentages can be thought of as fractions that are based on a whole of 100; that is, one whole is equal to 100%. The word percent means "per hundred." Fractions can be expressed as a percentage by finding equivalent fractions with a denomination of 100. Example: $\frac{7}{10} = \frac{70}{100} = 70\%$; $\frac{1}{4} = \frac{25}{100} = 25\%$.

To express a *percentage as a fraction*, divide the percentage number by 100 and reduce the fraction to its simplest possible terms. Example: $60\% = \frac{60}{100} = \frac{3}{5}$; $96\% = \frac{96}{100} = \frac{24}{25}$.

> **Review Video: Percentages**
> Visit mometrix.com/academy and enter code: 141911

Real World Problems with Percentages

A percentage problem can be presented three main ways: (1) Find what percentage of some number another number is. Example: What percentage of 40 is 8? (2) Find what number is some percentage of a given number. Example: What number is 20% of 40? (3) Find what number another number is a given percentage of. Example: What number is 8 20% of?

The three components in all of these cases are the same: a **whole** (W), a **part** (P), and a **percentage** (%). These are related by the equation: $P = W \times \%$. This is the form of the equation you would use to solve problems of type (2). To solve types (1) and (3), you would use these two forms:

$$\% = \frac{P}{W} \text{ and } W = \frac{P}{\%}$$

The thing that frequently makes percentage problems difficult is that they are most often also word problems, so a large part of solving them is figuring out which quantities are what. Example: In a school cafeteria, 7 students choose pizza, 9 choose hamburgers, and 4 choose tacos. Find the percentage that chooses tacos. To find the whole, you must first add all of the parts: $7 + 9 + 4 = 20$. The percentage can then be found by dividing the part by the whole ($\% = \frac{P}{W}$): $\frac{4}{20} = \frac{20}{100} = 20\%$.

Example 1
What is 30% of 120?

The word "of" indicates multiplication, so 30% of 120 is found by multiplying 30% by 120. First, change 30% to a fraction or decimal. Recall that "percent" means per hundred, so $30\% = \frac{30}{100} = 0.30$. 120 times 0.3 is 36.

> **Review Video: Finding Percentage of Number Given Whole**
> Visit mometrix.com/academy and enter code: 932623

Example 2
What is 150% of 20?

150% of 20 is found by multiplying 150% by 20. First, change 150% to a fraction or decimal. Recall that "percent" means per hundred, so $150\% = \frac{150}{100} = 1.50$. So, $(1.50)(20) = 30$. Notice that 30 is greater than the original number of 20. This makes sense because you are finding a number that is more than 100% of the original number.

Example 3

What is 14.5% of 96?

Change 14.5% to a decimal before multiplying. $0.145 \times 96 = 13.92$. Notice that 13.92 is much smaller than the original number of 96. This makes sense because you are finding a small percentage of the original number.

Example 4

According to a survey, about 82% of engineers were highly satisfied with their job. If 145 engineers were surveyed, how many reported that they were highly satisfied?

82% of $145 = 0.82 \times 145 = 118.9$. Because you can't have 0.9 of a person, we must round up to say that 119 engineers reported that they were highly satisfied with their jobs.

Example 5

On Monday, Lucy spent 5 hours observing sales, 3 hours working on advertising, and 4 hours doing paperwork. On Tuesday, she spent 4 hours observing sales, 6 hours working on advertising, and 2 hours doing paperwork. What was the percent change for time spent on each task between the two days?

The three tasks are observing sales, working on advertising, and doing paperwork. To find the amount of change, compare the first amount with the second amount for each task. Then, write this difference as a percentage compared to the initial amount.

Amount of change for observing sales:

$$5 \text{ hours} - 4 \text{ hours} = 1 \text{ hour}$$

The percent of change is

$$\frac{\text{amount of change}}{\text{original amount}} \times 100\%. \frac{1 \text{ hour}}{5 \text{ hours}} \times 100\% = 20\%.$$

Lucy spent 20% less time observing sales on Tuesday than she did on Monday.

Amount of change for working on advertising:

$$6 \text{ hours} - 3 \text{ hours} = 3 \text{ hours}$$

The percent of change is

$$\frac{\text{amount of change}}{\text{original amount}} \times 100\%. \frac{3 \text{ hours}}{3 \text{ hours}} \times 100\% = 100\%.$$

Lucy spent 100% more time (or twice as much time) working on advertising on Tuesday than she did on Monday.

Amount of change for doing paperwork:

$$4 \text{ hours} - 2 \text{ hours} = 2 \text{ hours}$$

The percent of change is

- 138 -

$$\frac{\text{amount of change}}{\text{original amount}} \times 100\%. \frac{2 \text{ hours}}{4 \text{ hours}} \times 100\% = 50\%.$$

Lucy spent 50% less time (or half as much time) working on paperwork on Tuesday than she did on Monday.

Example 6

A patient was given 40 mg of a certain medicine. Later, the patient's dosage was increased to 45 mg. What was the percent increase in his medication?

To find the percent increase, first compare the original and increased amounts. The original amount was 40 mg, and the increased amount is 45 mg, so the dosage of medication was increased by 5 mg (45– 40 = 5). Note, however, that the question asks not by how much the dosage increased but by what percentage it increased. Percent increase $= \frac{\text{new amount} - \text{original amount}}{\text{original amount}} \times 100\%$.

So, $\frac{45 \text{ mg} - 40 \text{ mg}}{40 \text{ mg}} \times 100\% = \frac{5}{40} \times 100\% = 0.125 \times 100\% = 12.5\%$

The percent increase is 12.5%.

Example 7

A patient was given 100 mg of a certain medicine. The patient's dosage was later decreased to 88 mg. What was the percent decrease?

The medication was decreased by 12 mg:

$$(100 \text{ mg} - 88 \text{ mg} = 12 \text{ mg})$$

To find by what percent the medication was decreased, this change must be written as a percentage when compared to the original amount.

In other words, $\frac{\text{new amount} - \text{original amount}}{\text{original amount}} \times 100\% = \text{percent change}$

So $\frac{12 \text{ mg}}{100 \text{ mg}} \times 100\% = 0.12 \times 100\% = 12\%$.

The percent decrease is 12%.

Example 8

A barista used 125 units of coffee grounds to make a liter of coffee. The barista later reduced the amount of coffee to 100 units. By what percentage was the amount of coffee grounds reduced?

In this problem you must determine which information is necessary to answer the question. The question asks by what percentage the coffee grounds were reduced. Find the two amounts and perform subtraction to find their difference. The first pot of coffee used 125 units. The second time, the barista used 100 units. Therefore, the difference is 125 units − 100 units = 25 units. The percentage reduction can then be calculated as:

$$\frac{\text{change}}{\text{original}} = \frac{25}{125} = \frac{1}{5} = 20\%$$

Example 9

In a performance review, an employee received a score of 70 for efficiency and 90 for meeting project deadlines. Six months later, the employee received a score of 65 for efficiency and 96 for meeting project deadlines. What was the percent change for each score on the performance review?

To find the percent change, compare the first amount with the second amount for each score; then, write this difference as a percentage of the initial amount.

Percent change for efficiency score:

$$70 - 65 = 5; \quad \frac{5}{70} \approx 7.1\%$$

The employee's efficiency decreased by about 7.1%.

Percent change for meeting project deadlines score:

$$96 - 90 = 6; \quad \frac{6}{90} \approx 6.7\%$$

The employee increased his ability to meet project deadlines by about 6.7%.

Simplify

Example 1

How to simplify:

$$\frac{\frac{2}{5}}{\frac{4}{7}}$$

Dividing a fraction by a fraction may appear tricky, but it's not if you write out your steps carefully. Follow these steps to divide a fraction by a fraction.

Step 1: Rewrite the problem as a multiplication problem. Dividing by a fraction is the same as multiplying by its **reciprocal**, also known as its **multiplicative inverse**. The product of a number and its reciprocal is 1. Because $\frac{4}{7}$ times $\frac{7}{4}$ is 1, these numbers are reciprocals. Note that reciprocals can be found by simply interchanging the numerators and denominators. So, rewriting the problem as a multiplication problem gives $\frac{2}{5} \times \frac{7}{4}$.

Step 2: Perform multiplication of the fractions by multiplying the numerators by each other and the denominators by each other. In other words, multiply across the top and then multiply across the bottom.

$$\frac{2}{5} \times \frac{7}{4} = \frac{2 \times 7}{5 \times 4} = \frac{14}{20}$$

Step 3: Make sure the fraction is reduced to lowest terms. Both 14 and 20 can be divided by 2.

$$\frac{14}{20} = \frac{14 \div 2}{20 \div 2} = \frac{7}{10}$$

The answer is $\frac{7}{10}$.

Example 2

How to simplify:

$$\frac{1}{4} + \frac{3}{6}$$

Fractions with common denominators can be easily added or subtracted. Recall that the denominator is the bottom number in the fraction and that the numerator is the top number in the fraction.

The denominators of $\frac{1}{4}$ and $\frac{3}{6}$ are 4 and 6, respectively. The lowest common denominator of 4 and 6 is 12 because 12 is the least common multiple of 4 (multiples 4, 8, 12, 16, ...) and 6 (multiples 6, 12, 18, 24, ...). Convert each fraction to its equivalent with the newly found common denominator of 12.

$$\frac{1 \times 3}{4 \times 3} = \frac{3}{12}; \frac{3 \times 2}{6 \times 2} = \frac{6}{12}$$

Now that the fractions have the same denominator, you can add them.

$$\frac{3}{12} + \frac{6}{12} = \frac{9}{12}$$

Be sure to write your answer in lowest terms. Both 9 and 12 can be divided by 3, so the answer is $\frac{3}{4}$.

Example 3

How to simplify:

$$\frac{7}{8} - \frac{8}{16}$$

Fractions with common denominators can be easily added or subtracted. Recall that the denominator is the bottom number in the fraction and that the numerator is the top number in the fraction.

The denominators of $\frac{7}{8}$ and $\frac{8}{16}$ are 8 and 16, respectively. The lowest common denominator of 8 and 16 is 16 because 16 is the least common multiple of 8 (multiples 8, 16, 24 ...) and 16 (multiples 16, 32, 48, ...). Convert each fraction to its equivalent with the newly found common denominator of 16.

$$\frac{7 \times 2}{8 \times 2} = \frac{14}{16}; \frac{8 \times 1}{16 \times 1} = \frac{8}{16}$$

Now that the fractions have the same denominator, you can subtract them.

$$\frac{14}{16} - \frac{8}{16} = \frac{6}{16}$$

Be sure to write your answer in lowest terms. Both 6 and 16 can be divided by 2, so the answer is $\frac{3}{8}$.

Example 4

How to simplify:

$$\frac{1}{2} + \left(3\left(\frac{3}{4}\right) - 2\right) + 4$$

When simplifying expressions, first perform operations within groups. Within the set of parentheses are multiplication and subtraction operations. Perform the multiplication first to get $\frac{1}{2} + \left(\frac{9}{4} - 2\right) + 4$. Then, subtract two to obtain $\frac{1}{2} + \frac{1}{4} + 4$. Finally, perform addition from left to right:

$$\frac{1}{2} + \frac{1}{4} + 4 = \frac{2}{4} + \frac{1}{4} + \frac{16}{4} = \frac{19}{4}$$

Example 5

How to simplify: $0.22 + 0.5 - (5.5 + 3.3 \div 3)$

First, evaluate the terms in the parentheses $(5.5 + 3.3 \div 3)$ using order of operations. $3.3 \div 3 = 1.1$, and $5.5 + 1.1 = 6.6$.

Next, rewrite the problem: $0.22 + 0.5 - 6.6$.

Finally, add and subtract from left to right: $0.22 + 0.5 = 0.72$; $0.72 - 6.6 = -5.88$. The answer is -5.88.

Example 6

How to simplify:

$$\frac{3}{2} + (4(0.5) - 0.75) + 2$$

First, simplify within the parentheses:

$$\frac{3}{2} + (2 - 0.75) + 2 =$$

$$\frac{3}{2} + 1.25 + 2$$

Finally, change the fraction to a decimal and perform addition from left to right:

$$1.5 + 1.25 + 2 = 4.75$$

Example 7

How to simplify: $1.45 + 1.5 + (6 - 9 \div 2) + 45$

First, evaluate the terms in the parentheses using proper order of operations.

$$1.45 + 1.5 + (6 - 4.5) + 45$$

$$1.45 + 1.5 + 1.5 + 45$$

Finally, add from left to right.

$$1.45 + 1.5 + 1.5 + 45 = 49.45$$

Converting Percentages, Fractions, and Decimals

Converting decimals to percentages and percentages to decimals is as simple as moving the decimal point. To *convert from a decimal to a percentage*, move the decimal point **two places to the right**. To *convert from a percentage to a decimal*, move it **two places to the left**. Example: $0.23 = 23\%$; $5.34 = 534\%$; $0.007 = 0.7\%$; $700\%\ 7.00$; $86\% = 0.86$; $0.15\% = 0.0015$.

It may be helpful to remember that the percentage number will always be larger than the equivalent decimal number.

> **Review Video: <u>Converting Decimals to Fractions and Percentages</u>**
> Visit mometrix.com/academy and enter code: 986765

Example 1

Convert 15% to both a fraction and a decimal.

First, write the percentage over 100 because percent means "per one hundred." So, 15% can be written as $\frac{15}{100}$. Fractions should be written in the simplest form, which means that the numbers in the numerator and denominator should be reduced if possible. Both 15 and 100 can be divided by 5:

$$\frac{15 \div 5}{100 \div 5} = \frac{3}{20}$$

As before, write the percentage over 100 because percent means "per one hundred." So, 15% can be written as $\frac{15}{100}$. Dividing a number by a power of ten (10, 100, 1000, etc.) is the same as moving the decimal point to the left by the same number of spaces that there are zeros in the divisor. Since 100 has 2 zeros, move the decimal point two places to the left:

$$15\% = 0.15$$

In other words, when converting from a percentage to a decimal, drop the percent sign and move the decimal point two places to the left.

Example 2

Write 24.36% as a fraction and then as a decimal. Explain how you made these conversions.

24.36% written as a fraction is $\frac{24.36}{100}$, or $\frac{2436}{10,000}$, which reduces to $\frac{609}{2500}$. 24.36% written as a decimal is 0.2436. Recall that dividing by 100 moves the decimal two places to the left.

> **Review Video: <u>Converting Percentages to Decimals and Fractions</u>**
> Visit mometrix.com/academy and enter code: 287297

Example 3

Convert $\frac{4}{5}$ to a decimal and to a percentage.

To convert a fraction to a decimal, simply divide the numerator by the denominator in the fraction. The numerator is the top number in the fraction and the denominator is the bottom number in a fraction. So $\frac{4}{5} = 4 \div 5 = 0.80 = 0.8$.

Percent means "per hundred." $\frac{4 \times 20}{5 \times 20} = \frac{80}{100} = 80\%$.

Example 4

Convert $3\frac{2}{5}$ to a decimal and to a percentage.

The mixed number $3\frac{2}{5}$ has a whole number and a fractional part. The fractional part $\frac{2}{5}$ can be written as a decimal by dividing 5 into 2, which gives 0.4. Adding the whole to the part gives 3.4. Alternatively, note that $3\frac{2}{5} = 3\frac{4}{10} = 3.4$

To change a decimal to a percentage, multiply it by 100.

$3.4(100) = 340\%$. Notice that this percentage is greater than 100%. This makes sense because the original mixed number $3\frac{2}{5}$ is greater than 1.

> **Review Video: Converting Fractions to Percentages and Decimals**
> Visit mometrix.com/academy and enter code: 306233

Scientific Notation

Scientific notation is a way of writing large numbers in a shorter form. The form $a \times 10^n$ is used in scientific notation, where a is greater than or equal to 1, but less than 10, and n is the number of places the decimal must move to get from the original number to a. Example: The number 230,400,000 is cumbersome to write. To write the value in scientific notation, place a decimal point between the first and second numbers, and include all digits through the last non-zero digit ($a = 2.304$). To find the appropriate power of 10, count the number of places the decimal point had to move ($n = 8$). The number is positive if the decimal moved to the left, and negative if it moved to the right. We can then write 230,400,000 as 2.304×10^8. If we look instead at the number 0.00002304, we have the same value for a, but this time the decimal moved 5 places to the right ($n = -5$). Thus, 0.00002304 can be written as 2.304×10^{-5}. Using this notation makes it simple to compare very large or very small numbers. By comparing exponents, it is easy to see that 3.28×10^4 is smaller than 1.51×10^5, because 4 is less than 5.

> **Review Video: Scientific Notation**
> Visit mometrix.com/academy and enter code: 976454

Operations with Decimals

Adding and Subtracting Decimals

When adding and subtracting decimals, the decimal points must always be aligned. Adding decimals is just like adding regular whole numbers. Example: $4.5 + 2 = 6.5$.

If the problem-solver does not properly align the decimal points, an incorrect answer of 4.7 may result. An easy way to add decimals is to align all of the decimal points in a vertical column visually.

This will allow one to see exactly where the decimal should be placed in the final answer. Begin adding from right to left. Add each column in turn, making sure to carry the number to the left if a column adds up to more than 9. The same rules apply to the subtraction of decimals.

Multiplying Decimals

A simple multiplication problem has two components: a **multiplicand** and a **multiplier**. When multiplying decimals, work as though the numbers were whole rather than decimals. Once the final product is calculated, count the number of places to the right of the decimal in both the multiplicand and the multiplier. Then, count that number of places from the right of the product and place the decimal in that position.

For example, 12.3×2.56 has three places to the right of the respective decimals. Multiply 123×256 to get 31488. Now, beginning on the right, count three places to the left and insert the decimal. The final product will be 31.488.

Dividing Decimals

Every division problem has a **divisor** and a **dividend**. The dividend is the number that is being divided. In the problem $14 \div 7$, 14 is the dividend and 7 is the divisor. In a division problem with decimals, the divisor must be converted into a whole number. Begin by moving the decimal in the divisor to the right until a whole number is created. Next, move the decimal in the dividend the same number of spaces to the right. For example, 4.9 into 24.5 would become 49 into 245. The decimal was moved one space to the right to create a whole number in the divisor, and then the same was done for the dividend. Once the whole numbers are created, the problem is carried out normally: $245 \div 49 = 5$.

Operations with Fractions

Adding and Subtracting Fractions

If two fractions have a common denominator, they can be added or subtracted simply by adding or subtracting the two numerators and retaining the same denominator. Example: $\frac{1}{2} + \frac{1}{4} = \frac{2}{4} + \frac{1}{4} = \frac{3}{4}$. If the two fractions do not already have the same denominator, one or both of them must be manipulated to achieve a common denominator before they can be added or subtracted.

Multiplying Fractions

Two fractions can be multiplied by multiplying the two numerators to find the new numerator and the two denominators to find the new denominator. Example: $\frac{1}{3} \times \frac{2}{3} = \frac{1 \times 2}{3 \times 3} = \frac{2}{9}$.

> **Review Video: Multiplying Fractions**
> Visit mometrix.com/academy and enter code: 638849

Dividing Fractions

Two fractions can be divided by flipping the numerator and denominator of the second fraction and then proceeding as though it were a multiplication. Example: $\frac{2}{3} \div \frac{3}{4} = \frac{2}{3} \times \frac{4}{3} = \frac{8}{9}$.

> **Review Video: Dividing Fractions**
> Visit mometrix.com/academy and enter code: 300874

Rational Numbers from Least to Greatest

Example

Order the following rational numbers from least to greatest: 0.55, 17%, $\sqrt{25}$, $\frac{64}{4}, \frac{25}{50}$, 3.

Recall that the term **rational** simply means that the number can be expressed as a ratio or fraction. The set of rational numbers includes integers and decimals. Notice that each of the numbers in the problem can be written as a decimal or integer:

$$17\% = 0.1717$$
$$\sqrt{25} = 5$$
$$\frac{64}{4} = 16$$
$$\frac{25}{50} = \frac{1}{2} = 0.5$$

So, the answer is 17%, $\frac{25}{50}$, 0.55, 3, $\sqrt{25}$, $\frac{64}{4}$.

Rational Numbers from Greatest to Least

Example

Order the following rational numbers from greatest to least: 0.3, 27%, $\sqrt{100}$, $\frac{72}{9}, \frac{1}{9}$, 4.5

Recall that the term **rational** simply means that the number can be expressed as a ratio or fraction. The set of rational numbers includes integers and decimals. Notice that each of the numbers in the problem can be written as a decimal or integer:

$$27\% = 0.27$$
$$\sqrt{100} = 10$$
$$\frac{72}{9} = 8$$
$$\frac{1}{9} \approx 0.11$$

So, the answer is $\sqrt{100}, \frac{72}{9}, 4.5, 0.3, 27\%, \frac{1}{9}$.

Common Denominators with Fractions

When two fractions are manipulated so that they have the same denominator, this is known as finding a **common denominator**. The number chosen to be that common denominator should be the **least common multiple** of the two original denominators. Example: $\frac{3}{4}$ and $\frac{5}{6}$; the least common multiple of 4 and 6 is 12. Manipulating to achieve the common denominator: $\frac{3}{4} = \frac{9}{12}$; $\frac{5}{6} = \frac{10}{12}$.

Factors and Greatest Common Factor

Factors are numbers that are multiplied together to obtain a **product**. For example, in the equation $2 \times 3 = 6$, the numbers 2 and 3 are factors. A **prime number** has only two factors (1 and itself), but other numbers can have many factors.

A **common factor** is a number that divides exactly into two or more other numbers. For example, the factors of 12 are 1, 2, 3, 4, 6, and 12, while the factors of 15 are 1, 3, 5, and 15. The common factors of 12 and 15 are 1 and 3.

A **prime factor** is also a prime number. Therefore, the prime factors of 12 are 2 and 3. For 15, the prime factors are 3 and 5.

The **greatest common factor** (GCF) is the largest number that is a factor of two or more numbers. For example, the factors of 15 are 1, 3, 5, and 15; the factors of 35 are 1, 5, 7, and 35. Therefore, the greatest common factor of 15 and 35 is 5.

Multiples and Least Common Multiple

The least common multiple (**LCM**) is the smallest number that is a multiple of two or more numbers. For example, the multiples of 3 include 3, 6, 9, 12, 15, etc.; the multiples of 5 include 5, 10, 15, 20, etc. Therefore, the least common multiple of 3 and 5 is 15.

Pre-Algebra

Proportions and Ratios

<u>Proportions</u>

A proportion is a relationship between two quantities that dictates how one changes when the other changes. A **direct proportion** describes a relationship in which a quantity increases by a set amount for every increase in the other quantity, or decreases by that same amount for every decrease in the other quantity. Example: Assuming a constant driving speed, the time required for a car trip increases as the distance of the trip increases. The distance to be traveled and the time required to travel are directly proportional.

Inverse proportion is a relationship in which an increase in one quantity is accompanied by a decrease in the other, or vice versa. Example: the time required for a car trip decreases as the speed increases, and increases as the speed decreases, so the time required is inversely proportional to the speed of the car.

> **Review Video: <u>Proportions</u>**
> Visit mometrix.com/academy and enter code: 505355

<u>Ratios</u>

A **ratio** is a comparison of two quantities in a particular order. Example: If there are 14 computers in a lab, and the class has 20 students, there is a student to computer ratio of 20 to 14, commonly written as 20:14. Ratios are normally reduced to their smallest whole number representation, so 20:14 would be reduced to 10:7 by dividing both sides by 2.

> **Review Video: <u>Ratios</u>**
> Visit mometrix.com/academy and enter code: 996914

Real World Problems with Proportions and Ratios

<u>Example 1</u>

A child was given 100 mg of chocolate every two hours. How much chocolate will the child receive in five hours?

Using proportional reasoning, since five hours is two and a half times as long as two hours, the child will receive two and a half times as much chocolate, 2.5×100 mg $= 250$ mg, in five hours.

To compute the answer methodically, first write the amount of chocolate per 2 hours as a ratio.

$$\frac{100 \text{ mg}}{2 \text{ hours}}$$

Next create a proportion to relate the different time increments of 2 hours and 5 hours.

$\frac{100 \text{ mg}}{2 \text{ hours}} = \frac{x \text{ mg}}{5 \text{ hours}}$, where x is the amount of chocolate the child receives in five hours. Make sure to keep the same units in either the numerator or denominator. In this case the numerator units must be mg for both ratios and the denominator units must be hours for both ratios.

Use cross multiplication and division to solve for x:

$$\frac{100 \text{ mg}}{2 \text{ hours}} = \frac{x \text{ mg}}{5 \text{ hours}}$$
$$100(5) = 2(x)$$
$$500 = 2x$$
$$500 \div 2 = 2x \div 2$$
$$250 = x$$

Therefore, the child receives 250 mg every five hours.

> **Review Video: Proportions in the Real World**
> Visit mometrix.com/academy and enter code: 221143

Example 2

At a school, for every 20 female students there are 15 male students. This same student ratio happens to exist at another school. If there are 100 female students at the second school, how many male students are there?

One way to find the number of male students is to set up and solve a proportion.

$$\frac{\text{number of female students}}{\text{number of male students}} = \frac{20}{15} = \frac{100}{\text{number of male students}}$$

Represent the unknown number of male students as the variable x.

$$\frac{20}{15} = \frac{100}{x}$$

Follow these steps to solve for x:

1. Cross multiply. $20 \times x = 15 \times 100$.

$$20x = 1500$$

2. Divide each side of the equation by 20.

$$x = 75$$

Or, notice that: $\frac{20 \times 5}{15 \times 5} = \frac{100}{75}$, so $x = 75$.

Example 3

In a hospital emergency room, there are 4 nurses for every 12 patients. What is the ratio of nurses to patients? If the nurse-to-patient ratio remains constant, how many nurses must be present to care for 24 patients?

The ratio of nurses to patients can be written as 4 to 12, 4:12, or $\frac{4}{12}$. Because four and twelve have a common factor of four, the ratio should be reduced to 1:3, which means that there is one nurse present for every three patients. If this ratio remains constant, there must be eight nurses present to care for 24 patients.

Example 4

In a bank, the banker-to-customer ratio is 1:2. If seven bankers are on duty, how many customers are currently in the bank?

Use proportional reasoning or set up a proportion to solve. Because there are twice as many customers as bankers, there must be fourteen customers when seven bankers are on duty. Setting up and solving a proportion gives the same result:

$$\frac{\text{number of bankers}}{\text{number of customers}} = \frac{1}{2} = \frac{7}{\text{number of customers}}$$

Represent the unknown number of patients as the variable x.

$$\frac{1}{2} = \frac{7}{x}$$

To solve for x, cross multiply:

$1 \times x = 7 \times 2$, so $x = 14$.

Constant of Proportionality

When two quantities have a proportional relationship, there exists a **constant of proportionality** between the quantities; the product of this constant and one of the quantities is equal to the other quantity. For example, if one lemon costs $0.25, two lemons cost $0.50, and three lemons cost $0.75, there is a proportional relationship between the total cost of lemons and the number of lemons purchased. The constant of proportionality is the **unit price**, namely $0.25/lemon. Notice that the total price of lemons, t, can be found by multiplying the unit price of lemons, p, and the number of lemons, n: $t = pn$.

Slope

On a graph with two points, (x_1, y_1) and (x_2, y_2), the **slope** is found with the formula $m = \frac{y_2 - y_1}{x_2 - x_1}$; where $x_1 \neq x_2$ and m stands for slope. If the value of the slope is **positive**, the line has an *upward direction* from left to right. If the value of the slope is **negative**, the line has a *downward direction* from left to right.

Unit Rate as the Slope

A new book goes on sale in bookstores and online stores. In the first month, 5,000 copies of the book are sold. Over time, the book continues to grow in popularity. The data for the number of copies sold is in the table below.

# of Months on Sale	1	2	3	4	5
# of Copies Sold (In Thousands)	5	10	15	20	25

So, the number of copies that are sold and the time that the book is on sale is a proportional relationship. In this example, an equation can be used to show the data: $y = 5x$, where x is the number of months that the book is on sale. Also, y is the number of copies sold. So, the slope is $\frac{\text{rise}}{\text{run}} = \frac{5}{1}$. This can be reduced to 5.

Work/Unit Rate

Unit rate expresses a quantity of one thing in terms of one unit of another. For example, if you travel 30 miles every two hours, a unit rate expresses this comparison in terms of one hour: in one hour you travel 15 miles, so your unit rate is 15 miles per hour. Other examples are how much one ounce of food costs (price per ounce) or figuring out how much one egg costs out of the dozen (price per 1 egg, instead of price per 12 eggs). The denominator of a unit rate is always 1. Unit rates are used to compare different situations to solve problems. For example, to make sure you get the best deal when deciding which kind of soda to buy, you can find the unit rate of each. If Soda #1 costs $1.50 for a 1-liter bottle, and soda #2 costs $2.75 for a 2-liter bottle, it would be a better deal to buy Soda #2, because its unit rate is only $1.375 per 1-liter, which is cheaper than Soda #1. Unit rates can also help determine the length of time a given event will take. For example, if you can paint 2 rooms in 4.5 hours, you can determine how long it will take you to paint 5 rooms by solving for the unit rate per room and then multiplying that by 5.

Example 1

Janice made $40 during the first 5 hours she spent babysitting. She will continue to earn money at this rate until she finishes babysitting in 3 more hours. Find how much money Janice earned babysitting and how much she earns per hour.

Janice will earn $64 babysitting in her 8 total hours (adding the first 5 hours to the remaining 3 gives the 8 hour total). This can be found by setting up a proportion comparing money earned to babysitting hours. Since she earns $40 for 5 hours and since the rate is constant, she will earn a proportional amount in 8 hours: $\frac{40}{5} = \frac{x}{8}$. Cross multiplying will yield $5x = 320$, and division by 5 shows that $x = 64$.

Janice earns $8 per hour. This can be found by taking her total amount earned, $64, and dividing it by the total number of hours worked, 8. Since $\frac{64}{8} = 8$, Janice makes $8 in one hour. This can also be found by finding the unit rate, money earned per hour: $\frac{64}{8} = \frac{x}{1}$. Since cross multiplying yields $8x = 64$, and division by 8 shows that $x = 8$, Janice earns $8 per hour.

Example 2

The McDonalds are taking a family road trip, driving 300 miles to their cabin. It took them 2 hours to drive the first 120 miles. They will drive at the same speed all the way to their cabin. Find the speed at which the McDonalds are driving and how much longer it will take them to get to their cabin.

The McDonalds are driving 60 miles per hour. This can be found by setting up a proportion to find the unit rate, the number of miles they drive per one hour: $\frac{120}{2} = \frac{x}{1}$. Cross multiplying yields $2x = 120$ and division by 2 shows that $x = 60$.

Since the McDonalds will drive this same speed, it will take them another 3 hours to get to their cabin. This can be found by first finding how many miles the McDonalds have left to drive, which is $300 - 120 = 180$. The McDonalds are driving at 60 miles per hour, so a proportion can be set up to determine how many hours it will take them to drive 180 miles: $\frac{180}{x} = \frac{60}{1}$. Cross multiplying yields $60x = 180$, and division by 60 shows that $x = 3$. This can also be found by using the formula $D = r \times t$ (or Distance = rate $\times$ time), where $180 = 60 \times t$, and division by 60 shows that $t = 3$.

Example 3

It takes Andy 10 minutes to read 6 pages of his book. He has already read 150 pages in his book that is 210 pages long. Find how long it takes Andy to read 1 page and also find how long it will take him to finish his book if he continues to read at the same speed.

It takes Andy 1 minute and 40 seconds to read one page in his book. This can be found by finding the unit rate per one page, by dividing the total time it takes him to read 6 pages by 6. Since it takes him 10 minutes to read 6 pages, $\frac{10}{6} = 1\frac{2}{3}$ minutes, which is 1 minute and 40 seconds.

It will take Andy another 100 minutes, or 1 hour and 40 minutes to finish his book. This can be found by first figuring out how many pages Andy has left to read, which is $210 - 150 = 60$. Since it is now known that it takes him $1\frac{2}{3}$ minutes to read each page, then that rate must be multiplied by however many pages he has left to read (60) to find the time he'll need: $60 \times 1\frac{2}{3} = 100$, so it will take him 100 minutes, or 1 hour and 40 minutes, to read the rest of his book.

Algebra

Function and Relation

When expressing functional relationships, the **variables** x and y are typically used. These values are often written as the **coordinates** (x, y). The x-value is the independent variable and the y-value is the dependent variable. A **relation** is a set of data in which there is not a unique y-value for each x-value in the dataset. This means that there can be two of the same x-values assigned to different y-values. A relation is simply a relationship between the x and y-values in each coordinate but does not apply to the relationship between the values of x and y in the data set. A **function** is a relation where one quantity depends on the other. For example, the amount of money that you make depends on the number of hours that you work. In a function, each x-value in the data set has one unique y-value because the y-value depends on the x-value.

> **Review Video: Definition of a Function**
> Visit mometrix.com/academy and enter code: 784611

Determining a Function

You can determine whether an equation is a **function** by substituting different values into the equation for x. These values are called input values. All possible input values are referred to as the **domain**. The result of substituting these values into the equation is called the output, or **range**. You can display and organize these numbers in a data table. A **data table** contains the values for x and y, which you can also list as coordinates. In order for a function to exist, the table cannot contain any repeating x-values that correspond with different y-values. If each x-coordinate has a unique y-coordinate, the table contains a function. However, there can be repeating y-values that correspond with different x-values. An example of this is when the function contains an exponent. For example, if $x^2 = y$, $2^2 = 4$, and $(-2)^2 = 4$.

Equation Using Independent and Dependent Variables

To write an equation, you must first assign **variables** to the unknown values in the problem and then translate the words and phrases into expressions containing numbers and symbols. For example, if Ray earns $10 an hour, this can be represented by the expression $10x$, where x is equal to the number of hours that Ray works. The value of x represents the number of hours because it is the **independent variable**, or the amount that you can choose and can manipulate. To find out how much money he earns in y hours, you would write the equation $10x = y$. The variable y is the **dependent variable** because it depends on x and cannot be manipulated. Once you have the equation for the function, you can choose any number of hours to find the corresponding amount that he earns. For example, if you want to know how much he would earn working 36 hours, you would substitute 36 in for x and multiply to find that he would earn $360.

Writing a Function Rule Using a Table

If given a set of data, place the corresponding x and y-values into a table and analyze the relationship between them. Consider what you can do to each x-value to obtain the corresponding y-value. Try adding or subtracting different numbers to and from x and then try multiplying or dividing different numbers to and from x. If none of these **operations** give you the y-value, try combining the operations. Once you find a rule that works for one pair, make sure to try it with each additional set of ordered pairs in the table. If the same operation or combination of operations satisfies each set of coordinates, then the table contains a function. The rule is then used to write the equation of the function in "$y =$" form.

Equations and Graphing

When algebraic functions and equations are shown graphically, they are usually shown on a *Cartesian coordinate plane*. The Cartesian coordinate plane consists of two number lines placed perpendicular to each other, and intersecting at the zero point, also known as the origin. The horizontal number line is known as the x-axis, with positive values to the right of the origin, and negative values to the left of the origin. The vertical number line is known as the y-axis, with positive values above the origin, and negative values below the origin. Any point on the plane can be identified by an ordered pair in the form (x, y), called coordinates. The x-value of the coordinate is called the abscissa, and the *y*-value of the coordinate is called the ordinate. The two number lines divide the plane into *four quadrants*: I, II, III, and IV.

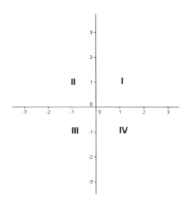

Before learning the different forms in which equations can be written, it is important to understand some terminology. A ratio of the change in the vertical distance to the change in horizontal distance is called the *slope*. On a graph with two points, (x_1, y_1) and (x_2, y_2), the slope is represented by the formula $s = \frac{y_2 - y_1}{x_2 - x_1}$; $x_1 \neq x_2$. If the value of the slope is positive, the line slopes upward from left to right. If the value of the slope is negative, the line slopes downward from left to right. If the *y*-coordinates are the same for both points, the slope is 0 and the line is a *horizontal line*. If the *x*-coordinates are the same for both points, there is no slope and the line is a *vertical line*. Two or more lines that have equal slopes are *parallel lines*. *perpendicular lines* have slopes that are negative reciprocals of each other, such as $\frac{a}{b}$ and $\frac{-b}{a}$.

> **Review Video: Graphs of Functions**
> Visit mometrix.com/academy and enter code: 492785

Equations are made up of monomials and polynomials. A *monomial* is a single variable or product of constants and variables, such as x, $2x$, or $\frac{2}{x}$. There will never be addition or subtraction symbols in a monomial. Like monomials have like variables, but they may have different coefficients. *Polynomials* are algebraic expressions which use addition and subtraction to combine two or more monomials. Two terms make a binomial; three terms make a trinomial; etc.. The d*egree of a monomial* is the sum of the exponents of the variables. The *degree of a polynomial* is the highest degree of any individual term.

As mentioned previously, equations can be written many ways. Below is a list of the many forms equations can take.

- Standard Form: $Ax + By = C$; the slope is $\frac{-A}{B}$ and the y-intercept is $\frac{C}{B}$
- *Slope Intercept Form*: $y = mx + b$, where m is the slope and b is the *y*-intercept
- Point-Slope Form: $y - y_1 = m(x - x_1)$, where m is the slope and (x_1, y_1) is a point on the line
- Two-Point Form: $\frac{y - y_1}{x - x_1} = \frac{y_2 - y_1}{x_2 - x_1}$, where (x_1, y_1) and (x_2, y_2) are two points on the given line

- *Intercept Form:* $\frac{x}{x_1} + \frac{y}{y_1} = 1$, where $(x_1, 0)$ is the point at which a line intersects the x-axis, and $(0, y_1)$ is the point at which the same line intersects the y-axis

Equations can also be written as $ax + b = 0$, where $a \neq 0$. These are referred to as **one variable linear equations**. A solution to such an equation is called a **root**. In the case where we have the equation $5x + 10 = 0$, if we solve for x we get a solution of $x = -2$. In other words, the root of the equation is -2. This is found by first subtracting 10 from both sides, which gives $5x = -10$. Next, simply divide both sides by the coefficient of the variable, in this case 5, to get $x = -2$. This can be checked by plugging -2 back into the original equation $(5)(-2) + 10 = -10 + 10 = 0$.

The **solution set** is the set of all solutions of an equation. In our example, the solution set would simply be -2. If there were more solutions (there usually are in multivariable equations) then they would also be included in the solution set. When an equation has no true solutions, this is referred to as an **empty set**. Equations with identical solution sets are *equivalent equations*. An **identity** is a term whose value or determinant is equal to 1.

Manipulation of Functions

Horizontal and vertical shift occur when values are added to or subtracted from the x or y values, respectively.

If a constant is added to the y portion of each point, the graph shifts up. If a constant is subtracted from the y portion of each point, the graph shifts down. This is represented by the expression $f(x) \pm k$, where k is a constant.

If a constant is added to the x portion of each point, the graph shifts left. If a constant is subtracted from the x portion of each point, the graph shifts right. This is represented by the expression $f(x \pm k)$, where k is a constant.

Stretch, compression, and reflection occur when different parts of a function are multiplied by different groups of constants. If the function as a whole is multiplied by a real number constant greater than 1, $(k \times f(x))$, the graph is stretched vertically. If k in the previous equation is greater than zero but less than 1, the graph is compressed vertically. If k is less than zero, the graph is reflected about the x-axis, in addition to being either stretched or compressed vertically if k is less than or greater than -1, respectively. If instead, just the x-term is multiplied by a constant greater than 1 $(f(k \times x))$, the graph is compressed horizontally. If k in the previous equation is greater than zero but less than 1, the graph is stretched horizontally. If k is less than zero, the graph is reflected about the y-axis, in addition to being either stretched or compressed horizontally if k is greater than or less than -1, respectively.

Classification of Functions

There are many different ways to classify functions based on their structure or behavior. Listed here are a few common classifications.

Constant functions are given by the equation $y=b$ or $f(x) = b$, where b is a real number. There is no independent variable present in the equation, so the function has a constant value for all x. The graph of a constant function is a horizontal line of slope 0 that is positioned b units from the x-axis. If b is positive, the line is above the x-axis; if b is negative, the line is below the x-axis.

Identity functions are identified by the equation $y=x$ or $f(x) = x$, where every value of y is equal to its corresponding value of x. The only zero is the point $(0, 0)$. The graph is a diagonal line with slope 1.

In **linear functions**, the value of the function changes in direct proportion to x. The rate of change, represented by the slope on its graph, is constant throughout. The standard form of a linear equation is $ax + by = c$, where a, b, and c are real numbers. As a function, this equation is commonly written as $y = mx + b$ or $f(x) = mx + b$. This is known as the slope-intercept form, because the coefficients give the slope of the graphed function (m) and its y-intercept (b). Solve the equation $mx + b = 0$ for x to get $x = -\frac{b}{m}$, which is the only zero of the function. The domain and range are both the set of all real numbers.

A **polynomial function** is a function with multiple terms and multiple powers of x, such as:

$$f(x) = a_n x^n + a_{n-1} x^{n-1} + a_{n-2} x^{n-2} + \cdots + a_1 x + a_0$$

where n is a non-negative integer that is the highest exponent in the polynomial, and $a_n \neq 0$. The domain of a polynomial function is the set of all real numbers. If the greatest exponent in the polynomial is even, the polynomial is said to be of even degree and the range is the set of real numbers that satisfy the function. If the greatest exponent in the polynomial is odd, the polynomial is said to be odd and the range, like the domain, is the set of all real numbers.

> **Review Video:** Simplifying Rational Polynomial Functions
> Visit mometrix.com/academy and enter code: 351038

A **quadratic function** is a polynomial function that follows the equation pattern $y = ax^2 + bx + c$, or $f(x) = ax^2 + bx + c$, where a, b, and c are real numbers and $a \neq 0$. The domain of a quadratic function is the set of all real numbers. The range is also real numbers, but only those in the subset of the domain that satisfy the equation. The root(s) of any quadratic function can be found by plugging the values of a, b, and c into the **quadratic formula**:

$$x = \frac{-b \pm \sqrt{b^2 - 4ac}}{2a}$$

If the expression $b^2 - 4ac$ is negative, you will instead find complex roots.

A quadratic function has a parabola for its graph. In the equation $f(x) = ax^2 + bx + c$, if a is positive, the parabola will open upward. If a is negative, the parabola will open downward. The axis of symmetry is a vertical line that passes through the vertex. To determine whether or not the parabola will intersect the x-axis, check the number of real roots. An equation with two real roots will cross the *x*-axis twice. An equation with one real root will have its vertex on the *x*-axis. An equation with no real roots will not contact the *x*-axis.

A **rational function** is a function that can be constructed as a ratio of two polynomial expressions: $f(x) = \frac{p(x)}{q(x)}$, where $p(x)$ and $q(x)$ are both polynomial expressions and $q(x) \neq 0$. The domain is the set of all real numbers, except any values for which $q(x) = 0$. The range is the set of real numbers that satisfies the function when the domain is applied. When you graph a rational function, you will have vertical asymptotes wherever $q(x) = 0$. If the polynomial in the numerator is of lesser degree than the polynomial in the denominator, the *x*-axis will also be a horizontal asymptote. If the numerator and denominator have equal degrees, there will be a horizontal asymptote not on the *x*-axis. If the degree of the numerator is exactly one greater than the degree of the denominator, the graph will have an oblique, or diagonal, asymptote. The asymptote will be along the line $y = \frac{p_n}{q_{n-1}}x + \frac{p_{n-1}}{q_{n-1}}$, where p_n and q_{n-1} are the coefficients of the highest degree terms in their respective polynomials.

A **square root function** is a function that contains a radical and is in the format $f(x) = \sqrt{ax + b}$. The domain is the set of all real numbers that yields a positive radicand or a radicand equal to zero. Because square root values are assumed to be positive unless otherwise identified, the range is all real numbers from zero to infinity. To find the zero of a square root function, set the radicand equal to zero and solve for *x*. The graph of a square root function is always to the right of the zero and always above the *x*-axis.

An **absolute value function** is in the format $f(x) = |ax + b|$. Like other functions, the domain is the set of all real numbers. However, because absolute value indicates positive numbers, the range is limited to positive real numbers. To find the zero of an absolute value function, set the portion inside the absolute value sign equal to zero and solve for x.

An absolute value function is also known as a piecewise function because it must be solved in pieces – one for if the value inside the absolute value sign is positive, and one for if the value is negative. The function can be expressed as

$$f(x) = \begin{cases} ax + b \text{ if } ax + b \geq 0 \\ -(ax + b) \text{ if } ax + b < 0 \end{cases}$$

This will allow for an accurate statement of the range.

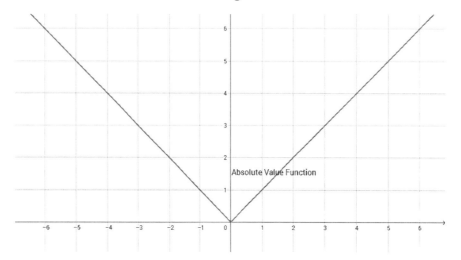

Absolute Value Function

Exponential functions are equations that have the format $y = b^x$, where base $b > 0$ and $b \neq 1$. The exponential function can also be written $f(x) = b^x$.

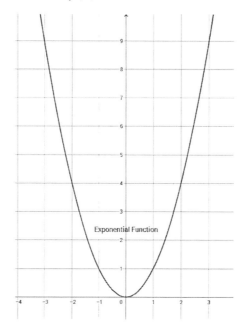

Exponential Function

Logarithmic functions are equations that have the format $y = \log_b x$ or $f(x) = \log_b x$. The base b may be any number except one; however, the most common bases for logarithms are base 10 and base e. The log base e is known the natural logarithm, or ln, expressed by the function $f(x) = \ln x$.

Any logarithm that does not have an assigned value of b is assumed to be base 10: $\log x = \log_{10} x$. Exponential functions and logarithmic functions are related in that one is the inverse of the other. If

$f(x) = b^x$, then $f^{-1}(x) = \log_b x$. This can perhaps be expressed more clearly by the two equations: $y = b^x$ and $x = \log_b y$.

The following properties apply to logarithmic expressions:

$$\log_b 1 = 0$$
$$\log_b b = 1$$
$$\log_b b^p = p$$
$$\log_b MN = \log_b M + \log_b N$$
$$\log_b \frac{M}{N} = \log_b M - \log_b N$$
$$\log_b M^p = p \log_b M$$

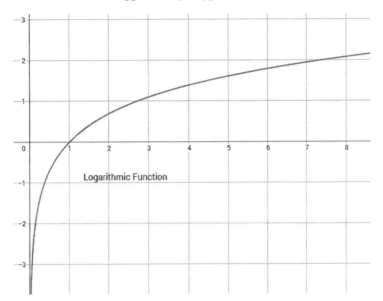

Logarithmic Function

In a **one-to-one function**, each value of x has exactly one value for y (this is the definition of a function) *and* each value of y has exactly one value for x. While the vertical line test will determine if a graph is that of a function, the horizontal line test will determine if a function is a one-to-one function. If a horizontal line drawn at any value of y intersects the graph in more than one place, the graph is not that of a one-to-one function. Do not make the mistake of using the horizontal line test exclusively in determining if a graph is that of a one-to-one function. A one-to-one function must pass both the vertical line test and the horizontal line test. One-to-one functions are also **invertible functions**.

A **monotone function** is a function whose graph either constantly increases or constantly decreases. Examples include the functions $f(x) = x$, $f(x) = -x$, or $f(x) = x^3$.

An **even function** has a graph that is symmetric with respect to the y-axis and satisfies the equation $f(x) = f(-x)$. Examples include the functions $f(x) = x^2$ and $f(x) = ax^n$, where a is any real number and n is a positive even integer.

An **odd function** has a graph that is symmetric with respect to the origin and satisfies the equation $f(x) = -f(-x)$. Examples include the functions $f(x) = x^3$ and $f(x) = ax^n$, where a is any real number and n is a positive odd integer.

Algebraic functions are those that exclusively use polynomials and roots. These would include polynomial functions, rational functions, square root functions, and all combinations of these functions, such as polynomials as the radicand. These combinations may be joined by addition, subtraction, multiplication, or division, but may not include variables as exponents.

Transcendental functions are all functions that are non-algebraic. Any function that includes logarithms, trigonometric functions, variables as exponents, or any combination that includes any of these is not algebraic in nature, even if the function includes polynomials or roots.

Related Concepts

According to the **fundamental theorem of algebra**, every non-constant, single variable polynomial has exactly as many roots as the polynomial's highest exponent. For example, if x^4 is the largest exponent of a term, the polynomial will have exactly 4 roots. However, some of these roots may have multiplicity or be non-real numbers. For instance, in the polynomial function $f(x) = x^4 - 4x + 3$, the only real roots are 1 and -1. The root 1 has multiplicity of 2 and there is one non-real root $(-1 - \sqrt{2}i)$.

The **remainder theorem** is useful for determining the remainder when a polynomial is divided by a binomial. The Remainder Theorem states that if a polynomial function $f(x)$ is divided by a binomial $x - a$, where a is a real number, the remainder of the division will be the value of $f(a)$. If $f(a) = 0$, then a is a root of the polynomial.

The **factor theorem** is related to the Remainder Theorem and states that if $f(a) = 0$ then $(x - a)$ is a factor of the function.

According to the **rational root theorem,** any rational root of a polynomial function $f(x) = a_n x^n + a_{n-1} x^{n-1} + \cdots + a_1 x + a_0$ with integer coefficients will, when reduced to its lowest terms, be a positive or negative fraction such that the numerator is a factor of a_0 and the denominator is a factor of a_n. For instance, if the polynomial function $f(x) = x^3 + 3x^2 - 4$ has any rational roots, the numerators of those roots can only be factors of 4 (1, 2, 4), and the denominators can only be factors of 1 (1). The function in this example has roots of 1 $\left(\text{or } \frac{1}{1}\right)$ and -2 $\left(\text{or } -\frac{2}{1}\right)$.

Variables that vary directly are those that either both increase at the same rate or both decrease at the same rate. For example, in the functions $f(x) = kx$ or $f(x) = kx^n$, where k and n are positive, the value of $f(x)$ increases as the value of x increases and decreases as the value of x decreases.

Variables that vary inversely are those where one increases while the other decreases. For example, in the functions $f(x) = \frac{k}{x}$ or $f(x) = \frac{k}{x^n}$ where k is a positive constant, the value of y increases as the value of x decreases, and the value of y decreases as the value of x increases.

In both cases, k is the constant of variation.

Applying the Basic Operations to Functions

For each of the basic operations, we will use these functions as examples: $f(x) = x^2$ and $g(x) = x$.

To find the sum of two functions f and g, assuming the domains are compatible, simply add the two functions together: $(f + g)(x) = f(x) + g(x) = x^2 + x$

To find the difference of two functions f and g, assuming the domains are compatible, simply subtract the second function from the first: $(f - g)(x) = f(x) - g(x) = x^2 - x$.

To find the product of two functions f and g, assuming the domains are compatible, multiply the two functions together: $(f \cdot g)(x) = f(x) \cdot g(x) = x^2 \cdot x = x^3$.

To find the quotient of two functions f and g, assuming the domains are compatible, divide the first function by the second: $\frac{f}{g}(x) = \frac{f(x)}{g(x)} = \frac{x^2}{x} = x \, ; x \neq 0$.

The example given in each case is fairly simple, but on a given problem, if you are looking only for the value of the sum, difference, product or quotient of two functions at a particular x-value, it may be simpler to solve the functions individually and then perform the given operation using those values.

The composite of two functions f and g, written as $(f \circ g)(x)$ simply means that the output of the second function is used as the input of the first. This can also be written as $f(g(x))$. In general, this can be solved by substituting $g(x)$ for all instances of x in $f(x)$ and simplifying. Using the example functions $f(x) = x^2 - x + 2$ and $g(x) = x + 1$, we can find that $(f \circ g)(x)$ or $f(g(x))$ is equal to $f(x + 1) = (x + 1)^2 - (x + 1) + 2$, which simplifies to $x^2 + x + 2$.

It is important to note that $(f \circ g)(x)$ is not necessarily the same as $(g \circ f)(x)$. The process is not commutative like addition or multiplication expressions. If $(f \circ g)(x)$ does equal $(g \circ f)(x)$, the two functions are inverses of each other.

Solve Equations in One Variable

Manipulating Equations

Sometimes you will have variables missing in equations. So, you need to find the missing variable. To do this, you need to remember one important thing: *whatever you do to one side of an equation, you need to do to the other side.* If you subtract 100 from one side of an equation, you need to subtract 100 from the other side of the equation. This will allow you to change the form of the equation to find missing values.

Example

Ray earns $10 an hour at his job. Write an equation for his earnings as a function of time spent working. Determine how long Ray has to work in order to earn $360.

The number of dollars that Ray earns is dependent on the number of hours he works, so earnings will be represented by the dependent variable y and hours worked will be represented by the independent variable x. He earns 10 dollars per hour worked, so his earning can be calculated as

$$y = 10x$$

To calculate the number of hours Ray must work in order to earn $360, plug in 360 for y and solve for x:

$$360 = 10x$$

$$x = \frac{360}{10} = 36$$

- 161 -

So, Ray must work 36 hours in order to earn $360.

Solving One Variable Linear Equations

Another way to write an equation is $ax + b = 0$ where $a \neq 0$. This is known as a **one-variable linear equation**. A solution to an equation is called a **root**. Consider the following equation:

$$5x + 10 = 0$$

If we solve for x, the solution is $x = -2$. In other words, the root of the equation is –2.

The first step is to subtract 10 from both sides. This gives $5x = -10$.

Next, divide both sides by the **coefficient** of the variable. For this example, that is 5. So, you should have $x = -2$. You can make sure that you have the correct answer by substituting –2 back into the original equation. So, the equation now looks like this: $(5)(-2) + 10 = -10 + 10 = 0$.

Example 1

$\frac{45\%}{12\%} = \frac{15\%}{x}$. Solve for x.

First, cross multiply; then, solve for x: $\frac{45\%}{12\%} = \frac{15\%}{x}$

$$\frac{0.45}{0.12} = \frac{0.15}{x}$$
$$0.45(x) = 0.12(0.15)$$
$$0.45x = 0.0180$$
$$0.45x \div 0.45 = 0.0180 \div 0.45$$
$$x = 0.04 = 4\%$$

Alternatively, notice that $\frac{45\% \div 3}{12\% \div 3} = \frac{15\%}{4\%}$. So, $x = 4\%$.

Example 2

How do you solve for x in the proportion $\frac{0.50}{2} = \frac{1.50}{x}$?

First, cross multiply; then, solve for x.

$$\frac{0.50}{2} = \frac{1.50}{x}$$
$$0.50(x) = 2(1.50)$$
$$0.50x = 3$$
$$0.50x \div 0.50 = 3 \div 0.50$$
$$x = 6$$

Or, notice that $\frac{0.50 \times 3}{2 \times 3} = \frac{1.50}{6}$, so $x = 6$.

Example 3

$\frac{40}{8} = \frac{x}{24}$. Find x.

One way to solve for x is to first cross multiply.

$$\frac{40}{8} = \frac{x}{24}$$
$$40(24) = 8(x)$$
$$960 = 8x$$
$$960 \div 8 = 8x \div 8$$
$$x = 120$$

Or, notice that:

$$\frac{40 \times 3}{8 \times 3} = \frac{120}{24}, \text{ so } x = 120$$

Other Important Concepts

Commonly in algebra and other upper-level fields of math you find yourself working with mathematical expressions that do not equal each other. The statement comparing such expressions with symbols such as < (less than) or > (greater than) is called an *inequality*. An example of an inequality is $7x > 5$. To solve for x, simply divide both sides by 7 and the solution is shown to be $x > \frac{5}{7}$. Graphs of the solution set of inequalities are represented on a number line. Open circles are used to show that an expression approaches a number but is never quite equal to that number.

> **Review Video: Inequalities**
> Visit mometrix.com/academy and enter code: 347842

Conditional inequalities are those with certain values for the variable that will make the condition true and other values for the variable where the condition will be false. **Absolute inequalities** can have any real number as the value for the variable to make the condition true, while there is no real number value for the variable that will make the condition false. Solving inequalities is done by following the same rules as for solving equations with the exception that when multiplying or dividing by a negative number the direction of the inequality sign must be flipped or reversed. **double inequalities** are situations where two inequality statements apply to the same variable expression. An example of this is $-c < ax + b < c$.

A **weighted mean**, or weighted average, is a mean that uses "weighted" values. The formula is weighted mean $= \frac{w_1 x_1 + w_2 x_2 + w_3 x_3 \dots + w_n x_n}{w_1 + w_2 + w_3 + \dots + w_n}$. Weighted values, such as $w_1, w_2, w_3, \dots w_n$ are assigned to each member of the set $x_1, x_2, x_3, \dots x_n$. If calculating weighted mean, make sure a weight value for each member of the set is used.

Graphing Inequalities

Graph the inequality $10 > -2x + 4$.

In order to **graph the inequality** $10 > -2x + 4$, you must first solve for x. The opposite of addition is subtraction, so subtract 4 from both sides. This results in $6 > -2x$. Next, the opposite of multiplication is division, so divide both sides by -2. Don't forget to flip the inequality symbol since you are dividing by a negative number. This results in $-3 < x$. You can rewrite this as $x > -3$. To graph an inequality, you create a number line and put a circle around the value that is being compared to x. If you are graphing a greater than or less than inequality, as the one shown, the circle remains open. This represents all of the values excluding -3. If the inequality happens to be a greater than or equal to or less than or equal to, you draw a closed circle around the value. This would represent all of the values including the number. Finally, take a look at the values that the

- 163 -

solution represents and shade the number line in the appropriate direction. You are graphing all of the values greater than -3 and since this is all of the numbers to the right of -3, shade this region on the number line.

Determining Solutions to Inequalities

Determine whether $(-2, 4)$ is a solution of the inequality $y \geq -2x + 3$.

To determine whether a coordinate is a **solution of an inequality**, you can either use the inequality or its graph. Using $(-2, 4)$ as (x, y), substitute the values into the inequality to see if it makes a true statement. This results in $4 \geq -2(-2) + 3$. Using the integer rules, simplify the right side of the inequality by multiplying and then adding. The result is $4 \geq 7$, which is a false statement. Therefore, the coordinate is not a solution of the inequality. You can also use the **graph** of an inequality to see if a coordinate is a part of the solution. The graph of an inequality is shaded over the section of the coordinate grid that is included in the solution. The graph of $y \geq -2x + 3$ includes the solid line $y = -2x + 3$ and is shaded to the right of the line, representing all of the points greater than and including the points on the line. This excludes the point $(-2, 4)$, so it is not a solution of the inequality.

Calculations Using Points

Sometimes you need to perform calculations using only points on a graph as input data. Using points, you can determine what the **midpoint** and **distance** are. If you know the equation for a line you can calculate the distance between the line and the point.

To find the **midpoint** of two points (x_1, y_1) and (x_2, y_2), average the x-coordinates to get the x-coordinate of the midpoint, and average the y-coordinates to get the y-coordinate of the midpoint. The formula is Midpoint $= \left(\frac{x_1 + x_2}{2}, \frac{y_1 + y_2}{2}\right)$.

The **distance** between two points is the same as the length of the hypotenuse of a right triangle with the two given points as endpoints, and the two sides of the right triangle parallel to the x-axis and y-axis, respectively. The length of the segment parallel to the x-axis is the difference between the x-coordinates of the two points. The length of the segment parallel to the y-axis is the difference between the y-coordinates of the two points. Use the Pythagorean theorem $a^2 + b^2 = c^2$ or $c = \sqrt{a^2 + b^2}$ to find the distance. The formula is distance $= \sqrt{(x_2 - x_1)^2 + (y_2 - y_1)^2}$.

When a line is in the format $Ax + By + C = 0$, where A, B, and C are coefficients, you can use a point (x_1, y_1) not on the line and apply the formula $d = \frac{|Ax_1 + By_1 + C|}{\sqrt{A^2 + B^2}}$ to find the distance between the line and the point (x_1, y_1).

Example
Find the distance and midpoint between points $(2, 4)$ and $(8, 6)$.

Midpoint

$$\text{Midpoint} = \left(\frac{x_1 + x_2}{2}, \frac{y_1 + y_2}{2}\right)$$
$$\text{Midpoint} = \left(\frac{2 + 8}{2}, \frac{4 + 6}{2}\right)$$
$$\text{Midpoint} = \left(\frac{10}{2}, \frac{10}{2}\right)$$

- 164 -

$$\text{Midpoint} = (5,5)$$

Distance

$$\text{Distance} = \sqrt{(x_2 - x_1)^2 + (y_2 - y_1)^2}$$
$$\text{Distance} = \sqrt{(8 - 2)^2 + (6 - 4)^2}$$
$$\text{Distance} = \sqrt{(6)^2 + (2)^2}$$
$$\text{Distance} = \sqrt{36 + 4}$$
$$\text{Distance} = \sqrt{40} \text{ or } 2\sqrt{10}$$

Systems of Equations

Systems of equations are a set of simultaneous equations that all use the same variables. A solution to a system of equations must be true for each equation in the system. *Consistent systems* are those with at least one solution. *Inconsistent systems* are systems of equations that have no solution.

> **Review Video: Systems of Equations**
> Visit mometrix.com/academy and enter code: 658153

Substitution

To solve a system of linear equations by *substitution*, start with the easier equation and solve for one of the variables. Express this variable in terms of the other variable. Substitute this expression in the other equation and solve for the other variable. The solution should be expressed in the form (x, y). Substitute the values into both of the original equations to check your answer. Consider the following problem.

Solve the system using substitution:

$$x + 6y = 15$$

$$3x - 12y = 18$$

Solve the first equation for x:

$$x = 15 - 6y$$

Substitute this value in place of x in the second equation, and solve for y:

$$3(15 - 6y) - 12y = 18$$

$$45 - 18y - 12y = 18$$

$$30y = 27$$

$$y = \frac{27}{30} = \frac{9}{10} = 0.9$$

Plug this value for y back into the first equation to solve for x:

$$x = 15 - 6(0.9) = 15 - 5.4 = 9.6$$

Check both equations if you have time:

$$9.6 + 6(0.9) = 9.6 + 5.4 = 15$$

$$3(9.6) - 12(0.9) = 28.8 - 10.8 = 18$$

Therefore, the solution is (9.6, 0.9).

<u>Elimination</u>

To solve a system of equations using *elimination*, begin by rewriting both equations in standard form $Ax + By = C$. Check to see if the coefficients of one pair of like variables add to zero. If not, multiply one or both of the equations by a non-zero number to make one set of like variables add to zero. Add the two equations to solve for one of the variables. Substitute this value into one of the original equations to solve for the other variable. Check your work by substituting into the other equation. Next, we will solve the same problem as above, but using the addition method.

Solve the system using elimination:

$$x + 6y = 15$$

$$3x - 12y = 18$$

If we multiply the first equation by 2, we can eliminate the y terms:

$$2x + 12y = 30$$

$$3x - 12y = 18$$

Add the equations together and solve for x:

$$5x = 48$$

$$x = \frac{48}{5} = 9.6$$

Plug the value for x back into either of the original equations and solve for y:

$$9.6 + 6y = 15$$

$$y = \frac{15 - 9.6}{6} = 0.9$$

Check both equations if you have time:

$$9.6 + 6(0.9) = 9.6 + 5.4 = 15$$

$$3(9.6) - 12(0.9) = 28.8 - 10.8 = 18$$

Therefore, the solution is (9.6, 0.9).

<u>Graphically</u>

To solve a system of linear equations **graphically**, plot both equations on the same graph. The solution of the equations is the point where both lines cross. If the lines do not cross (are parallel), then there is **no solution**.

For example, consider the following system of equations:

$$y = 2x + 7$$
$$y = -x + 1$$

Since these equations are given in slope-intercept form, they are easy to graph; the y intercepts of the lines are $(0, 7)$ and $(0, 1)$. The respective slopes are 2 and -1, thus the graphs look like this:

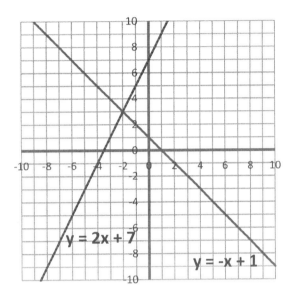

The two lines intersect at the point $(-2, 3)$, thus this is the solution to the system of equations.

Solving a system graphically is generally only practical if both coordinates of the solution are integers; otherwise the intersection will lie between gridlines on the graph and the coordinates will be difficult or impossible to determine exactly. It also helps if, as in this example, the equations are in slope-intercept form or some other form that makes them easy to graph. Otherwise, another method of solution (by substitution or elimination) is likely to be more useful.

Solving A System of Equations Consisting of a Linear Equation and a Quadratic Equation

Algebraically

Generally, the simplest way to solve a system of equations consisting of a linear equation and a quadratic equation algebraically is through the method of **substitution**. One possible strategy is to solve the linear equation for y and then substitute that expression into the quadratic equation. After expansion and combining like terms, this will result in a new quadratic equation for x which, like all quadratic equations, may have zero, one, or two solutions. Plugging each solution for x back into one of the original equations will then produce the corresponding value of y.

For example, consider the following system of equations:

$$x + y = 1$$
$$y = (x + 3)^2 - 2$$

We can solve the linear equation for y to yield $y = -x + 1$.

Substituting this expression into the quadratic equation produces $-x + 1 = (x + 3)^2 - 2$

- 167 -

We can simplify this equation:

$$-x + 1 = (x + 3)^2 - 2$$

$$-x + 1 = x^2 + 6x + 9 - 2$$

$$-x + 1 = x^2 + 6x + 7$$

$$x^2 + 7x + 6 = 0$$

This quadratic equation can be factored as $(x + 1)(x + 6) = 0$. It therefore has two solutions: $x_1 = -1$ and $x_2 = -6$. Plugging each of these back into the original linear equation yields $y_1 = -x_1 + 1 = -(-1) + 1 = 2$ and $y_2 = -x_2 + 1 = -(-6) + 1 = 7$. Thus this system of equations has two solutions, $(-1, 2)$ and $(-6, 7)$.

It may help to check your work by putting each x and y value back into the original equations and verifying that they do provide a solution.

Graphically

To solve a system of equations consisting of a linear equation and a quadratic equation **graphically**, plot both equations on the same graph. The linear equation will of course produce a straight line, while the quadratic equation will produce a parabola. These two graphs will intersect at zero, one, or two points; each point of intersection is a solution of the system.

For example, consider the following system of equations:

$$y = -2x + 2$$
$$y = -2x^2 + 4x + 2$$

The linear equation describes a line with a y-intercept of $(0, 2)$ and a slope of -2.

To graph the quadratic equation, we can first find the vertex of the parabola: the x-coordinate of the vertex is $h = -\frac{b}{2a} = -\frac{4}{2(-2)} = 1$, and the y coordinate is $k = -2(1)^2 + 4(1) + 2 = 4$. Thus, the vertex lies at $(1, 4)$. To get a feel for the rest of the parabola, we can plug in a few more values of x to find more points; by putting in $x = 2$ and $x = 3$ in the quadratic equation, we find that the points $(2, 2)$ and $(3, -4)$ lie on the parabola; by symmetry thus do $(0, 2)$ and $(-1, -4)$. We can now plot both equations:

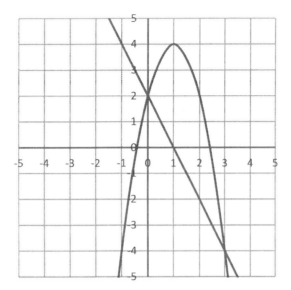

These two curves intersect at the points $(0, 2)$ and $(3, -4)$, thus these are the solutions of the equation.

Polynomial Algebra

To multiply two binomials, follow the **FOIL** method. FOIL stands for:

- First: Multiply the first term of each binomial
- Outer: Multiply the outer terms of each binomial
- Inner: Multiply the inner terms of each binomial
- Last: Multiply the last term of each binomial

Using FOIL $(Ax + By)(Cx + Dy) = ACx^2 + ADxy + BCxy + BDy^2$.

<u>Example</u>

Use the FOIL method on binomials $(x + 2)$ and $(x - 3)$.

$$\text{First: } (x + 2)(x - 3) = (x)(x) = x^2$$

$$\text{Outer: } (x + 2)\ (x - 3) = (x)(-3) = -3x$$

$$\text{Inner: } (x + 2)\ (x - 3) = (2)(x) = 2x$$

$$\text{Last: } (x + 2)(x - 3) = (2)(-3) = -6$$

Combine like Terms:

$$(x^2) + (-3x) + (2x) + (-6) = x^2 - x - 6$$

Review Video: <u>Multiplying Terms Using the FOIL Method</u>
Visit mometrix.com/academy and enter code: 854792

- 169 -

To divide polynomials, begin by arranging the terms of each polynomial in order of one variable. You may arrange in ascending or descending order, but make sure to be consistent with both polynomials. To get the first term of the quotient, divide the first term of the dividend by the first term of the divisor. Multiply the first term of the quotient by the entire divisor and subtract that product from the dividend. Repeat for the second and successive terms until you either get a remainder of zero or a remainder whose degree is less than the degree of the divisor. If the quotient has a remainder, write the answer as a mixed expression in the form: quotient $+ \frac{\text{remainder}}{\text{divisor}}$.

Rational expressions are fractions with polynomials in both the numerator and the denominator; the value of the polynomial in the denominator cannot be equal to zero. To add or subtract rational expressions, first find the common denominator, then rewrite each fraction as an equivalent fraction with the common denominator. Finally, add or subtract the numerators to get the numerator of the answer, and keep the common denominator as the denominator of the answer. When multiplying rational expressions factor each polynomial and cancel like factors (a factor which appears in both the numerator and the denominator). Then, multiply all remaining factors in the numerator to get the numerator of the product, and multiply the remaining factors in the denominator to get the denominator of the product. Remember – cancel entire factors, not individual terms. To divide rational expressions, take the reciprocal of the divisor (the rational expression you are dividing by) and multiply by the dividend.

> **Review Video: Simplifying Rational Polynomial Functions**
> Visit mometrix.com/academy and enter code: 351038

Below are patterns of some special products to remember: *perfect trinomial squares*, the *difference between two squares*, the *sum and difference of two cubes*, and *perfect cubes*.

- Perfect trinomial squares: $x^2 + 2xy + y^2 = (x + y)^2$ or $x^2 - 2xy + y^2 = (x - y)^2$
- Difference between two squares: $x^2 - y^2 = (x + y)(x - y)$
- Sum of two cubes: $x^3 + y^3 = (x + y)(x^2 - xy + y^2)$
- Note: the second factor is *not* the same as a perfect trinomial square, so do not try to factor it further.
- Difference between two cubes: $x^3 - y^3 = (x - y)(x^2 + xy + y^2)$
- Again, the second factor is *not* the same as a perfect trinomial square.
- Perfect cubes: $x^3 + 3x^2y + 3xy^2 + y^3 = (x + y)^3$ and $x^3 - 3x^2y + 3xy^2 - y^3 = (x - y)^3$

In order to **factor a polynomial**, first check for a common monomial factor. When the greatest common monomial factor has been factored out, look for patterns of special products: differences of two squares, the sum or difference of two cubes for binomial factors, or perfect trinomial squares for trinomial factors. If the factor is a trinomial but not a perfect trinomial square, look for a factorable form, such as $x^2 + (a + b)x + ab = (x + a)(x + b)$ or $(ac)x^2 + (ad + bc)x + bd = (ax + b)(cx + d)$. For factors with four terms, look for groups to factor. Once you have found the factors, write the original polynomial as the product of all the factors. Make sure all of the polynomial factors are prime. Monomial factors may be prime or composite. Check your work by multiplying the factors to make sure you get the original polynomial.

Solving Quadratic Equations

The **quadratic formula** is used to solve quadratic equations when other methods are more difficult. To use the quadratic formula to solve a quadratic equation, begin by rewriting the equation in standard form $ax^2 + bx + c = 0$, where a, b, and c are coefficients. Once you have identified the values of the coefficients, substitute those values into the quadratic formula $x = \frac{-b \pm \sqrt{b^2 - 4ac}}{2a}$. Evaluate the equation and simplify the expression. Again, check each root by substituting into the original equation. In the quadratic formula, the portion of the formula under the radical $(b^2 - 4ac)$ is called the **discriminant**. If the discriminant is zero, there is only one root: $-\frac{b}{2a}$. If the discriminant is positive, there are two different real roots. If the discriminant is negative, there are no real roots.

To solve a quadratic equation by factoring, begin by rewriting the equation in standard form, if necessary. Factor the side with the variable then set each of the factors equal to zero and solve the resulting linear equations. Check your answers by substituting the roots you found into the original equation. If, when writing the equation in standard form, you have an equation in the form $x^2 + c = 0$ or $x^2 - c = 0$, set $x^2 = -c$ or $x^2 = c$ and take the square root of c. If $c = 0$, the only real root is zero. If c is positive, there are two real roots—the positive and negative square root values. If c is negative, there are no real roots because you cannot take the square root of a negative number.

> **Review Video: Factoring Quadratic Equations**
> Visit mometrix.com/academy and enter code: 336566

To solve a quadratic equation by **completing the square**, rewrite the equation so that all terms containing the variable are on the left side of the equal sign, and all the constants are on the right side of the equal sign. Make sure the coefficient of the squared term is 1. If there is a coefficient with the squared term, divide each term on both sides of the equal side by that number. Next, work with the coefficient of the single-variable term. Square half of this coefficient and add that value to both sides. Now you can factor the left side (the side containing the variable) as the square of a binomial. $x^2 + 2ax + a^2 = C \Rightarrow (x + a)^2 = C$, where x is the variable, and a and C are constants. Take the square root of both sides and solve for the variable. Substitute the value of the variable in the original problem to check your work.

Quadratic Function

A *quadratic function* is a function in the form $y = ax^2 + bx + c$, where a does not equal 0. While a linear function forms a line, a quadratic function forms a **parabola**, which is a u-shaped figure that either opens upward or downward. A parabola that opens upward is said to be a **positive quadratic function** and a parabola that opens downward is said to be a **negative quadratic function**. The shape of a parabola can differ, depending on the values of a, b, and c. All parabolas contain a **vertex**, which is the highest possible point, the **maximum**, or the lowest possible point, the **minimum**. This is the point where the graph begins moving in the opposite direction. A quadratic function can have zero, one, or two solutions, and therefore, zero, one, or two x-intercepts. Recall that the x-intercepts are referred to as the zeros, or roots, of a function. A quadratic function will have only one y-intercept. Understanding the basic components of a quadratic function can give you an idea of the shape of its graph.

Example graph of a positive quadratic function:

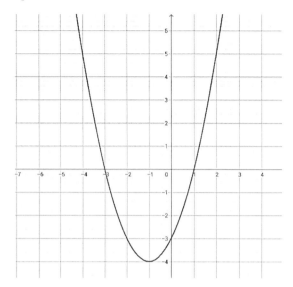

Simplifying Polynomial Expressions

A polynomial is a group of monomials added or subtracted together. Simplifying polynomials requires combining like terms. The like terms in a polynomial expression are those that have the same variable raised to the same power. It is often helpful to connect the like terms with arrows or lines in order to separate them from the other monomials. Once you have determined the like terms, you can rearrange the polynomial by placing them together. Remember to include the sign that is in front of each term. Once the like terms are placed together, you can apply each operation and simplify. When adding and subtracting polynomials, only add and subtract the **coefficient**, or the number part; the variable and exponent stay the same.

Position of Parabola

A **quadratic function** is written in the form $y = ax^2 + bx + c$. Changing the leading coefficient, a, in the equation changes the direction of the parabola. If the value of a is **positive**, the graph opens upward. The vertex of this parabola is the **minimum** value of the graph. If the value of a is **negative**, the graph opens downward. The vertex of this parabola is the **maximum** value of the graph. The leading coefficient, a, also affects the width of the parabola. The closer a is to 0, the wider the parabola will be. The values of b and c both affect the position of the parabola on the graph. The effect from changing b depends on the sign of a. If a is negative, increasing the value of b moves the parabola to the right and decreasing the value of b moves it to the left. If a is positive, changes to b have the opposite effect. The value of c in the quadratic equation represents the y-intercept and therefore, moves the parabola up and down the y-axis. The larger the c-value, the higher the parabola is on the graph.

Finding Roots

Find the roots of $y = x^2 + 6x - 16$ and explain why these values are important.

The **roots** of a quadratic equation are the solutions when $ax^2 + bx + c = 0$. To find the roots of a quadratic equation, first replace y with 0. If $0 = x^2 + 6x - 16$, then to find the values of x, you can factor the equation if possible. When factoring a quadratic equation where $a = 1$, find the factors of c that add up to b. That is the factors of -16 that add up to 6. The factors of -16 include, -4 and 4,

- 172 -

−8 and 2 and −2 and 8. The factors that add up to equal 6 are −2 and 8. Write these factors as the product of two binomials, $0 = (x - 2)(x + 8)$. You can verify that these are the correct factors by using FOIL to multiply them together. Finally, since these binomials multiply together to equal zero, set them each equal to zero and solve for x. This results in $x - 2 = 0$, which simplifies to $x = 2$ and $x + 8 = 0$, which simplifies to $x = -8$. Therefore, the roots of the equation are 2 and −8. These values are important because they tell you where the graph of the equation crosses the x-axis. The points of intersection are $(2, 0)$ and $(-8, 0)$.

> **Review Video: Finding the Missing Roots**
> Visit mometrix.com/academy and enter code: 198376

Solving Quadratic Equations

<u>Methods</u>

One way to find the solution or solutions of a quadratic equation is to use its **graph**. The solution(s) of a quadratic equation are the values of x when $y = 0$. On the graph, $y = 0$ is where the parabola crosses the x-axis, or the x-intercepts. This is also referred to as the **roots**, or zeros of a function. Given a graph, you can locate the x-intercepts to find the solutions. If there are no x-intercepts, the function has no solution. If the parabola crosses the x-axis at one point, there is one solution and if it crosses at two points, there are two solutions. Since the solutions exist where $y = 0$, you can also solve the equation by substituting 0 in for y. Then, try factoring the equation by finding the factors of ac that add up to equal b. You can use the guess and check method, the box method, or grouping. Once you find a pair that works, write them as the product of two binomials and set them equal to zero. Finally, solve for x to find the solutions. The last way to solve a quadratic equation is to use the

quadratic formula. The quadratic formula is $x = \frac{-b \pm \sqrt{b^2 - 4ac}}{2a}$. Substitute the values of a, b, and c into the formula and solve for x. Remember that ± refers to two different solutions. Always check your solutions with the original equation to make sure they are valid.

<u>Example</u>

List the steps used in solving $y = 2x^2 + 8x + 4$.

First, substitute 0 in for y in the quadratic equation:

$$0 = 2x^2 + 8x + 4$$

Next, try to factor the quadratic equation. If $a \neq 1$, list the factors of ac, or 8:

$$(1, 8), (-1, -8), (2, 4), (-2, -4)$$

Look for the factors of ac that add up to b, or 8. Since none do, the equation cannot be factored with whole numbers. Substitute the values of a, b, and c into the quadratic formula, $x = \frac{-b \pm \sqrt{b^2 - 4ac}}{2a}$:

$$x = \frac{-8 \pm \sqrt{8^2 - 4(2)(4)}}{2(2)}$$

Use the order of operations to simplify:

$$x = \frac{-8 \pm \sqrt{64 - 32}}{4}$$

$$x = \frac{-8 \pm \sqrt{32}}{4}$$

Reduce and simplify:

$$x = \frac{-8 \pm \sqrt{(16)(2)}}{4}$$

$$x = \frac{-8 \pm 4\sqrt{2}}{4}$$

$$x = -2 \pm \sqrt{2}$$

$$x = -2 + \sqrt{2} \text{ and } x = -2 - \sqrt{2}$$

Check both solutions with the original equation to make sure they are valid.

Simplify the square roots and round to two decimal places.

$$x = -3.41 \text{ and } x = -0.586$$

Laws of Exponents

Multiply $(2x^4)^2(xy)^4 \cdot 4y^3$ using the **laws of exponents**.

According the order of operations, the first step in simplifying expressions is to evaluate within the parentheses. Moving from left to right, the first set of parentheses contains a power raised to a power. The rules of exponents state that when a power is raised to a power, you *multiply* the exponents. Since $4 \times 2 = 8$, $(2x^4)^2$ can be written as $4x^8$. The second set of parentheses raises a product to a power. The **rules of exponents** state that you raise every value within the parentheses to the given power. Therefore, $(xy)^4$ can be written as x^4y^4. Combining these terms with the last term gives you, $4x^8 \cdot x^4y^4 \cdot 4y^3$. In this expression, there are powers with the same base. The rules of exponents state that you *add* powers with the same base, while multiplying the coefficients. You can group the expression as $(4x^8 \cdot x^4) \cdot (y^4 \cdot 4y^3)$ to organize the values with the same base. Then, using this rule add the exponents. The result is $4x^{12} \cdot 4y^7$, or $16x^{12}y^7$.

> **Review Video: Laws of Exponents**
> Visit mometrix.com/academy and enter code: 532558

Using Given Roots to Find Quadratic Equation

<u>Example</u>

Find a quadratic equation whose real roots are $x = 2$ and $x = -1$.

One way to find the roots of a quadratic equation is to factor the equation and use the **zero product property**, setting each factor of the equation equal to zero to find the corresponding root. We can

- 174 -

use this technique in reverse to find an equation given its roots. Each root corresponds to a linear equation which in turn corresponds to a factor of the quadratic equation.

For example, the root $x=2$ corresponds to the equation $x - 2 = 0$, and the root $x = -1$ corresponds to the equation $x + 1 = 0$.

These two equations correspond to the factors $(x - 2)$ and $(x+1)$, from which we can derive the equation $(x - 2)(x + 1) = 0$, or $x^2 - x - 2 = 0$.

Any integer multiple of this entire equation will also yield the same roots, as the integer will simply cancel out when the equation is factored. For example, $2x^2 - 2x - 4 = 0$ factors as

$2(x - 2)(x + 1) = 0$.

Simplifying Rational Expressions

To *simplify a rational expression*, factor the numerator and denominator completely. Factors that are the same and appear in the numerator and denominator have a ratio of 1. The denominator, $(1 - x^2)$, is a difference of squares. It can be factored as $(1 - x)(1 + x)$. The factor $1 - x$ and the numerator $x - 1$ are opposites and have a ratio of –1. Rewrite the numerator as $-1(1 - x)$. So, the rational expression can be simplified as follows:

$$\frac{x - 1}{1 - x^2} = \frac{-1(1 - x)}{(1 - x)(1 + x)} = \frac{-1}{1 + x}$$

(Note that since the original expression is defined for $x \neq \{-1, 1\}$, the simplified expression has the same restrictions.)

Matrix Basics

A **matrix** (plural: matrices) is a rectangular array of numbers or variables, often called **elements**, which are arranged in columns and rows. A matrix is generally represented by a capital letter, with its elements represented by the corresponding lowercase letter with two subscripts indicating the row and column of the element. For example, n_{ab} represents the element in row a column b of matrix N.

$$N = \begin{bmatrix} n_{11} & n_{12} & n_{13} \\ n_{21} & n_{22} & n_{23} \end{bmatrix}$$

A matrix can be described in terms of the number of rows and columns it contains in the format $a \times b$, where a is the number of rows and b is the number of columns. The matrix shown above is a 2×3 matrix. Any $a \times b$ matrix where $a = b$ is a square matrix. A **vector** is a matrix that has exactly one column (**column vector**) or exactly one row (**row vector**).

The **main diagonal** of a matrix is the set of elements on the diagonal from the top left to the bottom right of a matrix. Because of the way it is defined, only square matrices will have a main diagonal. For the matrix shown below, the main diagonal consists of the elements $n_{11}, n_{22}, n_{33}, n_{44}$.

$$\begin{bmatrix} n_{11} & n_{12} & n_{13} & n_{14} \\ n_{21} & n_{22} & n_{23} & n_{24} \\ n_{31} & n_{32} & n_{33} & n_{34} \\ n_{41} & n_{42} & n_{43} & n_{44} \end{bmatrix}$$

A 3×4 matrix such as the one shown below would not have a main diagonal because there is no straight line of elements between the top left corner and the bottom right corner that joins the elements.

$$\begin{bmatrix} n_{11} & n_{12} & n_{13} & n_{14} \\ n_{21} & n_{22} & n_{23} & n_{24} \\ n_{31} & n_{32} & n_{33} & n_{34} \end{bmatrix}$$

A **diagonal matrix** is a square matrix that has a zero for every element in the matrix except the elements on the main diagonal. All the elements on the main diagonal must be nonzero numbers.

$$\begin{bmatrix} n_{11} & 0 & 0 & 0 \\ 0 & n_{22} & 0 & 0 \\ 0 & 0 & n_{33} & 0 \\ 0 & 0 & 0 & n_{44} \end{bmatrix}$$

If every element on the main diagonal of a diagonal matrix is equal to one, the matrix is called an **identity matrix**. The identity matrix is often represented by the letter I.

$$I = \begin{bmatrix} 1 & 0 & 0 & 0 \\ 0 & 1 & 0 & 0 \\ 0 & 0 & 1 & 0 \\ 0 & 0 & 0 & 1 \end{bmatrix}$$

A **zero matrix** is a matrix that has zero as the value for every element in the matrix.

$$\begin{bmatrix} 0 & 0 & 0 & 0 \\ 0 & 0 & 0 & 0 \\ 0 & 0 & 0 & 0 \\ 0 & 0 & 0 & 0 \end{bmatrix}$$

The zero matrix is the *identity for matrix addition*. Do not confuse the zero matrix with the identity matrix.

The **negative of a matrix** is also known as the additive inverse of a matrix. If matrix N is the given matrix, then matrix $-N$ is its negative. This means that every element n_{ab} is equal to $-n_{ab}$ in the negative. To find the negative of a given matrix, change the sign of every element in the matrix and keep all elements in their original corresponding positions in the matrix.

If two matrices have the same order and all corresponding elements in the two matrices are the same, then the two matrices are **equal matrices**.

A matrix N may be **transposed** to matrix N^T by changing all rows into columns and changing all columns into rows. The easiest way to accomplish this is to swap the positions of the row and column notations for each element. For example, suppose the element in the second row of the third column of matrix N is $n_{23} = 6$. In the transposed matrix N^T, the transposed element would be $n_{32} = 6$, and it would be placed in the third row of the second column.

$$N = \begin{bmatrix} 1 & 2 & 3 \\ 4 & 5 & 6 \end{bmatrix}; \ N^T = \begin{bmatrix} 1 & 4 \\ 2 & 5 \\ 3 & 6 \end{bmatrix}$$

To quickly transpose a matrix by hand, begin with the first column and rewrite a new matrix with those same elements in the same order in the first row. Write the elements from the second column of the original matrix in the second row of the transposed matrix. Continue this process until all columns have been completed. If the original matrix is identical to the transposed matrix, the matrices are symmetric.

The **determinant** of a matrix is a scalar value that is calculated by taking into account all the elements of a square matrix. A determinant only exists for square matrices. Finding the determinant of a 2×2 matrix is as simple as remembering a simple equation. For a 2×2 matrix $M = \begin{bmatrix} m_{11} & m_{12} \\ m_{21} & m_{22} \end{bmatrix}$, the determinant is obtained by the equation $|M| = m_{11}m_{22} - m_{12}m_{21}$. Anything larger than 2×2 requires multiple steps. Take matrix $N = \begin{bmatrix} a & b & c \\ d & e & f \\ g & h & j \end{bmatrix}$. The determinant of N is

calculated as $|N| = a \begin{vmatrix} e & f \\ h & j \end{vmatrix} - b \begin{vmatrix} d & f \\ g & j \end{vmatrix} + c \begin{vmatrix} d & e \\ g & h \end{vmatrix}$ or $|N| = a(ej - fh) - b(dj - fg) + c(dh - eg)$.

There is a shortcut for 3×3 matrices: add the products of each unique set of elements diagonally left-to-right and subtract the products of each unique set of elements diagonally right-to-left. In matrix N, the left-to-right diagonal elements are (a, e, j), (b, f, g), and (c, d, h). The right-to-left diagonal elements are (a, f, h), (b, d, j), and (c, e, g). $\det(N) = aej + bfg + cdh - afh - bdj - ceg$.

Calculating the determinants of matrices larger than 3×3 is rarely, if ever, done by hand.

The **inverse** of a matrix M is the matrix that, when multiplied by matrix M, yields a product that is the identity matrix. Multiplication of matrices will be explained in greater detail shortly. Not all matrices have inverses. Only a square matrix whose determinant is not zero has an inverse. If a matrix has an inverse, that inverse is unique to that matrix. For any matrix M that has an inverse, the inverse is represented by the symbol M^{-1}. To calculate the inverse of a 2×2 square matrix, use the following pattern:

$$M = \begin{bmatrix} m_{11} & m_{12} \\ m_{21} & m_{22} \end{bmatrix}; \ M^{-1} = \begin{bmatrix} \dfrac{m_{22}}{|M|} & \dfrac{-m_{12}}{|M|} \\ \dfrac{-m_{21}}{|M|} & \dfrac{m_{11}}{|M|} \end{bmatrix}$$

Another way to find the inverse of a matrix by hand is use an augmented matrix and elementary row operations. An **augmented matrix** is formed by appending the entries from one matrix onto the end of another. For example, given a 2×2 invertible matrix $N = \begin{bmatrix} a & b \\ c & d \end{bmatrix}$, you can find the inverse N^{-1} by creating an augmented matrix by appending a 2×2 identity matrix: $\begin{bmatrix} a & b & | & 1 & 0 \\ c & d & | & 0 & 1 \end{bmatrix}$.

To find the inverse of the original 2×2 matrix, perform elementary row operations to convert the original matrix on the left to an identity matrix: $\begin{bmatrix} 1 & 0 & e & f \\ 0 & 1 & g & h \end{bmatrix}$.

Elementary row operations include multiplying a row by a non-zero scalar, adding scalar multiples of two rows, or some combination of these. For instance, the first step might be to multiply the second row by $\frac{b}{d}$ and then subtract it from the first row to make its second column a zero. The end result is that the 2×2 section on the right will become the inverse of the original matrix: $N^{-1} = \begin{bmatrix} e & f \\ g & h \end{bmatrix}$.

Calculating the inverse of any matrix larger than 2×2 is cumbersome and using a graphing calculator is recommended.

Basic Operations with Matrices

There are two categories of basic operations with regard to matrices: operations between a matrix and a scalar, and operations between two matrices.

Scalar Operations

A scalar being added to a matrix is treated as though it were being added to each element of the matrix:

$$M + 4 = \begin{bmatrix} m_{11} + 4 & m_{12} + 4 \\ m_{21} + 4 & m_{22} + 4 \end{bmatrix}$$

The same is true for the other three operations.

Subtraction:

$$M - 4 = \begin{bmatrix} m_{11} - 4 & m_{12} - 4 \\ m_{21} - 4 & m_{22} - 4 \end{bmatrix}$$

Multiplication:

$$M \times 4 = \begin{bmatrix} m_{11} \times 4 & m_{12} \times 4 \\ m_{21} \times 4 & m_{22} \times 4 \end{bmatrix}$$

Division:

$$M \div 4 = \begin{bmatrix} m_{11} \div 4 & m_{12} \div 4 \\ m_{21} \div 4 & m_{22} \div 4 \end{bmatrix}$$

Matrix Addition and Subtraction

All four of the basic operations can be used with operations between matrices (although division is usually discarded in favor of multiplication by the inverse), but there are restrictions on the situations in which they can be used. Matrices that meet all the qualifications for a given operation are called **conformable matrices**. However, conformability is specific to the operation; two matrices that are conformable for addition are not necessarily conformable for multiplication.

For two matrices to be conformable for addition or subtraction, they must be of the same dimension; otherwise the operation is not defined. If matrix M is a 3×2 matrix and matrix N is a

2×3 matrix, the operations $M + N$ and $M - N$ are meaningless. If matrices M and N are the same size, the operation is as simple as adding or subtracting all of the corresponding elements:

$$\begin{bmatrix} m_{11} & m_{12} \\ m_{21} & m_{22} \end{bmatrix} + \begin{bmatrix} n_{11} & n_{12} \\ n_{21} & n_{22} \end{bmatrix} = \begin{bmatrix} m_{11} + n_{11} & m_{12} + n_{12} \\ m_{21} + n_{21} & m_{22} + n_{22} \end{bmatrix}$$

$$\begin{bmatrix} m_{11} & m_{12} \\ m_{21} & m_{22} \end{bmatrix} - \begin{bmatrix} n_{11} & n_{12} \\ n_{21} & n_{22} \end{bmatrix} = \begin{bmatrix} m_{11} - n_{11} & m_{12} - n_{12} \\ m_{21} - n_{21} & m_{22} - n_{22} \end{bmatrix}$$

The result of addition or subtraction is a matrix of the same dimension as the two original matrices involved in the operation.

Matrix Multiplication

The first thing it is necessary to understand about matrix multiplication is that it is not commutative. In scalar multiplication, the operation is commutative, meaning that $a \times b = b \times a$. For matrix multiplication, this is not the case: $A \times B \neq B \times A$. The terminology must be specific when describing matrix multiplication. The operation $A \times B$ can be described as A multiplied (or **post-multiplied**) by B, or B **pre-multiplied** by A.

For two matrices to be conformable for multiplication, they need not be of the same dimension, but specific dimensions must correspond. Taking the example of two matrices M and N to be multiplied $M \times N$, matrix M must have the same number of columns as matrix N has rows. Put another way, if matrix M has the dimensions $a \times b$ and matrix N has the dimensions $c \times d$, b must equal c if the two matrices are to be conformable for this multiplication. The matrix that results from the multiplication will have the dimensions $a \times d$. If a and d are both equal to 1, the product is simply a scalar. Square matrices of the same dimensions are always conformable for multiplication, and their product is always a matrix of the same size.

The simplest type of matrix multiplication is a 1×2 matrix (a row vector) times a 2×1 matrix (a column vector). These will multiply in the following way:

$$\begin{bmatrix} m_{11} & m_{12} \end{bmatrix} \times \begin{bmatrix} n_{11} \\ n_{21} \end{bmatrix} = m_{11}n_{11} + m_{12}n_{21}$$

The two matrices are conformable for multiplication because matrix M has the same number of columns as matrix N has rows. Because the other dimensions are both 1, the result is a scalar. Expanding our matrices to 1×3 and 3×1, the process is the same:

$$\begin{bmatrix} m_{11} & m_{12} & m_{13} \end{bmatrix} \times \begin{bmatrix} n_{11} \\ n_{21} \\ n_{31} \end{bmatrix} = m_{11}n_{11} + m_{12}n_{21} + m_{13}n_{31}$$

Once again, the result is a scalar. This type of basic matrix multiplication is the building block for the multiplication of larger matrices.

To multiply larger matrices, treat each **row from the first matrix** and each **column from the second matrix** as individual vectors and follow the pattern for multiplying vectors. The scalar value found from multiplying the first-row vector by the first column vector is placed in the first row, first column of the new matrix. The scalar value found from multiplying the second-row vector by the first column vector is placed in the second row, first column of the new matrix. Continue this pattern until each row of the first matrix has been multiplied by each column of the second vector.

Below is an example of the multiplication of a 3 × 2 matrix and a 2 × 3 matrix.

$$\begin{bmatrix} m_{11} & m_{12} \\ m_{21} & m_{22} \\ m_{31} & m_{32} \end{bmatrix} \times \begin{bmatrix} n_{11} & n_{12} & n_{13} \\ n_{21} & n_{22} & n_{23} \end{bmatrix} = \begin{bmatrix} m_{11}n_{11} + m_{12}n_{21} & m_{11}n_{12} + m_{12}n_{22} & m_{11}n_{13} + m_{12}n_{23} \\ m_{21}n_{11} + m_{22}n_{21} & m_{21}n_{12} + m_{22}n_{22} & m_{21}n_{13} + m_{22}n_{23} \\ m_{31}n_{11} + m_{32}n_{21} & m_{31}n_{12} + m_{32}n_{22} & m_{31}n_{13} + m_{32}n_{23} \end{bmatrix}$$

This process starts by taking the first column of the second matrix and running it through each row of the first matrix. Removing all but the first M row and first N column, we would see only the following:

$$[m_{11} \ \ m_{12}] \times \begin{bmatrix} n_{11} \\ n_{21} \end{bmatrix}$$

The first product would then be $m_{11}n_{11} + m_{12}n_{21}$. This process will be continued for each column of the N matrix to find the first full row of the product matrix, as shown below.

$$[m_{11} \ \ m_{12}] \times \begin{bmatrix} n_{11} \\ n_{21} \end{bmatrix} = [m_{11}n_{11} + m_{12}n_{21} \ \ \ \ m_{11}n_{12} + m_{12}n_{22} \ \ \ \ m_{11}n_{13} + m_{12}n_{23}]$$

After completing the first row, the next step would be to simply move to the second row of the M matrix and repeat the process until all of the rows have been finished. The result is a 3 × 3 matrix.

$$\begin{bmatrix} m_{11} & m_{12} \\ m_{21} & m_{22} \\ m_{31} & m_{32} \end{bmatrix} \times \begin{bmatrix} n_{11} & n_{12} & n_{13} \\ n_{21} & n_{22} & n_{23} \end{bmatrix} = \begin{bmatrix} m_{11}n_{11} + m_{12}n_{21} & m_{11}n_{12} + m_{12}n_{22} & m_{11}n_{13} + m_{12}n_{23} \\ m_{21}n_{11} + m_{22}n_{21} & m_{21}n_{12} + m_{22}n_{22} & m_{21}n_{13} + m_{22}n_{23} \\ m_{31}n_{11} + m_{32}n_{21} & m_{31}n_{12} + m_{32}n_{22} & m_{31}n_{13} + m_{32}n_{23} \end{bmatrix}$$

If the operation were done in reverse ($N \times M$), the result would be a 2 × 2 matrix.

$$\begin{bmatrix} n_{11} & n_{12} & n_{13} \\ n_{21} & n_{22} & n_{23} \end{bmatrix} \times \begin{bmatrix} m_{11} & m_{12} \\ m_{21} & m_{22} \\ m_{31} & m_{32} \end{bmatrix} = \begin{bmatrix} m_{11}n_{11} + m_{21}n_{12} + m_{31}n_{13} & m_{12}n_{11} + m_{22}n_{12} + m_{32}n_{13} \\ m_{11}n_{21} + m_{21}n_{22} + m_{31}n_{23} & m_{12}n_{21} + m_{22}n_{22} + m_{32}n_{23} \end{bmatrix}$$

Example

A sporting-goods store sells baseballs, volleyballs, and basketballs.

Baseballs	$3 each
Volleyballs	$8 each
Basketballs	$15 each

Here are the same store's sales numbers for one weekend:

	Baseballs	Volleyballs	Basketballs
Friday	5	4	4
Saturday	7	3	10
Sunday	4	3	6

Find the total sales for each day by multiplying matrices.

The first table can be represented by the following column-vector:

$$\begin{bmatrix} 3 \\ 8 \\ 15 \end{bmatrix}$$

And the second table can be represented by this matrix:

$$\begin{bmatrix} 5 & 4 & 4 \\ 7 & 3 & 10 \\ 4 & 3 & 6 \end{bmatrix}$$

Multiplying the second matrix by the first will result in a column vector showing the total sales for each day:

$$\begin{bmatrix} 5 & 4 & 4 \\ 7 & 3 & 10 \\ 4 & 3 & 6 \end{bmatrix} \times \begin{bmatrix} 3 \\ 8 \\ 15 \end{bmatrix} = \begin{bmatrix} 3 \times 5 + 8 \times 4 + 15 \times 4 \\ 3 \times 7 + 8 \times 3 + 15 \times 10 \\ 3 \times 4 + 8 \times 3 + 15 \times 6 \end{bmatrix} = \begin{bmatrix} 15 + 32 + 60 \\ 21 + 24 + 150 \\ 12 + 24 + 90 \end{bmatrix} = \begin{bmatrix} 107 \\ 195 \\ 126 \end{bmatrix}$$

From this, we can see that Friday's sales were \$107, Saturday's sales were \$195, and Sunday's sales were \$126.

Solving Systems of Equations

Matrices can be used to represent the coefficients of a system of linear equations and can be very useful in solving those systems. Take for instance three equations with three variables:

$$a_1 x + b_1 y + c_1 z = d_1$$

$$a_2 x + b_2 y + c_2 z = d_2$$

$$a_3 x + b_3 y + c_3 z = d_3$$

where all a, b, c, and d are known constants.

To solve this system, define three matrices:

$$A = \begin{bmatrix} a_1 & b_1 & c_1 \\ a_2 & b_2 & c_2 \\ a_3 & b_3 & c_3 \end{bmatrix}; \ D = \begin{bmatrix} d_1 \\ d_2 \\ d_3 \end{bmatrix}; \ X = \begin{bmatrix} x \\ y \\ z \end{bmatrix}$$

The three equations in our system can be fully represented by a single matrix equation:

$$AX = D$$

We know that the identity matrix times X is equal to X, and we know that any matrix multiplied by its inverse is equal to the identity matrix.

$$A^{-1}AX = IX = X; \text{thus } X = A^{-1}D$$

Our goal then is to find the inverse of A, or A^{-1}. Once we have that, we can pre-multiply matrix D by A^{-1} (post-multiplying here is an undefined operation) to find matrix X.

Systems of equations can also be solved using the transformation of an augmented matrix in a process similar to that for finding a matrix inverse. Begin by arranging each equation of the system in the following format:

$$a_1x + b_1y + c_1z = d_1$$

$$a_2x + b_2y + c_2z = d_2$$

$$a_3x + b_3y + c_3z = d_3$$

Define matrices A and D and combine them into augmented matrix A_a:

$$A = \begin{bmatrix} a_1 & b_1 & c_1 \\ a_2 & b_2 & c_2 \\ a_3 & b_3 & c_3 \end{bmatrix}; \; D = \begin{bmatrix} d_1 \\ d_2 \\ d_3 \end{bmatrix}; \; A_a = \begin{bmatrix} a_1 & b_1 & c_1 & d_1 \\ a_2 & b_2 & c_2 & d_2 \\ a_3 & b_3 & c_3 & d_3 \end{bmatrix}$$

To solve the augmented matrix and the system of equations, use elementary row operations to form an identity matrix in the first 3×3 section. When this is complete, the values in the last column are the solutions to the system of equations:

$$\begin{bmatrix} 1 & 0 & 0 & x \\ 0 & 1 & 0 & y \\ 0 & 0 & 1 & z \end{bmatrix}$$

If an identity matrix is not possible, the system of equations has no unique solution. Sometimes only a partial solution will be possible. The following are partial solutions you may find:

$$\begin{bmatrix} 1 & 0 & k_1 & x_0 \\ 0 & 1 & k_2 & y_0 \\ 0 & 0 & 0 & 0 \end{bmatrix}$$ gives the non-unique solution $x = x_0 - k_1z$; $y = y_0 - k_2z$

$$\begin{bmatrix} 1 & j_1 & k_1 & x_0 \\ 0 & 0 & 0 & 0 \\ 0 & 0 & 0 & 0 \end{bmatrix}$$ gives the non-unique solution $x = x_0 - j_1y - k_1z$

This process can be used to solve systems of equations with any number of variables, but three is the upper limit for practical purposes. Anything more ought to be done with a graphing calculator.

Geometric Transformations

The four *geometric transformations* are **translations**, **reflections**, **rotations**, and **dilations**. When geometric transformations are expressed as matrices, the process of performing the transformations is simplified. For calculations of the geometric transformations of a planar figure, make a $2 \times n$ matrix, where n is the number of vertices in the planar figure. Each column represents the rectangular coordinates of one vertex of the figure, with the top row containing the values of the x-coordinates and the bottom row containing the values of the y-coordinates. For example, given a planar triangular figure with coordinates (x_1, y_1), (x_2, y_2), and (x_3, y_3), the corresponding matrix is $\begin{bmatrix} x_1 & x_2 & x_3 \\ y_1 & y_2 & y_3 \end{bmatrix}$. You can then perform the necessary transformations on this matrix to determine the coordinates of the resulting figure.

Translation

A **translation** moves a figure along the x-axis, the y-axis, or both axes without changing the size or shape of the figure. To calculate the new coordinates of a planar figure following a translation, set up a matrix of the coordinates and a matrix of the translation values and add the two matrices.

$$\begin{bmatrix} h & h & h \\ v & v & v \end{bmatrix} + \begin{bmatrix} x_1 & x_2 & x_3 \\ y_1 & y_2 & y_3 \end{bmatrix} = \begin{bmatrix} h + x_1 & h + x_2 & h + x_3 \\ v + y_1 & v + y_2 & v + y_3 \end{bmatrix}$$

where h is the number of units the figure is moved along the x-axis (horizontally) and v is the number of units the figure is moved along the y-axis (vertically).

Reflection

To find the **reflection** of a planar figure over the x-axis, set up a matrix of the coordinates of the vertices and pre-multiply the matrix by the 2×2 matrix $\begin{bmatrix} 1 & 0 \\ 0 & -1 \end{bmatrix}$ so that $\begin{bmatrix} 1 & 0 \\ 0 & -1 \end{bmatrix} \begin{bmatrix} x_1 & x_2 & x_3 \\ y_1 & y_2 & y_3 \end{bmatrix} = \begin{bmatrix} x_1 & x_2 & x_3 \\ -y_1 & -y_2 & -y_3 \end{bmatrix}$. To find the reflection of a planar figure over the y-axis, set up a matrix of the coordinates of the vertices and pre-multiply the matrix by the 2×2 matrix $\begin{bmatrix} -1 & 0 \\ 0 & 1 \end{bmatrix}$ so that $\begin{bmatrix} -1 & 0 \\ 0 & 1 \end{bmatrix} \begin{bmatrix} x_1 & x_2 & x_3 \\ y_1 & y_2 & y_3 \end{bmatrix} = \begin{bmatrix} -x_1 & -x_2 & -x_3 \\ y_1 & y_2 & y_3 \end{bmatrix}$. To find the reflection of a planar figure over the line $y = x$, set up a matrix of the coordinates of the vertices and pre-multiply the matrix by the 2×2 matrix $\begin{bmatrix} 0 & 1 \\ 1 & 0 \end{bmatrix}$ so that $\begin{bmatrix} 0 & 1 \\ 1 & 0 \end{bmatrix} \begin{bmatrix} x_1 & x_2 & x_3 \\ y_1 & y_2 & y_3 \end{bmatrix} = \begin{bmatrix} y_1 & y_2 & y_3 \\ x_1 & x_2 & x_3 \end{bmatrix}$. Remember that the order of multiplication is important when multiplying matrices. The commutative property does not apply.

Rotation

To find the coordinates of the figure formed by rotating a planar figure about the origin θ degrees in a counterclockwise direction, set up a matrix of the coordinates of the vertices and pre-multiply the matrix by the 2×2 matrix $\begin{bmatrix} \cos\theta & \sin\theta \\ -\sin\theta & \cos\theta \end{bmatrix}$. For example, if you want to rotate a figure 90° clockwise around the origin, you would have to convert the degree measure to 270° counterclockwise and solve the 2×2 matrix you have set as the pre-multiplier: $\begin{bmatrix} \cos 270° & \sin 270° \\ -\sin 270° & \cos 270° \end{bmatrix} = \begin{bmatrix} 0 & -1 \\ 1 & 0 \end{bmatrix}$. Use this as the pre-multiplier for the matrix $\begin{bmatrix} x_1 & x_2 & x_3 \\ y_1 & y_2 & y_3 \end{bmatrix}$ and solve to find the new coordinates.

Dilation

To find the **dilation** of a planar figure by a scale factor of k, set up a matrix of the coordinates of the vertices of the planar figure and pre-multiply the matrix by the 2×2 matrix $\begin{bmatrix} k & 0 \\ 0 & k \end{bmatrix}$ so that $\begin{bmatrix} k & 0 \\ 0 & k \end{bmatrix} \begin{bmatrix} x_1 & x_2 & x_3 \\ y_1 & y_2 & y_3 \end{bmatrix} = \begin{bmatrix} kx_1 & kx_2 & kx_3 \\ ky_1 & ky_2 & ky_3 \end{bmatrix}$. This is effectively the same as multiplying the matrix by the scalar k, but the matrix equation would still be necessary if the figure were being dilated by different factors in vertical and horizontal directions. The scale factor k will be greater than 1 if the figure is being enlarged, and between 0 and 1 if the figure is being shrunk. Again, remember that when multiplying matrices, the order of the matrices is important. The commutative property does not apply, and the matrix with the coordinates of the figure must be the second matrix.

Geometry and Measurement

Lines and Planes

A **point** is a fixed location in space; has no size or dimensions; commonly represented by a dot.

A **line** is a set of points that extends infinitely in two opposite directions. It has length, but no width or depth. A line can be defined by any two distinct points that it contains. A line segment is a portion of a line that has definite endpoints. A ray is a portion of a line that extends from a single point on that line in one direction along the line. It has a definite beginning, but no ending.

A **plane** is a two-dimensional flat surface defined by three non-collinear points. A plane extends an infinite distance in all directions in those two dimensions. It contains an infinite number of points, parallel lines and segments, intersecting lines and segments, as well as parallel or intersecting rays. A plane will never contain a three-dimensional figure or skew lines. Two given planes will either be parallel or they will intersect to form a line. A plane may intersect a circular conic surface, such as a cone, to form conic sections, such as the parabola, hyperbola, circle or ellipse.

Perpendicular lines are lines that intersect at right angles. They are represented by the symbol $\perp$. The shortest distance from a line to a point not on the line is a perpendicular segment from the point to the line.

Parallel lines are lines in the same plane that have no points in common and never meet. It is possible for lines to be in different planes, have no points in common, and never meet, but they are not parallel because they are in different planes.

A **bisector** is a line or line segment that divides another line segment into two equal lengths. A perpendicular bisector of a line segment is composed of points that are equidistant from the endpoints of the segment it is dividing.

Intersecting lines are lines that have exactly one point in common. Concurrent lines are multiple lines that intersect at a single point.

A **transversal** is a line that intersects at least two other lines, which may or may not be parallel to one another. A transversal that intersects parallel lines is a common occurrence in geometry.

Angles

An **angle** is formed when two lines or line segments meet at a common point. It may be a common starting point for a pair of segments or rays, or it may be the intersection of lines. Angles are represented by the symbol $\angle$.

The **vertex** is the point at which two segments or rays meet to form an angle. If the angle is formed by intersecting rays, lines, and/or line segments, the vertex is the point at which four angles are formed. The pairs of angles opposite one another are called vertical angles, and their measures are equal.

An *acute* angle is an angle with a degree measure less than 90°.

A *right* angle is an angle with a degree measure of exactly 90°.

An *obtuse* angle is an angle with a degree measure greater than 90° but less than 180°.

A *straight angle* is an angle with a degree measure of exactly 180°. This is also a semicircle.

A *reflex angle* is an angle with a degree measure greater than 180° but less than 360°.

A *full angle* is an angle with a degree measure of exactly 360°.

Two angles whose sum is exactly 90° are said to be **complementary**. The two angles may or may not be adjacent. In a right triangle, the two acute angles are complementary.

Two angles whose sum is exactly 180° are said to be **supplementary**. The two angles may or may not be adjacent. Two intersecting lines always form two pairs of supplementary angles. Adjacent supplementary angles will always form a straight line.

Two angles that have the same vertex and share a side are said to be **adjacent**. Vertical angles are not adjacent because they share a vertex but no common side.

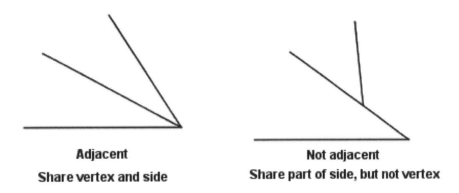

Adjacent
Share vertex and side

Not adjacent
Share part of side, but not vertex

When two parallel lines are cut by a transversal, the angles that are between the two parallel lines are **interior angles**. In the diagram below, angles 3, 4, 5, and 6 are interior angles.

When two parallel lines are cut by a transversal, the angles that are outside the parallel lines are **exterior angles**. In the diagram below, angles 1, 2, 7, and 8 are exterior angles.

When two parallel lines are cut by a transversal, the angles that are in the same position relative to the transversal and a parallel line are *corresponding angles*. The diagram below has four pairs of corresponding angles: angles 1 and 5; angles 2 and 6; angles 3 and 7; and angles 4 and 8. Corresponding angles formed by parallel lines are congruent.

When two parallel lines are cut by a transversal, the two interior angles that are on opposite sides of the transversal are called *alternate interior angles*. In the diagram below, there are two pairs of alternate interior angles: angles 3 and 6, and angles 4 and 5. Alternate interior angles formed by parallel lines are congruent.

When two parallel lines are cut by a transversal, the two exterior angles that are on opposite sides of the transversal are called *alternate exterior angles*.

In the diagram below, there are two pairs of alternate exterior angles: angles 1 and 8, and angles 2 and 7. Alternate exterior angles formed by parallel lines are congruent.

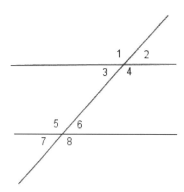

When two lines intersect, four angles are formed. The non-adjacent angles at this vertex are called vertical angles. Vertical angles are congruent. In the diagram, $\angle ABD \cong \angle CBE$ and $\angle ABC \cong \angle DBE$.

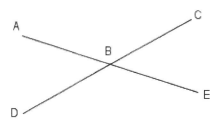

Polygons

Each straight line segment of a polygon is called a **side**.

The point at which two sides of a polygon intersect is called the **vertex**. In a polygon, the number of sides is always equal to the number of vertices.

A polygon with all sides congruent and all angles equal is called a **regular polygon**.

A line segment from the center of a polygon perpendicular to a side of the polygon is called the **apothem**. In a regular polygon, the apothem can be used to find the area of the polygon using the formula $A = \frac{1}{2}ap$, where a is the apothem and p is the perimeter.

A line segment from the center of a polygon to a vertex of the polygon is called a **radius**. The radius of a regular polygon is also the radius of a circle that can be circumscribed about the polygon.

Triangle – 3 sides

Quadrilateral – 4 sides

Pentagon – 5 sides

Hexagon – 6 sides

Heptagon – 7 sides

Octagon – 8 sides

Nonagon – 9 sides

Decagon – 10 sides

Dodecagon – 12 sides

More generally, an *n*-gon is a polygon that has *n* angles and *n* sides.

The sum of the interior angles of an *n*-sided polygon is $(n-2)180°$. For example, in a triangle $n = 3$, so the sum of the interior angles is $(3-2)180° = 180°$. In a quadrilateral, $n = 4$, and the sum of the angles is $(4-2)180° = 360°$. The sum of the interior angles of a polygon is equal to the sum of the interior angles of any other polygon with the same number of sides.

A **diagonal** is a line segment that joins two non-adjacent vertices of a polygon.

A **convex polygon** is a polygon whose diagonals all lie within the interior of the polygon.

A **concave polygon** is a polygon with a least one diagonal that lies outside the polygon. In the diagram below, quadrilateral *ABCD* is concave because diagonal $\overline{AC}$ lies outside the polygon.

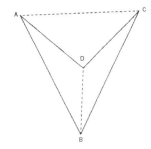

The number of diagonals a polygon has can be found by using the formula: number of diagonals $= \frac{n(n-3)}{2}$, where *n* is the number of sides in the polygon. This formula works for all polygons, not just regular polygons.

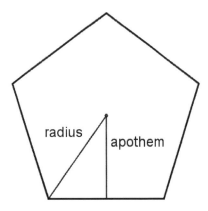

Congruent figures are geometric figures that have the same size and shape. All corresponding angles are equal, and all corresponding sides are equal. It is indicated by the symbol ≅.

Congruent polygons

Similar figures are geometric figures that have the same shape, but do not necessarily have the same size. All corresponding angles are equal, and all corresponding sides are proportional, but they do not have to be equal. It is indicated by the symbol ~.

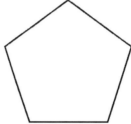

Similar polygons

Note that all congruent figures are also similar, but not all similar figures are congruent.

Review Video: Polygons, Similarity, and Congruence
Visit mometrix.com/academy and enter code: 686174

Line of Symmetry

A **line of symmetry** is a line that divides a figure or object into two symmetric parts. Each symmetric half is congruent to the other. An object may have no lines of symmetry, one line of symmetry, or more than one line of symmetry.

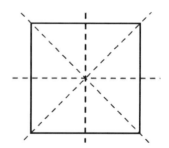

No lines of symmetry   One line of symmetry   Multiple lines of symmetry

Quadrilateral: A closed two-dimensional geometric figure composed of exactly four straight sides. The sum of the interior angles of any quadrilateral is 360°.

Parallelogram

A **parallelogram** is a quadrilateral that has exactly two pairs of opposite parallel sides. The sides that are parallel are also congruent. The opposite interior angles are always congruent, and the consecutive interior angles are supplementary. The diagonals of a parallelogram bisect each other. Each diagonal divides the parallelogram into two congruent triangles.

Trapezoid

Traditionally, a **trapezoid** is a quadrilateral that has exactly one pair of parallel sides. Some math texts define trapezoid as a quadrilateral that has at least one pair of parallel sides. Because there are no rules governing the second pair of sides, there are no rules that apply to the properties of the diagonals of a trapezoid.

Rectangles, rhombuses, and squares are all special forms of parallelograms.

Rectangle

A **rectangle** is a parallelogram with four right angles. All rectangles are parallelograms, but not all parallelograms are rectangles. The diagonals of a rectangle are congruent.

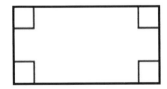

Rhombus

A **rhombus** is a parallelogram with four congruent sides. All rhombuses are parallelograms, but not all parallelograms are rhombuses. The diagonals of a rhombus are perpendicular to each other.

Review Video: Diagonals of Parallelograms, Rectangles, and Rhombi
Visit mometrix.com/academy and enter code: 320040

Square

A **square** is a parallelogram with four right angles and four congruent sides. All squares are also parallelograms, rhombuses, and rectangles. The diagonals of a square are congruent and perpendicular to each other.

A quadrilateral whose diagonals bisect each other is a **parallelogram**. A quadrilateral whose opposite sides are parallel (2 pairs of parallel sides) is a parallelogram.

A quadrilateral whose diagonals are perpendicular bisectors of each other is a **rhombus**. A quadrilateral whose opposite sides (both pairs) are parallel and congruent is a rhombus.

A parallelogram that has a right angle is a **rectangle**. (Consecutive angles of a parallelogram are supplementary. Therefore if there is one right angle in a parallelogram, there are four right angles in that parallelogram.)

A rhombus with one right angle is a **square**. Because the rhombus is a special form of a parallelogram, the rules about the angles of a parallelogram also apply to the rhombus.

- 190 -

Area and Perimeter Formulas

Triangle

The *perimeter of any triangle* is found by summing the three side lengths; $P = a + b + c$. For an equilateral triangle, this is the same as $P = 3s$, where s is any side length, since all three sides are the same length.

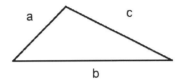

Square

The *area of a square* is found by using the formula $A = s^2$, where and s is the length of one side.

The *perimeter of a square* is found by using the formula $P = 4s$, where s is the length of one side. Because all four sides are equal in a square, it is faster to multiply the length of one side by 4 than to add the same number four times. You could use the formulas for rectangles and get the same answer.

> **Review Video: Area and Perimeter of a Square**
> Visit mometrix.com/academy and enter code: 620902

Rectangle

The *area of a rectangle* is found by the formula $A = lw$, where A is the area of the rectangle, l is the length (usually considered to be the longer side) and w is the width (usually considered to be the shorter side). The numbers for l and w are interchangeable.

The *perimeter of a rectangle* is found by the formula $P = 2l + 2w$ or $P = 2(l + w)$, where l is the length, and w is the width. It may be easier to add the length and width first and then double the result, as in the second formula.

> **Review Video: Area and Perimeter of a Rectangle**
> Visit mometrix.com/academy and enter code: 933707

Parallelogram

The *area of a parallelogram* is found by the formula $A = bh$, where b is the length of the base, and h is the height. Note that the base and height correspond to the length and width in a rectangle, so this formula would apply to rectangles as well. Do not confuse the height of a parallelogram with the length of the second side. The two are only the same measure in the case of a rectangle.

The *perimeter of a parallelogram* is found by the formula $P = 2a + 2b$ or $P = 2(a + b)$, where a and b are the lengths of the two sides.

> **Review Video: Area and Perimeter of a Parallelogram**
> Visit mometrix.com/academy and enter code: 718313

<u>Trapezoid</u>

The *area of a trapezoid* is found by the formula $A = \frac{1}{2}h(b_1 + b_2)$, where h is the height (segment joining and perpendicular to the parallel bases), and b_1 and b_2 are the two parallel sides (bases). Do not use one of the other two sides as the height unless that side is also perpendicular to the parallel bases.

The *perimeter of a trapezoid* is found by the formula $P = a + b_1 + c + b_2$, where a, b_1, c, and b_2 are the four sides of the trapezoid.

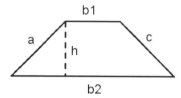

Triangles

An **equilateral triangle** is a triangle with three congruent sides. An equilateral triangle will also have three congruent angles, each 60°. All equilateral triangles are also acute triangles.

An **isosceles triangle** is a triangle with two congruent sides. An isosceles triangle will also have two congruent angles opposite the two congruent sides.

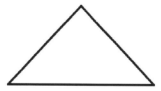

A **scalene triangle** is a triangle with no congruent sides. A scalene triangle will also have three angles of different measures. The angle with the largest measure is opposite the longest side, and the angle with the smallest measure is opposite the shortest side.

An **acute triangle** is a triangle whose three angles are all less than 90°. If two of the angles are equal, the acute triangle is also an isosceles triangle. If the three angles are all equal, the acute triangle is also an equilateral triangle.

A **right triangle** is a triangle with exactly one angle equal to 90°. All right triangles follow the Pythagorean theorem. A right triangle can never be acute or obtuse.

An **obtuse triangle** is a triangle with exactly one angle greater than 90°. The other two angles may or may not be equal. If the two remaining angles are equal, the obtuse triangle is also an isosceles triangle.

Terminology

Altitude of a triangle
A line segment drawn from one vertex perpendicular to the opposite side. In the diagram below, $\overline{BE}$, $\overline{AD}$, and $\overline{CF}$ are altitudes. The three altitudes in a triangle are always concurrent.

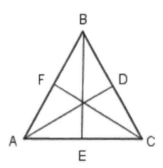

Height of a triangle
The length of the altitude, although the two terms are often used interchangeably.

Orthocenter of a triangle
The point of concurrency of the altitudes of a triangle. Note that in an obtuse triangle, the orthocenter will be outside the triangle, and in a right triangle, the orthocenter is the vertex of the right angle.

Median of a triangle
A line segment drawn from one vertex to the midpoint of the opposite side. This is not the same as the altitude, except the altitude to the base of an isosceles triangle and all three altitudes of an equilateral triangle.

Centroid of a triangle
The point of concurrency of the medians of a triangle. This is the same point as the orthocenter only in an equilateral triangle. Unlike the orthocenter, the centroid is always inside the triangle. The centroid can also be considered the exact center of the triangle. Any shape triangle can be perfectly balanced on a tip placed at the centroid. The centroid is also the point that is two-thirds the distance from the vertex to the opposite side.

Pythagorean Theorem

The side of a triangle opposite the right angle is called the **hypotenuse**. The other two sides are called the legs. The Pythagorean theorem states a relationship among the legs and hypotenuse of a right triangle: $a^2 + b^2 = c^2$, where a and b are the lengths of the legs of a right triangle, and c is the length of the hypotenuse. Note that this formula will only work with right triangles.

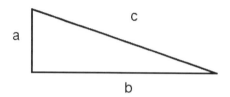

General Rules

The *triangle inequality theorem* states that the sum of the measures of any two sides of a triangle is always greater than the measure of the third side. If the sum of the measures of two sides were equal to the third side, a triangle would be impossible because the two sides would lie flat across the third side and there would be no vertex. If the sum of the measures of two of the sides was less than the third side, a closed figure would be impossible because the two shortest sides would never meet.

The sum of the measures of the interior angles of a triangle is always 180°. Therefore, a triangle can never have more than one angle greater than or equal to 90°.

In any triangle, the angles opposite congruent sides are congruent, and the sides opposite congruent angles are congruent. The largest angle is always opposite the longest side, and the smallest angle is always opposite the shortest side.

The line segment that joins the midpoints of any two sides of a triangle is always parallel to the third side and exactly half the length of the third side.

Similarity and Congruence Rules

Similar triangles are triangles whose corresponding angles are equal and whose corresponding sides are proportional. Represented by AA. Similar triangles whose corresponding sides are congruent are also congruent triangles.

Three sides of one triangle are congruent to the three corresponding sides of the second triangle. Represented as SSS.

Two sides and the included angle (the angle formed by those two sides) of one triangle are congruent to the corresponding two sides and included angle of the second triangle. Represented by SAS.

Two angles and the included side (the side that joins the two angles) of one triangle are congruent to the corresponding two angles and included side of the second triangle. Represented by ASA.

Two angles and a non-included side of one triangle are congruent to the corresponding two angles and non-included side of the second triangle. Represented by AAS.

Note that AAA is not a form for congruent triangles. This would say that the three angles are congruent, but says nothing about the sides. This meets the requirements for similar triangles, but not congruent triangles.

Area and Perimeter Formulas

The *perimeter of any triangle* is found by summing the three side lengths; $P = a + b + c$. For an equilateral triangle, this is the same as $P = 3s$, where s is any side length, since all three sides are the same length.

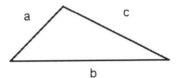

The area of any triangle can be found by taking half the product of one side length (base or b) and the perpendicular distance from that side to the opposite vertex (height or h). In equation form, $A = \frac{1}{2}bh$. For many triangles, it may be difficult to calculate h, so using one of the other formulas given here may be easier.

Another formula that works for any triangle is $A = \sqrt{s(s - a)(s - b)(s - c)}$, where A is the area, s is the semiperimeter $s = \frac{a+b+c}{2}$, and a, b, and c are the lengths of the three sides.

The area of an equilateral triangle can be found by the formula $A = \frac{\sqrt{3}}{4}s^2$, where A is the area and s is the length of a side. You could use the $30° - 60° - 90°$ ratios to find the height of the triangle and then use the standard triangle area formula, but this is faster.

The area of an isosceles triangle can be found by the formula, $A = \frac{1}{2}b\sqrt{a^2 - \frac{b^2}{4}}$, where A is the area, b is the base (the unique side), and a is the length of one of the two congruent sides. If you do not remember this formula, you can use the Pythagorean theorem to find the height so you can use the standard formula for the area of a triangle.

Rotation, Center of Rotation, and Angle of Rotation

A *rotation* is a transformation that turns a figure around a point called the **center of rotation**, which can lie anywhere in the plane. If a line is drawn from a point on a figure to the center of rotation, and another line is drawn from the center to the rotated image of that point, the angle between the two lines is the **angle of rotation**. The vertex of the angle of rotation is the center of rotation.

Reflection over a Line and Reflection in a Point

A reflection of a figure over a *line* (a "flip") creates a congruent image that is the same distance from the line as the original figure but on the opposite side. The **line of reflection** is the perpendicular bisector of any line segment drawn from a point on the original figure to its reflected image (unless the point and its reflected image happen to be the same point, which happens when a figure is reflected over one of its own sides).

A reflection of a figure in a *point* is the same as the rotation of the figure 180° about that point. The image of the figure is congruent to the original figure. The **point of reflection** is the midpoint of a line segment which connects a point in the figure to its image (unless the point and its reflected image happen to be the same point, which happens when a figure is reflected in one of its own points).

<u>Example</u>

Use the coordinate plane of the given image below to reflect the image across the *y*-axis.

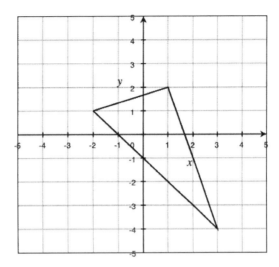

To reflect the image across the *y*-axis, replace each *x*-coordinate of the points that are the vertex of the triangle, *x*, with its negative, −*x*.

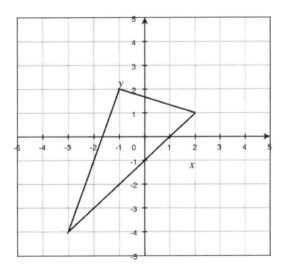

Translation

A *translation* is a transformation which slides a figure from one position in the plane to another position in the plane. The original figure and the translated figure have the same size, shape, and orientation.

Review Video: Translation
Visit mometrix.com/academy and enter code: 718628

Transforming a Given Figure Using Rotation, Reflection, and Translation

To **rotate** a given figure: 1. Identify the point of rotation. 2. Using tracing paper, geometry software, or by approximation, recreate the figure at a new location around the point of rotation.

- 197 -

To **reflect** a given figure: 1. Identify the line of reflection. 2. By folding the paper, using geometry software, or by approximation, recreate the image at a new location on the other side of the line of reflection.

To **translate** a given figure: 1. Identify the new location. 2. Using graph paper, geometry software, or by approximation, recreate the figure in the new location. If using graph paper, make a chart of the x- and y-values to keep track of the coordinates of all critical points.

Evidence of Transformation

To identify that a figure has been *rotated*, look for evidence that the figure is still face-up, but has changed its orientation.

To identify that a figure has been *reflected* across a line, look for evidence that the figure is now face-down.

To identify that a figure has been *translated*, look for evidence that a figure is still face-up and has not changed orientation; the only change is location.

To identify that a figure has been *dilated*, look for evidence that the figure has changed its size but not its orientation.

Dilation

A **dilation** is a transformation which proportionally stretches or shrinks a figure by a **scale factor**. The dilated image is the same shape and orientation as the original image but a different size. A polygon and its dilated image are similar.

Example 1

Use the coordinate plane to create a dilation of the given image below, where the dilation is the enlargement of the original image.

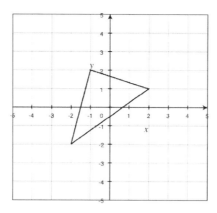

An enlargement can be found by multiplying each coordinate of the coordinate pairs located at the triangles vertices by a constant. If the figure is enlarged by a factor of 2, the new image would be:

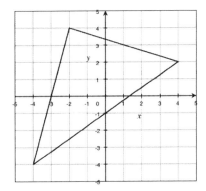

Trigonometric Formulas

In the diagram below, angle C is the **right angle**, and side c is the **hypotenuse**. Side a is the side adjacent to angle B and side b is the side adjacent to angle A. These formulas will work for any acute angle in a right triangle. They will *not* work for any triangle that is not a right triangle. Also, they will not work for the right angle in a right triangle, since there are not distinct adjacent and opposite sides to differentiate from the hypotenuse.

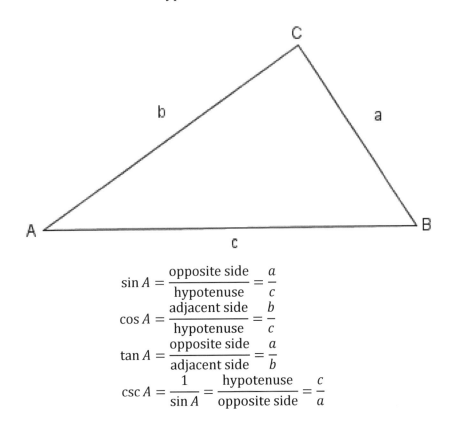

$$\sin A = \frac{\text{opposite side}}{\text{hypotenuse}} = \frac{a}{c}$$

$$\cos A = \frac{\text{adjacent side}}{\text{hypotenuse}} = \frac{b}{c}$$

$$\tan A = \frac{\text{opposite side}}{\text{adjacent side}} = \frac{a}{b}$$

$$\csc A = \frac{1}{\sin A} = \frac{\text{hypotenuse}}{\text{opposite side}} = \frac{c}{a}$$

$$\sec A = \frac{1}{\cos A} = \frac{\text{hypotenuse}}{\text{adjacent side}} = \frac{c}{b}$$

$$\cot A = \frac{1}{\tan A} = \frac{\text{adjacent side}}{\text{opposite side}} = \frac{b}{a}$$

Laws of Sines and Cosines

The **law of sines** states that $\frac{\sin A}{a} = \frac{\sin B}{b} = \frac{\sin C}{c}$, where A, B, and C are the angles of a triangle, and a, b, and c are the sides opposite their respective angles. This formula will work with all triangles, not just right triangles.

The **law of cosines** is given by the formula $c^2 = a^2 + b^2 - 2ab(\cos C)$, where a, b, and c are the sides of a triangle, and C is the angle opposite side c. This formula is similar to the *pythagorean theorem*, but unlike the pythagorean theorem, it can be used on any triangle.

> **Review Video: Cosine**
> Visit mometrix.com/academy and enter code: 361120

Circles

The **center** is the single point inside the circle that is **equidistant** from every point on the circle. (Point O in the diagram below.)

> **Review Video: Points of a Circle**
> Visit mometrix.com/academy and enter code: 420746

The **radius** is a line segment that joins the center of the circle and any one point on the circle. All radii of a circle are equal. (Segments OX, OY, and OZ in the diagram below.)

The **diameter** is a line segment that passes through the center of the circle and has both endpoints on the circle. The length of the diameter is exactly twice the length of the radius. (Segment XZ in the diagram below.)

The **area of a circle** is found by the formula $A = \pi r^2$, where r is the length of the radius. If the diameter of the circle is given, remember to divide it in half to get the length of the radius before proceeding.

> **Review Video: The Diameter, Radius, and Circumference of Circles**
> Visit mometrix.com/academy and enter code: 448988

The **circumference** of a circle is found by the formula $C = 2\pi r$, where r is the radius. Again, remember to convert the diameter if you are given that measure rather than the radius.

Concentric circles are circles that have the same center, but not the same length of radii. A bulls-eye target is an example of concentric circles.

An **arc** is a portion of a circle. Specifically, an arc is the set of points between and including two points on a circle. An arc does not contain any points inside the circle. When a segment is drawn from the endpoints of an arc to the center of the circle, a sector is formed.

A **central angle** is an angle whose vertex is the center of a circle and whose legs intercept an arc of the circle. Angle *XOY* in the diagram above is a central angle. A minor arc is an arc that has a measure less than 180°. The measure of a central angle is equal to the measure of the minor arc it intercepts. A major arc is an arc having a measure of at least 180°. The measure of the major arc can be found by subtracting the measure of the central angle from 360°.

A **semicircle** is an arc whose endpoints are the endpoints of the diameter of a circle. A semicircle is exactly half of a circle.

An **inscribed angle** is an angle whose vertex lies on a circle and whose legs contain chords of that circle. The portion of the circle intercepted by the legs of the angle is called the intercepted arc. The measure of the intercepted arc is exactly twice the measure of the inscribed angle. In the following diagram, angle *ABC* is an inscribed angle. $\widehat{AC} = 2(m\angle ABC)$

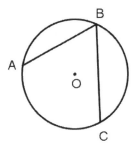

Any angle inscribed in a semicircle is a right angle. The intercepted arc is 180°, making the inscribed angle half that, or 90°. In the diagram below, angle *ABC* is inscribed in semicircle *ABC*, making angle *ABC* equal to 90°.

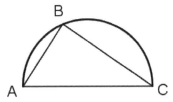

A **chord** is a line segment that has both endpoints on a circle. In the diagram below, $\overline{EB}$ is a chord.

Secant: A line that passes through a circle and contains a chord of that circle. In the diagram below, $\overleftrightarrow{EB}$ is a secant and contains chord $\overline{EB}$.

A **tangent** is a line in the same plane as a circle that touches the circle in exactly one point. While a line segment can be tangent to a circle as part of a line that is tangent, it is improper to say a tangent can be simply a line segment that touches the circle in exactly one point. In the diagram below, $\overleftrightarrow{CD}$ is tangent to circle A. Notice that $\overline{FB}$ is not tangent to the circle. $\overline{FB}$ is a line segment that touches the circle in exactly one point, but if the segment were extended, it would touch the circle in a second point. The point at which a tangent touches a circle is called the point of tangency. In the diagram below, point B is the point of tangency.

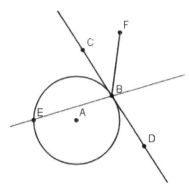

A **secant** is a line that intersects a circle in two points. Two secants may intersect inside the circle, on the circle, or outside the circle. When the two secants intersect on the circle, an inscribed angle is formed.

When two secants intersect inside a circle, the measure of each of two vertical angles is equal to half the sum of the two intercepted arcs. In the diagram below, m$\angle AEB = \frac{1}{2}(\widehat{AB} + \widehat{CD})$ and m$\angle BEC = \frac{1}{2}(\widehat{BC} + \widehat{AD})$.

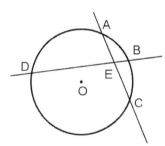

When two secants intersect outside a circle, the measure of the angle formed is equal to half the difference of the two arcs that lie between the two secants. In the diagram below, m$\angle E = \frac{1}{2}(\widehat{AB} - \widehat{CD})$.

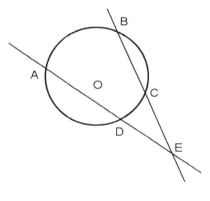

The **arc length** is the length of that portion of the circumference between two points on the circle. The formula for arc length is $s = \frac{\pi r \theta}{180°}$ where s is the arc length, r is the length of the radius, and θ is the angular measure of the arc in degrees, or $s = r\theta$, where θ is the angular measure of the arc in radians (2π radians = 360 degrees).

A **sector** is the portion of a circle formed by two radii and their intercepted arc. While the arc length is exclusively the points that are also on the circumference of the circle, the sector is the entire area bounded by the arc and the two radii.

The **area of a sector** of a circle is found by the formula, $A = \frac{\theta r^2}{2}$, where A is the area, θ is the measure of the central angle in radians, and r is the radius. To find the area when the central angle is in degrees, use the formula, $A = \frac{\theta \pi r^2}{360}$, where θ is the measure of the central angle in degrees and r is the radius.

A circle is inscribed in a polygon if each of the sides of the polygon is tangent to the circle. A polygon is inscribed in a circle if each of the vertices of the polygon lies on the circle.

A circle is circumscribed about a polygon if each of the vertices of the polygon lies on the circle. A polygon is circumscribed about the circle if each of the sides of the polygon is tangent to the circle.

If one figure is inscribed in another, then the other figure is circumscribed about the first figure.

Circle circumscribed about a pentagon
Pentagon inscribed in a circle

Other Conic Sections

Ellipse

An **ellipse** is the set of all points in a plane, whose total distance from two fixed points called the foci (singular: focus) is constant, and whose center is the midpoint between the foci.

The standard equation of an ellipse that is taller than it is wide is $\frac{(y-k)^2}{a^2} + \frac{(x-h)^2}{b^2} = 1$, where a and b are coefficients. The center is the point (h, k) and the foci are the points $(h, k + c)$ and $(h, k - c)$, where $c^2 = a^2 - b^2$ and $a^2 > b^2$.

The major axis has length $2a$, and the minor axis has length $2b$.

Eccentricity (e) is a measure of how elongated an ellipse is, and is the ratio of the distance between the foci to the length of the major axis. Eccentricity will have a value between 0 and 1. The closer to 1 the eccentricity is, the closer the ellipse is to being a circle. The formula for eccentricity is $= \frac{c}{a}$.

Parabola

Parabola: The set of all points in a plane that are equidistant from a fixed line, called the **directrix**, and a fixed point not on the line, called the **focus**.

Axis: The line perpendicular to the directrix that passes through the focus.

For parabolas that open up or down, the standard equation is $(x - h)^2 = 4c(y - k)$, where h, c, and k are coefficients. If c is positive, the parabola opens up. If c is negative, the parabola opens down. The vertex is the point (h, k). The directrix is the line having the equation $y = -c + k$, and the focus is the point $(h, c + k)$.

For parabolas that open left or right, the standard equation is $(y - k)^2 = 4c(x - h)$, where k, c, and h are coefficients. If c is positive, the parabola opens to the right. If c is negative, the parabola opens to the left. The vertex is the point (h, k). The directrix is the line having the equation $x = -c + h$, and the focus is the point $(c + h, k)$.

Hyperbola

A **hyperbola** is the set of all points in a plane, whose distance from two fixed points, called foci, has a constant difference.

The standard equation of a horizontal hyperbola is $\frac{(x-h)^2}{a^2} - \frac{(y-k)^2}{b^2} = 1$, where a, b, h, and k are real numbers. The center is the point (h, k), the vertices are the points $(h + a, k)$ and $(h - a, k)$, and the foci are the points that every point on one of the parabolic curves is equidistant from and are found using the formulas $(h + c, k)$ and $(h - c, k)$, where $c^2 = a^2 + b^2$. The asymptotes are two lines the graph of the hyperbola approaches but never reaches, and are given by the equations $y = \left(\frac{b}{a}\right)(x - h) + k$ and $y = -\left(\frac{b}{a}\right)(x - h) + k$.

A **vertical hyperbola** is formed when a plane makes a vertical cut through two cones that are stacked vertex-to-vertex.

The standard equation of a vertical hyperbola is $\frac{(y-k)^2}{a^2} - \frac{(x-h)^2}{b^2} = 1$, where a, b, k, and h are real numbers. The center is the point (h, k), the vertices are the points $(h, k + a)$ and $(h, k - a)$, and the foci are the points that every point on one of the parabolic curves is equidistant from and are found using the formulas $(h, k + c)$ and $(h, k - c)$, where $c^2 = a^2 + b^2$. The asymptotes are two lines the graph of the hyperbola approaches but never reach, and are given by the equations $y = \left(\frac{a}{b}\right)(x - h) + k$ and $y = -\left(\frac{a}{b}\right)(x - h) + k$.

Solids

The **surface area of a solid object** is the area of all sides or exterior surfaces. For objects such as prisms and pyramids, a further distinction is made between base surface area (B) and lateral surface area (LA). For a prism, the total surface area (SA) is $SA = LA + 2B$. For a pyramid or cone, the total surface area is $SA = LA + B$.

The **surface area of a sphere** can be found by the formula $A = 4\pi r^2$, where r is the radius. The volume is given by the formula $V = \frac{4}{3}\pi r^3$, where r is the radius. Both quantities are generally given in terms of π.

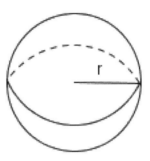

The **volume of any prism** is found by the formula $V = Bh$, where B is the area of the base, and h is the height (perpendicular distance between the bases). The surface area of any prism is the sum of the areas of both bases and all sides. It can be calculated as $SA = 2B + Ph$, where P is the perimeter of the base.

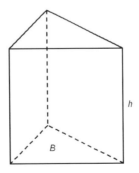

For a *rectangular prism*, the **volume** can be found by the formula $V = lwh$, where V is the volume, l is the length, w is the width, and h is the height. The surface area can be calculated as $SA = 2lw + 2hl + 2wh$ or $SA = 2(lw + hl + wh)$.

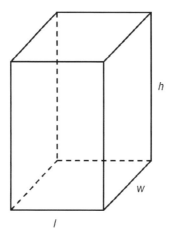

The **volume of a cube** can be found by the formula $V = s^3$, where s is the length of a side. The surface area of a cube is calculated as $SA = 6s^2$, where SA is the total surface area and s is the length of a side. These formulas are the same as the ones used for the volume and surface area of a rectangular prism, but simplified since all three quantities (length, width, and height) are the same.

> **Review Video: Volume and Surface Area of a Cube**
> Visit mometrix.com/academy and enter code: 664455

The **volume of a cylinder** can be calculated by the formula $V = \pi r^2 h$, where r is the radius, and h is the height. The surface area of a cylinder can be found by the formula $SA = 2\pi r^2 + 2\pi rh$. The first term is the base area multiplied by two, and the second term is the perimeter of the base multiplied by the height.

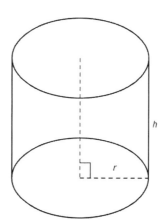

> **Review Video: Volume and Surface Area of a Right Circular Cylinder**
> Visit mometrix.com/academy and enter code: 226463

The **volume of a pyramid** is found by the formula $V = \frac{1}{3}Bh$, where B is the area of the base, and h is the height (perpendicular distance from the vertex to the base). Notice this formula is the same as $\frac{1}{3}$ times the volume of a prism. Like a prism, the base of a pyramid can be any shape.

Finding the **surface area of a pyramid** is not as simple as the other shapes we've looked at thus far. If the pyramid is a right pyramid, meaning the base is a regular polygon and the vertex is directly over the center of that polygon, the surface area can be calculated as $SA = B + \frac{1}{2}Ph_s$, where P is the perimeter of the base, and h_s is the slant height (distance from the vertex to the midpoint of one side of the base). If the pyramid is irregular, the area of each triangle side must be calculated individually and then summed, along with the base.

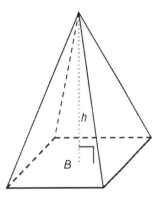

The **volume of a cone** is found by the formula $V = \frac{1}{3}\pi r^2 h$, where r is the radius, and h is the height. Notice this is the same as $\frac{1}{3}$ times the volume of a cylinder. The surface area can be calculated as $SA = \pi r^2 + \pi r s$, where s is the slant height. The slant height can be calculated using the Pythagorean Thereom to be $\sqrt{r^2 + h^2}$, so the surface area formula can also be written as $SA = \pi r^2 + \pi r\sqrt{r^2 + h^2}$.

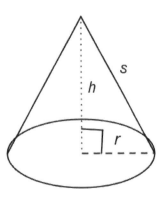

Probability

Probability Terminology

Probability is a branch of statistics that deals with the likelihood of something taking place. One classic example is a coin toss. There are only two possible results: heads or tails. The likelihood, or probability, that the coin will land as heads is 1 out of 2 ($\frac{1}{2}$, 0.5, 50%). Tails has the same probability. Another common example is a 6-sided die roll. There are six possible results from rolling a single die, each with an equal chance of happening, so the probability of any given number coming up is 1 out of 6.

<u>Terms frequently used in probability</u>

- **Event** – a situation that produces results of some sort (a coin toss)
- **Compound event** – event that involves two or more independent events (rolling a pair of dice; taking the sum)
- **Outcome** – a possible result in an experiment or event (heads, tails)
- **Desired outcome** (or success) – an outcome that meets a particular set of criteria (a roll of 1 or 2 if we are looking for numbers less than 3)
- **Independent events** – two or more events whose outcomes do not affect one another (two coins tossed at the same time)
- **Dependent events** – two or more events whose outcomes affect one another (two cards drawn consecutively from the same deck)
- **Certain outcome** – probability of outcome is 100% or 1
- **Impossible outcome** – probability of outcome is 0% or 0
- **Mutually exclusive outcomes** – two or more outcomes whose criteria cannot all be satisfied in a single event (a coin coming up heads and tails on the same toss)

> **Review Video: Intro to Probability**
> Visit mometrix.com/academy and enter code: 212374

Calculating Probability

Probability is the likelihood of a certain outcome occurring for a given event. The **theoretical probability** can usually be determined without actually performing the event. The likelihood of a outcome occurring, or the probability of an outcome occurring, is given by the formula

$$P(A) = \frac{\text{Number of acceptable outcomes}}{\text{Number of possible outcomes}}$$

where $P(A)$ is the probability of an outcome A occurring, and each outcome is just as likely to occur as any other outcome. If each outcome has the same probability of occurring as every other possible outcome, the outcomes are said to be equally likely to occur. The total number of acceptable outcomes must be less than or equal to the total number of possible outcomes. If the two are equal, then the outcome is certain to occur and the probability is 1. If the number of acceptable outcomes is zero, then the outcome is impossible and the probability is 0.

> **Review Video: Theoretical and Experimental Probability**
> Visit mometrix.com/academy and enter code: 444349

Example:

There are 20 marbles in a bag and 5 are red. The theoretical probability of randomly selecting a red marble is 5 out of 20, ($\frac{5}{20} = \frac{1}{4}$, 0.25, or 25%).

Permutations and Combinations

When trying to calculate the probability of an event using the $\frac{\text{desired outcomes}}{\text{total outcomes}}$ formula, you may frequently find that there are too many outcomes to individually count them. **Permutation** and **combination formulas** offer a shortcut to counting outcomes. A permutation is an arrangement of a specific number of a set of objects in a specific order. The number of **permutations** of r items given a set of n items can be calculated as $_nP_r = \frac{n!}{(n-r)!}$. Combinations are similar to permutations, except there are no restrictions regarding the order of the elements. While ABC is considered a different permutation than BCA, ABC and BCA are considered the same combination. The number of **combinations** of r items given a set of n items can be calculated as $_nC_r = \frac{n!}{r!(n-r)!}$ or $_nC_r = \frac{_nP_r}{r!}$.

Example:

Suppose you want to calculate how many different 5-card hands can be drawn from a deck of 52 cards. This is a combination since the order of the cards in a hand does not matter. There are 52 cards available, and 5 to be selected. Thus, the number of different hands is $_{52}C_5 = \frac{52!}{5! \times 47!} = 2,598,960$.

Complement of an Event

Sometimes it may be easier to calculate the possibility of something not happening, or the **complement of an event**. Represented by the symbol $\bar{A}$, the complement of A is the probability that event A does not happen. When you know the probability of event A occurring, you can use the formula $P(\bar{A}) = 1 - P(A)$, where $P(\bar{A})$ is the probability of event A not occurring, and $P(A)$ is the probability of event A occurring.

Addition Rule

The **addition rule** for probability is used for finding the probability of a compound event. Use the formula $P(A \text{ or } B) = P(A) + P(B) - P(A \text{ and } B)$, where $P(A \text{ and } B)$ is the probability of both events occurring to find the probability of a compound event. The probability of both events occurring at the same time must be subtracted to eliminate any overlap in the first two probabilities.

Conditional Probability

Conditional probability is the probability of an event occurring once another event has already occurred. Given event A and dependent event B, the probability of event B occurring when event A has already occurred is represented by the notation $P(A|B)$. To find the probability of event B occurring, take into account the fact that event A has already occurred and adjust the total number of possible outcomes. For example, suppose you have ten balls numbered 1–10 and you want ball number 7 to be pulled in two pulls. On the first pull, the probability of getting the 7 is $\frac{1}{10}$ because there is one ball with a 7 on it and 10 balls to choose from. Assuming the first pull did not yield a 7, the probability of pulling a 7 on the second pull is now $\frac{1}{9}$ because there are only 9 balls remaining for the second pull.

Multiplication Rule

The **multiplication rule** can be used to find the probability of two independent events occurring using the formula $P(A \text{ and } B) = P(A) \times P(B)$, where $P(A \text{ and } B)$ is the probability of two independent events occurring, $P(A)$ is the probability of the first event occurring, and $P(B)$ is the probability of the second event occurring.

The multiplication rule can also be used to find the probability of two dependent events occurring using the formula $P(A \text{ and } B) = P(A) \times P(B|A)$, where $P(A \text{ and } B)$ is the probability of two dependent events occurring and $P(B|A)$ is the probability of the second event occurring after the first event has already occurred.

Before using the multiplication rule, you MUST first determine whether the two events are *dependent* or *independent*.

Use a **combination of the multiplication** rule and the rule of complements to find the probability that at least one outcome of the element will occur. This given by the general formula $P(\text{at least one event occurring}) = 1 - P(\text{no outcomes occurring})$. For example, to find the probability that at least one even number will show when a pair of dice is rolled, find the probability that two odd numbers will be rolled (no even numbers) and subtract from one. You can always use a tree diagram or make a chart to list the possible outcomes when the sample space is small, such as in the dice-rolling example, but in most cases it will be much faster to use the multiplication and complement formulas.

Expected Value

Expected value is a method of determining expected outcome in a random situation. It is really a sum of the weighted probabilities of the possible outcomes. Multiply the probability of an event occurring by the weight assigned to that probability (such as the amount of money won or lost). A practical application of the expected value is to determine whether a game of chance is really fair. If the sum of the weighted probabilities is equal to zero, the game is generally considered fair because the player has a fair chance to at least to break even. If the expected value is less than zero, then players lose more than they win. For example, a lottery drawing might allow the player to choose any three-digit number, 000–999. The probability of choosing the winning number is 1:1000. If it costs \$1 to play, and a winning number receives \$500, the expected value is $\left(-\$1 \cdot \frac{999}{1{,}000}\right) + \left(\$500 \cdot \frac{1}{1{,}000}\right) = -0.499$ or $-\$0.50$. You can expect to lose on average 50 cents for every dollar you spend.

Empirical Probability

Most of the time, when we talk about probability, we mean theoretical probability. **Empirical probability**, or experimental probability or relative frequency, is the number of times an outcome occurs in a particular experiment or a certain number of observed events. While theoretical probability is based on what *should* happen, experimental probability is based on what *has* happened. Experimental probability is calculated in the same way as theoretical, except that actual outcomes are used instead of possible outcomes.

Theoretical and experimental probability do not always line up with one another. Theoretical probability says that out of 20 coin-tosses, 10 should be heads. However, if we were actually to toss 20 coins, we might record just 5 heads. This doesn't mean that our theoretical probability is incorrect; it just means that this particular experiment had results that were different from what was predicted. A practical application of empirical probability is the insurance industry. There are no set functions that define lifespan, health, or safety. Insurance companies look at factors from hundreds of thousands of individuals to find patterns that they then use to set the formulas for insurance premiums.

Objective Probability

Objective probability is based on mathematical formulas and documented evidence. Examples of objective probability include raffles or lottery drawings where there is a pre-determined number of possible outcomes and a predetermined number of outcomes that correspond to an event. Other cases of objective probability include probabilities of rolling dice, flipping coins, or drawing cards. Most gambling games are based on objective probability.

Subjective Probability

Subjective probability is based on personal or professional feelings and judgments. Often, there is a lot of guesswork following extensive research. Areas where subjective probability is applicable include sales trends and business expenses. Attractions set admission prices based on subjective probabilities of attendance based on varying admission rates in an effort to maximize their profit.

Sample Space

The total set of all possible results of a test or experiment is called a **sample space**, or sometimes a universal sample space. The sample space, represented by one of the variables S, Ω, or U (for universal sample space) has individual elements called outcomes. Other terms for outcome that may be used interchangeably include elementary outcome, simple event, or sample point. The number of outcomes in a given sample space could be infinite or finite, and some tests may yield multiple unique sample sets. For example, tests conducted by drawing playing cards from a standard deck would have one sample space of the card values, another sample space of the card suits, and a third sample space of suit-denomination combinations. For most tests, the sample spaces considered will be finite.

An **event**, represented by the variable E, is a portion of a sample space. It may be one outcome or a group of outcomes from the same sample space. If an event occurs, then the test or experiment will generate an outcome that satisfies the requirement of that event. For example, given a standard deck of 52 playing cards as the sample space, and defining the event as the collection of face cards, then the event will occur if the card drawn is a J, Q, or K. If any other card is drawn, the event is said to have not occurred.

For every sample space, each possible outcome has a specific likelihood, or probability, that it will occur. The probability measure, also called the **distribution**, is a function that assigns a real number probability, from zero to one, to each outcome. For a probability measure to be accurate, every outcome must have a real number probability measure that is greater than or equal to zero and less than or equal to one. Also, the probability measure of the sample space must equal one, and the probability measure of the union of multiple outcomes must equal the sum of the individual probability measures.

Probabilities of events are expressed as real numbers from zero to one. They give a numerical value to the chance that a particular event will occur. The probability of an event occurring is the sum of the probabilities of the individual elements of that event. For example, in a standard deck of 52 playing cards as the sample space and the collection of face cards as the event, the probability of drawing a specific face card is $\frac{1}{52} = 0.019$, but the probability of drawing any one of the twelve face cards is $12(0.019) = 0.228$. Note that rounding of numbers can generate different results. If you multiplied 12 by the fraction $\frac{1}{52}$ before converting to a decimal, you would get the answer $\frac{12}{52} = 0.231$.

Tree Diagram

For a simple sample space, possible outcomes may be determined by using a **tree diagram** or an organized chart. In either case, you can easily draw or list out the possible outcomes. For example, to determine all the possible ways three objects can be ordered, you can draw a tree diagram:

You can also make a chart to list all the possibilities:

First object	Second object	Third object
●	X	O
●	O	X
O	●	X
O	X	●
X	●	O
X	O	●

Either way, you can easily see there are six possible ways the three objects can be ordered.

If two events have no outcomes in common, they are said to be **mutually exclusive**. For example, in a standard deck of 52 playing cards, the event of all card suits is mutually exclusive to the event of all card values. If two events have no bearing on each other so that one event occurring has no influence on the probability of another event occurring, the two events are said to be independent. For example, rolling a standard six-sided die multiple times does not change that probability that a particular number will be rolled from one roll to the next. If the outcome of one event does affect the probability of the second event, the two events are said to be dependent. For example, if cards are drawn from a deck, the probability of drawing an ace after an ace has been drawn is different than the probability of drawing an ace if no ace (or no other card, for that matter) has been drawn.

In probability, the **odds in favor of an event** are the number of times the event will occur compared to the number of times the event will not occur. To calculate the odds in favor of an event, use the formula $\frac{P(A)}{1-P(A)}$, where $P(A)$ is the probability that the event will occur. Many times, odds in favor is given as a ratio in the form $\frac{a}{b}$ or $a{:}b$, where a is the probability of the event occurring and b is the complement of the event, the probability of the event not occurring. If the odds in favor are given as 2:5, that means that you can expect the event to occur two times for every 5 times that it does not occur. In other words, the probability that the event will occur is $\frac{2}{2+5} = \frac{2}{7}$.

In probability, the **odds against an event** are the number of times the event will not occur compared to the number of times the event will occur. To calculate the odds against an event, use the formula $\frac{1-P(A)}{P(A)}$, where $P(A)$ is the probability that the event will occur. Many times, odds against is given as a ratio in the form $\frac{b}{a}$ or $b{:}a$, where b is the probability the event will not occur (the complement of the event) and a is the probability the event will occur. If the odds against an event are given as 3:1, that means that you can expect the event to not occur 3 times for every one time it does occur. In other words, 3 out of every 4 trials will fail.

Experimental and Theoretical Probability

Probability, P(A), is the likelihood that event A will occur. Probability is often expressed as the ratio of ways an event can occur to the total number of **outcomes**, also called the **sample space**. For example, the probability of flipping heads on a two-sided coin can be written as $\frac{1}{2}$ since there is one side with heads and a total of two sides, which means that there are two possible outcomes. Probabilities can also be expressed as decimals or percentages.

Tree diagrams are used to list all possible outcomes. Suppose you are packing for vacation and have set aside 4 shirts, 3 pairs of pants, and 2 hats. How many possible outfits are there? To construct a tree diagram, start with the first group of events, the shirts. You can use letters to label each of the articles (SA refers to the first shirt, SB refers to the second shirt, and so on). Then, from each shirt draw branches to each pair of pants that it could be paired with. Next, from each pair of pants, draw a branch to each hat that it could be paired to and finally, repeat the process with the shoes. This method allows you to list all of the possible outcomes.

SA, PA, HA	SA, PB, HB
SA, PA, HB	SA, PC, HA
SB, PB, HA	SA, PC, HB
SB, PA, HA	SB, PB, HB
SB, PA, HB	SB, PC, HA
SB, PB, HA	SB, PC, HB
SC, PA, HA	SC, PB, HB
SC, PA, HB	SC, PC, HA
SC, PB, HA	SC, PC, HB
SD, PA, HA	SD, PB, HB
SD, PA, HB	SD, PC, HA
SD, PB, HA	SD, PC, HA

Altogether, there are 24 different combinations of shirts, pants, and hats.

A faster way to find the sample space without listing each individual outcome employs the **multiplication counting principle**. If one event can occur in a ways and a second event in b ways, then the two events can occur in $a \times b$ ways. In the previous example, there are 4 possible shirts, 3 possible pairs of pants, and 2 possible hats, so the possible number of combinations is $4 \times 3 \times 2$, or 24.

A similar principle is employed to determine the probability of two **independent events**. $P(A \ and \ B) = P(A) \times P(B)$, where A is the first event and B is the second such that the outcome of B does not depend on the outcome of A. For instance, suppose you choose a marble from a bag of 2 red marbles, 7 blue marbles, and 4 green marbles. The probability that you would choose a red marble, replace it, and then choose a green marble is found by multiplying the probabilities of each independent event:

$$\frac{2}{13} \times \frac{4}{13} = \frac{8}{169}, \text{ or } 0.047, \text{ or } 4.7\%$$

This method can also be used when finding the probability of more than 2 independent events.

When two events are dependent on one another, the likelihood of the second event is affected by the outcome of the first event. This formula for finding the probability of **dependent events** is $P(A \ then \ B) = P(A) \times P(B \ after \ A)$. The probability that you choose a 2 and then choose a 5 from a deck of 52 cards without replacement is

$$\frac{4}{52} \times \frac{4}{51} = \frac{1}{13} \times \frac{4}{51} = \frac{4}{663} \text{ or } 0.0060, \text{ or } 0.60\%$$

Note that there are four of each number in a deck of cards, so the probability of choosing a 2 is $\frac{4}{52}$. Since you keep this card out of the deck, there are only 51 cards to choose from when selecting a 5.

Thus far, the discussion of probability has been limited to **theoretical probability, which is used to predict the likelihood of an event. Experimental probability** expresses the ratio of the number of times an event actually occurs to the number of **trials** performed in an experiment. Theoretically, the probability of rolling a one on an unloaded, six-sided die is $\frac{1}{6}$. Suppose you conduct an experiment to determine whether a dice is a fair one and obtain these results.

Trial #	1	2	3	4	5	6	7	8	9	10	11	12	13	14	15	16	17	18	19	20
Outcome	6	1	2	6	4	2	1	3	4	5	4	1	6	6	4	5	6	4	1	6

Out of the 20 trials, you rolled a 1 six times. $\frac{6}{20} = \frac{3}{10} = 0.30$, or 30%. This probability is different than the theoretical probability of $\frac{1}{6}$ or 16.6%. You might conclude that the die is loaded, but it would be advisable to conduct more trials to verify your conclusion: the larger the number of trials, the more accurate the experimental probability.

Statistics

Statistics Terminology

Statistics is the branch of mathematics that deals with collecting, recording, interpreting, illustrating, and analyzing large amounts of **data**. The following terms are often used in the discussion of data and **statistics**:

- **Data** – the collective name for pieces of *information* (singular is datum).
- **Quantitative data** – measurements (such as length, mass, and speed) that provide information about *quantities* in numbers
- **Qualitative data** – information (such as colors, scents, tastes, and shapes) that *cannot be measured* using numbers

- **Discrete data** – information that can be expressed only by a *specific value*, such as whole or half numbers. For example, since people can be counted only in whole numbers, a population count would be discrete data.
- **Continuous data** – information (such as time and temperature) that can be expressed by *any value within a given range*
- **Primary data** – information that has been *collected* directly from a survey, investigation, or experiment, such as a questionnaire or the recording of daily temperatures. Primary data that has not yet been organized or analyzed is called raw data.
- **Secondary data** – information that has been collected, sorted, and *processed* by the researcher
- **Ordinal data** – information that *can be placed in numerical order*, such as age or weight
- **Nominal data** – information that *cannot be placed in numerical order*, such as names or places.

Statistics

Population

In statistics, the **population** is the entire collection of people, plants, etc., that data can be collected from. For example, a study to determine how well students in the area schools perform on a standardized test would have a population of all the students enrolled in those schools, although a study may include just a small sample of students from each school. A **parameter** is a numerical value that gives information about the population, such as the mean, median, mode, or standard deviation. Remember that the symbol for the mean of a population is μ and the symbol for the standard deviation of a population is σ.

Sample

A **sample** is a portion of the entire population. Whereas a parameter helped describe the population, a **statistic** is a numerical value that gives information about the sample, such as mean, median, mode, or standard deviation. Keep in mind that the symbols for mean and standard deviation are different when they are referring to a sample rather than the entire population. For a sample, the symbol for mean is $\bar{x}$ and the symbol for standard deviation is s. The mean and standard deviation of a sample may or may not be identical to that of the entire population due to a sample only being a subset of the population. However, if the sample is random and large enough, statistically significant values can be attained. Samples are generally used when the population is too large to justify including every element or when acquiring data for the entire population is impossible.

Inferential Statistics

Inferential statistics is the branch of statistics that uses samples to make predictions about an entire population. This type of statistics is often seen in political polls, where a sample of the population is questioned about a particular topic or politician to gain an understanding about the attitudes of the entire population of the country. Often, exit polls are conducted on election days using this method. Inferential statistics can have a large margin of error if you do not have a valid sample.

Sampling Distribution

Statistical values calculated from various samples of the same size make up the **sampling distribution**. For example, if several samples of identical size are randomly selected from a large population and then the mean of each sample is calculated, the distribution of values of the means would be a sampling distribution.

The **sampling distribution of the mean** is the distribution of the sample mean, $\bar{x}$, derived from random samples of a given size. It has three important characteristics. First, the mean of the sampling distribution of the mean is equal to the mean of the population that was sampled. Second, assuming the standard deviation is non-zero, the standard deviation of the sampling distribution of the mean equals the standard deviation of the sampled population divided by the square root of the sample size. This is sometimes called the standard error. Finally, as the sample size gets larger, the sampling distribution of the mean gets closer to a normal distribution via the Central Limit Theorem.

Survey Study

A **survey study** is a method of gathering information from a small group in an attempt to gain enough information to make accurate general assumptions about the population. Once a survey study is completed, the results are then put into a summary report.

Survey studies are generally in the format of surveys, interviews, or questionnaires as part of an effort to find opinions of a particular group or to find facts about a group.

It is important to note that the findings from a survey study are only as accurate as the sample chosen from the population.

Correlational Studies

Correlational studies seek to determine how much one variable is affected by changes in a second variable. For example, correlational studies may look for a relationship between the amount of time a student spends studying for a test and the grade that student earned on the test or between student scores on college admissions tests and student grades in college.

It is important to note that correlational studies cannot show a cause and effect, but rather can show only that two variables are or are not potentially correlated.

Experimental Studies

Experimental studies take correlational studies one step farther, in that they attempt to prove or disprove a cause-and-effect relationship. These studies are performed by conducting a series of experiments to test the hypothesis. For a study to be scientifically accurate, it must have both an experimental group that receives the specified treatment and a control group that does not get the treatment. This is the type of study pharmaceutical companies do as part of drug trials for new medications. Experimental studies are only valid when proper scientific method has been followed. In other words, the experiment must be well-planned and executed without bias in the testing process, all subjects must be selected at random, and the process of determining which subject is in which of the two groups must also be completely random.

Observational Studies

Observational studies are the opposite of experimental studies. In observational studies, the tester cannot change or in any way control all of the variables in the test. For example, a study to determine which gender does better in math classes in school is strictly observational. You cannot change a person's gender, and you cannot change the subject being studied. The big downfall of observational studies is that you have no way of proving a cause-and-effect relationship because you cannot control outside influences. Events outside of school can influence a student's performance in school, and observational studies cannot take that into consideration.

Random Samples

For most studies, a **random sample** is necessary to produce valid results. Random samples should not have any particular influence to cause sampled subjects to behave one way or another. The goal is for the random sample to be a **representative sample**, or a sample whose characteristics give an accurate picture of the characteristics of the entire population. To accomplish this, you must make sure you have a proper **sample size**, or an appropriate number of elements in the sample.

Biases

In statistical studies, biases must be avoided. **Bias** is an error that causes the study to favor one set of results over another. For example, if a survey to determine how the country views the president's job performance only speaks to registered voters in the president's party, the results will be skewed because a disproportionately large number of responders would tend to show approval, while a disproportionately large number of people in the opposite party would tend to express disapproval.

Extraneous Variables

Extraneous variables are, as the name implies, outside influences that can affect the outcome of a study. They are not always avoidable, but could trigger bias in the result.

Data Organization

Example

A nurse found the heart rates of ten different patients to be 76, 80, 90, 86, 70, 76, 72, 88, 88, and 68 beats per minute. Organize this information in a table.

There are several ways to organize data in a table. The table below is an example.

Patient Number	1	2	3	4	5	6	7	8	9	10
Heart Rate (bpm)	76	80	90	86	70	76	72	88	88	68

When making a table, be sure to label the columns and rows appropriately.

Data Analysis

Measures of Central Tendency

The **measure of central tendency** is a statistical value that gives a general tendency for the center of a group of data. There are several different ways of describing the measure of central tendency. Each one has a unique way it is calculated, and each one gives a slightly different perspective on the data set. Whenever you give a measure of central tendency, always make sure the units are the same. If the data has different units, such as hours, minutes, and seconds, convert all the data to the same unit, and use the same unit in the measure of central tendency. If no units are given in the data, do not give units for the measure of central tendency.

Mean

The **statistical mean** of a group of data is the same as the arithmetic average of that group. To find the mean of a set of data, first convert each value to the same units, if necessary. Then find the sum of all the values, and count the total number of data values, making sure you take into consideration each individual value. If a value appears more than once, count it more than once. Divide the sum of the values by the total number of values and apply the units, if any. Note that the mean does not have to be one of the data values in the set, and may not divide evenly.

- 217 -

$$\text{mean} = \frac{\text{sum of the data values}}{\text{quantity of data values}}$$

The mean of the data set {88, 72, 61, 90, 97, 68, 88, 79, 86, 93, 97, 71, 80, 84, 89, 72, 91, 95, 89, 83, 94, 90, 63, 69, 89} would be the sum of the twenty-five numbers divided by 25:

$$\frac{88 + 72 + 61 + 90 + 97 + \cdots + 94 + 90 + 63 + 69 + 89}{25}$$

$$= \frac{2078}{25}$$

$$= 83.12$$

While the mean is relatively easy to calculate and averages are understood by most people, the mean can be very misleading if used as the sole measure of central tendency. If the data set has outliers (data values that are unusually high or unusually low compared to the rest of the data values), the mean can be very distorted, especially if the data set has a small number of values. If unusually high values are countered with unusually low values, the mean is not affected as much. For example, if five of twenty students in a class get a 100 on a test, but the other 15 students have an average of 60 on the same test, the class average would appear as 70. Whenever the mean is skewed by outliers, it is always a good idea to include the median as an alternate measure of central tendency.

> **Review Video: Mean, Median, and Mode**
> Visit mometrix.com/academy and enter code: 286207

Median

The **statistical median** is the value in the middle of the set of data. To find the median, list all data values in order from smallest to largest or from largest to smallest. Any value that is repeated in the set must be listed the number of times it appears. If there are an odd number of data values, the median is the value in the middle of the list. If there is an even number of data values, the median is the arithmetic mean of the two middle values.

Mode

The **statistical mode** is the data value that occurs the most number of times in the data set. It is possible to have exactly one mode, more than one mode, or no mode. To find the mode of a set of data, arrange the data like you do to find the median (all values in order, listing all multiples of data values). Count the number of times each value appears in the data set. If all values appear an equal number of times, there is no mode. If one value appears more than any other value, that value is the mode. If two or more values appear the same number of times, but there are other values that appear fewer times and no values that appear more times, all of those values are the modes.

The big disadvantage of using the median as a measure of central tendency is that is relies solely on a value's relative size as compared to the other values in the set. When the individual values in a set of data are evenly dispersed, the median can be an accurate tool. However, if there is a group of rather large values or a group of rather small values that are not offset by a different group of values, the information that can be inferred from the median may not be accurate because the distribution of values is skewed.

The main disadvantage of the mode is that the values of the other data in the set have no bearing on the mode. The mode may be the largest value, the smallest value, or a value anywhere in between in the set. The mode only tells which value or values, if any, occurred the most number of times. It does not give any suggestions about the remaining values in the set.

Dispersion

The **measure of dispersion** is a single value that helps to "interpret" the measure of central tendency by providing more information about how the data values in the set are distributed about the measure of central tendency. The measure of dispersion helps to eliminate or reduce the disadvantages of using the mean, median, or mode as a single measure of central tendency, and give a more accurate picture of the dataset as a whole. To have a measure of dispersion, you must know or calculate the range, standard deviation, or variance of the data set.

Range

The **range** of a set of data is the difference between the greatest and lowest values of the data in the set. To calculate the range, you must first make sure the units for all data values are the same, and then identify the greatest and lowest values. Use the formula $range = highest\ value - lowest\ value$. If there are multiple data values that are equal for the highest or lowest, just use one of the values in the formula. Write the answer with the same units as the data values you used to do the calculations.

Standard Deviation

Standard deviation is a measure of dispersion that compares all the data values in the set to the mean of the set to give a more accurate picture. To find the standard deviation of a population, use the formula

$$\sigma = \sqrt{\frac{\sum_{i=1}^{n}(x_i - \bar{x})^2}{n}}$$

where σ is the standard deviation of a population, x represents the individual values in the data set, $\bar{x}$ is the mean of the data values in the set, and n is the number of data values in the set. The higher the value of the standard deviation is, the greater the variance of the data values from the mean. The units associated with the standard deviation are the same as the units of the data values.

Variance

The **variance** of a population, or just variance, is the square of the standard deviation of that population. While the mean of a set of data gives the average of the set and gives information about where a specific data value lies in relation to the average, the variance of the population gives information about the degree to which the data values are spread out and tell you how close an individual value is to the average compared to the other values. The units associated with variance are the same as the units of the data values squared.

Percentile

Percentiles and **quartiles** are other methods of describing data within a set. *Percentiles* tell what percentage of the data in the set fall below a specific point. For example, achievement test scores are often given in percentiles. A score at the 80th percentile is one which is equal to or higher than 80 percent of the scores in the set. In other words, 80 percent of the scores were lower than that score.

Quartile

Quartiles are percentile groups that make up quarter sections of the data set. The first quartile is the 25th percentile. The second quartile is the 50th percentile; this is also the median of the dataset. The third quartile is the 75th percentile.

Skewness

Skewness is a way to describe the symmetry or asymmetry of the distribution of values in a dataset. If the distribution of values is symmetrical, there is no skew. In general the closer the mean of a data set is to the median of the data set, the less skew there is. Generally, if the mean is to the right of the median, the data set is *positively skewed*, or right-skewed, and if the mean is to the left of the median, the data set is *negatively skewed*, or left-skewed. However, this rule of thumb is not infallible. When the data values are graphed on a curve, a set with no skew will be a perfect bell curve. To estimate skew, use the formula

$$\text{skew} = \frac{\sqrt{n(n-1)}}{n-2} \left(\frac{\frac{1}{n}\sum_{i=1}^{n}(x_i - \bar{x})^3}{\left(\frac{1}{n}\sum_{i=1}^{n}(x_i - \bar{x})^2\right)^{\frac{3}{2}}} \right)$$

where n is the number of values is the set, x_i is the ith value in the set, and $\bar{x}$ is the mean of the set.

Simple Regression

In statistics, **simple regression** is using an equation to represent a relation between an independent and dependent variables. The independent variable is also referred to as the explanatory variable or the predictor, and is generally represented by the variable x in the equation. The dependent variable, usually represented by the variable y, is also referred to as the response variable. The equation may be any type of function – linear, quadratic, exponential, etc. The best way to handle this task is to use the regression feature of your graphing calculator. This will easily give you the curve of best fit and provide you with the coefficients and other information you need to derive an equation.

Line of Best Fit

In a scatter plot, the **line of best fit** is the line that best shows the trends of the data. The line of best fit is given by the equation $\hat{y} = ax + b$, where a and b are the regression coefficients. The regression coefficient a is also the slope of the line of best fit, and b is also the *y*-coordinate of the point at which the line of best fit crosses the *x*-axis. Not every point on the scatter plot will be on the line of best fit. The differences between the y-values of the points in the scatter plot and the corresponding y-values according to the equation of the line of best fit are the residuals. The line of best fit is also called the least-squares regression line because it is also the line that has the lowest sum of the squares of the residuals.

Correlation Coefficient

The **correlation coefficient** is the numerical value that indicates how strong the relationship is between the two variables of a linear regression equation. A correlation coefficient of –1 is a perfect negative correlation. A correlation coefficient of +1 is a perfect positive correlation. Correlation coefficients close to –1 or +1 are very strong correlations. A correlation coefficient equal to zero indicates there is no correlation between the two variables. This test is a good indicator of whether or not the equation for the line of best fit is accurate. The formula for the correlation coefficient is

$$r = \frac{\sum_{i=1}^{n}(x_i - \bar{x})(y_i - \bar{y})}{\sqrt{\sum_{i=1}^{n}(x_i - \bar{x})^2}\sqrt{\sum_{i=1}^{n}(y_i - \bar{y})^2}}$$

where r is the correlation coefficient, n is the number of data values in the set, (x_i, y_i) is a point in the set, and $\bar{x}$ and $\bar{y}$ are the means.

Z-Score

A **z-score** is an indication of how many standard deviations a given value falls from the mean. To calculate a z-score, use the formula $= \frac{x - \mu}{\sigma}$, where x is the data value, μ is the mean of the data set, and σ is the standard deviation of the population. If the z-score is positive, the data value lies above the mean. If the z-score is negative, the data value falls below the mean. These scores are useful in interpreting data such as standardized test scores, where every piece of data in the set has been counted, rather than just a small random sample. In cases where standard deviations are calculated from a random sample of the set, the z-scores will not be as accurate.

Central Limit Theorem

According to the **central limit theorem**, regardless of what the original distribution of a sample is, the distribution of the means tends to get closer and closer to a normal distribution as the sample size gets larger and larger (this is necessary because the sample is becoming more all-encompassing of the elements of the population). As the sample size gets larger, the distribution of the sample mean will approach a normal distribution with a mean of the population mean and a variance of the population variance divided by the sample size.

Shape of Data Distribution

Symmetry and Skewness

Symmetry is a characteristic of the shape of the plotted data. Specifically, it refers to how well the data on one side of the median *mirrors* the data on the other side.

A **skewed data** set is one that has a distinctly longer or fatter tail on one side of the peak or the other. A data set that is *skewed left* has more of its values to the left of the peak, while a set that is *skewed right* has more of its values to the right of the peak. When actually looking at the graph, these names may seem counterintuitive since, in a left-skewed data set, the bulk of the values seem to be on the right side of the graph, and vice versa. However, if the graph is viewed strictly in relation to the peak, the direction of skewness makes more sense.

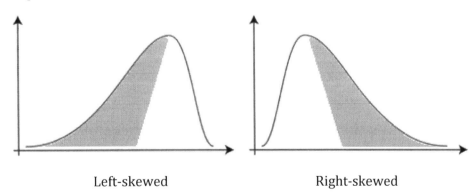

Left-skewed   Right-skewed

Unimodal vs. Bimodal

If a distribution has a single peak, it would be considered **unimodal**. If it has two discernible peaks it would be considered **bimodal**. Bimodal distributions may be an indication that the set of data being considered is actually the combination of two sets of data with significant differences.

Uniformity

A uniform distribution is a distribution in which there is *no distinct peak or variation* in the data. No values or ranges are particularly more common than any other values or ranges.

Displaying Information

Charts and Tables

Charts and tables are ways of organizing information into separate rows and columns that are labeled to identify and explain the data contained in them. Some charts and tables are organized horizontally, with row lengths giving the details about the labeled information. Other charts and tables are organized vertically, with column heights giving the details about the labeled information.

Frequency Tables

Frequency tables show how frequently each unique value appears in the set. A *relative frequency table* is one that shows the proportions of each unique value compared to the entire set. Relative frequencies are given as percents; however, the total percent for a relative frequency table will not necessarily equal 100 percent due to rounding. An example of a frequency table with relative frequencies is below.

Favorite Color	Frequency	Relative Frequency
Blue	4	13%
Red	7	22%
Purple	3	9%
Green	6	19%
Cyan	12	38%

Pictographs

A **pictograph** is a graph, generally in the horizontal orientation, that uses pictures or symbols to represent the data. Each pictograph must have a key that defines the picture or symbol and gives the quantity each picture or symbol represents. Pictures or symbols on a pictograph are not always shown as whole elements. In this case, the fraction of the picture or symbol shown represents the same fraction of the quantity a whole picture or symbol stands for. For example, a row with $3\frac{1}{2}$ ears of corn, where each ear of corn represents 100 stalks of corn in a field, would equal $3\frac{1}{2} \cdot 100 = 350$ stalks of corn in the field.

Circle Graphs

Circle graphs, also known as *pie charts*, provide a visual depiction of the relationship of each type of data compared to the whole set of data. The circle graph is divided into sections by drawing radii to create central angles whose percentage of the circle is equal to the individual data's percentage of the whole set. Each 1% of data is equal to 3.6° in the circle graph. Therefore, data represented by a 90° section of the circle graph makes up 25% of the whole. When complete, a circle graph often looks like a pie cut into uneven wedges. The pie chart below shows the data from the frequency table referenced earlier where people were asked their favorite color.

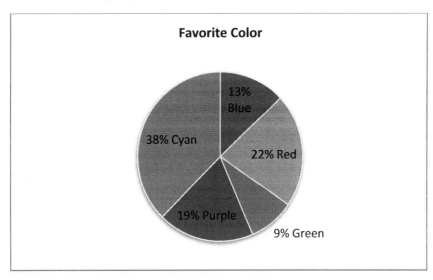

Line Graphs

Line graphs have one or more lines of varying styles (solid or broken) to show the different values for a set of data. The individual data are represented as ordered pairs, much like on a Cartesian plane. In this case, the x- and y-axes are defined in terms of their units, such as dollars or time. The individual plotted points are joined by line segments to show whether the value of the data is increasing (line sloping upward), decreasing (line sloping downward) or staying the same (horizontal line). Multiple sets of data can be graphed on the same line graph to give an easy visual comparison. An example of this would be graphing achievement test scores for different groups of students over the same time period to see which group had the greatest increase or decrease in performance from year-to-year (as shown below).

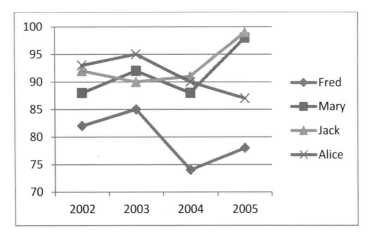

Line Plots

A **line plot**, also known as a *dot plot*, has plotted points that are not connected by line segments. In this graph, the horizontal axis lists the different possible values for the data, and the vertical axis lists the number of times the individual value occurs. A single dot is graphed for each value to show the number of times it occurs. This graph is more closely related to a bar graph than a line graph. Do not connect the dots in a line plot or it will misrepresent the data.

> **Review Video: Line Plot**
> Visit mometrix.com/academy and enter code: 754610

Stem and Leaf Plots

A **stem and leaf plot** is useful for depicting groups of data that fall into a range of values. Each piece of data is separated into two parts: the first, or left, part is called the stem; the second, or right, part is called the leaf. Each stem is listed in a column from smallest to largest. Each leaf that has the common stem is listed in that stem's row from smallest to largest. For example, in a set of two-digit numbers, the digit in the tens place is the stem, and the digit in the ones place is the leaf. With a stem and leaf plot, you can easily see which subset of numbers (10s, 20s, 30s, etc.) is the largest. This information is also readily available by looking at a histogram, but a stem and leaf plot also allows you to look closer and see exactly which values fall in that range. Using all of the test scores from above, we can assemble a stem and leaf plot like the one below.

Test Scores								
7	4	8						
8	2	5	7	8	8			
9	0	0	1	2	2	3	5	8	9

Bar Graphs

A **bar graph** is one of the few graphs that can be drawn correctly in two different configurations – both horizontally and vertically. A bar graph is similar to a line plot in the way the data is organized on the graph. Both axes must have their categories defined for the graph to be useful. Rather than placing a single dot to mark the point of the data's value, a bar, or thick line, is drawn from zero to the exact value of the data, whether it is a number, percentage, or other numerical value. Longer bar lengths correspond to greater data values. To read a bar graph, read the labels for the axes to find the units being reported. Then look where the bars end in relation to the scale given on the corresponding axis and determine the associated value.

The bar chart below represents the responses from our favorite color survey.

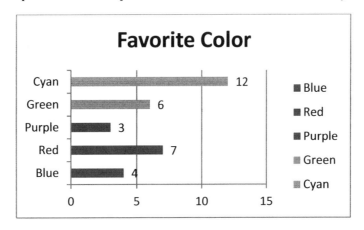

Histograms

At first glance, a **histogram** looks like a vertical bar graph. The difference is that a bar graph has a separate bar for each piece of data and a histogram has one continuous bar for each *range* of data. For example, a histogram may have one bar for the range 0–9, one bar for 10–19, etc. While a bar graph has numerical values on one axis, a histogram has numerical values on both axes. Each range is of equal size, and they are ordered left to right from lowest to highest. The height of each column on a histogram represents the number of data values within that range. Like a stem and leaf plot, a histogram makes it easy to glance at the graph and quickly determine which range has the greatest quantity of values. A simple example of a histogram is below.

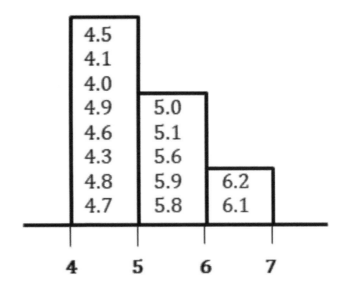

Bivariate Data

Bivariate data is simply data from two different variables. (The prefix *bi-* means *two*.) In a *scatter plot*, each value in the set of data is plotted on a grid similar to a Cartesian plane, where each axis represents one of the two variables. By looking at the pattern formed by the points on the grid, you can often determine whether or not there is a relationship between the two variables, and what that relationship is, if it exists. The variables may be directly proportionate, inversely proportionate, or show no proportion at all. It may also be possible to determine if the data is linear, and if so, to find an equation to relate the two variables. The following scatter plot shows the relationship between preference for brand "A" and the age of the consumers surveyed.

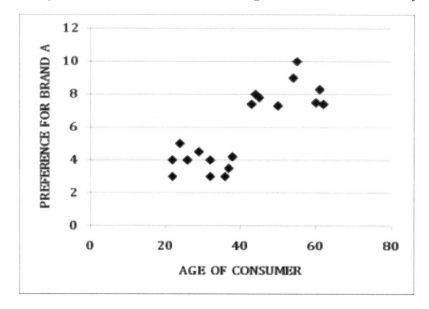

Scatter Plots

Scatter plots are also useful in determining the type of function represented by the data and finding the simple regression. Linear scatter plots may be positive or negative. Nonlinear scatter plots are generally exponential or quadratic. Below are some common types of scatter plots:

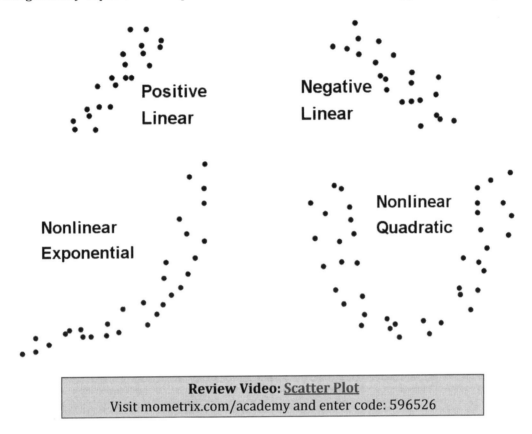

| **Review Video: Scatter Plot** |
| Visit mometrix.com/academy and enter code: 596526 |

5-Number Summary

The **5-number summary** of a set of data gives a very informative picture of the set. The five numbers in the summary include the minimum value, maximum value, and the three quartiles. This information gives the reader the range and median of the set, as well as an indication of how the data is spread about the median.

Box and Whisker Plots

A **box-and-whisker plot** is a graphical representation of the 5-number summary. To draw a box-and-whiskers plot, plot the points of the 5-number summary on a number line. Draw a box whose ends are through the points for the first and third quartiles. Draw a vertical line in the box through the median to divide the box in half. Draw a line segment from the first quartile point to the minimum value, and from the third quartile point to the maximum value.

The **68–95–99.7 rule** describes how a normal distribution of data should appear when compared to the mean. This is also a description of a normal bell curve. According to this rule, 68 percent of the data values in a normally distributed set should fall within one standard deviation of the mean (34 percent above and 34 percent below the mean), 95 percent of the data values should fall within two standard deviations of the mean (47.5 percent above and 47.5 percent below the mean), and 99.7 percent of the data values should fall within three standard deviations of the mean, again, equally distributed on either side of the mean. This means that only 0.3 percent of all data values should fall more than three standard deviations from the mean. On the graph below, the normal curve is centered on the y-axis. The x-axis labels are how many standard deviations away from the center you are.

Therefore, it is easy to see how the 68-95-99.7 rule can apply.

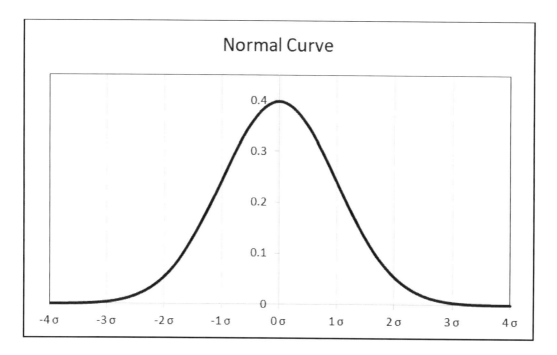

Shapes of Frequency Curves

The five general **shapes of frequency curves** are *symmetrical*, *u-shaped*, *skewed*, *j-shaped*, and *multimodal*. Symmetrical curves are also known as bell curves or normal curves. Values equidistant from the median have equal frequencies. U-shaped curves have two maxima – one at each end. Skewed curves have the maximum point off-center. Curves that are negative skewed, or left skewed, have the maximum on the right side of the graph so there is longer tail and lower slope on the left side. The opposite is true for curves that are positive-skewed, or right-skewed. J-shaped curves have a maximum at one end and a minimum at the other end. Multimodal curves have multiple maxima. For example, if the curve has exactly two maxima, it is called a bimodal curve.

Interpretation of Graphs

<u>Example</u>

The following graph shows the ages of five patients being cared for in a hospital:

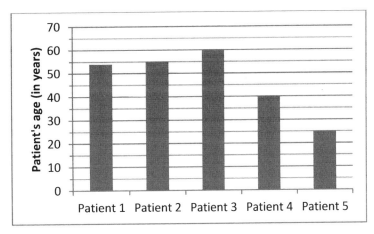

Determine the range of patient ages.

Patient 1 is 54 years old; Patient 2 is 55 years old; Patient 3 is 60 years old; Patient 4 is 40 years old; and Patient 5 is 25 years old. The range of patient ages is the age of the oldest patient minus the age of the youngest patient. In other words, $60 - 25 = 35$. The range of ages is 35 years.

Consistency between Studies

<u>Example</u>

In a drug study containing 100 patients, a new cholesterol drug was found to decrease low-density lipoprotein (LDL) levels in 25% of the patients. In a second study containing 50 patients, the same drug administered at the same dosage was found to decrease LDL levels in 50% of the patients. Are the results of these two studies **consistent** with one another?

Even though in both studies 25 people (25% of 100 is 25 and 50% of 50 is 25) showed improvements in their LDL levels, the results of the studies are inconsistent. The results of the second study indicate that the drug has a much higher efficacy (desired result) than the results of the first study. Because 50 out of 150 total patients showed improvement on the medication, one could argue that the drug is effective in one third (or approximately 33%) of patients. However, one should be wary of the reliability of results when they're not **reproducible** from one study to the next and when the **sample size** is fairly low.

Representations

Representations are the tools of symbols and materials. They are used to help students understand mathematics by giving them visual guides in their thinking. For example, the conventional symbols that indicate addition, subtraction, equality, and so on (into the higher realms of symbols used in geometry, algebra, and calculus) tell students, at a glance, the process that is being calculated. Materials that are used as representations are called **manipulatives**. These can be small plastic objects or pictures for the students to count, line up, or otherwise use to solve a problem. Representations make abstract concepts become concrete. They put mathematics into the students,' hands as well as heads, and the result is improved learning. Using familiar manipulatives with new problems helps the student to make connections and feel more confident and capable of expanding their skills.

Concepts Taught in Kindergarten Before Introducing Numbers

In kindergarten, children can be prepared for the study of mathematics by practicing certain concepts such as:

- **position** – top, middle, bottom, above, below, before, after, between, under, inside, outside, left, and right
- **visual attributes** – same and different colors, shapes, and sizes; identifying items that are out-of-place or don't belong
- **sorting** – by size, color, type, or shape; identifying an equal number, more, or fewer of a given item
- **graphing** – the use of picture graphs and using data from graphs
- **patterns** – identifying, copying, extending, and making patterns; finding patterns that are different or alike, making predictions from patterns
- **measurements** – longer and shorter; how much they weigh, heavier and lighter; how much an item can hold

Problem-Solving Strategies for Mathematics and Steps for Solving Word Problems

For any problem, the following **strategies** can be used according to their appropriateness to the type of problem or calculation: i) Use manipulatives or act out the problem, ii) draw a picture, iii) look for a pattern, iv) guess and check, v) use logical reasoning, vi) make an organized list, vii) make a table, viii) solve a simpler problem, and ix) work backward.

In order to solve a word problem, the following steps can be used:

- Achieve an understanding of the problem by reading it carefully, finding and separating the information needed to solve the problem, and discerning the ultimate question in the problem.
- Make a plan as to what needs to be done to solve the problem.
- Solve the problem using the plan from step 2.
- Review the word problem to make sure that the answer is the correct solution to the problem and makes sense.

Building Number Sense Among Students

It is important to think **flexibly** to develop number sense. Therefore, it is imperative to impress upon students that there is more than one right way to solve a problem. Otherwise, students will try to learn only one method of computation, rather than think about what makes sense or contemplate the possibility of an easier way. Some strategies for helping students develop number sense include the following:

- Frequently asking students to make their calculations mentally and rely on their reasoning ability. Answers can be checked manually afterwards, if needed.
- Having a class discussion about solutions the students found using their minds only and comparing the different approaches to solving the problem. Have the students explain their reasoning in their own words.

- Modeling the different ideas by tracking them on the board as the discussion progresses.
- Presenting problems to the students that can have more than one answer.

Using Manipulative Materials in Mathematics Classrooms

As with all classroom supplies, the students must understand that there are rules for their use, including how to store the materials when they are not in use. In addition:

- the teacher should discuss with the students the purpose of the manipulatives and how they will help the students to learn,
- the students should understand that the manipulatives are intended for use with specific problems and activities; however, time for free exploration should be made available so students are less tempted to play when assigned specific tasks,
- a chart posted in the classroom of the manipulatives with their names will help the students to gain familiarity with them and develop mathematical literacy skills, and
- loans of manipulatives for home use with a letter of explanation to the parents about the purpose and value of the manipulatives will encourage similar strategies with homework.

Implications of Mathematics Today

Today, mathematics is used throughout the world in many **fields**, including natural science, engineering, medicine, and the social sciences, such as economics. **Applied mathematics**, the application of mathematics to such fields, inspires and makes use of new mathematical discoveries and sometimes leads to the development of entirely new disciplines. Mathematicians also engage in **pure mathematics**, or mathematics for its own sake, without having any application in mind, although applications for what began as pure mathematics are often discovered later.

Connecting Math and Science to Real Life for Gifted Students

Since math and science are so often heavy in calculations and facts, students are usually not taught how these subjects relate to the real world. All students, especially gifted students, need to find meaning in an academic subject and understand how it **applies** in life. We may not appreciate enough that math and science are not like people whose opinions we can disagree with; they provide hard, objective, unchangeable facts. Teachers can show students the consequences of ignoring facts with examples like these: mathematicians and engineers advised not launching the Challenger space shuttle, but management overruled them, thereby leading to the deadly explosion. Pop singer Aaliyah died in a plane crash after pilot and crew ignored the mathematics indicating airplane overload and flew regardless. A mathematician proved racial bias in jury selection by calculating that the mathematical probability of fair selection was approximately 1 in 1,000,000,000,000,000.

Analyzing the Use of Appropriate Mathematical Concepts, Procedures, and Vocabulary when Evaluating Student Solutions

When evaluating student solutions, it is important to analyze the use of appropriate mathematical concepts, procedures, and vocabulary for a variety of reasons. First and foremost, we must be sure that we have provided adequate practice and instruction of **important concepts** before assessing them. Once we have established that instruction is sufficient, we must ensure that students are following the appropriate **procedures** when faced with various tasks and that those procedures are executed correctly. Finally, we must hold students accountable for using high-level **vocabulary** to ensure that students are able to read, understand, and communicate their mathematics thoughts at age- and grade-appropriate levels.

Correcting Student Errors

A student is asked to find the area of a rectangle measuring 8 feet by 4 feet. The student is able to break the rectangle into 32 squares but states that the area is 24 square feet. The student calculated the perimeter of the rectangle rather than the area. The perimeter of a rectangle is the sum of its sides. Here, the rectangle's sides measure 8 feet, 8 feet, 4 feet, and 4 feet, which total to 24 feet. To calculate area, the student must multiply the length by the width (8×4), which equals 32 square feet. To help the student correct his or her error, the teacher can explain that the student was on the right track when he or she broke the rectangle into 32 squares. Because area is the amount of unit squares that can be contained in a two-dimensional figure, the student could have also opted to simply count the unit squares he or she created, which would have also led him or her to the correct answer of 32 square feet.

Exploring Problem Structures with Unknowns in All Positions

It is important to provide students with the opportunity to explore and find solutions for **problem structures** to develop their higher-level thinking skills and problem-solving strategies. By exposing students to problems with unknowns in all positions, students are forced to not only memorize procedures but also to analyze the framework of a problem, make connections for relationships within the problem, and develop strategies for solving problems that may not follow specific rules or procedures. Problems that include put-together/take-apart scenarios are excellent problem structures for teachers to use in an effort to develop higher-level thinking skills. In addition, providing students the opportunity to use arrays to model their solutions provides teachers with a glimpse into the thought processes of each student's solution.

Unknown Addends

A teacher tells her students that she has five pieces of fruit in her refrigerator. Two are apples, and the rest are oranges. She asks the students how many oranges are in her refrigerator. In this type of problem, there is an **unknown addend**. When dealing with unknown addends and numbers up to 20 (typically in the elementary classroom), this type of problem is known as a put-together/take apart problem. Ideally, the teacher's goal is for the students to visualize this the scenario as $2 + ? = 5$. Depending on the students' approach (drawing a picture, subtracting, number facts, modeling, etc.), they may choose to put together or take apart the problem in a variety of ways. To analyze the students' process, the teacher should check that each student has developed a strategy that will result in correctly identifying the missing addend in a way that could be applied to other problems similar in nature, continually resulting in the correct answer.

Evaluating Validity of Mathematical Model or Argument when Analyzing a Solution

When assessing a student's **proficiency**, simply arriving at the correct answer does not validate true mastery of a mathematical concept. To determine that a student has truly mastered a skill or concept, that student must be able to explain or defend his or her **process** as well as the solution. By requiring a model or compelling students to defend their answers, teachers can truly assess the validity of each solution and determine whether or not each student has a true grasp of the concept being assessed. A teacher can be confident that a student has truly mastered a concept when that student can describe his or her process, explain the meaning behind his or her solution, and defend why that solution is logical and appropriate.

Analyzing Validity of Student's Mathematical Process

A teacher is assessing a student's ability to multiply two-digit numbers. A student in the class arrives at the correct answer without using the traditional algorithm. In mathematics, there is often more than one way to arrive at the correct answer. The focus of the teacher should be to analyze the **validity** of the student's mathematical process to determine if it is a process that could be applied to other multiplication problems, which would result in the correct answer. If the student has modeled his or her thought process, or can argue that the inventive strategy is applicable across all multiplication problems, then that student should be considered to have mastered the skill of multiplication. However, if the student's argument or model is not applicable to other multiplication problems, that student should be provided with more instruction and opportunity for improvement.

Using Individual Student Mathematics Assessment Data to Guide Instructional Decisions and Differentiate Instruction

Teachers should constantly **assess** student learning. These assessments should be quick in nature and offer immediate feedback to both the teacher and student. Assessments such as quick "exit tickets" at the end of each lesson can tell a teacher whether or not students achieved the objective of the day. If the majority of the class achieved mastery, the teacher should look to modify and reteach that lesson to the students who did not achieve mastery. On the other hand, if the majority of the class did not achieve mastery, the teacher should reflect on the way in which the lesson was presented and try another whole-class approach before moving on. By monitoring student learning on a constant basis, teachers are able to improve their teaching skills as well as identify and differentiate for struggling learners more quickly and effectively.

Creating Structured Experiences for Groups According to Cognitive Complexity of Tasks

Depending on the complexity of the task, teachers should modify the **delivery** of instruction. For less complex tasks, the teacher may opt for **whole-group instruction**, in which the entire class is introduced to a new concept together. Whole-group instruction usually includes a connection to prior knowledge, direct instruction, and some form of media. For more complex tasks, the teacher may choose **small-group instruction**, where students are grouped based on ability levels. The more accelerated learners are given a quicker, more direct form of instruction, whereas the struggling learners work independently at a math center or station activity. After a rotation, the struggling learners are given a modified form of instruction by the teacher, which has been differentiated and allows for more gradual release based on individual needs and abilities.

Distance Formula

A car is traveling at a speed of 40 miles per hour for 2.5 hours. How far, in miles, has the car traveled? The **distance formula** is $d = rt$, where d represents the distance, r represents the rate of speed, and t represents the time elapsed. The distance formula tells us that by multiplying the rate of speed by the time elapsed, we can determine the distance traveled. Here, when we substitute our rate, 40, for r and 2.5 for our time, t, we have the expression $d = 40(2.5)$. The product of 40 and 2.5 is 100, which simplifies our expression to $d = 100$. We can now conclude that the car has traveled a distance of 100 miles in 2.5 hours at a rate of 40 miles per hour.

Example Problems

<u>Problem 1</u>

The area of a closet is $25\frac{1}{4}$ square feet. New carpet (including labor and materials) costs $8.00 per square foot to install. What will it cost to re-carpet the entire closet?

To find the total cost to re-carpet the closet, we must multiply the area of the closet, $25\frac{1}{4}$, by the cost of the carpet, $8.00 per square foot. To multiply these values, we must convert both of them to improper fractions, creating the expression $\frac{101}{4} \times \frac{\$8}{1}$. We can use cross-cancellation to simplify our expression by dividing both 4 and 8 by 4, which changes our expression to $\frac{101}{1} \times \frac{\$2}{1}$. When we multiply across, we arrive at our product, $202.00. Without cross-cancellation, our product would be $\frac{808}{4}$, which still reduces to $202.00. It will cost $202.00 to re-carpet the closet.

<u>Problem 2</u>

A fish tank measures 5 feet long, 3 feet wide, and 3 feet tall. Each cubic foot of the tank holds 7.48 gallons of water. The fish tank is filled with water, leaving 6 inches of empty space at the top of the tank. How much water, in cubic feet, is in the fish tank?

To calculate the **volume of a rectangular prism** we would typically multiply the length, width, and height of the prism. However, the prompt tells us that 6 inches (or half a foot) of the tank is left empty. Given this information, we must use a measurement of 2.5 in place of 3 feet for the height of our tank. To calculate the volume of the portion of the tank filled with water we must multiply $5 \times 3 \times 2.5$, which equals 37.5 cubic feet. If each cubic foot holds 7.48 gallons of water, we can multiply 37.5 by 7.48 to determine the number of gallons of water contained in the tank. The product of 37.5 and 7.48 is 280.5. There are 280.5 gallons of water in the fish tank.

Foundations and Professional Roles and Responsibilities

Individuals with Disabilities Education Act

The Individuals with Disabilities Education Act (IDEA) includes six major principles that focus on students' rights and the responsibilities public schools have for educating children with disabilities. One of the main principles of the IDEA law is to provide a *free and appropriate public education* (FAPE) suited to the individual needs of a child with a disability. This requires schools to provide special education and related services to students identified as having disabilities. Another purpose of IDEA is to require schools to provide an *appropriate evaluation* of a child with a suspected disability and an *Individualized Education Program* (IEP) for a child with a disability who qualifies under IDEA. Students with IEPs are guaranteed *least restrictive environment* (LRE), or a guarantee that they are educated in the general education classroom as much as possible. IDEA also ensures *parent participation*, providing a role for parents as equal participants and decision makers. Lastly, *procedural safeguards* also serve to protect parents' rights to advocate for their children with disabilities.

People Protected by Parts B and C of IDEA Law

Early intervention services are provided to children with special needs from birth to age three under IDEA Part C. Children from birth to age 3 who are identified as having disabilities and qualify under IDEA receive Individualized Family Service Plans (IFSPs).

Special education and related services are provided to children with disabilities from ages 3 to 21 under IDEA Part B. Children ages 3 to 21 who are identified as having disabilities and qualify under IDEA receive educational documents, called Individualized Education Programs (IEPs).

Individualized Education Programs vs. Individualized Family Service Plans

IFSPs and IEPs are both educational documents provided under IDEA to service the rights of children with disabilities and their families. The major differences between IEPs and IFSPs, aside from the ages they service, is that IFSPs cover broader services for children with disabilities and their families. IFSP services are often provided in the children's homes. IEPs focus on special education and related services within the children's school settings.

Purpose of IEPs and Function of the PLOPs

An IEP is a written statement for a child with a disability. Its primary purposes are to establish measurable annual goals and to list the services needed to help the child with a disability meet the annual goals.

The IDEA law mandates that a statement of the child's academic achievement and functional performance be included within the IEP. This statement is called Present Levels of Performance (PLOPs). It provides a snapshot of the student's current performance in school. Present Levels of Performance should also report how a student's disability is affecting, or not affecting, progress in school.

The IDEA law mandates that an Annual Goals section be provided within the IEP. Annual goals lay out what a student is expected to learn within a 12-month period. These goals are influenced by the student's PLOPs and are developed using objective, measurable data based on the student's previous academic performance.

Child Find Law

Child Find is part of the Individuals with Disabilities Education Act (IDEA) and states that schools are legally required to find children who have disabilities and need special education or other services. According to the Child Find law, all school districts must have processes for identifying students who need special education and related services. Children with disabilities from birth to age 21, children who are homeschooled, and children in private schools are all covered by the Child Find law. Infants and toddlers can be identified and provided with services so that parents have the right tools in place to meet their children's needs before they enter grade school. The Child Find law does not mean that public schools need to agree to evaluate students when evaluations are requested. Schools may still refuse evaluation if school professionals do not suspect the children of having disabilities.

Steps to Implementing IEPs

The five important steps for an Individualized Education Program (IEP) process are a referral for special education services, an evaluation, determining eligibility, writing an IEP, and an IEP meeting. A referral can be initiated by a teacher, a special team in the school district, the student's parent, or another professional. An evaluation provides a snapshot of a student's background history, strengths, weaknesses, and academic, behavioral, or social needs. An IEP team of professionals uses the evaluation and any other reports regarding a student's progress to determine if the student is eligible for special education services. Once a student has been found eligible for special education, an IEP is written by a special education teacher or other specialist familiar with the student. The IEP meeting, either initial or annual, is held before the new IEP is implemented. The IEP team includes the parent, student, special education teacher, general education teacher, school psychologist, school administrator, appropriate related service professionals, and any other professionals or members that can comment on the student's strengths.

Manifestation Determination

Manifestation determination is a process defined by the Individuals with Disabilities Education Act (IDEA). The manifestation determination process is put into effect when a student receiving special education needs to be removed from the educational setting due to a suspension, expulsion or alternative placement. Manifestation determination is the process that determines if the disciplinary action resulted from a manifestation of the student's disability. This is important because if the action was a manifestation of the disability, the outcome of the disciplinary action may change. During the initial part of this process, relevant data is collected about the student and the circumstances of the offending behavior. The student's Individualized Education Program team determines whether or not the student's behavior was related to the disability. If they determine that the behavior was not related to the disability, the disciplinary action is carried out. If the behavior is determined to be related to the disability, the student is placed back into the original educational setting.

Provision of Title III of the Americans with Disabilities Act

Title III of ADA prohibits the discrimination of people with disabilities in public accommodations. Title III seeks to level the playing field of access for people with disabilities participating in public activities. Businesses open to the public, such as schools, restaurants, movie theaters, day care facilities, recreation facilities, doctor's offices, and restaurants, are required to comply with ADA standards. Additionally, commercial facilities, such as privately-owned businesses, factories, warehouses, and office buildings, are required to provide access per ADA standards. Title III of ADA outlines the general requirements of the reasonable modifications that businesses must provide. Title III also provides detailed, specific requirements for reasonable modifications within businesses and requires new construction and building alterations to abide by ADA regulations. Title III also outlines rules regarding enforcement of ADA regulations, such as the consequences for a person or persons participating in discrimination of a person with a disability. Title III provides for certification of state laws or local building codes. This means that a state's Assistant Attorney General may issue certification to a place of public accommodation or commercial facility that meets or exceeds the minimum requirements of Title III.

Larry P. v. Riles

The *Larry P. v. Riles* (1977) court case examined possible cultural discrimination of African-American students. The court case questioned whether an intelligence quotient (IQ) test was an accurate measurement of a student's true intelligence. The case argued that there was a disproportionate number of African-American students identified as needing special education services (EMR program services). The court plaintiff Larry P. argued that IQ tests were biased against African-American students, which resulted in their placements in limiting educational settings. The defendant Riles argued that the prevalence of African-American students in the EMR classes was due to genetics and social and environmental factors. The court ultimately ruled that the IQ tests were discriminatory and resulted in the disproportionate placement of African-American students in the EMR setting. It was determined that these particular assessments were culturally biased, and the students' performances would be more accurately measured using adaptive behavior assessments, diagnostic tests, observations, and other assessments.

Diana v. State Board of Education

Diana v. State Board of Education (1970) is a court case that examined the case of a student who was placed in special education after results of the Stanford Binet Intelligence test indicated she had a mild case of "mental retardation." This class-action lawsuit was developed on behalf of nine Mexican-American children, arguing that IQ scores were not an adequate measurement to determine special education placement in the EMR setting. The case argued that Mexican-American children might be at a disadvantage because the IQ tests were written and administered in English. This might possibly constitute discrimination. The plaintiffs in the case argued that IQ scores were not a valid measurement because the children might have been unable to comprehend the test written in English. In the conclusive results of this case, the court ordered children to be tested in their primary language, if it was not English. As a result of this case, IQ tests were no longer used as the sole assessments for determining special education placement. There was also increased focus on cultural and linguistic diversity in students.

Winkelman v. Parma City Board of Education

This court case began as an argument against a free and appropriate public education as required by the Individuals with Disabilities Education Act (IDEA). The parents of Jacob Winkelman believed their son was not provided with a FAPE in his special education setting in Parma City Schools. The disagreement became about whether or not children can be represented by their parents per IDEA law in federal court. The U.S Court of Appeals for the Sixth Circuit argued that IDEA protected the rights of the children and not the parents. In the end, the District Court ruled that parents could represent their children within disputes over a free and appropriate public education as constituted by IDEA. Ultimately, this settled the question of whether or not parents have rights under IDEA, in addition to their children. The court case determined that parents play a significant role in the education of their children on Individualized Education Programs (IEPs) and are IEP team members. Therefore, parents are entitled to litigate *pro se* for their children.

Honig v. Doe

Honig v. Doe (1998) was a Supreme Court case examining the violation of the Education for All Handicapped Children Act (EAHCA, an earlier version of the Individuals with Disabilities Education Act) against the California School Board. The offense occurred when a child was suspended for a violent behavior outburst that was related to his disability. The court case centered on two plaintiffs. Both were diagnosed with an Emotional Disturbance and qualified for special education under EAHCA. Following the violent incident, the school suspended the students and recommended them for expulsion. The plaintiff's case argued that the suspension/expulsion went against the stay-put provision of EAHCA, which states that children with disabilities must remain in their current educational placements during review proceedings unless otherwise agreed upon by both parents and educational representatives. The defendant argued that the violence of the situation marked an exception to the law. The court determined that schools are able to justify the placement removal of a student when maintaining a safe learning environment outweighs a student's right to a free and appropriate public education.

Pennsylvania Association for Retarded Children v. Commonwealth of Pennsylvania

The Commonwealth of Pennsylvania was accused by the Pennsylvania Association for Retarded Children (PARC 1971) of denying a free and appropriate public education to students with disabilities. The Commonwealth of Pennsylvania was accused of refusing to educate students who had not met the "mental age of 5." The groups argued before the District Court of the Eastern District of Pennsylvania. This case was significant because PARC was one of the first institutions in the country to challenge the placement of students with special needs. The plaintiffs argued that all children should and would benefit from some sort of educational instruction and training. Ultimately, this was the beginning of instituting the state requirement of a free and appropriate public education (FAPE) for all children in public education from ages 6-21. The Commonwealth of Pennsylvania was tasked with providing a FAPE and sufficient education and training for all eligible children receiving special education. They could no longer deny students based on their mental ages. This triggered other state institutions to make similar decisions and led to the creation of similar federal policies in the Education for All Handicapped Children Act (1974).

1990 Amendments to the IDEA

The Individuals with Disabilities Education Act (IDEA) replaced the Education for All Handicapped Children Act in 1990. IDEA amendments changed the age range for children to receive special education services to ages 3-21. IDEA also changed the language of the law, changing the focus onto the individuals with disabilities rather than the handicapped children. Therefore, the focus shifted from the conditions or disabilities to the individual children and their needs. IDEA amendments also categorized different disabilities. IDEA 1997 increased the emphasis on the individualized education plans for students with disabilities and increased parents' roles in the educational decision-making processes for their children with disabilities. Part B of the 1997 amendment provided services to children ages 3-5, mandating that their learning needs be outlined in Individualized Education Programs or Individualized Family Service Plans. Part C of IDEA provided financial assistance to the families of infants and toddlers with disabilities. Part C states that educational agencies must provide early intervention services that focus on children's developmental and medical needs, as well as the needs of their families. Part C also gives states the option to provide services to children who are at risk for developmental disabilities.

Effect of the Individuals with Disabilities Education Improvement Act of 2004 on IDEA

In 2004, the Individuals with Disabilities Education Act implemented the Individuals with Disabilities Improvement Act. IDEA was reauthorized to better meet the needs of children in special education programs and children with special needs. As a result of these changes:

- Special educators are required to achieve Highly Qualified Teacher status and be certified in special education.
- Individualized Education Programs must contain measurable annual goals and descriptions of how progress toward the goals will be measured and reported.
- Schools or agencies must provide science or research-based interventions as part of the evaluation process to determine if children have specific learning disabilities. This may be done in addition to assessments that measure achievement or intelligence.

The changes made to require science or research-based interventions resulted in many districts implementing Response to Intervention procedures. These procedures meet the IDEA 2004 requirement of providing interventions in addition to achievement reports or intelligence tests on the Individualized Education Programs for children with disabilities.

Development of Educational Laws Like Goals 2000 and No Child Left Behind

President Bill Clinton signed The National Educational Goals Act, also known as Goals 2000, into effect in the 1990s to trigger standardized educational reform. The act focused on outcomes-based education and was intended to be completed by the year 2000. The goals of this act included ensuring that children are ready to learn by the time they start school, increasing high school graduation rates, demonstration of competency by students in grades 4, 8, and 12 in core content areas, and positioning the United States as first in the world in mathematics and science achievement. Goals 2000 was withdrawn when President George W. Bush implemented the No Child Left Behind Act (NCLB) in 2001. NCLB also supported standards-based reform, and it mandated that states develop more skills-based assessments. The act emphasized state testing, annual academic progress, report cards, and increased teacher qualification standards. It also outlined changes in state funding. NCLB required schools to meet Adequate Yearly Progress (AYP). AYP was measured by results of achievement tests taken by students in each school district, and consequences were implemented for school districts that missed AYP during consecutive years.

Every Student Succeeds Act of 2015

NCLB was replaced in 2015 by the Every Student Succeeds Act (ESSA). ESSA built upon the foundations of NCLB and emphasized equal opportunity for students. ESSA currently serves as the main K-12 educational law in the United States. ESSA affects students in public education, including students with disabilities. The purpose of ESSA is to provide a quality education for all students. It also aims to address the achievement of disadvantaged students, including students living in poverty, minority groups, students receiving special education services, and students with limited English language skills. ESSA determined that states may decide educational plans as long as they follow the government's framework. ESSA also allows states to develop their own educational standards and mandates that the curriculum focus on preparing students for post-secondary educations or careers. The act requires students to be tested annually in math and reading during grades 3-8 and once in high school. Students must also be tested in science once in elementary school, middle school, and high school. School accountability was also mandated by ESSA. The act requires states to have plans in place for any schools that are underperforming.

ESL Rights for Students and Parents

As public schools experience an influx of English as a Second Language (ESL) students, knowledge of their rights becomes increasingly important. The Every Student Succeeds Act (ESSA) of 2015 addresses funding discrepancies for ESL students and families. ESSA allocates funds to schools and districts where low-income families comprise 40% or more of the enrollment. This is intended to assist with ESL students who are underperforming or at risk for underperforming. ESSA also provides funding for ESL students to become English proficient and find academic success. However, in order for schools and districts to receive this funding, they must avoid discrimination, track ESL student progress, assess ESL student English proficiency, and notify parents of their children's ESL status. Avoiding discrimination includes preventing the over-identification of ESL students for special education services. The referral and evaluation process must be carried out with caution to ensure that students' perceived disabilities are actual deficits and not related to their English language learning abilities.

Rehabilitation Act of 1973

The Rehabilitation Act of 1973 was the law that preceded IDEA 1975. The Rehab Act serves to protect the rights of people with disabilities in several ways.

- It protects people with disabilities against discrimination relating to employment.
- It provides students with disabilities equal access to the general education curriculum (Section 504).

Americans with Disabilities Act of 1990 (ADA)

The Americans with Disabilities Act (1990) also protects the rights of people with disabilities.

- The ADA provides equal employment for people with disabilities. This means employers must provide reasonable accommodations for people with disabilities in their job and work environments.
- It provides access for people with disabilities to both public and private places open to the public (i.e. access ramps and automatic doors).
- It provides telecommunications access to people with disabilities. This ensures people with hearing and speech disabilities can communicate over the telephone and internet.

Elementary and Secondary Education Act (ESEA)

The Elementary and Secondary Education Act (ESEA) also protects the rights of people with disabilities.

- Passed by President Johnson in 1965, ESEA was part of the president's "War on Poverty." The law sought to allow equal access to a quality education.
- ESEA extended more funding to secondary and primary schools and emphasized high standards and accountability.
- This law was authorized as No Child Left Behind (2001) under President Bush, then reauthorized as the Every Student Succeeds Act (ESSA) under President Obama.

Section 504

A Section 504 Plan comes from the civil rights law, Section 504 of the Rehabilitation Act of 1973, and protects the rights of individuals with disabilities. A 504 Plan is a formal plan or blueprint for how the school will provide services to a student with a disability. This essentially removes barriers for individuals with disabilities by ensuring that appropriate services are provided to meet their special needs. A 504 Plan includes:

- Accommodations: A 504 Plan includes accommodations a student with a disability may need to be successful in a regular education classroom. For example, a student with ADHD may need to sit near the front of the room to limit distractions.
- Related Services: A 504 Plan includes related services, such as speech therapy or occupational therapy, a student may need to be successful in the general education classroom.
- Modifications: Although it is rare for a 504 Plan to include modifications, sometimes they are included. Modifications change what the student is expected to do, such as being given fewer homework assignments.

504 Plans vs. Individualized Education Programs

- A 504 Plan and an Individualized Education Program are similar in that they serve as a blueprint for a student with a disability. However, a 504 Plan serves as a blueprint for how the student will have access to school, whereas the IEP serves as a blueprint for a student's special education experience.
- A 504 Plan helps level the playing field for a student with a disability by providing services and changes to the learning environment. An IEP provides individualized special education and related services to meet the unique needs of a student with a disability. Both IEPs and 504 Plans are provided at no cost to parents.
- The 504 Plan was established under the Rehabilitation Act of 1973 as a civil rights law. The Individualized Education Program was established under the Individuals with Disabilities Education Act (1975 and amended in 2004).
- Unlike an IEP, a 504 Plan does not have to be a planned, written document. An IEP is a planned, written document that includes unique annual learning goals and describes related services for the student with a disability.

Informed Parental Consent

The Individuals with Disabilities Education Act (IDEA) requires that parents be informed before a student is evaluated for special education services. IDEA mandates that a school district receive parental consent to initiate an evaluation of a student for special education services. Consent means the school district has fully informed the parent of their intentions or potential reasons for evaluation of the student. Legally, the request must be written in the parent's native language. This consent does not mean the parent gives consent for a student's placement in special education. In order for a student to be initially placed in special education or receive special education services, parental consent must be given for this issue separately. At any time, parents can withdraw consent for special education placement or special education services. Schools are able to file due process if they disagree with the parental withdrawal of consent. Parents also have a right to consent to parts of a student's Individualized Education Program (IEP), but not necessarily all of the IEP. Once parental consent is granted for all parts of the IEP, it can be implemented.

Tiers of the Response to Intervention Model

- *Tier 1: High Quality Classroom Instruction, Screening, and Group Interventions:* In Tier 1, all students are screened using universal screening and/or the results of statewide assessments. Students identified as at risk receive supplemental instruction. Students who make adequate progress are returned to their regular instruction. Students who do not make adequate progress move to Tier 2.
- *Tier 2: Targeted Interventions:* These interventions are designed to improve the progress of the students who did not make adequate progress in Tier 1. Targeted instruction is usually in the areas of reading and math and does not last longer than one grading period.
- *Tier 3: Intensive Interventions and Comprehensive Evaluation:* Students who are not successful in Tier 2 move on to Tier 3. They receive intensive interventions that target their specific deficits. Students who do not meet progress goals during intensive interventions are referred to receive comprehensive evaluations and are considered to be eligible for special education under IDEA.

Stakeholders in Special Education

Stakeholders that play roles in educating students with disabilities include the students, parents, general educators, administrators, and community members. Students should receive an educational curriculum based on strict standards, such as the Common Core Content Standards. This ensures that they receive good educational foundations from which to grow and expand upon during their school careers. Parents, legal guardians, and sometimes agencies act in the best interests of their children. If they do not think the Individualized Education Programs suit the needs of their children, they can request due process hearings in court. FAPE and LRE ensure that students are educated alongside peers in general education classrooms by general educators. General educators collaborate with special educators to create successful inclusion classrooms. When inclusion is done successfully, the students with disabilities meet their IEP goals.

Information to Be Evaluated During Multi-Factored Evaluations or Evaluation Team Reports

Multi-Factored Evaluations are processes required by the Individuals with Disabilities Education Act to determine if a student is eligible for special education. When a student is suspected of having a disability, the parent or school district can initiate the evaluation process. Student information that is evaluated in a Multi-Factored Evaluation includes background information, health information, vision testing, hearing testing, social and emotional development, general intelligence, past and current academic performance, communication needs, gross and fine motor abilities, results of aptitude or achievement tests, academic skills, and current progress toward Individualized Education Program (IEP) goals. Progress reporting on IEP goals is only appropriate during an annual MFE when a student has already qualified for special education services. The purpose of an MFE is to provide comprehensive information about a student for professionals working with the student. An MFE also helps determine what academic or behavioral goals or related services might be appropriate for a student with disabilities.

Free and Appropriate Public Education Components

The Individuals with Disabilities Education Act (IDEA) defines free and appropriate public education (FAPE) as an educational right for children with disabilities in the United States. FAPE stands for:

- Free: All students found eligible for special education services must receive free services, expensed to the public instead of the parents.
- Appropriate: Students are eligible for educations that are appropriate for their specific needs, as stated in their Individualized Education Programs (IEPs).
- Public: Students with disabilities have the right to be educated in public schools.
- Education: An education must be provided to any school-aged child with a disability. Education and services are defined in a student's IEP.

Ideally, FAPE components are put in place in order to guarantee the best education possible that also suits the individual needs of a student with a disability. FAPE should take place in the least restrictive environment, or the environment with the fewest barriers to learning for the individual student with a disability.

Multi-Factored Evaluation or Evaluation Team Report

A Multi-Factored Evaluation (MFE), sometimes referred to as an Evaluation Team Report (ETR), serves as a snapshot of a child's abilities, strengths, and weaknesses. An MFE is conducted to determine a student's eligibility for special education. Once a student with a disability qualifies for special education, an MFE is conducted at least every three years after the initial MFE date. MFEs are conducted for students ages 3 to 21 who are on IEPs. The purpose of the MFE is to influence a student's Individualized Education Program. An MFE reports on a student's current abilities and how the disability may affect educational performance. MFEs can also determine if a student qualifies for related services, such as occupational therapy or speech-language therapy. An MFE can be requested by a parent or school district when a child is suspected of having a disability. The school district typically has 30 days or less to respond to a parental request to evaluate a student, giving consent or refusal for an evaluation. While initial MFEs are conducted as a means to determine special education qualification, annual MFEs are conducted to address any changes in the needs or services of a student already receiving special education services.

Least Restrictive Environments to Deliver Special Education Services

Special education services are delivered to students that qualify with a disability defined by the Individuals with Disabilities Education Act (IDEA). IDEA law also requires that students who qualify for special education must receive special education services in least restrictive environments that provide the fewest barriers to their learning. A student's most appropriate instructional setting is written out in the Individualized Education Program (IEP). Some special education instructional settings include:

- no instructional setting
- mainstream setting
- resource room
- self-contained classroom
- homebound instruction

With no instructional setting, students participate in the general education curriculum but may receive related services, such as speech-language therapy or occupational therapy. In the mainstream setting, students are instructed in the general education classroom for most or part of the day and provided with special education supports, accommodations, modifications, and related services. A resource room is an environment where students receive remedial instruction when they cannot participate in the general curriculum for one or more subject areas. A self-contained classroom is a setting for students who need special education and related services for more than 50% of the day. Homebound instruction is for students who are homebound or hospital bound for more than four consecutive weeks.

Purpose of Special Education

Special education is specially designed instruction delivered to meet the individual needs of children with disabilities. Special education includes a free and appropriate education in the least restrictive environment. In the past, a special education model might consist of a self-contained classroom of students with special needs whose needs were addressed in that setting. Today, students who qualify for special education must receive instruction in free and appropriate settings. This means they receive special education services in settings that provide the fewest barriers to their learning. The most appropriate setting varies, depending on the student and the disability. The purpose of special education is to ensure that the unique needs of children with disabilities are addressed. In the public school setting, the Individuals with Disabilities Education Act mandates that students with disabilities receive free and appropriate public educations. The goal of special education is to create fair environments for students with special needs to learn. Ideally, the settings should enable students to learn to their fullest potential.

Due Process Rights Available to Parents and Legal Guardians

When parents or legal guardians and school districts cannot agree on components of a student with a disability's Individualized Education Program (IEP), parents and legal guardians have a right to due process. Due process is a legal right under the Individuals with Disabilities Education Act (IDEA) that usually involves the school district violating a legal rule. Examples of these violations include a school district not running an IEP meeting, failing to conduct a tri-annual evaluation, or failing to implement a student's IEP. Disputes often involve a student's instructional placement, appropriate accommodations or modifications, related services, or changes to IEPs. School districts' due process policies vary depending on the district. IDEA, however, mandates that a due process legal form be completed by the parent or legal guardian in order to move forward. This form must be completed within two years of a dispute. Mediation, or the process of coming to an agreement before filing due process, can be a solution to the dispute. IEP meetings, even when it is not time for an annual review, are also appropriate options for resolving a dispute before filing due process.

Purpose of Mediation in Lieu of a Parent or Legal Guardian Filing for Due Process

Mediation is a process used to address a dispute prior to a parent or legal guardian filing for due process. The purpose of mediation is to resolve a dispute between the parent or legal guardian of a student with a disability and the school district. Disputes occur when the parent or legal guardian does not agree with an IEP component, such as what related services are provided or the way a student's IEP is being implemented. Mediation is not a parent or legal guardian's legal right, but school districts often support mediation to offset a due process filing. Mediation involves the attempt to resolve a dispute and includes a meeting between the parent or legal guardian, school district member, and a neutral third party, such as a mediator provided by the state. States have lists of mediators available for these situations. Agreements that come out of the mediation process are put into writing and, if appropriate, put into a student's IEP. Disagreements can continue to be mediated, or the decision may be made to file due process. Prior to mediation, parents or legal

- 244 -

guardians and school districts have the option of holding IEP meetings (outside of annual meetings) to resolve disputes.

Maintaining Confidentiality and Privacy of Student Records

Similar to the Health Insurance Portability and Accountability Act of 1966 (HIPAA), FERPA is a law that protects privacy. However, FERPA is specific to the privacy of students. The FERPA law applies to any school or agency that receives funds from the U.S. Department of Education. This ensures that schools or agencies cannot share any confidential information about a student without a parent or student's written consent. Student educational records can be defined as records, files, documents, or other materials which contain a student's personal information. Individualized Education Programs and Evaluation Team Reports (ETRs) are examples of private documents under the FERPA law. The responsibility of a school covered by FERPA is to maintain confidentiality and privacy. The members of an IEP team, such as special educators, related service professionals, general educators, or other professionals, cannot share any identifying, private information about a student. Information addressing the needs of individual students found on an IEP, Evaluation Team Report, or other identifying document must remain confidential unless express written consent is given by the parent or legal guardian.

Pre-Referral/Referral Process for Identifying and Placing a Student with a Disability

The purpose of a pre-referral process for a child with a suspected disability is to attempt reasonable modifications and accommodations before the child is referred for special education services. Schools often have pre-referral teams whose purpose is to identify the strengths and needs of a child, put reasonable strategies into action, and evaluate the results of this pre-referral intervention. If the results do not show any change, another intervention can be attempted, or the student can be referred for a special education evaluation.

If a child is suspected of having a disability and did not succeed with pre-referral interventions, the school or parent can request an evaluation. During the evaluation process, the school compiles information to see if the student needs special education or related services. This information is used to determine if the student's disability is affecting school performance and if the student qualifies for special education. The evaluation lists and examines the student's strengths, weaknesses, and development and determines what supports the student needs in order to learn. An evaluation must be completed before special education services can be provided.

Role of a School Psychologist in the Special Education

School psychologists are certified members of school teams that support the needs of students and teachers. They help students with overall academic, social, behavioral, and emotional success. School psychologists are trained in data collection and analysis, assessments, progress monitoring, risk factors, consultation and collaboration, and special education services. In special education, school psychologists may work directly with students and collaborate with teachers, administrators, parents, and other professionals working with particular students. They may also be involved in counseling students' parents, the Response to Intervention process, and performing initial evaluations of students who are referred for special education services. School psychologists also work to improve academic achievement, promote positive behavior and health by implementing school-wide programs, support learning needs of diverse learners, maintain safe school environments, and strengthen and maintain good school-parent relationships.

Overrepresentation of Students from Diverse Backgrounds

34b. Disproportionate representation occurs when there is not an equal representation of students from different cultural and linguistic backgrounds identified for special education services. Students from different cultural and linguistic groups should be identified for special education services in similar proportions. This ensures that no one group is overrepresented and overidentified as having special needs due to their cultural or linguistic differences. Disproportionality can occur based on a child's sex, language proficiency, receipt of free and reduced lunch, or race and ethnicity. Historically, most disproportionality has been a civil rights issue and due to a child's cultural or linguistic background. Recently, the focus has been on the disproportional number of students who spend time in special education classrooms instead of being educated alongside regularly educated peers.

The referral process, Response to Intervention (RTI), provides safeguards against disproportionality. The RTI process requires instruction and intervention catered to the unique, specific needs of the individual student. The purpose of RTI is not the identification of a disability or entitlement to services. Instead, it focuses on data used to make educational decisions about individuals, classrooms, schools, or districts. Models like RTI address disproportionate representation, but they are not perfect.

Collaborating with IEP Team Members

It is important for Individualized Education Program (IEP) team members to collaborate with each other in order to certify that students are receiving educational plans that are suitable to their needs in the least restrictive environments. IEP team members include special education teachers, general education teachers, parents or legal guardians, students, school district representatives, and others knowledgeable about the students' performances. Each member brings a valuable piece of information about the students for instructional planning and IEP planning meetings. It is important for special educators to establish good relationships and collaborate with the students and parents or legal guardians in order to gauge the students' strengths and weaknesses. Collaboration is essential between the general and special educators in order to ensure that students' IEP goals and needs are being met in the appropriate settings. Collaboration with district team members or others like school psychologists is helpful for gaining insight on special education procedures or assessment results.

Communicating with Related Service Members Across All Special Education Settings

In order to provide students with disabilities the best educations possible, it is important for special educators and related service members to communicate effectively. Communication is important due to the degree of collaboration required between the special educators and the related service members. Related service members are often Individualized Education Program (IEP) team members and help students meet their IEP goals and objectives. Related service members, like speech pathologists and occupational therapists, also work on a consultation basis with special educators. They may also consult with general education teachers to ensure that students receive required related services in the general education or inclusive classroom settings. Special educators and related service members must collaborate in order to ensure the needs of the students are met, especially when IEP goals or objectives are out of the scope of the special educators' knowledge bases. For example, a speech pathologist might help a teacher address a student's fluency goal.

Communicating with Parents of Students with Disabilities

It is good practice to communicate with parents outside of progress reporting times and Individualized Education Program meetings. This is especially important for students with communication deficits who may not be able to communicate with their parents or legal guardians. Communication also helps prevent potential crises or problem behaviors and alerts parents or legal guardians before any major issues arise. Special educators should find methods of communication that work best for parents or legal guardians, such as phone calls, emails, or writing in daily communication logs. Email is beneficial for creating paper trails, especially for any discussions about educating students. However, email lacks tone and body language and can sometimes be misunderstood. Phone calls fulfill an immediate need to speak with a parent or legal guardian. However, there are no paper trails with phone calls, and they can also lead to misunderstanding. Phone calls may be time consuming, but they can be conducted on special occasions or when behavioral issues need to be discussed. Written communication logs are useful for writing brief summaries about students' days. With any mode of communication, it is essential to document what is communicated between the parents or legal guardians and the educators.

Roles of Parents/Legal Guardians and the School District During Evaluation

If parents or legal guardians suspect their children have disabilities, they can request that the school districts evaluate the children for special education. A parent or legal guardian can send a written evaluation request to the child's school, principal, and the school district's director or director of special education services. In some states, parents and legal guardians may be required to sign a school district form requesting the evaluation. Parents should follow up on the request and/or set a timeframe for the school district to respond. The school district may choose to implement the Response to Intervention (RTI) pre-referral process. RTI is a process by which the school gives the student special academic support before determining whether or not to move forward with the evaluation process. Not all states or school districts have the same method for applying RTI. Under IDEA, the timeframe for completion of RTI is 60 days. However, some states can set their own timelines. RTI should not be the only means by which the school district collects data on the student and should be part of a comprehensive evaluation conducted by the student's school.

Speech Language Pathologist

Speech language pathologists (SLP) provide interventions for children with communication disorders. They can assist, evaluate, prevent, and diagnose a variety of speech issues, from fluency to voice disorders. Before children reach grade school age, it is important that they receive early interventions for suspected communication disorders. SLPs are helpful with targeting speech or language issues, identifying at-risk students, or providing interventions for children and adults. SLPs also play a role in helping children develop good reading and writing skills, especially when deficits are evident. SLPs work collaboratively with special educators to deliver interventions to children with speech and language disorders in grade school. In schools, SLPs play a role in prevention, assessment, intervention, program design, data collection and analysis, and Individualized Education Program compliance. SLPs work with special educators, parents, students, reading specialists, occupational therapists, school psychologists, and others in order to provide effective services to students who require them.

Occupational Therapist

Students with special needs may need occupational therapy services. The amount of services students receive is defined on their Individualized Education Programs (IEPs). Occupational therapists (OTs) may help students on IEPs refine their fine motor skills, improve sensory processing deficits, improve visual skills, and improve self-care skills. OTs can also assist with behavior management, social skills, and improving attention and focus. When a student is identified as possibly needing OT services, the OT spends time observing the student in a variety of settings where the skill or skill deficit will be demonstrated. Prior to the student's IEP meeting, the OT typically meets with the student's teachers, parents, and other professionals in order to discuss observations, assessment results, and determinations. Determinations are then put into the IEP and implemented as related services. Fine motor skill instruction begins with the OT instructing the student on a particular skill. OTs can set up regimens for teachers and parents to generalize using the fine motor skills in the classroom and home environments.

Reasonable Accommodations for Students

According to the Americans with Disabilities Act, a reasonable accommodation is a change to workplace conditions, equipment, or environment that allow an individual to effectively perform a job. Title I under ADA requires businesses with more than 15 employees to abide by certain regulations, ensuring that their needs are reasonably met. Any change to the work environment or the way a job is performed that gives a person with a disability access to equal employment is considered a reasonable accommodation. Reasonable accommodations fall into three categories: changes to a job application process, changes to the work environment or to the way a job is usually done, and changes that enable an employee access to equal benefits and privileges that employees without disabilities receive. These effectively level the playing field for people with disabilities to receive the same benefits as their peers. It also allows for the fewest barriers to success in the workplace. Many communities have resources available to help people with disabilities find jobs. They also have resources that help employers make their workplaces accessible for people with disabilities.

Paraprofessional

The U.S. Department of Education requires paraprofessionals to have high school diplomas or equivalent under Title 1 law. Paraprofessionals (paras), sometimes called paraeducators, assist classroom teachers with classroom activities and help students with special needs. In a special education setting, a para works with a certified teacher to help deliver instruction and help students meet Individualized Education Program goals and objectives. Paras are not responsible for teaching new skills or introducing new goals and objectives to students. In this respect, special educators generally work alongside the paras and students to introduce new skills, goals, or objectives. At times, paras may be responsible for helping students maintain behavior plans, working with students who may be aggressive or violent, and providing physical assistance if necessary. Training is usually provided by the school district for situations when physical assistance is a possible necessity. Paras can also help take notes on students' progress toward meeting their goals or objectives. They can also discuss how students are progressing with behavior plans.

Behavior Issues of Students and Intervention Strategies

Behavior issues occur with students with and without disabilities. However, they may occur more frequently or to a higher degree for some students with disabilities. Behavior issues are often a manifestation of a child's disability. For example, students with Attention Deficit Hyperactivity Disorder may present with attention and focus issues and impulsivity. Common behavior issues include:

- emotional outbursts
- inattention and inability to focus
- impulsivity
- aggression
- abusive language
- oppositional defiance
- lying or stealing
- threatening adults or peers

Other behavior issues may include inappropriate sexual behavior, inability to control sexual behavior, self-harm, or self-harm attempts. Behavior issues can be avoided or remediated with classroom management skills, like setting clear and consistent classroom goals, setting time limits, and providing visuals to assist with transitions or concepts. When a student is in an aggressive state, it is important for the teacher to remain calm, provide choices for the student, and restate the consequences of any aggressive outbursts.

Managing Students with Emotional Disturbances

Managing a classroom of students with emotional disorders can be challenging and unpredictable. Students with emotional disorders have Individualized Education Program goals that focus on controlling or monitoring their daily behavior choices. However, this does not always mean they will engage in meeting these goals. It is important for educators to know how to manage issues students with emotional disorders may bring to the classroom. When creating resources and lesson plans, an educator should:

- establish a safety plan, which includes knowing how to implement a crisis prevention plan.
- maintain an environment that reduces stimulation and provides visual cues for expected behavior.
- implement intervention-based strategies for managing student behavior.
- collect and use data to identify triggers, track behaviors, and recognize successful strategies that produced positive outcomes.
- practice open communication about classroom expectations to students, parents, and other teachers.

Special education teachers can be good resources for many of these components, especially when students with emotional disorders are in inclusive settings.

Concept of Antecedents, Behavior, and Consequences as Stimuli Used in Behavior Analysis

Antecedents and consequences play a role in behavioral analysis, which is important for evaluating the behaviors of students. The purpose of behavior analysis is to gather information about a specific behavior demonstrated by a student. Antecedents refer to the actions or events that occur before the behavior occurs. It is important to recognize antecedents for behaviors to better understand under what circumstances the behavior is occurring. The behavior is the undesirable action that occurs as a result of the antecedent. Consequences are what happens immediately after the behavior occurs. These can be natural or enforced. A certain consequence might be what the student desires by doing the behavior. Understanding the antecedents, behavior, and consequences and the relationships between them for a particular behavior allows a professional to determine how to minimize or eliminate the behavior. In some circumstances, antecedents can be manipulated, changed, or removed in order to avoid the undesired behavior. Consequences can be manipulated, changed, or removed in order to avoid reinforcing the undesired behavior.

Behavior Rating Scale Assessments

Behavior rating scales address the needs of students referred to special education with emotional disorders. Problems with behavior are often the reason a student has been referred for special education. Behavior rating scales are used in determining a student's eligibility for special education. Behavior rating scales are also useful in addressing undesirable behaviors demonstrated by students with other disorders in special education. They are similar to adaptive behavior scales because teachers or other professionals can administer the scales with little training as long as they are familiar with the students. Behavior rating scales help rate the frequency and intensity of the behaviors for a particular student. Behavior frequency and intensity are often rated with numbered rating scales. They serve as starting points for learning more about a student's behavior so that behavior interventions and management can take place. These scales are norm-referenced, so the outcomes of the behavior rating scales are compared to the behaviors of others.

Negative and Positive Reinforcement Related to Applied Behavior Analysis

Part of applied behavior analysis is applying negative and positive reinforcement strategies. Reinforcement is a process that involves increasing the possibility of a desired behavior occurring. The goal of reinforcement is for the desired behavior to continue occurring in the future. Positive reinforcement works by providing a desired reward for a desired behavior. By reinforcing the desired behavior when it is exhibited, it increases the likelihood that the behavior will occur in the future. For example, parents may give a child an allowance for doing chores, and the allowance is the positive reinforcement for the behavior (the chores). In contrast, negative reinforcement is when a stimulus, usually an aversive stimulus, is removed to enforce a desired behavior. Negative reinforcement should not be seen as a punishment because a punishment is given to decrease a behavior. With negative reinforcement, the goal is for behaviors to increase by stopping, removing, or avoiding negative outcomes. An example of negative reinforcement is making a child finish dinner before receiving a popsicle. The popsicle is the reward for demonstrating the expected behavior.

Developing Positive Behavioral Interventions and Supports

Positive behavioral intervention and support (PBIS) plans can be implemented in classrooms or schoolwide to encourage specific, positive outcomes in groups of students with and without disabilities. A PBIS plan, such as an anti-bullying campaign, is put in place to encourage good behavior and/or school safety. The goal of a PBIS plan is to teach students appropriate behavior, just as they would learn any other academic subject. PBIS plans are put in place to teach students positive behavior or safety procedures that are incompatible with undesirable behaviors. Appropriate PBIS plans should be based on the results of data collected on targeted, large-scale behaviors. They should also be research based and proven effective. As with any behavioral plans, PBIS plans are most successful when student progress is monitored. An effective PBIS plan removes environmental triggers for behavior, reducing the chances of the behavior occurring in the first place. PBIS plans should change if they do not work or stop working.

Developing Functional Behavior Assessment

A functional behavior assessment (FBA) is a formal process used to examine student behavior. The goal of an FBA is to identify what is causing a specific behavior and evaluate how the behavior is affecting the student's educational performance. Once these factors are determined, the FBA is useful in implementing interventions for the specific behavior. When an FBA is developed, a student's behavior must be specifically defined. Then the teacher or other professional devises a plan for collecting data on the behavior. This is helpful in determining what may be causing the behavior, such as environmental triggers. Collected data is analyzed to determine the big picture for what may be causing the behavior. The analyzed data is used to formulate a hypothesis about what is causing the behavior, so the teacher or other professional can then implement the most appropriate plan for addressing the student's specific behavior. Often, this means implementing a behavior intervention plan, which includes introducing the student to actions or processes that are incompatible with the problem behavior. It is important to monitor the plan to ensure effectiveness or remediate certain steps.

Implementing Crisis Prevention Plans

Students with disabilities sometimes display symptoms of their particular disorders that require trained adults to implement crisis prevention plans. Some organizations, such as the Crisis Prevention Institute, specialize in crisis prevention and intervention training for professionals. Crisis prevention plans are put in place to help the students avoid the behaviors before they occur. The goal is to keep the students functioning appropriately in their environments by removing or being aware of possible behavioral triggers. Crisis prevention plans are important to have in place for when students' behaviors become safety concerns. It is helpful to recognize warning signs that crises may be starting, and this can be done by providing interventions when people exhibit behaviors that are typical for them. Clear structure and expectations allow students to understand direct consequences for undesired choices, prior to crisis mode. When students enter crisis mode, the crisis prevention plans provide clear processes that professionals can use to de-escalate the situations.

Developing Behavior Intervention Plans

A behavior intervention plan is based on a functional behavior assessment (FBA). A behavior intervention plan (BIP) is a formal plan that follows the results of an FBA. The purpose of the BIP is to teach the student actions, behaviors, or processes that are incompatible with the problem behavior. The BIP may be included on an Individualized Education Program or 504 Plan, or components of the BIP may be written out as IEP goals. Once an FBA is conducted, a BIP is put in place that describes the behavior, lists factors that trigger the target behavior, and lists any interventions that help the student avoid the behavior. The target behavior is the behavior that needs to be changed. The interventions determined by the FBA and listed in the BIP focus on the problem behavior. The interventions include problem-solving skills for the student to use instead of demonstrating the target behavior. When the interventions fail to target the problem behavior and/or are no longer effective for targeting the behavior, an FBA must be revisited and a new BIP should be developed.

Positive Classroom Discipline Strategies

Promoting positive classroom discipline is part of effective classroom management. This involves holding students accountable for their actions, and it starts with establishing clear and consistent consequences when poor choices are demonstrated. Students learn to predict consequences and self-correct their behaviors. It is helpful to give reminders before immediately resorting to consequences. Reminders help students remember the consequences for breaking rules regarding behavior. Pre-reminders are one way to enforce and remind students of expectations before diving into lessons. Nonverbal reminders, such as looks, touches, silence, or removal, are possible ways to distract students from engaging in poor choices. Removal involves tasks like sending students to throw things away. Spoken reminders can be used to further encourage self-management skills and should be used as precursors for reminding students about expectations instead of delivering immediate consequences.

Promoting Appropriate Behavior in Inclusive Learning Environments

Effective classrooms have good management strategies in place that promote good learning environments and minimize disruptions. When it comes to students with disabilities, planning classroom management strategies presents different challenges. In inclusive learning environments, it is important for teachers to keep all students on track with their learning. General educators and special educators can demonstrate effective classroom management strategies by figuring out what is causing students to act out or misbehave. Effective teachers understand how students' special needs come into play with expected classroom behaviors. They also promote positive classroom experiences, establish clear expectations for behavior, and reinforce positive behaviors. Teachers with effective classroom management strategies demonstrate good leadership and organizational skills. They collaborate with other professionals and students' parents to ensure the success of students with special needs in their classrooms. Lastly, effective classroom management includes setting goals for inclusive classrooms to achieve. Clear goals help establish good rapport with students with special needs because they know what is expected of them.

Supporting Mental Health Issues

Students with disabilities present mental health issues in some circumstances and in some educational settings. These students may not necessarily be diagnosed with emotional disturbances, as mental health issues can occur concurrently with other disabilities. General and special educators across all special education settings can support these students by learning how to recognize mental health issues in schools. Students' mental health symptoms may fluctuate on an hourly, daily, or weekly basis. Teachers can use observations and other research-based strategies for identifying any issues. They may also already be aware of such issues or work in settings where mental health issues are predominant. Intervention techniques and supports rely on the individual needs of each specific student. Training in managing students with certain mental health disorders may also be useful. Occasionally, training in crisis prevention plans is required of teachers working with students who may become aggressive due to their disorders.

Working with Students with Physical Disabilities

Students with physical disabilities may be included in general education classrooms with accommodations if their disabilities do not coexist with other disabilities, such as learning disabilities. They may also be placed in inclusive settings or partially inclusive settings with Individualized Education Program goals, depending on their least restrictive environments. In these settings, it is essential for educators to practice instructional strategies that facilitate the learning processes and accommodate the needs of students with physical disabilities. Classrooms should be arranged so they can be navigated easily by everyone. This includes giving students using wheelchairs adequate aisle space and work space. Partner work is helpful for students with physical disabilities, who may struggle with handwriting or using keyboards. Partners can assist the students with skills like note taking, which may be difficult for students with physical disabilities. Additionally, assignments can include accommodations or modifications to meet the specific needs of students with physical disabilities. For example, text-to-speech software can be provided for students who struggle with using regular keyboards.

TExES Special Education Practice Test

1. A new high school student is being assessed. He reads a 500 word text. He misreads 35 words. At what level is he reading?

    a. Instructional level.
    b. Independent level.
    c. Unsatisfactory level.
    d. Merit level.

2. According to the Assistive Technology Act, assistive devices are:

    a. Electronic devices that support learning such as computers, calculators, student responders, electronic self-teaching books and electronic reading devices.
    b. Any mechanical, electrical or electronic device that helps teachers streamline efficiency.
    c. Any device that could help a disabled student in school or life functions.
    d. Experimental, high-tech teaching tools that teachers can obtain by participating in one of 67 government funded research projects.

3. In the first week of school, a resource teacher asks her high school students to make lists of things they know how to do well. How is this activity <u>most</u> useful to the teacher?

    a. It establishes a feeling of success in her students from the start.
    b. It is an informal assessment of their writing skills and gives the teacher an idea of each student's interests and abilities.
    c. It is a formal assessment of prior knowledge.
    d. It invites further discussion of each student's unique contributions and will help the class bond with mutual respect.

4. In the above example, how could the teacher use the students' lists in her lesson planning?

    a. On the last day of school, she can return the lists and ask the students to add the new skills they've learned, so they can see how far they've come.
    b. She can have the students exchange lists so they can find other students who share the same interests.
    c. She can use the lists when planning independent reading and research projects for each student.
    d. All of the above.

5. A seventh grader with mild intellectual disabilities is having considerable trouble with algebra. His stepfather is trying to help, but the more he drills the girl, the less she seems to understand. The teacher suggests:

    a. He continues drilling and enhances with pop quizzes. It may take the student longer to understand algebraic terms, expressions and equations, but with hard work he will eventually learn them.
    b. He calls a moratorium on at-home algebra work. The student is becoming less willing to work at school and the teacher is concerned he is losing confidence due to failure at home.
    c. He continues drilling but breaks the study sessions into no more than 3 five-minute periods per day.
    d. He substitutes fun activities for math drills. Incorporating algebra blocks, math games, and applications of algebra to real-life situations will make math more fun and more relevant.

6. Augmentative and Alternative Communication (AAC) devices, forearm crutches and a head pointer are assistive devices that might be used by a student with:

    a. Severe intellectual disabilities.
    b. Cerebral palsy.
    c. Tourette syndrome.
    d. Minor skeletal birth defects.

7. A four year old child has difficulty sorting plastic cubes, circles and triangles by color and shape, doesn't recognize patterns or groups and doesn't understand the relationship between little/big, tall/short, many/few. The child enjoys counting, but does not say the numbers in proper order nor recognize the meaning of different numbers. This child most likely:

    a. Is exhibiting signs of intellectual disabilities.
    b. Is developing within an acceptable range.
    c. Has dysgraphia.
    d. Has dyscalculia.

8. Response to Intervention (RTI) is:

    a. Parents, classroom teacher, special education teacher and other caring persons stage an intervention to express how a student's socially unacceptable behavior upsets them.
    b. An opportunity for a student to openly and freely respond to specific interventions without fear of reprimand.
    c. A strategy for diagnosing learning disabilities in which a student receives research-supported interventions to correct an academic delay. If the interventions do not result in considerable improvement, the failure to respond suggests causal learning disabilities.
    d. A formal complaint lodged by a parent or guardian in response to what they consider an intrusion by a teacher into private matters.

9. Sixth graders Alfie and Honesty ride the same bus. Honesty constantly teases Alfie. Alfie is embarrassed because he believes she is berating him. The bus driver told their teacher it was possible that Honesty is actually interested in Alfie, but doesn't express it well. The best form of conflict resolution would be for the teacher to:

    a. Take Honesty aside and explain boys don't like overly aggressive girls.
    b. Take Honesty aside and teach her less embarrassing methods of getting a boy's attention.
    c. Explain to Alfie that Honesty probably teases him because she likes him and he should take it as a compliment.
    d. Suggest to Alfie that if he is disturbed by Honesty's teasing, he have a calm, assertive conversation with her and tell her he doesn't like it and insist she stop.

10. A special education teacher is creating a developmental history for a high school student. She wants to know when the teen reached certain behavioral, academic and developmental milestones. She should consult:

    a. The student's previous teachers. This information should be in the file.
    b. The student. Involving him in the process will make him more interested in his progress.
    c. The student's doctor and therapist. These professionals know how to elicit and document this information.
    d. The parent or guardian because he or she has known the student from the beginning.

11. When transitioning from one subject to another and when she becomes anxious, a student always taps her front tooth 5 times then opens and closes her eyes 11 times before leaving her desk. The child most likely has:

    a. Repetitive Disorder
    b. Obsessive Compulsive Disorder
    c. Anxiety Disorder
    d. Depression

12. By law, a child with a disability is defined as one with:

    a. Intellectual disabilities, hearing, speech, language, visual, orthopedic or other health impairments, emotional disturbance, autism, brain injury caused by trauma or specific learning disabilities and needs special education and related services.
    b. Intellectual disabilities, emotional disturbance, autism, brain injury caused by trauma or specific learning disabilities who needs special education and related services.
    c. A child who is unable to reach the same academic goals as his peers, regardless of cause, and needs special education and related services.
    d. The term "disability" is no longer used. The correct term is "other ability".

13. Which classroom environment is most likely to support a student with ADHD?

    a. Students with ADHD become bored easily so a classroom with distinct areas for a multitude of activities will stimulate her. When she loses interest in one area, she can move to the next and continue learning.
    b. Students with ADHD are highly aggressive and easily fall into depression. The teacher needs to provide a learning environment in which sharp objects such as scissors, tacks or sharpened pencils are eliminated. This ensures greater safety for both student and teacher.
    c. Students with ADHD are highly creative. A room with brightly colored mobiles, a multitude of visual and physical textures (such as striped rugs and fuzzy pillows) and plenty of art-based games will stimulate and encourage learning.
    d. Students with ADHD are extremely sensitive to distractions. A learning environment in which visual and audio distractions have been eliminated is best. Low lighting, few posters and a clean whiteboard help the student focus.

14. A resource teacher notices one of her students has made the same reading error numerous times the past few days. She decides the student wrongly believes that 'ou' is always pronounced as it is in the word *through.*She corrects this misunderstanding by showing the student word families containing words like *though, ought, ground*. This strategy is called:

    a. Corrective feedback
    b. Positive reinforcement
    c. Consistent repetition
    d. Corrective support

15. A kindergarten teacher has a new student who will not make eye contact with anyone so she doesn't appear to be listening. She often rocks back and forth and does not stop when asked or give any indication she has heard. She avoids physical contact. Sometimes the teacher must take her arm to guide her from one place to another. Occasionally the student erupts, howling in terror and fury. The most likely diagnosis is:

    a. Asperger's Syndrome
    b. Obsessive-Compulsive Disorder
    c. Autism
    d. Antisocial Psychosis

16. A special education teacher shows parents of a dyslexic child a study that examined brain scans of dyslexic and non-dyslexic readers. The study demonstrated that dyslexics use (the) _____ side(s) of their brains while non-dyslexics use (the) _____ side.

    a. Both, the left.
    b. Both, the right.
    c. Left, right.
    d. Right, left.

17. A student with _____ has a great deal of difficulty with the mechanical act of writing. She drops her pencil, cannot form legible letters and cannot decode what she has written.

    a. A nonverbal learning disorder
    b. Dyslexia
    c. Dyspraxia
    d. Dysgraphia

18. A resource room teacher has a middle school student recently diagnosed with depression. The student has been put on an antidepressant. The teacher knows the student may develop certain transitory reactions to the medication. One reaction might be:

    a. Extreme sleepiness.
    b. Increased, persistent thirst.
    c. Anxiety, coupled with an urge to verbalize a continuous inner dialogue.
    d. Inappropriate anger.

19. Reading comprehension should be evaluated:

    a. Every two months using various informal assessments. Done more than twice a year, assessments place undue stress on both student and teacher and do not indicate enough change to be worth it.
    b. With a combination of informal and formal assessments including: standardized testing, awareness of grades, systematically charted data over a period of time and teacher notes.
    c. With bi-weekly self-assessment rubrics to keep the student aware of his progress.
    d. By testing the student before reading a particular text to determine which vocabulary words he already knows and can correctly use.

20. A diabetic first grader is very pale, trembling and covered in a fine sweat. The teacher attempts to talk to the child, but the girl's response is confused and she seems highly irritable She is most likely experiencing:

    a. Diabetic hypoglycemia.
    b. Lack of sleep.
    c. Hunger.
    d. Diabetic hyperglycemia.

21. an intellectually disabled teen has been offered a job by an elderly neighbor. The neighbor wants the teen to work alongside her in the garden twice a week. They will plant seeds, transplant larger plants, weed, lay mulch, water and fertilize. Later in the season, they will cut flowers and arrange bouquets, pick produce and sell them at the neighbor's roadside stand. The neighbor, the teen's mother and special education teacher meet to discuss the proposal. The plan is:

    a. Tentatively accepted. Because the teen is excited about having a job, her mother and teacher reluctantly agree. They both know the girl is likely to lose interest quickly and caution the neighbor that if she truly needs help she may want to look elsewhere. However, no one wants to disappoint the girl and all decide the experience will be good for her.
    b. Rejected. Despite the teen's insistence that she can manage these tasks, her mother and teacher believe that she cannot. They fear trying will set her up for failure.
    c. Tentatively rejected. The teacher and her mother are very uncomfortable with the neighbor's offer. They suspect the elderly woman is simply lonely or may be a predator who has selected an intellectually disabled victim because such children are particularly vulnerable.
    d. Enthusiastically accepted. The adults discuss a background check and the possibility that the teen might discover gardening is not for her and want to quit. However, this is most likely to happen early in her employment, giving the neighbor sufficient time to find another helper. The teacher is pleased because the girl will learn new skills through modeling and repetition. The mother is pleased because the experience will add to the girl's self-esteem and show her she is capable of learning. The elderly neighbor is pleased because she is compassionate and truly needs help. The girl is delighted the neighbor recognizes her potential and sees her as valuable.

22. Dr. Gee reads the following sentence to a group of 5th graders: "The turquoise sky is reflected in the still lake. Fat white clouds floated on the lake's surface as though the water was really another sky. It was such a beautiful day. The students were to write the word "beautiful" in the blank. One student wrote 'pretty' instead. This suggests:

    a. The student doesn't know the meaning of the word 'beautiful'.
    b. The student is highly creative and believes he can substitute a word with a similar meaning.
    c. The student did not know how to spell 'beautiful'.
    d. The student did not hear what the teacher said. He heard 'pretty' instead of 'beautiful.'

23. Autism Spectrum Disorder is also known as:

    a. Pervasive Spectrum Disorder
    b. Asperger's Syndrome
    c. Variable Developmental Disorder
    d. Artistic Continuum Syndrome

24. A third grade boy is new to the school. His teacher has noticed he happily plays with other children, redirects his attention without upset when another child rejects his offer to play and doesn't mind playing on his own. However, the boy doesn't pay attention when academic instruction is given. He continues to speak with other children, draws, or distracts himself. The teacher reminds him repeatedly to listen and follow instruction. When he does not, she moves him to a quiet desk away from the others. When isolated, the boy puts his head on the desk and weeps uncontrollably, or stares at a fixed spot and repeats to himself, "I hate myself, I hate myself. I should be dead." During these episodes, the teacher cannot break through to the student; his disconnection seems complete. The teacher has requested a conference with his parents, but they do not speak English and have not responded to her offer of a translator. The teacher should:

a. Establish a consistent set of expectations for the child. He needs to understand there are appropriate times for play and for learning.

b. Isolate the boy first thing. His behavior suggests manipulation. By third grade children fully understand they are expected to pay attention when the teacher is speaking. The boy is punishing the teacher with tears and repetitive self-hate, consciously or unconsciously attempting to make the teacher feel guilty.

c. Immediately refer him to the counselor. The boy is exhibiting serious emotional distress suggesting abuse or neglect at home or outside of school.

d. Recognize the child's highly sensitive nature; offer comfort when he acts out self-loathing. Carefully explain why he must learn to pay attention so he will use reason instead of emotion when making future choices.

25. A student with Asperger's Syndrome is most likely to display which set of behaviors?

a. He is confrontational, argumentative and inflexible.

b. He is fearful, shy and highly anxious.

c. He is socially distant, focused on certain subjects to the point of obsession and inflexible.

d. He is flighty, tearful and exhibits repetitive, ritualized behavior.

26. A special education teacher working with a group of third graders is about to begin a unit on birds. She asks the children what they know about birds. They tell her birds fly, lay eggs and build nests. She asks the students to draw a picture of a bird family. Some children draw birds in flight; one draws a mother bird with a nest of babies; another draws an egg with the baby bird inside the egg. These pre-reading activities are useful because:

a. They help assess prior knowledge.

b. They establish a framework in which to integrate the new information.

c. They create a sense of excitement and curiosity.

d. All of the above.

27. Verbal dyspraxia is:

a. Trouble with the physical act of writing.

b. Refusal to speak.

c. Misplacing letters within words.

d. A motor skill development disorder which includes inconsistent speech errors.

28. A resource room teacher has a small group of second and third graders who are struggling with reading comprehension. A useful strategy would be to:

    a. Present a list of vocabulary before students read a particular text.

    b. Ask students to create a play about the story.

    c. Read a story aloud. Ask students to raise their hands when they hear an unfamiliar word.

    d. Have each child keep a book of new vocabulary words. Whenever an unfamiliar word is seen or heard the student should enter the word in her personal dictionary.

29. Tourette syndrome is characterized by:

    a. Facial twitches, grunts, inappropriate words and body spasms.

    b. Inappropriate words, aggressive behavior and tearful episodes.

    c. Facial twitches, grunts, extreme shyness and refusal to make eye contact.

    d. Refusal to make eye contact, rocking, spinning of objects and ritualized behavior.

30. A second grader finds it impossible to remain in her seat. She wanders around the room, sprawls on the floor and rolls back and forth when asked to do math problems and jumps up and down when waiting in line. When the teacher tells her to sit down, she rolls her eyes in apparent disgust and looks to other students for support. When she finds a student looking back, she laughs and makes a face. The teacher has noticed when a reward is attached to good behavior; the girl is consistently able to control her actions for long periods of time. But when reprimanded without the promise of a reward, she becomes angry, tearful and pouts. This child is most likely manifesting:

    a. Tourette's Syndrome

    b. Attention Deficit Hyperactivity Disorder

    c. Lack of sufficiently developed behavior and social skills

    d. Psychosis

31. ADHD refers to:

    a. Attention Deficit Hyperactivity Disorder

    b. Anxiety/ Depression Hyperactivity Disorder

    c. Aggression-Depression Hyperactivity Disorder

    d. Atkinson, Draper and Hutchinson Disability

32. Rate, accuracy and prosody are elements of:

    a. Reading fluency

    b. Reading comprehension

    c. Math fluency

    d. Algebraic function

33. When a diabetic student goes into insulin shock, she should:

    a. Call her parents to come get her.

    b. Drink a soda or eat some hard candy.

    c. Drink a high-protein shake.

    d. Put her head on the desk and wait for the episode to pass.

34. Strategies to increase reading fluency for English Language Learners include:

    a. Tape-assisted reading.

    b. Reading aloud while students follow along in their books.

    c. Asking parents to read with the child each evening.

    d. A and B.

35. How could a teacher effectively use a picture book of folk tales from an English Language Learner's country of origin?

    a. Share the book with other students to educate them about the ELL's culture.

    b. Ask the ELL to rewrite the folk tale, modernizing it and using the United States as the setting.

    c. Ask the student to tell one folk tale in her native language. The teacher writes key English words and asks the child to find them in the book. When the child finds the words, they read them together.

    d. None of the above. It's best to encourage the student to forget about her first country as quickly as possible to help her acclimate. Folktales from her country will only make her homesick.

36. What kind of load does the previous example employ?

    a. Cognitive load

    b. Language load

    c. Bilingual load

    d. Cultural load

37. A teacher asks an English Language Learner to do a picture walk through a book and describe what he thinks the story is about. This helps the student's awareness of the story's _____.

    a. Deeper meaning

    b. Theme

    c. Context

    d. Events

38. Language load is:

    a. The weight of books in a child's backpack or the damage to the child's body the weight may cause in the future.

    b. The vocabulary a child has upon entering a new classroom.

    c. The number of unrecognizable words an English Language Learner encounters when reading a passage or listening to a teacher.

    d. The number of languages a person has mastered.

39. When working with English Language Learners, teachers should:

    a. Avoid idioms and slang; involve students in hands-on activities; reference students' prior knowledge; speak slowly.

    b. Speak slowly; use monosyllabic words when possible; repeat each sentence three times; use idioms but not slang.

    c. Use monosyllabic words when possible; repeat key instructions three times but not in a row; reference students' prior knowledge; have students keep a journal of new vocabulary words.

    d. Use both idioms and slang; reference students' prior knowledge; speak at a normal rate of speed; involve students in hands-on activities.

40. Word recognition is:

    a. One of the building blocks of learning.

    b. Useful only to fluent readers.

    c. Culturally based.

    d. Especially important to English Language Learners and students with reading disabilities.

41. Assessing silent reading fluency can best be accomplished by:

a. Having the student or summarize the material to determine how much was understood.
b. Giving a written test which covers plot, theme, character development, sequence of events, rising action, climax, falling action and outcome. A student must test at a 95% accuracy rate to be considered fluent at silent reading.
c. Giving a three minute Test of Silent Contextual Reading Fluency four times a year.
d. Silent reading fluency cannot be assessed. It is a private act between the reader and the text and does not invite critique.

42. Explicit instruction includes:

a. Clarifying the goal, modeling strategies and offering explanations geared to a student's level of understanding.
b. Determining the goal, offering strategies and asking questions designed to ascertain if understanding has been reached.
c. Reassessing the goal, developing strategies and determining if further reassessing of the goal is required.
d. Objectifying the goal, assessing strategies and offering explanations geared to a student's level of understanding.

43. An ORF is:

a. An Oral Reading Fluency assessment.
b. An Occasional Reading Function assessment.
c. An Oscar Reynolds Feinstein assessment.
d. An Overt Reading Failure assessment.

44. The four types of Bilingual Special Education Instructional Delivery Models include:

a. Bilingual Support Model, Coordinated Services Model, Integrated Bilingual Special Education, Bilingual Special Education Model.
b. Bilingual Instructional Education, Coordinating Instruction, Disintegrative Support, Bilingual Special Education Model.
c. Integrated, Disintegrative, Bilingual Support, Corresponding Services.
d. Special Instructional Education, Bilingual Instruction, Bilingual Delivery, Special Support Education.

45. The Individuals with Disabilities Education Act (IDEA) requires that members of an IEP team include:

a. All teachers involved with the student, the parent(s) or guardian and the student (if appropriate).
b. The classroom teacher, a special education teacher, the parent(s) or guardian, a representative of the local education agency knowledgeable about specialized instruction, someone to interpret instructional implications, the student (if appropriate) and other people invited by the parents or the school.
c. The classroom teacher, a special education teacher, the principal or AP and the parent(s) or guardian.
d. All teachers involved with the student, the principal or AP, the parent(s) or guardian and the student (if appropriate).

46. At the beginning of each month, a student reads a page or two from a book he hasn't seen before. The resource teacher notes the total number of words in the section and the number of times the student leaves out or misreads a word. If the student reads with more than a 10% error rate, he is:

a. Reading with full comprehension.
b. Probably bored and his attention is wandering.
c. Reading at a frustration level.
d. Missing contextual clues.

47. A Cloze test evaluates a student's:

a. Reading fluency
b. Understanding of context and vocabulary
c. Phonemic skills
d. Ability to apply the Alphabetic Principle to previously unknown material.

48. A Kindergarten teacher is showing students the written alphabet. The teacher pronounces a phoneme and one student points to it on the alphabet chart. The teacher is presenting:

a. Letter-sound correspondence
b. Rote memorization
c. Predictive Analysis
d. Segmentation

49. A ninth grade special education teacher is giving students strategies for taking a Maze test. There will be several paragraphs in which some words have been blanked out. There are five possible answers for each blank. The best approach is to:

a. Read all answers; mark out any that are illogical. 'Plug in' the remaining words and mark out those that are grammatically incorrect or do not sound right. Think about context clues.
b. Read the first answer. If it is logical and sounds correct, select that word and move on to the next question.
c. Cover the answers and try to guess what the correct word is. Look at the five choices. Select the one closest in meaning to the word guessed.
d. Do the first and last questions then one in the middle. Look for a pattern and select the remaining words accordingly.

50. A resource teacher wants to design a lesson that will help first and second graders learn sight words so all the students can read their lists. She should teach them how to:

a. Divide sight words into syllables. Considering one syllable at a time provides a sense of control and increases confidence.
b. Recognize word families. Organizing similar words allows patterns to emerge.
c. Sound out the words by vocalizing each letter. Using this approach, students will be able to sound out any sight word.
d. Memorize their lists by using techniques such as songs, mnemonic devices and other fun activities. By definition, sight words cannot be decoded but must be recognized on sight.

51. Phonological awareness activities are:

a. Oral
b. Visual
c. Both A and B.
d. Semantically based.

52. It is important to teach life skills to developmentally delayed students to prepare them for life after school. Which of the following skills sets should these students be taught?

    a. Count money, plan meals, grocery shop, recognize safety concerns.
    b. Count money, order delivery meals, dating skills, how to drive.
    c. How to drive, style and hygiene tips, social strategies, dating skills.
    d. Stock market investment, hairdressing, house painting, pet care.

53. A special education teacher has done intervention with an eighth grade student with a reading disability. The student can now successfully use tactics to understand the meanings of unfamiliar words, knows words such as *crucial, criticism* and *witness* have multiple meanings and considers what she already knows to figure out a word's meaning. These features of effective reading belong to which category?

    a. Word recognition
    b. Vocabulary
    c. Content
    d. Comprehension

54. Emergent writers understand letters represent sounds, words begin with a sound that can be written as a letter and writing is a way one person captures an idea another person will read. Emergent writers pass through the following stages:

    a. Scripting the end-sound to a word (KT=cat); leaving space between words; writing from the top left to the top right and from top to bottom of the page.
    b. Scripting the end-sound to a word (KT=cat); writing from the top left to the top right and from top to bottom of the page; separating the words from one another with a space in between.
    c. Leaving space between the initial letters that represent words; writing from the top left to the top right and from top to bottom of the page; scripting the final sound of each word and the initial sound (KT=cat).
    d. Drawing a picture beside each of the initial sounds to represent the entire word; scripting the end-sound to a word (KT=cat); scripting the interior sounds that compose the entire word (KAT=cat).

55. As defined by the Individuals with Disabilities Education Act (IDEA), Secondary Transition is a synchronized group of activities that are:

    a. Results-oriented and include post-school activities, vocational education, employment support and adult services and considers the individual's strengths, preferences and interests.
    b. Socially structured and consider the individual's strengths, preferences and interests and vocational requirements.
    c. Designed to support vocational training, results-oriented and have a strong social component.
    d. Selected by the parent(s) or guardian because the student cannot choose for himself.

56. A resource teacher can facilitate the greatest achievement in emergent writers who are scripting initial and final sounds by:

    a. Suggesting they write a book to build confidence, teach sequencing, and encourage them to deeply explore ideas.
    b. Asking they read their stories to other students.
    c. Inviting a reporter to write about her emergent writers.
    d. Inviting parents or guardians for a tea party at which the children will read their stories aloud.

57. At what point should the teacher in the above example offer the children picture books and ask them to read to her?

    a. When the children are able to script initial sounds, end sounds and interior sounds. She should wait until this point to avoid frustration.

    b. After the teacher has read the picture books several times, the children can 'practice reading' to her, while learning to handle books, turn pages, and pay attention to context clues.

    c. After the children have learned the sight words.

    d. From the first day of school. Picture walks help young readers understand books are arranged sequentially. Pictures provide narrative coherence and contextual clues. Holding a book and turning pages also gives young readers a familiarity with them.

58. How can a teacher teach spelling effectively?

    a. Students who have an understanding of letter-sound association do not need to be taught to spell. If they can say a word, they can spell it.

    b. Students who have an understanding of letter-sound association and can identify syllables and recognize when the base word has a Latin, Greek or Indo-European ancestry don't need to be taught to spell. They can deduce what is most likely the correct spelling using a combination of these strategies. A teacher who posts charts organizing words into their ancestor families, phonemic units and word-sound families is efficiently teaching spelling. The rest is up to the student.

    c. Students who spell poorly will be at a disadvantage for the rest of their lives. It is essential students spend at least 15 minutes a day drilling spelling words until they know them forward and backward. The teacher should alternate between students individually writing a new word 25 times and the entire class chanting the words.

    d. Students should be taught writing is a process. By applying spelling patterns found in word families, the spelling of many words can be deduced.

59. A special education teacher gives a struggling reader a story with key words missing:

The children were hungry. They went into the _____. They found bread, peanut _____ and jelly in the cupboard. They made _____. They _ _ the sandwiches. Then they were not _____ anymore.

The student is able to complete the sentences by paying attention to:

    a. Syntax. Word order can provide enough hints that a reader can predict what happens next.

    b. Pretext. By previewing the story, the student can determine the missing words.

    c. Context. By considering other words in the story, the student can deduce the missing words.

    d. Sequencing. By ordering the ideas, the student can determine the missing words.

60. Collaborative Strategic Reading (CSR) depends upon which two practices?

    a. Cooperative learning and reading comprehension.

    b. Reading and metacognition.

    c. Reading comprehension and metacognition.

    d. Cooperative learning and metacognition.

61. Before being assigned to a special education classroom, a student must:

    a. Agree to the reassignment.

    b. Have an Individualized Education Plan developed.

    c. Have an Independent Education Policy developed.

    d. Be seen by an educational psychologist to confirm her diagnosis.

62. When asked a question, the new student answers with as few words as possible. He prefers to draw airplanes over and over again rather than play with the other children. The classroom teacher isn't sure how to help the child. The special education teacher suggests the teacher:

    a. Leave the child alone. He is likely adjusting to the new situation and will come out of his shell soon enough.

    b. Remind other children in the class to include the new student.

    c. Observe the child over the course of a week or two. Draw him into conversation to determine if vocabulary is limited. Note how the child interacts with others in the class. Does he initiate conversation? If another child initiates, does he respond?

    d. Refer him to the school counselor immediately. It is likely the child is suffering from serious problems at home.

63. A special education teacher feels some of his strategies aren't effective. He asked a specialist to help him improve. The specialist suggests he:

    a. Begin a journal in which he considers strategies he has used. Which seemed to work? Which didn't, and why?

    b. Meet with the specialist to discuss the teacher's goals.

    c. Permit the specialist arrive unannounced for observation. This will prevent the teacher from unconsciously over-preparing.

    d. Set up a video camera and record several student sessions to review. They can effectively collaborate at that time.

64. An eighth grade student is able to decode many words and has a borderline/acceptable vocabulary, but his reading comprehension is quite low. He can be helped with intervention offering:

    a. Strategies to increase comprehension and develop vocabulary.

    b. Strategies to increase comprehension and learn to identify syntax.

    c. Strategies to improve understanding of both content and context.

    d. Strategies to develop vocabulary and improve understanding of both content and context.

65. Research indicates oral language competency in emergent readers is essential because:

    a. It enhances students' phonemic awareness and increases vocabulary.

    b. The more verbally expressive emergent readers are, the more confident they become. These students will embrace both academic and independent reading levels.

    c. Strong oral language skills invite students to consider a plethora of ideas. The more they ask, the richer their background knowledge.

    d. It demonstrates to students their ideas are important and worth sharing.

66. A teacher has shown a mentally challenged student a website that integrates music and video clips with a variety of educational games about a topic the student has shown interest in. The student is initially intimidated and fears interacting with the program might result in her breaking the computer. The teacher reassures her she cannot harm the machine and shows the girl how to manipulate the mouse and keyboard. The teacher reminds the student what she already knows about the subject. As the student becomes more comfortable with the mouse, she focuses on the images and sounds, at times responding to the program conversationally, telling it what she knows about dinosaurs. The teacher is using the computer along with which teaching strategy?

    a. Modular instruction.
    b. Scaffolding.
    c. Linking.
    d. Transmutation.

67. A student has been identified with a cluster of learning disabilities. She will be joining a special education classroom. She is understandably nervous about making the change to a different teacher and group of classmates. In order to help her make the transition, the child should:

    a. Have a party to which her new classmates are invited along with some friends from the fifth-grade class she is leaving.
    b. Prepare to begin classes with her new teacher the next day. Once the decision has been made, nothing will be gained by postponing the inevitable.
    c. Be brave and understand life will be full of transitions. This is an opportunity to learn new skills that will serve her well in the future.
    d. Visit the classroom, meet the teacher and her new classmates and be given the opportunity to ask questions about the change she is about to make.

68. A student is taking a reading test in which several words have been replaced with blanks. Below each blank is a series of three possible answers. The student chooses the right answer from each set. The student is taking:

    a. A Cloze test, which is a type of Maze test.
    b. A Maze test, which is a type of Cloze test.
    c. A multiple-choice quiz.
    d. A vocabulary test incorporating a type of multiple-choice quiz.

69. A high school student is not a strong reader. She loses her place often and misreads key words. She doesn't try to correct her errors, even when they make no sense. She can give only a rudimentary summary of what she read. Which type of instructional focus would be most beneficial?

    a. Well-organized coaching in decoding, sight words, vocabulary and comprehension several times a week. The more systematic the lessons, the better the chance the intervention will succeed.
    b. Weekly instruction on one area of reading; more, and the student will become overwhelmed and likely shut down.
    c. Instruction aimed at helping her become self-motivated and disciplined in her approach to learning.
    d. Strategies to help her understand the general meaning so that she can gather context clues.

70. A teacher has a student with dyscalculia who has trouble organizing addition and subtraction problems on paper. She can best help him by:

    a. Encouraging memorization of number families. Committing them to memory is the only way.
    b. Demonstrating a problem in different ways. Write a problem on the board:
    11 - 3. Gather 11 books and take 3 of them away. Draw 11 x's on the board and erase 3.
    c. Use graph paper to help him organize. Show him how to write the problems, keeping each number in a box aligned with other numbers.
    d. Make a game of addition and subtraction problems. Divide the class into groups and let them compete to see which group can solve the most problems.

71. A child has been losing strength in her muscles over a period of time. The loss is very gradual, but the teacher is concerned and would like the child to see a doctor. The possible diagnosis is:

    a. Cerebral Palsy
    b. Muscular Dystrophy
    c. Muscular Sclerosis
    d. Spastic Muscular and Nerve Disorder

72. A middle school student is preparing to transition from a self-contained special education classroom to a general education classroom. This transition should be made:

    a. With proper preparation. A student this age needs to acclimate socially and can best do so with the same group of students in every class.
    b. At the beginning of the next school year so the student doesn't have a stigma when joining the new group.
    c. One class at a time with the special education teacher supervising academic and social progress.
    d. By transitioning into classes he is most interested in because he is most likely to succeed with subjects he cares about. The confidence he gains from academic success will support him as he transitions into classes he's less interested in.

73. The four required activities described by the Assistive Technology Act (AT ACT) of 1998 are a public awareness program, coordinating activities among state agencies, technical assistance and training and

    a. Specialized training for special education teachers and support.
    b. Outreach to underrepresented religious groups, ethnicities and urban populations.
    c. Outreach to underrepresented and rural populations.
    d. New technologies training on a quarterly basis for special education teachers and support.

74. Behavior problems in special education students are most effectively handled with:

    a. Zero tolerance.
    b. Positive Behavioral Support (PBS)
    c. Acceptance and tolerance
    d. Positive Behavioral Control (PBC)

75. A teacher suspects one of her kindergarteners has a learning disability in math. Why would the teacher suggest intervention to the child's concerned parents rather than assessment as the first step?

a. She wouldn't; assessment should precede intervention.

b. She wouldn't; kindergarteners develop new skills at radically different rates. Suggesting either intervention or assessment at this point is premature. The teacher would more likely observe the child over a three month period to note her development before including the parents about her concern.

c. Assessing a young child for learning disabilities often leads to an incorrect conclusion because a student must be taught the subject before it's possible to assess her understanding of it. Intervention teaches the child specific skills to correct her misconceptions. If the intervention fails, assessment is the next step.

d. Assessment at this stage is unnecessary and wastes time and money. Since an assessment that resulted in a diagnosis of a learning disability would recommend intervention to correct it, it is more efficient to proceed directly to intervention.

76. A high school student struggles with applied math problems. He is given the following word math problem. He selects a. 55 hours.

A train travelled from point A to point B in 3.5 hours. The same train travelled from point B to point C in 2.75 hours. Another train left point C 1.25 hours after the first train arrived at point C. This train travelled to point D in 45 minutes. The first train returns to point B in only 2.5 hours. How long did it take to travel from point A to point D?
a. 55 hours
b. 97.60 hours
c. 8.25 hours
d. 19.75 hours

The student most likely:

a. Knows he lacks the skills to solve word problems. He arbitrarily selected the first answer without attempting to solve the problem.

b. Tried to solve the problem. He aligned all the numbers as they appeared so that 45 minutes were added with 5 in the ones column and 4 in the tens column. He also added 2.5 hours, which isn't required to solve the problem.

c. Tried to solve the problem by estimating and chose the most likely answer.

d. Selected the correct answer.

77. The teacher in the above example wants to give the student something he can manipulate to arrive at the correct answer. The student should be given:

a. Graph paper so he can properly align the numbers.

b. A blank page to make a visual representation of the problem.

c. A calculator.

d. A digital clock that can be manually moved forward.

78. The teacher knows there are several ways to arrive at the correct answer. She also knows if she explains them to the student, he will not only be able to understand where he made errors, but he might also see the relationships between various methods of solving applied math problems. The teacher should show the student how to:

   a. Estimate the answer; convert all of the numbers to minutes and divide the answer by 60 to determine the number of hours and minutes; determine the percentage of an hour 45 minutes is, and write that number as .75; create a graph.
   b. Estimate the answer; add the relevant numbers by removing the decimal points, then insert a decimal point in the answer; use a calculator to avoid problems in addition.
   c. Estimate the answer; remove all decimal points; add all of the numbers; divide by 60 using a calculator; make a graph;
   d. Estimate; create a graph; use a digital clock; add the relevant numbers together by removing the decimal points, then insert a decimal point in the answer.

79. The answer in the above word problem is:

   a. 8.75 hours
   b. 97.60 hours
   c. 8.25 hours
   d. none of the above

80. IDEA requires that students identified with learning disabilities or other special needs be educated in _____ learning environment appropriate for their needs.

   a. The safest
   b. The least restrictive
   c. The most appropriate
   d. The most desirable

81. Ella, a high school student with some mental challenges, is a verbal linguistic learner. This means she learns best using:

   a. Oral and written materials.
   b. Materials in both her native language and English.
   c. Songs combined with movements.
   d. All types of visual aids.

82. Howard Gardner's theory of Multiple Intelligences organizes learners into what types of intelligences?

   a. Verbal linguistic, mathematical, musically attuned, visual special, body embraced, interpersonal, naturistic, existential.
   b. Emphatic, recessive, aggressive, assertive, dogmatic, apologetic, determined, elusive.
   c. Verbal linguistic, mathematical logical, musical, visual spatial, body kinesthetic, interpersonal, naturistic, existential.
   d. Dramatic, musical, verbal, mathematical, dance-oriented, sports-oriented, scientific, socially concerned.

83. Jacob, a high school student, destroyed his motorcycle in an accident on a rainy night. He did not appear to be seriously injured. A previously excellent student, after the accident he became extremely moody and defiant. His school work became spotty. While on occasion he does quite well, more often he fails to turn in homework or doesn't write down the assignment. These behaviors are often found in:

a. All teenagers and should not be cause for alarm.
b. Emotionally troubled teens; sometimes these teens 'act out' by putting themselves in danger, such as riding a motorcycle in bad weather.
c. Traumatic brain injury.
d. Students learning they are responsible for their own actions. Jacob is most likely angry his motorcycle was destroyed and is expressing his reluctance to take responsibility by behaving like a child.

84. Lead teaching, learning centers / learning stations, resource services, team teaching and consultation are all used in:

a. Innovative teaching
b. Strategic teaching
c. Collaborative teaching
d. Self-contained classrooms

85. A special education teacher has a child who doesn't understand the relationship between ones, tens and hundreds. He is a Bodily Kinesthetic learner. The teacher should:

a. Draw a colorful chart and put the numbers in the appropriate columns.
b. Teach him how an abacus works.
c. Create a song and dance about the numbers families.
d. Show him the relationship using Monopoly money.

86. Binh, a high school senior, is concerned his school records might contain inaccurate information. He has requested them. By law, the school must:

a. Obtain permission from his parents first.
b. Provide the records within 7 days.
c. Provide the records within 45 days.
d. The school can refuse; by law, they own the records and may share them as they see fit, regardless of requests.

87. Identifying specific skills deficient in special education math students is important so the teacher can decide how to remediate. Problems can include an inability to recall math facts, understand mathematical operations and formulas and how rules are used in solving problems or focusing on attention to details. Such students might be:

a. Able to solve math problems when they haven't been taught an operation required to do so.
b. Unable to locate errors in their own work.
c. Able to solve math problems in another language.
d. Unable to count higher than 100.

88. What steps are taken to identify specific skill deficits in math?

    a. Standardized assessment tests, examining areas of weakness in student work to determine patterns, teacher observations, interviews with student.

    b. Standardized assessment tests, examining areas of weakness in student work to determine patterns, teacher observations, interviews with parent(s).

    c. Teacher observations coupled with examining areas of weakness in student work are sufficient.

    d. None of the above.

89. A fifth-grade lead teacher and the special education teacher have scheduled a parent conference to discuss the behavior problems of the student. They anticipate the boy's mother will be anxious and defensive as she has been at previous conferences. The best approach for the teachers to take is to:

    a. Draw the parent out about issues in her own life so that she will feel reassured and trusting. Point out possible connections between the mother's emotions about her own life and her son's behaviors and reactions.

    b. Be very firm with the mother, explain the penalties and disciplines her son can expect if the behavior continues and stress neither the parent nor the child has input regarding punishment.

    c. Stress the teachers will not do anything without the parent's approval since they do not want to face liability issues.

    d. Begin by welcoming the mother and telling her about her son's academic improvements. Stress the teachers, the mother and the child share goals for the student's success. Explain the behavior problems and ask if the mother has any insights to share.

90. At the beginning of the week, a special education teacher asked a group of students to generate a list of verbs that make visual or sound pictures. She suggests students think of verbs that mean ways of walking, talking, eating, sitting and playing. The students spend the remainder of the week compiling the list. They notice interesting verbs as they read books, remark on less common verbs they hear in conversation or on television and locate interesting verbs in signs, magazines and other printed materials. One child begins to draw pictures to illustrate some of the verbs. Two children collaborate to create a play in which they demonstrate some of the verbs in a dance. A boy writes a song incorporating the list of verbs. The project is extremely successful. At the end of the week the students have created the following list:

TIPTOE, SCOOT, MUMBLE, MUNCH, LEAP, SPIN, DIVE, POUNCE, GLIDE, SLITHER, MOAN, WHISPER, GRUMBLE, NIBBLE, SHRILL, HOLLER, PERCH, LEAN, STOMP, MARCH, GIGGLE, HOP, STRUT, SLOUCH, GULP, HOWL, WHINE, SLURP, CROUCH, DRIBBLE, DROOL, HOOT, YELP, YOWL, GROWL, WHISTLE, SHRIEK, SNICKER, INSULT, COMPLIMENT, PLEAD, BARK, WIGGLE, TWIST, SLINK, TODDLE, TRUDGE, WANDER, STROLL.

The teacher's goal is to:

    a. Enhance students' understanding of theme by encouraging them to make connections between categories of verbs.

    b. Enhance students' vocabulary by encouraging them to find examples in the world around them.

    c. Enhance students' understanding of context by encouraging them to explore verbs for contextual clues.

    d. Enhance students' sense of curiosity by directing their attention to a number of different resources they may not have considered.

91. In the previous example, how could the teacher extend the lesson and apply it across the curriculum?

   a. Create a Word Wall with the words the students collected.
   b. Have students work on a class dictionary, putting the words in alphabetical order and explaining what they mean.
   c. Ask students to create a chart noting which verbs have 1, 2 or 3 syllables, which verbs contain double letters, which verbs are also nouns and which verbs have common word-endings.
   d. All of the above.

92. A classroom teacher has a student with learning disabilities that affect her ability to do math. The teacher consults with the special education teacher and decides she will modify the work the child is given by reducing the number of problems, let her have extra time to finish, and provide her with a multiplication chart. The teacher is:

   a. Giving the student an unfair advantage. Letting her have extra time should be sufficient.
   b. Giving the student an unfair advantage. Providing a multiplication chart should be sufficient. With that, she should get her work done on time.
   c. Making appropriate modifications. Each child is different. In this case, she consulted with the special education teacher and concluded the child needs multiple supports.
   d. Modifying the student's work because it makes it easier on the teacher. There is less to explain and less to grade.

93. Explain the philosophy of inclusion.

   a. All children should be included in decisions affecting their education.
   b. Children with special needs are as much a part of the educational community as any other child and necessary services that allow these students to participate in the learning community should be provided.
   c. Parents are part of a child's learning community and should be included in academic decisions.
   d. All teachers and support persons, including Para pros, translators and other assistants, should be allowed to participate in academic decisions.

94. The ADA is:

   a. The Americans with Disabilities Act.
   b. The Anti-Discrimination Act.
   c. The American Diabetes Association.
   d. The Alternatives to Discrimination Act.

95. A teacher working with students who have math disabilities has had success with a variety of multi-sensory techniques including:

   a. Estimating, converting fractions, multiplication families, graphic organizers.
   b. Graphic organizers, math textbooks, multi-step problems, converting fractions.
   c. Memorizing tables, drawing graphs, converting fractions, charting information.
   d. Power point presentations that include music, manipulatives, graphic organizers, clapping games.

96. The development of an IEP is a(n) _____ process.

    a. Indirect.
    b. Collaborative.
    c. Mathematical.
    d. Single.

97. A middle school Language Arts teacher begins each class with 10 minutes of journal writing. Students are free to write about whatever they choose. She reminds them this is the perfect place to react to something they've read, write about a problem and try to think of solutions, track a project they've undertaken and otherwise interact honestly with themselves. The teacher should periodically:

    a. Collect the journals and select an entry to edit; this will show the student how his writing can improve.
    b. Suggest new and innovative ways students can use their journals, including automatic writing, found poetry, lists, and collages.
    c. Collect and review the journals to identify students at risk for drugs, alcohol or sexual abuse.
    d. Say nothing about the journals during the school year. They are intensely private and discussing them in any way with the students violates trust.

98. A high school student has been diagnosed with ODD. Some of the manifestations of the diagnosis are:

    a. Obsessive and compulsive activities such as hand washing, counting and ritualistic behaviors.
    b. He is self-occupied, depressed and disorganized. He keeps to himself, is considered odd by his classmates and could be suicidal.
    c. The student is overly occupied with others, defending them from imagined slights and determined they recognize his concern as real rather than psychotic.
    d. He goes out of his way to annoy others, is defiant and goes into childish rages in which he blames others.

99. A teacher is introducing a new subject to her special education student. She reminds the student what she knows about the subject, offers a graphic organizer with which she can organize her learning, teaches key vocabulary and models an activity the student will undertake in her study. The teacher is providing:

    a. Building Blocks.
    b. Strategic Framing.
    c. Multiple Learning Styles Techniques.
    d. Scaffolding.

100. The Family Educational Rights and Privacy Act (FERPA) is a federal law that addresses student rights regarding their records. Among the rights the law protects are the right to:

    a. Obtain requested records within 45 days; request amendment of inaccurate information or information that violates the student's privacy; be notified before personal information is shared with third parties; file a complaint with the U.S. Dept. of Education should the school fail to fulfill these requests.
    b. Obtain records within 45 days and make amendments at the request of parents only.
    c. Obtain records within 45 days and make amendments at the request of both parents and student. Neither parent(s) nor students can obtain or amend documents alone.
    d. Be notified of all requests for personal information by third parties.

Answer Key and Explanations

1. A: Instructional level. In one minute, a student who reads with 95-100% accuracy is at an independent reading level. A student who reads with 90-95% accuracy is at an Instructional level. A student who reads with less than 90% accuracy is at a frustration level.

2. C: Any device that could help a disabled student in education or life functioning. The Assistive Technology Act of 1998 is the primary legislation regarding assistive technology for disabled students and adults. The act funds 56 state programs concerned with the assistive technology needs of individuals with disabilities. Assistive devices include wheelchairs, hearing aids, glare-reduction screens, Braille devices, voice-recognition software, screen magnifiers and a wealth of other tools.

3. B: It is an informal assessment of their writing and also gives the teacher an idea of each student's interests, abilities and skills. This assignment gives the teacher an idea of her students' writing abilities at the beginning of the year. She can return to this piece of writing during the school year to assess progress.

4. D: All of the above. The writing prompt is multipurpose. The teacher can use it in a number of ways, including planning independent reading and research projects for each student, inviting students to share their writing to find others with the same interests and as a way of demonstrating to each student their academic growth at the end of the school year.

5. D: He substitutes more enjoyable algebra activities for math drills. Incorporating manipulables such as algebra blocks, math games and applications of algebra to real-life situations, will make math both greater fun and more relevant. When both parent and child are enjoying the work, they will accomplish more in a shorter period of time and the child will feel happy and successful, which encourages her to embrace further learning opportunities.

6. B: Cerebral palsy. Cerebral palsy is an umbrella term that groups neurological childhood disorders that affect muscular control. It does not worsen over time and the cause is located in damaged areas of the brain that control muscle movement. Depending upon the severity of the disorder, a child with cerebral palsy might benefit from an AAC device to help in speaking, forearm crutches to assist in walking or a head pointer for a child whose best motor control is his head.

7. D: Dyscalculia. Dyscalculia defines a range of difficulties in math, such as the inability to understand numbers' meanings, measurements, patterns, mathematical terms and the application of mathematic principals. Early clues include a young child's inability to group items by size or color, recognize patterns or understand the meaning or order of numbers.

8. C: A strategy for diagnosing learning disabilities in which a student with an academic delay receives research-supported interventions to correct the delay. If the interventions do not result in considerable academic improvement, the failure to respond suggests causal learning disabilities.

9. D: Suggest to Alfie that if he is disturbed by Honesty's teasing, he might have a calm, assertive conversation with her in which he tells her he doesn't like it and insist she stop. By encouraging Alfie to act on his own, it shows him he has primary responsibility for taking care of himself. By offering social strategies, he learns a set of skills that will serve him throughout life. If Honesty continues to tease him, he can ask a teacher to step in, but doing so without his invitation is inappropriate.

10. D: The student's parent or guardian, who has known the student throughout his life, is the correct answer. When compiling a developmental history it's best to consult people who have had a close personal relationship with the student over his lifetime. They are the most likely to possess the greatest amount of information regarding the student's development over time.

11. B: Obsessive Compulsive Disorder (OCD). Children and adults with OCD typically engage in a series of highly ritualized behaviors that are rigidly performed when they feel stressed. Behaviors include tapping, snapping fingers, blinking, counting and so forth.

12. A: Intellectual disabilities, hearing, speech, language, visual, orthopedic or other health impairments, emotional disturbance, autism, brain injury caused by trauma, or specific learning disabilities who needs special education and related services. Children with one or more of these conditions are legally entitled to services and programs designed to help them achieve at the highest level of their ability.

13. D: Students with ADHD are extremely sensitive to distractions. A learning environment in which visual and audio distractions have been eliminated is best. Low lighting, few posters and a clean whiteboard will help minimize distractions.

14. A: Corrective feedback. Corrective feedback is offered to a student in order to explain why a particular error is, in fact, an error. Corrective feedback is specific; it locates where and how the student went astray so that similar errors can be avoided in the future.

15. C: Autism. Autistic children are typically very withdrawn, avoid eye contact and are not responsive to verbal or physical attempts to connect. Some autistic children fall into repetitive behaviors that are very difficult to arrest or prevent. These behaviors include rocking, spinning and handshaking.

16. A: Both, the left. Research using MRIs show dyslexics use both sides of their brains for activities such as reading, while non-dyslexics use only the left side.

17. D: Dysgraphia. Dysgraphic individuals cannot manage the physical act of writing. While many dysgraphics are highly intelligent and able to express themselves cogently, they have extreme difficulty holding a writing implement and shaping letters.

18. B: Extreme, persistent thirst. Although there are a number of antidepressants available, most of them share the side effect of a dry, cottony mouth that lasts for a few weeks at the beginning. The student is likely to ask for water frequently because this type of thirst isn't easily quenched. The teacher and the student should understand this side effect will ease and disappear with time.

19. B: With a combination of informal and formal assessments including standardized testing, awareness of grades, systematically charted data over a period of time and teacher notes. Comprehension and vocabulary cannot be sufficiently assessed with occasional, brief studies. Continuous observation, high-stakes and standardized testing, attention to grades and closely tracking the outcomes of objective-linked assessments are interrelated tools that, when systematically organized, offer a solid understanding of students' strengths and weaknesses.

20. A: Diabetic hypoglycemia. Diabetic hypoglycemia, also known as insulin reaction, occurs when blood sugar falls to a very low level. It is important to treat it quickly or the diabetic could faint, in which case an injection of glucagon is administered.

21. D: Enthusiastically accepted. The adults discuss a background check and the possibility the teen might discover gardening is not for her and want to quit. However, this is most likely to occur early in her employment, giving the neighbor sufficient time to find another helper. The teacher is pleased because the girl will learn new skills through modeling and repetition. The mother is pleased because the experience will add to the girl's self-esteem as well as show her she is capable of learning. The elderly neighbor is pleased because she is both compassionate and truly needs help. The girl is delighted the neighbor recognizes her potential and sees her as valuable.

22. C: The student did not know how to spell 'beautiful'. It is doubtful the student heard "pretty" instead of beautiful since the two sound nothing alike. It is equally unlikely he doesn't know the meaning of the word 'beautiful' since his substitution, 'pretty', is a synonym for beautiful. It is likely this child is creative, but that alone wouldn't be sufficient reason to replace one word with another. The most logical answer is that he simply didn't know how to spell 'beautiful'. He does know that some words mean almost the same thing, and since he already knew how to spell 'pretty', he incorrectly believed a synonym would be acceptable.

23. A: Pervasive Spectrum Disorders (PSD) is another name for Autism Spectrum Disorders (ASD). PSD causes disabilities in language, thought, emotion and empathy. The most severe form of PSD is autistic disorder. A much less severe form is Asperger's Syndrome.

24. C: Immediately refer him to the counselor. The boy is exhibiting serious emotional distress suggesting either abuse or neglect at home or elsewhere. While his behavior may seem manipulative, the fact that the boy is unreachable once he's in the highly charged emotional state in which he repeats, "I hate myself" suggests emotional trauma. The fact the child is socialized with peers, playing with them when invited and not taking rejection personally, suggests his emotional distress may be caused by an adult who has convinced him he is unworthy. A trained counselor is the best choice.

25. C: He is socially distant, focused on certain subjects to the point of obsession and inflexible. Asperger Syndrome is a mild form of autism. Children with this disorder typically do interact with teachers, other adults and sometimes other children; however, the interaction is rather remote and without emotional expression. They are also very focused on subjects of great interest to the abandonment of all others. When asked to redirect focus, Asperger children often become emphatically obstinate, refusing to shift focus.

26. D: All of the above is correct. This project gives the teacher the opportunity to evaluate what students already know, establishes a scaffold of accessible information to which the students can integrate new information and creates a sense of curiosity and excitement in the students, which encourages them to learn.

27. D: is correct: A motor skill development disorder which includes speech errors that don't clearly follow a pattern and so appear to be inconsistent. An example is a student who can pronounce /p/ when it is followed by a long i, as in pine, but not when followed by an ou diphthong, as in pout. Verbally dyspraxic individuals are unable to correctly place the tongue, lips and jaw for consistent sounds that can be organized into syllables. Dyspraxia appears to be a brain disorder in which the area that controls production of particular sounds is damaged.

28. B: Ask students to create a play about the story as the teacher reads aloud. This activity grounds the students in the story action as it is occurring. Acting it out insures understanding; otherwise, the students will most likely stop the teacher and ask for clarification. Furthermore, by acting it

out, students are incorporating understanding physically. They will be more likely to retain the story and be able to comprehend the meanings incorporated in it.

29. A: Twitches, grunts, inappropriate words, body spasms. Children and adults with Tourette syndrome are rarely aggressive nor are they reluctant to make eye contact or otherwise engage others. Tourette syndrome is characterized by explosive sounds, sometimes in the form of inappropriate words, more often just as meaningless syllables; muscular twitches of the face or elsewhere in the body and the complete inability to control these spasms. Tourette sufferers often also suffer from Obsessive Compulsive Disorder.

30. C: Lack of sufficiently developed behavior and social skills. The child may or may not be hyperactive, but the fact that she can control her behavior for extended periods if a reward is involved suggests the child is overly indulged outside of class. In addition, she appears to act out in an effort to seek peer admiration; this excludes the possibility of Tourette syndrome and Attention Deficit Hyperactivity Disorder. In the first case, she would be unlikely to seek approval. In the second, she would be unlikely to be able to control herself under certain circumstances. There is nothing in her behavior to suggest psychosis.

31. A: Attention Deficit Hyperactivity Disorder. Children with ADHD exhibit a myriad of symptoms including: disorganization, easily distracted and frustrated, defensive, immature, impulsive, often interrupts conversations and hyperactive behaviors.

32. A: Reading fluency. Fluent readers are able to read smoothly and comfortably at a steady pace. The more quickly a child reads, the greater the chance of leaving out a word or substituting one word for another, i.e., wink instead of *sink*. Fluent readers are able to maintain accuracy without sacrificing rate. Fluent readers also stress important words in a text, group words into rhythmic phrases and read with intonation (prosody).

33. B: Drink a soda or eat some hard candy. Diabetes is a metabolic disorder that prevents proper processing of food, resulting in a lack of enough insulin for the blood to transport sugar. Insulin shock, also known as hypoglycemia, is typically brought on by a diabetic's failure to take insulin or to eat often enough. It is a serious condition that must be dealt with immediately.

34. D: A and B. Any opportunity for an ELL to hear spoken English while simultaneously seeing it in print will help facilitate reading fluency.

35. C: Asking the student to tell her one folk tale from the book in her native language. The teacher writes key English words and asks the child to find those words in the book. When the child finds the words, they read them together. The teacher might also suggest the child write the new English words in a notebook and extend the lesson by having the child write sentences using the words.

36. D: Cultural load. Cultural load is concerned with how the relationship between language and culture can help or hinder learning. By using a familiar folk tale, the student is given the opportunity to learn new words in a culturally familiar context.

37. D: Events. A picture walk invites a reader to prepare for the act of reading the text by previewing the illustrations in order to understand the events that will unfold in the story.

38. C: The number of unrecognizable words an English Language Learner encounters when reading or listening. Language load is one of the barriers ELLs face. Rephrasing, dividing complex sentences into smaller units and teaching essential vocabulary before the student begins reading are all strategies which can lighten the load.

39. A: Avoid idioms and slang; involve students in hands-on activities; reference students' prior knowledge; speak slowly. Informal use of speech such as idioms and slang are likely to confuse ELLs. Involving students in hands-on activities such as group reading and language play makes the experience more meaningful and more immediate. New knowledge can only be absorbed by attaching it to prior knowledge so referencing what students already know is essential. Speaking slowly to English Language Learners is important since they are processing what is being said at a slower rate than a native speaker.

40. D: Especially important to English Language Learners and students with reading disabilities. Word recognition is the process of identifying a word's meaning and pronunciation. While it is important to all readers, it is essential to ELLs.

41. C: Giving a three minute Test of Silent Contextual Reading Fluency four times a year. This test presents a student with a string of text in which no spaces between words appear; punctuation is also removed. The student must divide one word from another by marking where division should occur. When presented with a strand such as: Thesmalldogherdedthefluffysheepintothebarn would ideally be sectioned as The/small/dog/herded/the/fluffy/sheep/into/the/barn. The more words a student accurately separates, the higher the silent reading fluency score.

42. A: Clarifying the goal, modeling strategies and offering explanations geared to a student's level of understanding. Well-organized teaching that offers simple steps and frequent references to previously learned material defines explicit instruction.

43. A: An ORF is an Oral Reading Fluency assessment. An ORF, also called Curriculum-Based Measurement (CBM) is a one-minute assessment in which the student reads a grade-level text aloud. The test supervisor notes errors the reader doesn't self-correct and the number of words read correctly.

44. A: Bilingual Support Model, Coordinated Services Model, Integrated Bilingual Special Education, Bilingual Special Education Model. The *Bilingual Support Model* teams bilingual paraprofessionals with English-speaking special educators to assist with the IEP implementation. The bilingual assistant gives instruction in areas specified in the IEP. In the *Coordinated Services Model, the team* consists of an English speaking special education teacher and a bilingual educator.
The *Integrated Bilingual Special Education model is applied in districts with bilingual special education teachers who can give* instruction in the native language, English as Second Language (ESL) training and transition assistance as the student gains proficiency. The *Bilingual Special Education Model* integrates all school personnel who focus on bilingual special education instruction and services. All professionals have been trained in bilingual special education.

45. B: The classroom teacher, a special education teacher, parents or guardian, a representative of the local education agency knowledgeable about specialized instruction, someone to interpret instructional implications, the student if appropriate and other people invited by the parents or the school. IDEA defines the IEP team as a group of people responsible for developing, reviewing and revising the Individualized Education Program for a disabled student.

46. C: Reading at a Frustration reading level. At a Frustration reading level, a student is unable to unlock meaning from a text regardless of teacher support or strategies. The reader is at this level when he has less than 90% accuracy in word recognition and less than 50% in comprehension, retelling a story is illogical or incomplete and the student cannot accurately answer questions about the text.

47. B: Understanding of context and vocabulary. A Cloze test presents a reader with a text in which certain words are blocked out. The reader must determine probable missing words based on context clues. In order to supply these words, the reader must already know them.

48. A: Letter-sound correspondence. Letter-sound correspondence is the relationship between a spoken sound and the letters predictably used in English to transcribe them.

49. A: Read all answers; mark out any that are illogical. Next 'plug in' the remaining words and mark out those that are grammatically incorrect or do not sound right. Finally, think about context clues. Maze and Cloze tests are related. In a Cloze test, the reader uses context clues and familiar vocabulary to decide which words have been left out of a text. A Maze test supplies a number of possible answers and the reader must select the correct one. Possible answers can be syntactically possible but illogical, syntactically impossible but make semantic sense and both illogical and grammatically impossible.

50. D: Memorize their lists by using techniques such as songs, mnemonic devices and other fun activities. By definition, sight words cannot be decoded but must be recognized on sight.

51. A: Oral. Phonological awareness is the understanding of the sounds within a spoken word. While phonological awareness contributes to fluent reading skills, activities designed to develop an awareness of word-sounds are, by definition, oral.

52. A: Count money, plan meals, grocery shop, recognize safety concerns. These are among the most basic life skills developmentally delayed students must master. Other life skills include specific occupational skills, home maintenance, clothes selection and care, food preparation and personal hygiene.

53. A: Word recognition. Elements of word recognition include strategies to decode unfamiliar words, considering alternate word meanings to decode a text and the ability to apply prior knowledge to determine a word's meaning.

54. C: Scripting the end-sound to a word KT=cat; leaving space between words; writing from the top left to the top right and from top to bottom of the page. Each of these steps is progressively more abstract. Scripting the end-sound to a word helps a young writer recognize words have beginnings and endings. This naturally leads to the willingness to separate words with white space so they stand as individual entities. Once this step is reached, the child realizes English, writing progresses from left to right and from the top of the page to the bottom.

55. A: Are results-oriented, includes post-school activities, vocational education, employment support, adult services and considers the individual's strengths, preferences and interests. Additional activities that compose Secondary Transition are instruction, related services, community experiences, the development of employment and other post-school adult living objectives and, if appropriate, acquisition of daily living skills and functional vocational evaluation.

56. B: Asking they read their stories to other students. Emergent writers scripting initial and final sounds will gain the most immediate and relevant satisfaction by moving around the room, reading what they've written to other students.

57. D: From the first day of school. Picture walks give young readers the idea books are arranged sequentially. Pictures provide narrative coherence and context clues. Holding a book and turning pages gives young readers a familiarity with them.

58. D: Students should be taught that writing is a process. By applying spelling patterns found in word families, the spelling of many words can be deduced.

59. C: Context. By considering the other words in the story, the student can deduce the missing words. Referring to other words when a reader encounters an unfamiliar or missing word, can often unlock meaning.

60. A: Cooperative learning and reading comprehension. CSR is group of four reading strategies that students with learning disabilities can use to decipher and understand texts. Small groups of students at various reading levels support one another by going through the strategies as they read aloud or silently. Before reading, the group *previews*, applying prior knowledge and prediction. Next readers target words or syllables they didn't understand called *clunks* and apply a number of strategies to decode the *clunks.* Third, students *get the gist* by determining the most important character, setting, event or idea. Finally, the students *wrap it up* by creating questions to discuss their understanding of the text and summarize its meaning.

61. B: Have an Individualized Education Plan written for her. An IEP is a requirement of law. The plan, written by a team of individuals including her classroom teacher, the special education teacher, her parent s, the student if appropriate and other interested individuals, establishes objectives and goals and offers a time-line in which to reach them.

62. C: Observe the child over the course of a week or two. Draw him into conversation to determine if vocabulary is limited. Note how the child interacts with others in the class. Does he initiate conversation? If another child initiates, does he respond? Once the teacher has observed, she is in a better position to offer information to the special education teacher or counselor and to determine her best course of action.

63. B: Meet with the specialist to discuss the teacher's goals. It isn't possible to determine if strategies are effective or determine a future course unless the teacher has a firm grasp of his goals and expectations.

64. A: Strategies to increase comprehension and to build vocabulary. He should receive instruction focused on just the areas in which he is exhibiting difficulty. Improved vocabulary will give him greater comprehension skills. Strategies focused on enhancing comprehension together with a stronger vocabulary will provide the greatest help.

65. A: It enhances students' phonemic awareness and increases vocabulary. Strength in oral language helps emergent readers because reading relies largely upon the ability to decode words with knowledge about what sounds the letters represent. A large vocabulary helps the reader recognize words whose sounds are properly decoded but whose meanings aren't familiar. Unfamiliar words slow reading fluency.

66. B: Scaffolding. Scaffolding is an umbrella teaching approach which offers a multitude of supports. Scaffolding includes prior knowledge, mnemonic devices, modeling, graphs, charts, graphic organizers and information needed prior to starting the lesson such as vocabulary or mathematical formulas.

67. D: Visit the classroom, meet the teacher and her new classmates and be given the opportunity to ask questions about the change she is about to make. When she is able to visualize what the classroom looks like, meet the people that will become her new educational 'family' and have her concerns and questions addressed, she will feel more confident about the transition.

68. B: A Maze test, which is a type of Cloze test. A Cloze test offers a text with key words blanked out and the student must determine the most likely words based upon context and his vocabulary. A Maze test offers a number of possible answers and the student must read very carefully in order to make the correct selection.

69. A: Well-organized coaching in decoding, sight words, vocabulary and comprehension several times a week. The more systematic the lessons, the better the chance the intervention will succeed.

70. C: Use graph paper to help him organize. Show him how to write the problems, keeping each number in a box aligned with other numbers. This will help him determine which numbers are in the ones group, the tens group, the hundreds group and so on.

71. B: Muscular dystrophy. There are 20 types of muscular dystrophy, a genetically inherited disease that frequently first manifests in childhood. By contrast, muscular sclerosis almost never appears in childhood. Cerebral palsy is not a deteriorating disease, as is muscular dystrophy.

72. C: One class at a time, with the special education teacher supervising his academic and social progress. It is important to make this transition slowly, to permit the special education teacher to remain in the student's life as both academic and emotional support and the student to adjust to her larger classes and students she doesn't know as well.

73. C: Outreach to underrepresented and rural populations. The four required activities of the AT ACT of 1998 are: a public awareness program, coordinate activities among state agencies, technical assistance and training and outreach to underrepresented and rural populations.

74. B: Positive Behavior Support. The Individuals with Disabilities Education Act of 1997 is the recommended method of dealing with behavioral problems in children with disabilities.

75. C: Assessing a young child for learning disabilities often leads to an incorrect conclusion because a student must be taught the subject before it is possible to assess her understanding of it. Intervention teaches the child specific skills to correct her misconceptions. If the intervention fails, assessment is the next step. Many experts recommend such assessment should not be undertaken until a child is at least six years of age.

76. B: Tried to solve the problem. He aligned all the numbers as they appeared so that 45 minutes were added with 5 in the ones column and 4 in the tens column. He also added 2.5 hours, which isn't required to solve the problem.

77. D: A digital clock that can be manually moved forward. This student's error is the result of two misunderstandings. The first is that 45 minutes is represented as 5 in the ones column and 4 in the tens column, but that 2.5 hours is represented with .5 in the tens column and 3 in the ones column. The second misunderstanding is the student includes the red herring 2.5 hours, which should not be in the equation. With a digital clock that can be manually moved forward, the student can begin at 0:00 and move the clock forward as he adds the numbers. The teacher can remind him 45 minutes is not 45 hours and it is irrelevant the first train returned to point B in 2.5 hours.

78. A: Estimate the answer; convert all of the numbers to minutes and divide the answer by 60 to determine the number of hours and minutes; Determine the percentage of an hour 45 minutes is, and write that number as .75; create a graph.

79. C: 8.25 hours. 3.5 hours+2.75 hours=6.25 hours+1.25 hours=7.5 hours +.75 hour=8.25 hours.

80. B: Least restrictive. IDEA requires the least restrictive environment (LRE) appropriate to a child's needs is the proper learning environment so children are not unnecessarily isolated from non-disabled children. The student's IEP team is responsible for determining the LRE.

81. A: Oral and written materials. Verbal linguistic learners love language in all its forms. They often enjoy tongue twisters, mnemonic devices, poetry, word games and crossword puzzles.

82. C: Verbal linguistic, mathematical logical, musical, visual spatial, body kinesthetic, interpersonal, naturalistic, existential. Harvard Professor Howard Gardner cites his theory of multiple intelligences, also called learning styles, as an answer to how teachers can most effectively reach all their students. It is especially important to recognize the learning styles of students with learning disabilities and design lessons for those students accordingly.

83. C: Traumatic brain injury. Although Jacob appears to have escaped unhurt, his dramatic change in classroom behavior suggests he may be suffering from TBI. Other symptoms of TBI are: hyperactivity, impulsivity, memory and communication problems, sexually uninhibited, improper language, failure to recognize social cues, inability to focus, and physical problems such as balance.

84. C: Collaborative teaching. Classrooms with a lead teacher often include a specialized teacher to listen to the lesson then work with special needs children. Other methods are: learning centers or stations in which collaborating teachers are responsible for different areas, assigning special needs students into a resource room, team teaching and/or consultation by the special education teacher to the classroom teacher.

85. B: Teach him how an abacus works. An abacus gives both a visual/tactile demonstration of how numbers work and allows a child who processes information through hand/body movement to physically experience numerical relationships.

86. C: Provide the records within 45 days. The Family Educational Rights and Privacy Act (FERPA) is a federal law that addresses student rights regarding their records. Among FERPA regulations is the requirement that a student be given records within 45 days of making the request.

87. B: Unable to locate errors in their own work. This is the only logical answer. Answers a, c and d do not make sense in context.

88. A: Standardized assessment tests, examining areas of weakness in student work to determine patterns, teacher observations and interviews with the student. At this point the teacher is well-prepared to plan instruction.

89. D: Begin by welcoming the mother and discussing her son's academic improvements. Stress that the teachers, the mother and the child share goals for the student's success. Explain the behavior problems and ask if the mother has insights to share. It's important to keep communication open.

90. B: Enhance students' vocabulary by encouraging them to find examples in the world around them. Often children have richer vocabularies than they realize. This project simultaneously encourages students to remember words they already know and to learn other words with similar meanings.

91. D: All of the above. There is often a multitude of ways a teacher can apply skills and information learned in one lesson to other subjects. In this case, vocabulary building is enhanced with a word wall; logic and reasoning skills are developed by putting the words into alphabetical order then

carefully considering how to define them; and both math skills and word recognition ability are improved by creating a chart demonstrating a variety of ways one can categorize a list of words.

92. C: Making appropriate modifications. Each child is different. In this case, she has consulted with the special education teacher and concluded the child needs multiple supports.

93. B: Children with special needs are as much a part of the educational community as any other child and necessary services that allow these students to participate in the learning community should be provided.

94. A: The Americans with Disabilities Act. The ADA is a federal act prohibiting discrimination based on disability in the areas of employment, state and local government, public accommodations, commercial facilities, transportation and telecommunications.

95. D: Power point presentations that include music, manipulatives, graphic organizers and clapping games. Multi-sensory techniques include visual, audio, tactile and kinesthetic approaches to teaching.

96. B: Collaborative. The creation of an Individualized Education Plan (IEP) involves classroom and special education teachers, family members, the student (if appropriate) and other interested parties who collaborate in the student's best interests.

97. B: Suggest new and innovative ways students can use their journals including automatic writing, found poetry, lists and collages. While journals are intensely personal and should never be read without the student's permission, teachers can certainly inspire students to use the journals to explore their ideas in innovative ways.

98. D: He goes out of his way to annoy others, is defiant and goes into childish rages in which he blames others. This student has been diagnosed with Oppositional Defiant Disorder, a psychiatric disorder characterized by noncompliance, tantrums, extremely irritating conduct, refusal to follow rules, argumentative behavior and blaming others.

99. D: Scaffolding is an umbrella teaching approach that offers a learner a multitude of supports and encourages her to reach out in many directions to enhance learning. Elements of scaffolding include prior knowledge, mnemonic devices, modeling, graphs, charts, graphic organizers and information the student will need prior to undertaking the lesson, such as vocabulary or mathematical formulas.

100. A: Obtain requested records within 45 days; request amendment of inaccurate information or information that violates the student's privacy; be notified before personal information is shared with third parties; file a complaint with the U.S. Department of Education should the school fail to fulfill these requests. FERPA is a federal law that addresses student rights regarding records.

How to Overcome Test Anxiety

Just the thought of taking a test is enough to make most people a little nervous. A test is an important event that can have a long-term impact on your future, so it's important to take it seriously and it's natural to feel anxious about performing well. But just because anxiety is normal, that doesn't mean that it's helpful in test taking, or that you should simply accept it as part of your life. Anxiety can have a variety of effects. These effects can be mild, like making you feel slightly nervous, or severe, like blocking your ability to focus or remember even a simple detail.

If you experience test anxiety—whether severe or mild—it's important to know how to beat it. To discover this, first you need to understand what causes test anxiety.

Causes of Test Anxiety

While we often think of anxiety as an uncontrollable emotional state, it can actually be caused by simple, practical things. One of the most common causes of test anxiety is that a person does not feel adequately prepared for their test. This feeling can be the result of many different issues such as poor study habits or lack of organization, but the most common culprit is time management. Starting to study too late, failing to organize your study time to cover all of the material, or being distracted while you study will mean that you're not well prepared for the test. This may lead to cramming the night before, which will cause you to be physically and mentally exhausted for the test. Poor time management also contributes to feelings of stress, fear, and hopelessness as you realize you are not well prepared but don't know what to do about it.

Other times, test anxiety is not related to your preparation for the test but comes from unresolved fear. This may be a past failure on a test, or poor performance on tests in general. It may come from comparing yourself to others who seem to be performing better or from the stress of living up to expectations. Anxiety may be driven by fears of the future—how failure on this test would affect your educational and career goals. These fears are often completely irrational, but they can still negatively impact your test performance.

> **Review Video:** 3 Reasons You Have Test Anxiety
> Visit mometrix.com/academy and enter code: 428468

Elements of Test Anxiety

As mentioned earlier, test anxiety is considered to be an emotional state, but it has physical and mental components as well. Sometimes you may not even realize that you are suffering from test anxiety until you notice the physical symptoms. These can include trembling hands, rapid heartbeat, sweating, nausea, and tense muscles. Extreme anxiety may lead to fainting or vomiting. Obviously, any of these symptoms can have a negative impact on testing. It is important to recognize them as soon as they begin to occur so that you can address the problem before it damages your performance.

> **Review Video: 3 Ways to Tell You Have Test Anxiety**
> Visit mometrix.com/academy and enter code: 927847

The mental components of test anxiety include trouble focusing and inability to remember learned information. During a test, your mind is on high alert, which can help you recall information and stay focused for an extended period of time. However, anxiety interferes with your mind's natural processes, causing you to blank out, even on the questions you know well. The strain of testing during anxiety makes it difficult to stay focused, especially on a test that may take several hours. Extreme anxiety can take a huge mental toll, making it difficult not only to recall test information but even to understand the test questions or pull your thoughts together.

> **Review Video: How Test Anxiety Affects Memory**
> Visit mometrix.com/academy and enter code: 609003

Effects of Test Anxiety

Test anxiety is like a disease—if left untreated, it will get progressively worse. Anxiety leads to poor performance, and this reinforces the feelings of fear and failure, which in turn lead to poor performances on subsequent tests. It can grow from a mild nervousness to a crippling condition. If allowed to progress, test anxiety can have a big impact on your schooling, and consequently on your future.

Test anxiety can spread to other parts of your life. Anxiety on tests can become anxiety in any stressful situation, and blanking on a test can turn into panicking in a job situation. But fortunately, you don't have to let anxiety rule your testing and determine your grades. There are a number of relatively simple steps you can take to move past anxiety and function normally on a test and in the rest of life.

> **Review Video: How Test Anxiety Impacts Your Grades**
> Visit mometrix.com/academy and enter code: 939819

Physical Steps for Beating Test Anxiety

While test anxiety is a serious problem, the good news is that it can be overcome. It doesn't have to control your ability to think and remember information. While it may take time, you can begin taking steps today to beat anxiety.

Just as your first hint that you may be struggling with anxiety comes from the physical symptoms, the first step to treating it is also physical. Rest is crucial for having a clear, strong mind. If you are tired, it is much easier to give in to anxiety. But if you establish good sleep habits, your body and mind will be ready to perform optimally, without the strain of exhaustion. Additionally, sleeping well helps you to retain information better, so you're more likely to recall the answers when you see the test questions.

Getting good sleep means more than going to bed on time. It's important to allow your brain time to relax. Take study breaks from time to time so it doesn't get overworked, and don't study right before bed. Take time to rest your mind before trying to rest your body, or you may find it difficult to fall asleep.

> **Review Video: The Importance of Sleep for Your Brain**
> Visit mometrix.com/academy and enter code: 319338

Along with sleep, other aspects of physical health are important in preparing for a test. Good nutrition is vital for good brain function. Sugary foods and drinks may give a burst of energy but this burst is followed by a crash, both physically and emotionally. Instead, fuel your body with protein and vitamin-rich foods.

Also, drink plenty of water. Dehydration can lead to headaches and exhaustion, especially if your brain is already under stress from the rigors of the test. Particularly if your test is a long one, drink water during the breaks. And if possible, take an energy-boosting snack to eat between sections.

> **Review Video: How Diet Can Affect your Mood**
> Visit mometrix.com/academy and enter code: 624317

Along with sleep and diet, a third important part of physical health is exercise. Maintaining a steady workout schedule is helpful, but even taking 5-minute study breaks to walk can help get your blood pumping faster and clear your head. Exercise also releases endorphins, which contribute to a positive feeling and can help combat test anxiety.

When you nurture your physical health, you are also contributing to your mental health. If your body is healthy, your mind is much more likely to be healthy as well. So take time to rest, nourish your body with healthy food and water, and get moving as much as possible. Taking these physical steps will make you stronger and more able to take the mental steps necessary to overcome test anxiety.

> **Review Video: How to Stay Healthy and Prevent Test Anxiety**
> Visit mometrix.com/academy and enter code: 877894

Mental Steps for Beating Test Anxiety

Working on the mental side of test anxiety can be more challenging, but as with the physical side, there are clear steps you can take to overcome it. As mentioned earlier, test anxiety often stems from lack of preparation, so the obvious solution is to prepare for the test. Effective studying may be the most important weapon you have for beating test anxiety, but you can and should employ several other mental tools to combat fear.

First, boost your confidence by reminding yourself of past success—tests or projects that you aced. If you're putting as much effort into preparing for this test as you did for those, there's no reason you should expect to fail here. Work hard to prepare; then trust your preparation.

Second, surround yourself with encouraging people. It can be helpful to find a study group, but be sure that the people you're around will encourage a positive attitude. If you spend time with others who are anxious or cynical, this will only contribute to your own anxiety. Look for others who are motivated to study hard from a desire to succeed, not from a fear of failure.

Third, reward yourself. A test is physically and mentally tiring, even without anxiety, and it can be helpful to have something to look forward to. Plan an activity following the test, regardless of the outcome, such as going to a movie or getting ice cream.

When you are taking the test, if you find yourself beginning to feel anxious, remind yourself that you know the material. Visualize successfully completing the test. Then take a few deep, relaxing breaths and return to it. Work through the questions carefully but with confidence, knowing that you are capable of succeeding.

Developing a healthy mental approach to test taking will also aid in other areas of life. Test anxiety affects more than just the actual test—it can be damaging to your mental health and even contribute to depression. It's important to beat test anxiety before it becomes a problem for more than testing.

> **Review Video: Test Anxiety and Depression**
> Visit mometrix.com/academy and enter code: 904704

Study Strategy

Being prepared for the test is necessary to combat anxiety, but what does being prepared look like? You may study for hours on end and still not feel prepared. What you need is a strategy for test prep. The next few pages outline our recommended steps to help you plan out and conquer the challenge of preparation.

Step 1: Scope Out the Test

Learn everything you can about the format (multiple choice, essay, etc.) and what will be on the test. Gather any study materials, course outlines, or sample exams that may be available. Not only will this help you to prepare, but knowing what to expect can help to alleviate test anxiety.

Step 2: Map Out the Material

Look through the textbook or study guide and make note of how many chapters or sections it has. Then divide these over the time you have. For example, if a book has 15 chapters and you have five days to study, you need to cover three chapters each day. Even better, if you have the time, leave an extra day at the end for overall review after you have gone through the material in depth.

If time is limited, you may need to prioritize the material. Look through it and make note of which sections you think you already have a good grasp on, and which need review. While you are studying, skim quickly through the familiar sections and take more time on the challenging parts. Write out your plan so you don't get lost as you go. Having a written plan also helps you feel more in control of the study, so anxiety is less likely to arise from feeling overwhelmed at the amount to cover. A sample plan may look like this:

- Day 1: Skim chapters 1–4, study chapter 5 (especially pages 31–33)
- Day 2: Study chapters 6–7, skim chapters 8–9
- Day 3: Skim chapter 10, study chapters 11–12 (especially pages 87–90)
- Day 4: Study chapters 13–15
- Day 5: Overall review (focus most on chapters 5, 6, and 12), take practice test

Step 3: Gather Your Tools

Decide what study method works best for you. Do you prefer to highlight in the book as you study and then go back over the highlighted portions? Or do you type out notes of the important information? Or is it helpful to make flashcards that you can carry with you? Assemble the pens, index cards, highlighters, post-it notes, and any other materials you may need so you won't be distracted by getting up to find things while you study.

If you're having a hard time retaining the information or organizing your notes, experiment with different methods. For example, try color-coding by subject with colored pens, highlighters, or post-it notes. If you learn better by hearing, try recording yourself reading your notes so you can listen while in the car, working out, or simply sitting at your desk. Ask a friend to quiz you from your flashcards, or try teaching someone the material to solidify it in your mind.

Step 4: Create Your Environment

It's important to avoid distractions while you study. This includes both the obvious distractions like visitors and the subtle distractions like an uncomfortable chair (or a too-comfortable couch that makes you want to fall asleep). Set up the best study environment possible: good lighting and a comfortable work area. If background music helps you focus, you may want to turn it on, but otherwise keep the room quiet. If you are using a computer to take notes, be sure you don't have any other windows open, especially applications like social media, games, or anything else that could distract you. Silence your phone and turn off notifications. Be sure to keep water close by so you stay hydrated while you study (but avoid unhealthy drinks and snacks).

Also, take into account the best time of day to study. Are you freshest first thing in the morning? Try to set aside some time then to work through the material. Is your mind clearer in the afternoon or evening? Schedule your study session then. Another method is to study at the same time of day that you will take the test, so that your brain gets used to working on the material at that time and will be ready to focus at test time.

Step 5: Study!

Once you have done all the study preparation, it's time to settle into the actual studying. Sit down, take a few moments to settle your mind so you can focus, and begin to follow your study plan. Don't give in to distractions or let yourself procrastinate. This is your time to prepare so you'll be ready to fearlessly approach the test. Make the most of the time and stay focused.

Of course, you don't want to burn out. If you study too long you may find that you're not retaining the information very well. Take regular study breaks. For example, taking five minutes out of every hour to walk briskly, breathing deeply and swinging your arms, can help your mind stay fresh.

As you get to the end of each chapter or section, it's a good idea to do a quick review. Remind yourself of what you learned and work on any difficult parts. When you feel that you've mastered the material, move on to the next part. At the end of your study session, briefly skim through your notes again.

But while review is helpful, cramming last minute is NOT. If at all possible, work ahead so that you won't need to fit all your study into the last day. Cramming overloads your brain with more information than it can process and retain, and your tired mind may struggle to recall even previously learned information when it is overwhelmed with last-minute study. Also, the urgent nature of cramming and the stress placed on your brain contribute to anxiety. You'll be more likely to go to the test feeling unprepared and having trouble thinking clearly.

So don't cram, and don't stay up late before the test, even just to review your notes at a leisurely pace. Your brain needs rest more than it needs to go over the information again. In fact, plan to finish your studies by noon or early afternoon the day before the test. Give your brain the rest of the day to relax or focus on other things, and get a good night's sleep. Then you will be fresh for the test and better able to recall what you've studied.

Step 6: Take a practice test

Many courses offer sample tests, either online or in the study materials. This is an excellent resource to check whether you have mastered the material, as well as to prepare for the test format and environment.

Check the test format ahead of time: the number of questions, the type (multiple choice, free response, etc.), and the time limit. Then create a plan for working through them. For example, if you have 30 minutes to take a 60-question test, your limit is 30 seconds per question. Spend less time on the questions you know well so that you can take more time on the difficult ones.

If you have time to take several practice tests, take the first one open book, with no time limit. Work through the questions at your own pace and make sure you fully understand them. Gradually work up to taking a test under test conditions: sit at a desk with all study materials put away and set a timer. Pace yourself to make sure you finish the test with time to spare and go back to check your answers if you have time.

After each test, check your answers. On the questions you missed, be sure you understand why you missed them. Did you misread the question (tests can use tricky wording)? Did you forget the information? Or was it something you hadn't learned? Go back and study any shaky areas that the practice tests reveal.

Taking these tests not only helps with your grade, but also aids in combating test anxiety. If you're already used to the test conditions, you're less likely to worry about it, and working through tests until you're scoring well gives you a confidence boost. Go through the practice tests until you feel comfortable, and then you can go into the test knowing that you're ready for it.

Test Tips

On test day, you should be confident, knowing that you've prepared well and are ready to answer the questions. But aside from preparation, there are several test day strategies you can employ to maximize your performance.

First, as stated before, get a good night's sleep the night before the test (and for several nights before that, if possible). Go into the test with a fresh, alert mind rather than staying up late to study.

Try not to change too much about your normal routine on the day of the test. It's important to eat a nutritious breakfast, but if you normally don't eat breakfast at all, consider eating just a protein bar. If you're a coffee drinker, go ahead and have your normal coffee. Just make sure you time it so that the caffeine doesn't wear off right in the middle of your test. Avoid sugary beverages, and drink enough water to stay hydrated but not so much that you need a restroom break 10 minutes into the test. If your test isn't first thing in the morning, consider going for a walk or doing a light workout before the test to get your blood flowing.

Allow yourself enough time to get ready, and leave for the test with plenty of time to spare so you won't have the anxiety of scrambling to arrive in time. Another reason to be early is to select a good seat. It's helpful to sit away from doors and windows, which can be distracting. Find a good seat, get out your supplies, and settle your mind before the test begins.

When the test begins, start by going over the instructions carefully, even if you already know what to expect. Make sure you avoid any careless mistakes by following the directions.

Then begin working through the questions, pacing yourself as you've practiced. If you're not sure on an answer, don't spend too much time on it, and don't let it shake your confidence. Either skip it and come back later, or eliminate as many wrong answers as possible and guess among the remaining ones. Don't dwell on these questions as you continue—put them out of your mind and focus on what lies ahead.

Be sure to read all of the answer choices, even if you're sure the first one is the right answer. Sometimes you'll find a better one if you keep reading. But don't second-guess yourself if you do immediately know the answer. Your gut instinct is usually right. Don't let test anxiety rob you of the information you know.

If you have time at the end of the test (and if the test format allows), go back and review your answers. Be cautious about changing any, since your first instinct tends to be correct, but make sure you didn't misread any of the questions or accidentally mark the wrong answer choice. Look over any you skipped and make an educated guess.

At the end, leave the test feeling confident. You've done your best, so don't waste time worrying about your performance or wishing you could change anything. Instead, celebrate the successful completion of this test. And finally, use this test to learn how to deal with anxiety even better next time.

Review Video: 5 Tips to Beat Test Anxiety
Visit mometrix.com/academy and enter code: 570656

Important Qualification

Not all anxiety is created equal. If your test anxiety is causing major issues in your life beyond the classroom or testing center, or if you are experiencing troubling physical symptoms related to your anxiety, it may be a sign of a serious physiological or psychological condition. If this sounds like your situation, we strongly encourage you to seek professional help.

Thank You

We at Mometrix would like to extend our heartfelt thanks to you, our friend and patron, for allowing us to play a part in your journey. It is a privilege to serve people from all walks of life who are unified in their commitment to building the best future they can for themselves.

The preparation you devote to these important testing milestones may be the most valuable educational opportunity you have for making a real difference in your life. We encourage you to put your heart into it—that feeling of succeeding, overcoming, and yes, conquering will be well worth the hours you've invested.

We want to hear your story, your struggles and your successes, and if you see any opportunities for us to improve our materials so we can help others even more effectively in the future, please share that with us as well. **The team at Mometrix would be absolutely thrilled to hear from you!** So please, send us an email (support@mometrix.com) and let's stay in touch.

If you'd like some additional help, check out these other resources we offer for your exam:

http://MometrixFlashcards.com/TExES

Additional Bonus Material

Due to our efforts to try to keep this book to a manageable length, we've created a link that will give you access to all of your additional bonus material.

Please visit http://www.mometrix.com/bonus948/texesspedec12 to access the information.